Racism in the Modern World

Historical Perspectives on Cultural Transfer and Adaptation

Edited by

Manfred Berg and Simon Wendt

berghahn

NEW YORK · OXFORD

www.berghahnbooks.com

First published in 2011 by

Berghahn Books

www.berghahnbooks.com

©2011, 2014 Manfred Berg and Simon Wendt

First paperback edition published in 2014

The printing of this volume has been made possible by the
generous support of the Thyssen Foundation and the
Heidelberg Center for American Studies.

Library of Congress Cataloging-in-Publication Data

Racism in the modern world : historical perspectives on cultural transfer
and adaptation / edited by Manfred Berg and Simon Wendt.
     p. cm.
  Includes bibliographical references and index.
  ISBN 978-0-85745-076-0 (hardback) -- ISBN 978-0-85745-077-7 (institutional ebook) -- ISBN 978-1-78238-085-6 (paperback) --
ISBN 978-1-78238-086-3 (retail ebook)
  1. Racism. 2. Racism--History. I. Berg, Manfred, 1959- II. Wendt, Simon.
  HT1521.R4185 2011
  305.8--dc22

                                                                           2011009335

British Library Cataloguing in Publication Data

A catalogue record for this book is available from the British Library

Printed on acid-free paper

ISBN: 978-1-78238-085-6 paperback
ISBN: 978-1-78238-086-3 retail ebook

Contents

Introduction

Racism in the Modern World: Historical Perspectives on Cultural Transfer and Adaptation

Manfred Berg and Simon Wendt

Although the term only gained currency during the 1920s and 1930s, racism, both as a set of ideas and as social practice, has a much longer history. Broadly speaking, the concept has been predicated on the belief that humankind is divided into distinctive entities, commonly called races, which are delineated by descent and phenotype and regarded as primordial, static, and homogeneous. Moreover, the assertion that race determines not only physical appearance but also intellectual abilities and culture has been a key tenet of racism. Finally, its advocates have tried to establish a natural hierarchy of supposedly superior and inferior races from which they have inferred the claim that the former have a right to rule and exploit the latter. As a consequence, racist ideas have been employed in justifying colonial conquest, slavery, and genocide as well as the segregation of and discrimination against purportedly inferior races. Arguably, no part of the globe has remained untouched by racism, and although racist ideologies came under increasing attack during the 1930s and 1940s, the World War II era did not usher in an age of racial egalitarianism. In the United States, racial segregation was not abolished until the mid-1960s. South African Apartheid persisted until the early 1990s. In the twenty-first century, racism, while being less clearly identifiable, continues to affect modern society.[1]

Not surprisingly, scholars have been keenly interested in the question of why and how racism developed into such a powerful historical force. Because racist ideas played a salient role in the process of European expansion and in establishing the global dominance of the so-called white race, the focus has largely been on the emergence of racism in Europe and North America and on its impact on the rest of the world. Viewed from this perspective, racism appears to have been a Western ideology tailor-made to legitimize the subjugation and exploitation of non-white peoples.[2] To be sure, there are perfectly sound reasons why this approach has dominated the study of racism for decades. No expert in the field would seriously dispute that Europeans and their descendents all over the world have been the chief propagandists and beneficiaries of racist ideologies and practices. But then again, racism did not exclusively target non-white people and racist ideas and customs were not solely confined to the United States or Western Europe. For example, in the Middle East notions of race have influenced the development of slavery as well as regional identities. Historical research has demonstrated that racial categories and racial hierarchies were a significant aspect of intellectual discourse in modern China. Imperial Japan used similar notions of racial superiority to occupy and colonize China and Korea.[3]

Furthermore, the challenge that the new global history has mounted against Eurocentric interpretations of world history has also affected the study of racism.[4] Ironically, the notion that Westerners simply imposed racism on the rest of the world in a top-down fashion may well reflect a Eurocentric interpretation of a Eurocentric ideology. This volume, therefore, seeks to explore additional and alternative explanations of racism's historical significance by going beyond the dominant paradigms, which have focused on the development of racism within the framework of Western nation states, on the spread of white supremacy, and on the oppression of blacks by whites.[5] Instead, it proposes to take a closer look at the complex processes of diffusion, transfer, adaptation, and transformation of racial ideas in various parts of the world, including their interaction with indigenous traditions.

Scholars have begun to examine these issues from different angles. A global perspective conceives of racism as one of the grand cultural, social, and political forces that transcend the boundaries of nation-states or even continents and have shaped the history of the modern world. For instance, inasmuch as historians are interested in global movements, understood as shared visions of common destiny and purpose, they will consider racism a most appropriate subject.[6] When racism reached the pinnacle of respectability as a scientific theory in the late nineteenth and early twentieth centuries, its proponents claimed that the struggle between the races was the major driving force of world history and that the fate of humanity and civilization depended on the global supremacy of the white race. In the same vein, many anti-racists viewed racism and colonial oppression as a global challenge for all non-white peoples.[7]

Of course, the focus on global processes and forces begs the question of how they manifested themselves in specific cultural and historical contexts. The sociologist Roland Robertson has coined the phrase "glocalization" to capture the "simultaneity and inter-penetration of what are conventionally called the global and the local, the universal and the particular."[8] With regard to racist ideologies, this means that indigenous populations did not simply adopt certain ideas about race that were introduced into their societies by Western colonial authorities, scientists, and military personnel, but that they actively adapted them within the local contexts of their native environments. Hence, glocalization becomes part of a larger transnational history that Ian Tyrrell succinctly defines as the study of "the movement of peoples, ideas, technologies and institutions across national boundaries."[9] If we want to understand how racist ideologies were disseminated within and beyond the Western world and how Western nations, in turn, were influenced by racial practices and debates in the colonial periphery, a transnational or transcultural perspective is imperative. For example, in his work on Brazil and the United States, historian George Reid Andrews shows that there was an "extended, century-long conversation between the two countries ... on the topic of race," which, among other things, contributed to critical discussions of Brazil's racial identity.[10]

While historians often combine transnational and comparative history, these two approaches pursue different scholarly interests. "Through comparisons," Peter Kolchin, an eminent comparativist, characterizes the method, "the historian seeks to establish similarities and differences between common processes in two or more locations or eras," trying to establish either generalizations or distinctiveness or point to "significance that would be less evident in isolation."[11] For example, the comparative work of the late George Fredrickson and others on white supremacy in the United States and South Africa has demonstrated that race relations in these two societies did not simply mirror a fixed set of racist doctrines but "can only be understood within a broader historical context that is itself constantly evolving and thus altering the terms under which whites and nonwhites interact."[12] However, in recent years critics have argued that the histories of nations, societies, and cultures in the modern world are so closely entangled and interconnected that comparisons make little sense because the isolation of variables is simply impossible. Still, without the analytical rigor of the comparative method transnational history may easily lose direction and focus.[13]

Although some enthusiastic promoters of global and transnational history seem to suggest that in the age of globalization their approach is the only meaningful way of writing history, national or regional case studies, based on the expertise of specialists, remain indispensable building blocks for the bigger scholarly edifice. Preferably, such case studies relate to the concepts of global history, consider transnational influences, and invoke asymmetrical comparisons, but they also remind us of the importance of cultural, geographic, and historical specificity. Frank Dikötter's work on race in China certainly falls into this category of enriched and enriching case studies.[14]

Obviously, these four approaches are not mutually exclusive but should be combined in pragmatic ways. Methodological pluralism is especially suitable for a volume that seeks to explore the global ramifications of racism. All contributors to this book are specialists in their respective fields but they are united in their efforts to integrate their work into a more comprehensive perspective. Still, readers should be aware that in a field as politicized and fraught with controversy as the study of racism, there is little consensus among scholars even on such basic categories as terminology and definitions. In particular, the authors of this collection disagree over two key questions that are closely intertwined. First, should racism be defined narrowly or broadly? Second, to what extent must racism be understood as an essentially Western ideology? Both questions require some background.

Several contributors insist that, for the sake of analytical rigor, the term should be confined to ideologies based on explicitly biological and hereditary theories of human difference or to what is frequently called scientific racism. A definition along these lines is Pierre van den Berghe's oft-cited characterization of racism as "any set of beliefs that organic, genetically transmitted differences (whether real or imagined) between human groups are intrinsically associated with the presence or absence of certain socially relevant abilities or characteristics, hence that such differences are a legitimate basis of invidious distinctions between groups socially defined as races."[15] While the focus on biological determinism avoids the danger that racism becomes a polemical catch-all phrase for all kinds of prejudices against ethnic, religious, and social groups, it also appears highly restrictive. To begin with, it ties the history of racism to the rise of scientific thought during the Enlightenment and leaves out earlier manifestations of racial prejudice. Historians have intensely argued over the origins of racism, including the question of whether the xenophobia and ethnocentrism of ancient cultures should be considered racist. Many scholars also maintain that medieval and early modern forms of religious hatred, especially against the Jewish and Muslim populations of Europe, should be viewed as a form of proto-racism.[16] Restrictive definitions of racism predicated on the presence of some kind of biologist concept are even more controversial within the context of the European conquest of the Americas, including the large-scale eradication of indigenous populations, the transatlantic slave trade, and the establishment of plantation slavery in the New World. Arguably, odious racial and cultural stereotypes were closely related to conquest and enslavement both as preconditions and as consequences.[17]

Undeniably, the Enlightenment became a watershed moment in the development of modern racism. During the eighteenth century, early attempts to classify human groups into races gave credence to the idea of biological determinism and dichotomous assumptions about superiority and inferiority based on physical characteristics. At the same time, the celebrated principle that "all men are created equal," extolled by the American Declaration of Independence, required new justifications for the continued exclusion of slaves, aboriginal peoples, and other oppressed groups. The advent of reason and egalitarianism thus both challenged and reinforced notions of race and racism. By creating an imagined community of a superior ruling race, racism, in effect, democratized the privileges of descent that in the age of feudalism had been confined to the nobility. The United States can be seen as the best example of such a "*Herrenvolk* democracy." While priding itself on its egalitarian roots, the new nation sanctioned chattel slavery until the Civil War, sought to maintain the "purity" of the white race, and condoned racist violence, racial segregation, and disfranchisement.[18]

Yet many historians contest that the emphasis on scientific discourse encompasses the complexity and variety of racism as a social, political, and cultural phenomenon. Thus, another group of contributors to this volume insists that the definition of racism must be expanded to include essentialist notions of cultural difference and hierarchy. The proposition that the discrepancies in social achievement among various ethnic groups are the result of cultural rather than biogenetic differences, they argue, amounts to a functional equivalent of racism or what Christian Geulen calls "racism without race."[19] In a post-racist age, when old-style biologist racism is no longer acceptable, discrimination and hostility towards immigrants and minorities is usually justified in terms of cultural essentialism rather than racial inferiority. Then again, traditional scientific racism still surfaces occasionally as it did in the infamous "Bell Curve" debate on race, ethnicity, and intelligence in the United States in the mid-1990s. There is also concern that recent scientific research on diseases that appear to be common only in certain ethnic groups that were traditionally regarded as races may revive and revalidate the view of race as a biological reality.[20]

The intricate relationship between racism and culture figures prominently in this book. To be sure, all authors agree that race is not a valid biological category but a social and cultural construction. They also acknowledge the challenge of "reconstructing" racist ideologies and practices in vastly different historical and cultural contexts as well as the highly flexible and malleable character of racism. In fact, scholars who utilize comparative and transnational approaches are perfectly aware that they do not deal with a monolithic and static doctrine of racism but with the history of different racisms, "each historically specific and articulated in a different way with the societies in which they appear," as the British sociologist Stuart Hall phrased it as early as 1978.[21]

Yet, the following essays nevertheless differ in their assessment of the extent to which race has been an essentially Western ideology that was spread across the globe as a consequence of Western imperialism. Several contributors challenge such models of imposition and diffusion and advocate an "interactive model," to borrow the term used by Frank Dikötter. Dikötter and others seek to demonstrate that racial ideas pre-existed in non-Western cultures. Echoing Robertson's concept of "glocalization," these authors argue that Western ideas were not passively adopted but creatively adapted to specific local conditions and contexts. Other contributors caution against applying Western categories to understand indigenous traditions lest we only reproduce the colonialist perspective.

Moreover, the relationship between racism and imperialism is more complex than is often acknowledged. Surely, racist ideologies played an important role in the imperialist ventures of Western nations, whose leaders frequently legitimized military occupation and exploitation in Africa and Asia with the alleged racial inferiority of the regions' inhabitants and the mission to civilize the "savages." But racism could also work as a barrier against imperialism as it did in the United States, where the guardians of white supremacy were opposed to incorporating additional non-whites into the body politic.[22] Thus, both the propagandists and the opponents of imperialism fostered the emergence of a white racial identity in imperialist nations. Over the past twenty years, "whiteness" has developed into a burgeoning field of study and an analytical concept that seeks to explore the circumstances under which people of European descent came to believe they are white. The fascinating studies on whiteness and immigration in American history have demonstrated that U.S. authorities and mainstream society used whiteness to classify immigrants and thereby offered a new racialized identity that immigrants embraced, adapted, or rejected.[23] Yet recent scholarship on whiteness has little to say about how Western notions of whiteness differed from and came to influence similar racial identities in other countries. Several essays in this volume help to fill this void by scrutinizing the construction of whiteness in colonial settings such as India, the Philippines, and Australia. Other authors are interested in the formation of non-white racial identities such as "yellowness."

It would be illusory to believe that all aspects of race and racism in the modern world could be covered in one volume. Obviously, this book makes no claim to geographical or topical comprehensiveness. Certain gaps are a consequence of practical constraints; others are a result of the editors' decisions. For example, the history of white supremacy in North America and the history of European anti-Semitism, which George Fredrickson calls "the most conspicuous manifestations of racism," are not addressed in separate essays. The literature on these two topics is already vast and most general histories of racism treat them extensively. Instead we chose to invite contributions that deal with American white supremacy and European and German anti-Semitism within comparative or transnational frameworks. Of course, the Holocaust continues to be the most extreme example of how racist ideology was utilized to exterminate entire peoples stigmatized as "the racial other."[24]

Similarly, gender analysis does not play a salient role in this volume, although it is clear that many racial ideologies and practices, as a number of scholars have shown, are always gendered. U.S. historians in particular have analyzed the intricate tensions and interrelationships between racism and gender. In her path-breaking work *Manliness & Civilization,* for instance, Gail Bederman demonstrated how manhood and racial dominance were inextricably linked in American culture around 1900. American middle-class men conceptualized male dominance in terms of white supremacy and vice versa in discussions about lynching, American imperialism, as well as childrearing. Other scholars have explored the role that American women played in supporting racist hierarchies at home and abroad and the ways in which white feminists incorporated certain notions of white supremacy into their calls for women's liberation.[25]

Comparative and transnational perspectives on the history of racism and gender have gained more ground in recent years, but the historiography pertaining to this topic is still in its infancy. Most scholars who study this aspect of racism have focused on Western colonialism and imperialism, exploring, for instance, how women cooperated with men in perpetuating racial hierarchies in various colonial and imperial ventures abroad. More recent studies explore how colonizers imagined themselves in the colonies and what role masculinity and femininity played in related identity constructions. Others have analyzed how gender, sexual difference, and racism constructed each other in discourses on the legitimacy of slavery. In many of these works, there is an implicit awareness of the importance of processes of cultural transfer and translation, without which various forms of racism would not have developed. Few studies, however, explicitly address the various forms of exchange and adaptation that affected the interrelationship between racism and gender among both colonizers and colonized.[26]

One final clarification seems to be in order: by design the contributions to this volume primarily interrogate racist ideologies and discourses, even though most authors at least hint at the complex interrelationship between ideology and social practice. However, a fully-fledged analysis of racial practices and institutions would require another book that would have to be different in design and scope.

The first four essays of this collection explore the "big picture" of racism as a global phenomenon. Frank Dikötter (chapter 1) ponders the question of how and why racism, which he understands as an ideology that "equates social groups with biological units" (and therefore should be distinguished from other forms of invidious discrimination), developed into a belief system of global reach and appeal. Rejecting as Eurocentric the notion that the West imposed racism on the rest of the world, he proposes to rely on an "interactive model" based on the complex interplay between indigenous traditions, transcultural flows, and processes of local adaptation. Citing recent research on Native American, Chinese, and African cultures, he contends that skin color as a racial marker was not simply a European "import" but fitted in neatly with indigenous cognitive traditions. Furthermore, Dikötter argues that racist ideas had such a global appeal because they provided answers to the problem of political equality and were predicated on a highly adaptable language of science.

Like Dikötter, Benjamin Braude (chapter 2) understands racism as an ideology based on "hereditary determinism" that should not be confused with other forms of prejudice. Yet, while he thinks that racism is a specifically Western phenomenon, he is interested in the elementary historical circumstances that explain why imagined divisions of race developed in Europe and did not in other parts of the world, especially in the Islamic Near East. Braude urges us to ponder the history of prejudice in the premodern world, when notions of biology and heredity were radically different from our modern systems of knowledge. He then undertakes a sweeping comparison of geographic, cultural, social, and political differences between Europe and the Near East since the Middle Ages that in his view explain why racism emerged in the former but could not develop in the latter. His argument, he insists, is not to exonerate the Islamic world from group prejudice and mass violence but to demonstrate that they did not stem from racist ideologies.

In contrast to Dikötter and Braude, Christian Geulen (chapter 3) advocates a broad definition of racism. He believes that it would be misleading to portray racism as "a deterministic ideology of fixed differences and racial hierarchies" with culture as the supposedly flexible and benign alternative concept of explaining human difference and constructing identity.[27] Geulen seeks to demonstrate that the relationship between racism and culture has been much more intricate throughout the twentieth century and that the idiom of culture has been an integral part of the history of racism. Modern racists, he argues, have always conceived of races as malleable rather than static entities and of culture as a powerful force in the making of races. For example, according to Geulen, racial hygiene and eugenics had much more in common with cultural anthropology than is often assumed. Since World War II, Geulen further claims, racial discourse has been transformed into the idiom of culture (as in the notorious Clash of Civilizations) at a time when culture "has become the most important and most trusted category for collective identity and belonging." Even without a biological concept of race, racism has survived in the form of cultural essentialism.

In his comparative essay on racism and genocide (chapter 4), Boris Barth insists on the need to define both terms narrowly. Racism should be understood as the "biologization of the social sphere," whereas the term genocide should be confined to those cases of mass murder in the twentieth century that were perpetrated by the state with the intent to exterminate entire groups.[28] Although this leaves us with relatively few instances that can be indisputably regarded as genocide, Barth nevertheless concludes that "genocide in the twentieth century always had an ethnic dimension or was based on racist ideas." Viewed from this perspective, racism does not automatically lead to genocide, but it appears to be a necessary precondition, especially when it is coupled with fantasies of ethnic cleansing, pan-nationalist ideologies of conquest, or eugenicist utopianism. While racist ideologies may exist and even thrive in democratic societies, Barth believes that democracies are structurally incapable of perpetrating full-scale genocide.

The next four chapters open up transnational perspectives on racism in the Americas. In his essay on the racialization of slavery in nineteenth-century Cuba, a time period when the island experienced a stunning sugar boom based on mass slavery, Michael Zeuske (chapter 5) emphasizes class. He seeks to demonstrate that the Cuban planter elite used race to create a separate *clase negra* that included both slaves and free blacks. Yet his study of Francisco de Arango y Parreño (1765–1837), a leading member of the planter class and leading Cuban intellectual, also shows that racial ideologies were highly flexible as economic and political circumstances changed. Arango started out as a racist defender of slavery but subsequently metamorphosed into an abolitionist and advocate of racial equality. Arango's basic economic and racial ideas, however, remained relatively stable. Although this Cuban intellectual's calls for a color-blind Cuban nation were not heeded during his lifetime, they foreshadowed the highly ambivalent ways in which Cuban nationalism dealt with the legacies of race and slavery in the late nineteenth and early twentieth centuries.

The historiographies of racism and anti-Semitism tend to be treated as separate fields of inquiry. Claudia Bruns explores the intersections of both ideologies in chapter 6. Her biographical approach focuses on the life of Wilhelm Marr (1819–1904), the "founding father" of German racial anti-Semitism. As a young man, Marr was a democratic socialist and advocate of republican ideals. After the failure of the Revolution of 1848, he migrated to the New World and spent more than a decade in the United States and Central America. The sympathies Marr felt for the plight of enslaved and free blacks in the U.S. soon gave way to racist contempt. Bruns argues that Marr's racialization of Jews and his embrace of anti-Semitism after his return to Germany was heavily influenced by his experiences in the Americas. According to Bruns, anti-Semitism as an "intra-white" racism cannot be divorced from the colonial experience and the racism directed against blacks and other non-white peoples.

John David Smith also takes a biographical approach (chapter 7) in exploring the transatlantic dimensions of racial ideologies. His protagonist is Felix von Luschan (1854–1924), an Austrian professor of anthropology at the University of Berlin and the curator of the anthropological collection at Berlin's Royal Ethnological Museum. Between October 1914 and April 1915, Luschan lectured in the United States and, with the help of African-American leader Booker T. Washington, conducted anthropological field research among southern blacks. Although Luschan emphatically rejected the doctrines of scientific racism, he was nevertheless fascinated by the study of heredity and eugenics and viewed the U.S. as a "laboratory" for the study of race. Smith sees Luschan as highly ambivalent in his attitude toward racism. While he espoused cultural relativism and rejected notions of racial inferiority, Luschan retained the outlook of an "elitist nationalist" and a paternalist "colonialist." His studies in America, the essay concludes, did not help Luschan to clarify his views but rather exacerbated his ambivalent stance on race.

In his essay on race and empire in the Philippine-American colonial experience (chapter 8), Paul Kramer questions established notions of "export" and "projection" that he thinks still prevail in the practice of transnational history.[29] In contrast, he argues that race-making in Philippine-American history in the early twentieth century has to take into account dynamic processes that developed in both countries. Kramer insists that American and Philippine nationalism and related notions of race must be situated within a complex framework of interaction that includes the Spanish colonial legacies, colonial warfare, Philippine-American collaboration, ideas of state-building, and exclusionary U.S. immigration policies.

The following four essays focus on the degree to which Western racial thought was received and transformed in Asia. In their interrogation of caste and race in South Asia (chapter 9), Gita Dharampal-Frick and Katja Götzen contend that the racialization of caste is conceptually flawed and, in fact, mirrors the colonialist mind-set. In a sweeping survey from the early modern period to the present they seek to deconstruct the genealogy of the term and its misleading discursive linkage with European ideas of race. The concept of caste, they show, was first introduced by the Portuguese to make sense of Indian social hierarchies but retained polyvalent meanings. European Orientalists and missionaries then gradually racialized caste and linked it to the so-called Aryan race theory. The resulting image of Indian castes as racial entities, the authors conclude, is a colonialist misconception whose legacy is reflected in present-day condemnations of the caste system as racist.

Harald Fischer-Tiné reverses this perspective in chapter 10 by exploring how "whiteness" was constructed and maintained in nineteenth-century British India. In the first part of his essay he shows how the language of "scientific racism" gradually superseded environmentalist explanations of human diversity during the nineteenth century. He then goes on to explore the difficulties that colonial authorities faced in upholding the fictitious image of a unified "white" race, given that India's white colonial society was in itself highly stratified. Specifically, Fischer-Tiné analyzes the controversy over how to deal with white criminals and convicts in India, a group of people that caused enormous problems for the colonial administration in its endeavor to maintain British self-representations as a "ruling race."

In her account (chapter 11) of how Chinese reformers of the late nineteenth century appropriated Western ideas of race, Gotelind Müller utilizes Roland Robertson's concept of "glocalization" to emphasize the simultaneity of the global and local dimensions of transcultural flows. Western race concepts, she argues, were not an "imposed hegemonic discourse" but were tied in with the agendas of Chinese reformers trying to construct a modern Chinese national identity vis-à-vis the Western colonial powers but also vis-à-vis the Manchu dynasty and the Japanese. The process of "glocalizing" race in China thus highlights the enormous flexibility of racial categories.

In stark contrast to China, Japan not only succeeded in maintaining its independence from colonial rule but also in establishing the only modern empire built by a non-Western power. In chapter 12 Urs Zachmann first traces the reception of Western "scientific racism" in Japan, which, he contends, remained confined to a small group of academics. The author then looks at how racial attitudes manifested themselves in three fields of public policy, namely international relations, immigration and colonial rule. While the Japanese strictly rejected racial hierarchies in their interactions with the Western powers, they insisted on the cultural assimilation of their colonial subjects in Korea and Taiwan. Although he finds that Japanese attitudes in dealing with "other" peoples should be termed "culturalism" rather than racism, Zachmann raises the intriguing question whether enforced integration might fall under the definition of racism as well.

The final three contributions deal with South Africa and Australia. While both societies can be classified as cases of settler racism, they differ in that the white minority of South Africa established a rigid apartheid regime to oppress the black majority, whereas the white Australian majority conquered and marginalized the aboriginal minority. Christoph Marx discusses (chapter 13) the intellectual influences that shaped the racial ideas of Hendrik Verwoerd (1901–1966), the architect of the apartheid system in the 1950s and 1960s. Although Verwoerd studied psychology in Germany, Marx contests historians' claims that German racial thought and Nazi racism influenced his conceptions of the racial order of South Africa. Rather, according to Marx, Verwoerd's project of a postcolonial racist state based on strict segregation and cultural essentialism ought to be interpreted as an attempt to promote the racial and social improvement of poor whites. Verwoerd thus becomes a "technocratic racist" who tried to implement apartheid as an authoritarian modernization of state and society to benefit whites.

Gregory Smithers probes the construction of whiteness in settler colonies (chapter 14) by comparing the racial construction of white identity in the United States and Australia between the 1780s and 1930s. Smithers shows that missionaries, scholars, and political leaders regarded whiteness as the bedrock of civilization in far-flung settler colonies, which they believed could only endure if they produced racially and culturally homogeneous populations. Yet the differences between the United States and Australia are striking. While white Americans enforced segregation and anti-miscegenation laws, influential members of the Australian elite actually advocated interracial unions "to breed out the color." Smithers suggests that these attitudes reflected a self-confident belief in the preponderance of the white race, whereas American segregation mirrored the uneasiness of racists in a multiracial and multiethnic society.[30]

In the last chapter (chapter 15), Dirk Moses connects the transformation of "White Australia" into a multiracial and multicultural society with the current debates and conflicts that this process has triggered. On the one hand, racism and racial discourses persist among white traditionalists. On the other hand, critical race theorists denounce liberal anti-racism as "benign whiteness." The controversy over the "crisis of the indigenous community" in Australia, including problems such as alcoholism, child abuse, etc., serves as a case in point. Does government intervention amount to a paternalistic racism or, vice versa, does non-intervention reveal a racist attitude of indifference and neglect? Moses closely analyzes the debate among indigenous intellectuals over whether indiginity should be preserved and defended on the basis of a racial essentialism or whether the indigenous community should seek a new identity based on "peoplehood" within modern Australia.

It is likely that this volume will raise as many questions as it answers. The essays that follow clearly demonstrate that it is necessary to probe the history of particular racisms rather than explore a general history of racism. They also show the importance of historicity and context, without which the emergence and development of particular racisms cannot be fully understood. Nevertheless, the editors hope that the focus on cultural transfer and adaptation offers a common framework that will contribute to a more diverse and nuanced history of race and racism in the modern world.

Notes

1. The literature on the history of racism is vast. For the most accessible introductions and surveys, see George M. Fredrickson, *Racism: A Short History* (Princeton, 2002); Pierre L. Van den Berghe, *Race and Racism: A Comparative Perspective*, 2nd ed. (New York, 1978); Ivan Hannaford, *Race: The History of an Idea in the West* (Baltimore, 1996); Imanuel Geiss, *Geschichte des Rassismus* (Frankfurt, 1988); Georg L. Mosse, *Die Geschichte des Rassismus in Europa* (Frankfurt, 1990); Christian Delacampagne, *Die Geschichte des Rassismus* (Düsseldorf, 2005); Christian Geulen, *Geschichte des Rassismus* (München, 2007).
2. See, e.g., David E. Stannard, *American Holocaust. The Conquest of the New World* (New York, 1992).
3. See Bernard Lewis, *Race and Slavery in the Middle East: An Historical Inquiry* (New York, 1990); Benjamin Braude, "The Sons of Noah and the Construction of Ethnic and Geographical Identities in the Medieval and Early Modern Periods," *William and Mary Quarterly* 54, no. 1 (January 1997): 103–42; James H. Sweet, "The Iberian Roots of American Racism," *William and Mary Quarterly* 54, no. 1 (January 1997): 142–66; Frank Dikötter, *The Discourse of Race in Modern China* (London, 1992); Frank Dikötter, ed., *The Construction of Racial Identities in China and Japan: Historical and Contemporary Perspectives* (London, 1997); Mariko Asano Tamanoi, "Knowledge, Power, and Racial Classification: The 'Japanese' in 'Manchuria,'" *Journal of Asian Studies* 59, no. 2 (May 2000): 248–76; John W. Dower, *War Without Mercy: Race and Power in the Pacific War* (New York, 1987).
4. For a useful introduction to the approaches and topics of the new global history, see Bruce Mazlish and Akira Iriye, eds., *The Global History Reader* (New York, 2005); Bruce Mazlish, *The New Global History* (New York, 2006); Sebastian Conrad, Andreas Eckert, and Ulrike Freitag, eds., *Globalgeschichte: Theorien, Ansätze, Themen* (Frankfurt, 2007). For a highly influential critique of Eurocentrism, see Dipesh Chakrabarty, *Provincializing Europe: Postcolonial Thought and Historical Difference* (Princeton, 2000); see also Sebastian Conrad and Shalini Randeria, eds., *Jenseits des Eurozentrismus: Postkoloniale Perspektiven in den Geschichts- und Kulturwissenschaften* (Frankfurt, 2002).
5. There are countless studies on racism in the United States, Britain, and Germany. See, e.g., George M. Fredrickson, *The Black Image in the White Mind: The Debate on Afro-American Character and Destiny, 1817–1914* (New York, 1971); Thomas F. Gossett, *Race: The History of an Idea in America* (New York, 1963); Audrey Smedley, *Race in North America: Origin and Evolution of a Worldview*, 3rd ed. (Boulder, CO, 2007); John Solomos, *Race and Racism in Britain*, 3rd ed. (New York, 2003); Tony Ballantyne, *Orientalism and Race: Aryanism in the British Empire* (New York, 2002); Peter Walkenhorst, *Nation – Volk – Rasse: Radikaler Nationalismus im Deutschen Kaiserreich, 1890–1914* (Göttingen, 2007); Michael Burleigh and Wolfgang Wippermann, *The Racial State: Germany, 1933–1945* (Cambridge, UK, 1991). For a recent transnational history of

white supremacy, see Marilyn Lake and Henry Reynolds, *Drawing the Global Colour Line: White Men's Countries and the International Challenge of Racial Equality* (Cambridge, UK, 2008); see also Gerald Horne, "Race from Power: U.S. Foreign Policy and the General Crisis Of 'White Supremacy,'" in *Ambiguous Legacy: U.S. Foreign Relations in The "American Century,"* edited by Michael J. Hogan (Cambridge, 1999), 302–36.

6. See Conrad, et al., *Globalgeschichte*, 7–49.

7. See, e.g., Robert Knox, *The Races of Men: A Philosophical Enquiry into the Influence of Race over the Destinies of Nations*, 2nd ed. (London, 1862); Madison Grant, *The Passing of the Great Race* (New York, 1916); Lothrop Stoddard, *The Rising Tide of Color against White Supremacy* (New York, 1920). The work on the eugenics movement falls into this category. See Stefan Kühl, *Die Internationale der Rassisten: Aufstieg und Niedergang der internationalen Bewegung für Eugenik und Rassenhygiene im 20. Jahrhundert* (Frankfurt/M., 1997); Mark B. Adams, *The Wellborn Science: Eugenics in Germany, France, Brazil, and Russia* (New York, 1990). The historiography on the internationalism of African Americans has grown immensely over the past twenty years. See, e.g., Robin D.G. Kelley, "'But a Local Phase of a World Problem': Black History's Global Vision, 1883–1950," *Journal of American History* 86, no. 3 (1999): 1045–77; Brenda Gayle Plummer, *Rising Wind: Black Americans and U.S. Foreign Affairs, 1935–1960* (Chapel Hill and London, 1996).

8. Roland Robertson, "Globalisation or Glocalisation?," *Journal of International Communication* 1, no. 1 (1994): 38. See also Roland Robertson, "Glocalization: Time–Space and Homogeneity–Heterogeneity," in *Global Modernities*, edited by Mike Featherstone, Scott Lash, and Roland Robertson (London, 1995), 25–44.

9. Ian Tyrrell, *Transnational Nation: United States History in Global Perspective since 1789* (Basingstoke, 2007), 3. For methodological discussions of transnational history, see David Thelen, "The Nation and Beyond: Transnational Perspectives on United States History," *Journal of American History* 86, no. 3 (December 1999): 965–75; Gunilla-Friederike Budde, Sebastian Conrad, and Oliver Janz, eds., *Transnationale Geschichte: Themen, Tendenzen und Theorien* (Göttingen, 2006).

10. George Reid Andrews, "Brazilian Racial Democracy, 1900–90: An American Counterpoint," *Journal of Contemporary History* 31, no. 3 (July 1996): 483–507, 484. Recent work on colonialism emphasizes the repercussions of colonial experiences in the colonizing societies. See, e.g., Frank Becker, ed., *Rassenmischehen, Mischlinge, Rassentrennung: Zur Politik der Rasse im Deutschen Kolonialreich* (Stuttgart, 2004); Sebastian Conrad, *Deutsche Kolonialgeschichte* (München, 2008); Paul Kramer, *Blood of Government: Race, Empire, the United States, and the Philippines* (Chapel Hill, 2006). A study on transfer and interconnections within the Western world is Stefan Kühl, *The Nazi Connection: Eugenics, American Racism, and German National Socialism* (New York, 1994).

11. Peter Kolchin, "The South and the World," *Journal of Southern History* 75, no. 3 (2009): 565–80. On the scope and limitations of comparisons, see Jürgen Kocka, "Comparison and Beyond," *History and Theory* 42, no. 1 (February 2003): 39–44.

12. George M. Fredrickson, *White Supremacy: A Comparative Study in American and South African History* (Oxford, 1981), xvii. Fredrickson was the leading authority on comparative history of race and racism, see George M. Fredrickson, *The Comparative Imagination: On the History of Racism, Nationalism, and Social Movements* (Berkeley and Los Angeles, 1997); George M. Fredrickson, *Diverse Nations: Explorations in the History of Racial and Ethnic Pluralism* (Boulder, CO, 2008). Other important contributions to the field are Anthony W. Marx, *Making Race and Nation: A Comparison of South Africa, the United States, and Brazil* (New York, 1997); John W. Cell, *The Highest Stage of White Supremacy: The Origins of Segregation in South African and the American South* (Cambridge, 1982); Howard Lamar and Leonard Thompson, eds., *The Frontier in History: North America and Southern Africa Compared* (New Haven, 1981).

13. On the relationship between transnational and comparative history, see Johannes Paulmann, "Internationaler Vergleich und Interkultureller Transfer: Zwei Forschungsansätze zur Europäischen Geschichte des 18. bis 20. Jahrhunderts," *Historische Zeitschrift* 267, no. 3 (1998): 649–85; Micol Seigel, "Beyond Compare: Comparative Method after the Transnational Turn," *Radical History Review* 91 (Winter 2005): 62–90; Jürgen Osterhammel, *Geschichtswissenschaft jenseits des Nationalstaats: Studien zu Beziehungsgeschichte und Zivilisationsvergleich* (Göttigen, 2001); Jürgen Osterhammel, "Transnationale Geschichte: Erweiterung oder Alternative?," *Geschichte und Gesellschaft* 27, no. 3 (2001): 464–79.

14. Dikötter, *The Discourse of Race in Modern China*; Frank Dikötter, *Imperfect Conceptions: Medical Knowledge, Birth Defects, and Eugenics in China* (London: 1998).

15. Van den Berghe, *Race and Racism*, 9. A classic work on scientific racism is Stephen Jay Gould, *The Mismeasure of Man* (New York, 1981); see also William H. Tucker, *The Science and Politics of Racial Research* (Urbana and Chicago, 1994); Elazar Barkan, *The Retreat of Scientific Racism: Changing Concepts of Race in Britain and the United States between the World Wars* (Cambridge, 1992); Saul Dubow, *Scientific Racism in Modern South Africa* (Cambridge, 1995).

16. Frank M. Snowden Jr., *Before Color Prejudice: The Ancient View of Blacks* (Cambridge, MA, 1983); Benjamin Isaac, *The Invention of Racism in Classical Antiquity* (Princeton, 2004); Robert Bartlett, *The Making of Europe: Conquest, Colonization, and Cultural Change, 950–1350* (Princeton, 1993); Valentin Groebner, "Mit dem Feind schlafen: Nachdenken über Hautfarben, Sex und 'Rasse' im spätmittelalterlichen Europa," *Historische Anthropologie* 15, no. 3 (2007): 327–38; Sweet, "Iberian Roots"; Max S. Hering Torres, *Rassismus in der Vormoderne: Die "Reinheit des Blutes" im Spanien der Frühen Neuzeit* (Frankfurt, 2006); Rainer Walz, "Der Vormoderne Antisemitismus: Religiöser Fanatismus oder Rassenwahn?," *Historische Zeitschrift* 260, no. 3 (1995): 719–48.

17. Tzvetan Todorov, *The Conquest of America: The Question of the Other* (Norman, 1999); Ronald Sanders, *Lost Tribes and Promised Lands: The Origins of American Racism* (1978, reprint; New York, 1992); Winthrop D. Jordan, *White over Black:*

American Attitudes toward the Negro, 1550–1812 (Chapel Hill, 1968); Alden T. Vaughan, *Roots of American Racism. Essays on the Colonial Experience* (New York, 1995); Manfred Berg,"Die Ursprünge der Sklaverei in Nordamerika,"*Zeitschrift für Geschichtswissenschaft* 54 , no. 9 (2006): 741–60.

18. See H.F. Augstein, ed., *Race: The Origins of an Idea, 1760–1850* (Bristol, 1996); Andrew Valls, *Race and Racism in Modern Philosophy* (Ithaca, NY, 2005); Fredrickson, *Racism: A Short History*; Hannaford, *Race: The History of an Idea in the West*; Rayford Logan, *The Negro in American Life and Thought: The Nadir, 1877–1901* (New York, 1954); Leon Litwack, *Trouble in Mind: Black Southerners in the Age of Jim Crow* (New York, 1998). The term "Herrenvolk democracy" was first used by Pierre van den Berghe. Van den Berghe, *Race and Racism*, 18.

19. See Howard Schuman, "Free Will and Determinism in Public Beliefs about Race," in *Majority and Minority: The Dynamics of Race and Ethnicity in American Life*, 3rd ed. (Boston, 1999), 345–50; David O. Sears, "Egalitarian Values and Contemporary Racial Politics," in *Racialized Politics: The Debate About Racism in America*, edited by David O. Sears, Jim Sidanius, and Lawrence Bobo (Chicago, 2000), 75–117; Pierre-Andre Taguieff, *The Force of Prejudice: On Racism and Its Doubles* (Minneapolis, 2001); Wulf D. Hundt, *Rassismus* (Bielefeld, 2007).

20. See Priscilla Wald, "Blood and Stories: How Genomics is Rewriting Race, Medicine and Human History," *Patterns of Prejudice* 40, no. 4–5 (2006): 303–33; Robert Carter, "Genes, Genomes and Genealogies: The Return of Scientific Racism?," *Ethnic and Racial Studies* 30, no. 4 (2007): 546–56. See Richard J. Herrnstein and Charles Murray, *The Bell Curve: Intelligence and Class Structure in American Life* (New York, 1994); Russel Jacoby and Naomi Glauberman, eds., *The Bell Curve Debate: History, Documents, Opinions* (New York, 1995).

21. Stuart Hall, "Racism and Reaction," in *Five Views of Multi-Racial Britain*, edited by the Commission for Racial Equality (London, 1978), 26.

22. See Boris Barth and Jürgen Osterhammel, eds., *Zivilisierungsmissionen: Imperiale Weltverbesserung seit dem 18. Jahrhundert* (Konstanz, 2005); Frank Becker, "Zum Stellenwert des Rassismus im Spektrum der deutschen Kolonialideologie," in *Rassenmischehen—Mischlinge—Rassentrennung: Zur Politik der Rasse im deutschen Kolonialreich*, edited by Frank Becker (Stuttgart, 2004), 27–41; Alice L. Conklin, "Colonialism and Human Rights, A Contradiction in Terms? The Case of France in West Africa, 1895–1914," *American Historical Review* 103, no. 2 (April 1998): 419–42; Eric T.L. Love, *Race Over Empire: Racism & U.S. Imperialism, 1865–1900* (Chapel Hill, 2004); Michael Adas, *Machines as Measures of Men: Science, Technology, and Ideologies of Western Dominance* (Ithaca, 1990).

23. See Steve Garner, *Whiteness: An Introduction* (New York, 2007); Thomas K. Nakayama and Judith N. Martin, *Whiteness: The Communication of Social Identity* (Thousand Oaks, 1999); Richard Delgado and Jean Stefancic, *Critical White Studies: Looking Behind the Mirror* (Philadelphia, 1997); Allen Theodore, *The Invention of the White Race* (New York, 1994); David R. Roediger, *Working Toward Whiteness:*

How America's Immigrants Became White (New York, 2005); David R. Roediger, *Colored White: Transcending the Racial Past* (Berkeley, 2002); David R. Roediger, *The Wages of Whiteness: Race and the Making of the American Working Class*, rev. ed. (New York, 1999); Matthew Frye Jacobson, *Whiteness of a Different Color: European Immigrants and the Alchemy of Race* (Cambridge, 1998); Thomas A. Guglielmo, *White on Arrival: Italians, Race, Color, and Power in Chicago, 1890–1945* (New York, 2003). On the historiography of whiteness studies in the United States, see Daniel Wickberg, "Heterosexual White Male: Some Recent Inversions in American Cultural History," *Journal of American History* 92, no. 1 (June 2005): 136–57; Peter Kolchin, "Whiteness Studies: The New History of Race in America," *Journal of American History* 89, no. 1 (2002): 154–73.

24. Fredrickson, *A Short History of Racism*, 156; Geiss, *Geschichte des Rassismus*; George L. Mosse, *Toward the Final Solution: A History of European Racism* (Madison, WI, 1985); George L. Mosse, *Die Geschichte des Rassismus in Europa*; Audrey Smedley, *Race in North America: Origin and Evolution of a Worldview*; Norbert Finzsch and Dietmar Schirmer, eds., *Identity and Intolerance: Nationalism, Racism, and Xenophobia in Germany and the United States* (New York, 1998).

25. Gail Bederman, *Manliness & Civilization: A Cultural History of Gender and Race in the United States, 1880–1917* (Chicago, 1995); Glenda Elizabeth Gilmore, *Gender and Jim Crow: Women and the Politics of White Supremacy in North Carolina, 1896–1920* (Chapel Hill, 1996); Kathleeen M. Blee, *Women of the Klan: Racism and Gender in the 1920s* (Berkeley, 1991); Kathleen M. Blee, *Inside Organized Racism: Women in the Hate Movement* (Berkeley, 2003); Abby L. Ferber, ed., *Home-Grown Hate: Gender and Organized Racism* (New York, 2004); Louise Michelle Newman, *White Women's Rights: The Racial Origins of Feminism in the United States* (New York, 1999).

26. See Katharina Walgenbach, *"Die Weiße Frau als Trägerin deutscher Kultur": Koloniale Diskurse über Geschlecht, "Rasse" und Klasse im Kaiserreich* (Frankfurt, 2005); Cecily Jones, *Engendering Whiteness: White Women and Colonialism in Barbados and North Carolina, 1627–1865* (Manchester, 2007); Laura Briggs, *Reproducing Empire: Race, Sex, Science, and U.S. Imperialism in Puerto Rico* (Berkeley, 2002); Lora Wildenthal, *German Women for Empire, 1884–1945* (Durham, 2001); Jennifer L. Morgan, "'Some Could Suckle Over Their Shoulder': Male Travelers, Female Bodies, and the Gendering of Racial Ideology, 1500–1770," *William and Mary Quarterly* 54, no. 1 (January 1997): 167–92; Ann Laura Stoler, "Making Empire Respectable: The Politics of Race and Sexual Morality in Twentieth-Century Colonial Culture," in *Dangerous Liaisons: Gender, Nation, and Postcolonial Perspectives*, edited by Anne McClintock, Aamir Mufti, and Ella Shohat (Minneapolis, 1997), 344–73; Ann Laura Stoler, *Carnal Knowledge and Imperial Power: Race and the Intimate in Colonial Rule* (Berkeley 2002).

27. See also Geulen, *Rassismus*.

28. See also Boris Barth, *Genozid: Völkermord im 20. Jahrhundert, Geschichte – Theorien – Kontroversen* (München, 2007). It needs to be added that many scholars of European expansion and imperialism insist on a much broader definition of genocide that encompasses the extermination of indigenous peoples in the Americas and in Australia. See A. Dirk Moses, ed., *Genocide and Settler Society: Frontier Violence and Stolen Indigenous Children in Australian History* (New York, 2004); A. Dirk Moses, ed., *Empire, Colony, Genocide: Conquest, Occupation, and Subaltern Resistance in World History* (New York, 2008).
29. See also Kramer, *Blood of Government*.
30. See also Gregory D. Smithers, *Science, Sexuality, and Race in the United States and Australia, 1780s–1890s* (New York, 2009).

Chapter 1

The Racialization of the Globe: Historical Perspectives

Frank Dikötter

"This yellow river, it so happens, bred a nation identified by its yellow skin pigment. Moreover, this nation also refers to its earliest ancestor as the Yellow Emperor. Today, on the face of the earth, of every five human beings there is one that is a descendant of the Yellow Emperor."[1]

Definitions and Approaches

How do we explain the spread of racist belief systems around the globe? Before we attempt to answer this question it might be helpful to provide definitions of the terms "race" and "racism." In English alone, the Oxford English Dictionary provides a range of literary and scientific meanings, and it is obvious that the word had many legitimate definitions for different people in different times and different circumstances. As Michael Banton has shown, in English the term "race" only started referring to alleged biological differences between groups of people during the nineteenth century.[2] Nor is it a necessary precondition to use the word "race" in order to construct what many would consider to be racial categories of thought. At the turn of the century, many authors in Britain used the word "nation" to sustain racial frames of analysis; the "nation" was thought by some to correspond to a biologically homogeneous unit that could be improved through selective breeding. In Nazi Germany, German citizens were often described as a Volk, whereas "racial hygiene" was called Volksgesundheit. No historian would deny that the term Volk has a variety of ambiguous meanings, but it would be foolhardy to argue that it did not contribute to the invention of "the Aryans" as a group of people linked by blood.[3]

Rather than review the different definitions that have been proposed for "race" by the historical participants themselves, it may be more fruitful to focus on how boundaries have been drawn between human beings. Socially constructed "races," from this perspective, are population groups which are imagined to have boundaries based on biological characteristics, and can be contrasted to socially constructed "ethnicities," which are groups thought to be based on culturally acquired features: the ways in which boundaries are created and maintained are distinct, although they clearly overlap in many cases. Racism attempts to root culture in nature, to equate social groups with biological units, to primordialize the imagined or real bodily attributes of human beings: it takes a bodily feature—eye color, skin tone, hair texture—to construct systemic differences between human beings. A softer version of racism—seen to convey notions of hierarchy and oppression—is sometimes proposed by using the term "racialism," defined as the belief that the human species can be divided into equal yet distinct "races." But whether or not any hierarchy is implied between human groups, all worldviews which systematically purport to classify people on the basis of some physical signifier, be it skin color, body height, hair texture, or head-shape, are racist in that they define group boundaries along alleged natural lines.

Two main criticisms have been leveled against this approach. On the one hand it is argued that "scientific racism," as it is sometimes referred to, no longer represents the dominant form of discrimination, as references to the science that underpinned racism in the nineteenth century have largely disappeared. One of the key problems, it is alleged, is that after the exposure of "scientific racism" as a dangerous illusion, explicit racist statements are rarely made in public as they are no longer seen as acceptable, although racism per se has all but vanished. It is hiding behind notions of "culture" and "difference" and thus needs to be caught with a wider net. As Marek Kohn has argued in his *Race Gallery: The Return of Racial Science*,[4] this argument—popular during the Cold War—failed to foresee the remarkable versatility and persistence of scientific arguments in favor of a notion of race, as recent debates sparked by advances in genomics amply show: many social scientists have underestimated how a very rapidly evolving language of science has continued to reinvigorate racist belief systems, from genetics in earlier decades to DNA today.

A second reservation is that we should be concerned with the function rather than the contents of discourse: the intention of discrimination is what matters, not its particular ideological justification. But humanity has devised so many ways to discriminate—in the name of religion, status, or culture—that this approach would be of little help to historians, who would quickly be overwhelmed. For instance, large numbers of people were killed in the twentieth century in the name of "class" rather than exclusively as a consequence of "race"—some thirty to forty million were starved or beaten to death in communist China between 1959 and 1962. More fruitful is the recognition that racism as an organized belief system is a limited historical, ideological, and political phenomenon—one tool among others in the arsenal of horror devised by human beings to demean, oppress, or exterminate each other.

Now that we have a rough working definition of "racism," we can turn our critical attention to some common explanations of its global dimensions—three to be precise. One popular view is that racial classifications are widespread because they are real: I call this the "common-sense model," and it has long thrived on ideas attributed to biology. For many decades a broad range of historians, sociologists, anthropologists, and biologists—one thinks of Richard Lewontin and Stephen Gould—have denounced race as a powerful illusion with no real foundation in science,[5] but the very fact that science itself is a complex and ever-evolving field speaking in many voices means that new claims purporting to demonstrate the existence of "racial differences" continually reappear. Recent advances in genomics, for instance the Human Genome Project, have even led to folk notions of "race" being given renewed credibility today: not only do some biologists claim that the "five races" historically envisaged by Blumenbach and others several centuries ago really do exist, but it is also alleged that "black," "brown," "red," "yellow," and "white" people have significant differences at the genomic level that lead to their susceptibility to particular diseases.[6] Neil Risch, while fully aware of the potential misunderstanding that might be caused by discussing race and genetics together, recently contended—with a number of qualifications—that "self-ascribed race and continental ancestry often have relatively high predictive value" in medically significant terms: folk knowledge, it might be inferred, remains for the time being a good guide to genetic differences.[7] In a less subtle manner Armand Leroi, writing an editorial for the New York Times in March 2005, affirms the biological reality of race in the human species by proclaiming that "races are real." The point here is not to contend that science should be purged of the notion of "race," but rather that the field of science is so diverse and the interactions between biology and culture so complex that, as Troy Duster puts it, such an enterprise might not be practicable, possible or even desirable.[8] Finally, directly relevant to those of us working in the humanities, "race" is not only in favor again among some scientists: popular historians such as Niall Ferguson have also seized upon these debates to claim that the persistence of racism at a global level today is due to the behavior of humans, programed to protect their kin and fight racial outsiders: deep biological laws dictate that like attracts like, thus shaping human history to a much larger extent than many of us would like to acknowledge—or so we are told.[9]

A second and equally popular explanation discards science as mere myth and shows instead that global racism is embedded in the ideologies and structures of global capitalism. Put briefly, in the "imposition model" thinkers ranging from Oliver Cox to Fidel Castro believe that as Europeans conquered the globe, they created unequal systems of social relations in which cheap labor was essential: racism ensured that colonized people were regarded as inferior and could be bought and sold like any other commodity. More recently, Percy C. Hintzen has shown the fundamental role race has played in shaping Caribbean identity, which has served to hide a racialized division of labor and a racialized allocation of power and privilege: closely linked to constructions of créolité, notions of "white purity continue to reinforce and legitimise a system of globalised dependency."[10] In its latest and most general incarnation this approach posits that the fall of the Berlin Wall has ushered in a new era of globalization in which a corporate North perpetuates racism in its spoliation of a postcolonial South.

Less politically overt yet even more influential is the "diffusion model," or cloud to dust theory: "Westernization," it is held, has resulted in the spread of racism out of Europe into the rest of the world, as prejudice is copied and assimilated locally, displacing more traditional forms of discrimination. Negative attitudes about "blackness" are reproduced locally as global elites strive to identify with "whiteness." In Brazil, for instance, sophisticated social vocabularies indicate traces of whiteness, from a brancarao who is so light-skinned a mulatto as to appear almost white, all the way to a small and dark mulequinho. Probably the best example, however, is a series of studies on cosmetic surgery in Japan—most purporting to demonstrate how the racial ideology of whiteness has been internalized to such as extent that local women not only apply skin lighteners to appear more "Western" but also go under the knife in order to restructure their eyelids and heighten their nose bridges.[11]

All three explanatory models are powerful in their simplicity but ultimately fail by interpreting racism as a uniform phenomenon, as if there were only one form of racism which is universal in its origins, causes, meanings, and effects. They also replicate a Eurocentric bias, ignoring the persistent power of moral and cognitive traditions in Asia, Africa, Amer-

ica, and the Middle East: they portray human beings as mere passive re-
cipients of ideas and things foreign, when instead we should recognize the
importance of human agency, as historical agents around the globe interpreted, adapted, transformed, and possibly even rejected racism in their
own specific ways. Far from being fixed or static entities, the polyphony
and adaptability of racial discourse in different historical circumstances
should be recognized if their enduring appeal is to be understood. The interactive model of interpretation proposed here emphasizes the worldviews
constructed by local historical agents, analyzing the complex cognitive, social, and political dimensions behind the indigenization and appropriation
of racist belief systems: put briefly, it highlights inculturation where others
see acculturation.

But the interactive model, based on reception studies, immediately encounters a major challenge: if local understandings of racism are important,
we need detailed in-depth studies based on local languages, which have
been all but ignored by the three Eurocentric models introduced above.
Only in 1992 was the first systematic historical analysis of a racist belief
system outside Europe and America published, providing detailed evidence
about the emergence, spread, and consolidation of racism in the specific
case of China.[12] A body of work has since appeared on other parts of the
world as well, consolidating the interactive model of explanation which
sees appropriation, differential usage, and resignification as the keys to understanding the rapid spread of racist worldviews in parts of the globe
outside Europe.[13]

Cognitive Traditions and the Emergence of Racial Categories of Thought

The first significant point to emerge from the study of racism outside Europe is the importance of pre-existing cognitive and social traditions. In a
path-breaking article published in 1997 and entitled "How Indians got to
be Red," Nancy Shoemaker questioned the idea that Europeans were the
sole inventors of the idea of "redness."[14] The conventional wisdom assigns
the power to label to Europeans alone, as they are believed to have defined
Indians as "red" after witnessing how they wore red paint. Yet well before
the appearance of the term in any European language, American Indians,
in particular those in the Southeast, were calling themselves "red." Native
color symbolism—origin stories which referred to red people, red earth

and a red creator—rather than European terminology determined its use in council meetings in the 1720s, when most foreign explorers used the term brown or tawny. In Southeastern Indian languages—whether Natchez, Choctaw or Muskogee—the very word meaning Indian originated in the term for the color "red" and literally meant "man-red," being translated as "red man" or "red people." Red and white were complementary divisions indicating war and peace. Where Indians in the Southeast did not have an indigenous category, they called themselves "red" in response to the Europeans who presented themselves as "white" or to distinguish themselves from their "black" slaves. Here too important geographical distinctions existed: most Europeans in the Southeast started referring to themselves as "whites" in the early 1700s, no doubt because many Carolina colonists emigrated from Barbados, one of the first colonies to experience a shift in identity from "Christian" to "white." The Dutch in New Netherlands and the English in the Northeast continued to see the world in terms of Christians and Indians until about the 1730s, when they started describing themselves as "white"—a term which could be literally translated into native languages, unlike the notion of "Christian."

By the 1760s most Indians believed that differences in physical appearance were markers of clear distinctions between the two people; skin color served as a divine sign that indicated how the land belonged to the reds while the whites were intruders. Ironically both Indians and Europeans initially viewed themselves in similar ways, but gradually developed a "fiction of irresolute difference" which was signified in racial terms of "red" and "white": "Indian and European similarities enabled them to see their differences in sharper relief and, over the course of the eighteenth century, construct new identities that exaggerated the contrasts between them while ignoring what they had in common."[15]

In China, to turn to another part of the world, the color "yellow" had positive connotations well before the arrival of racist belief systems from abroad. In Europe the notion of a "yellow race" probably only originated at the end of the seventeenth century as a reaction to reports of the Jesuits in China on the symbolic value of the color yellow. The concept did not exist in the ancient world, and was not used by travelers of the Middle Ages such as Marco Polo, Pian del Carpini, Bento de Goes, or any of the Arab traders. In 1655, the first European mission to the Qing described the Chinese as having a white complexion, "equal to the Europeans," except for some Southerners whose skin was "slightly brown." The first scientific work in which the notion of a "yellow race" appeared was François Bernier's

"Etrennes adressées à Madame de la Sablière pour l'année 1688." In China, moreover, the meanings ascribed to the term "yellow" were very positive. Yellow, one of the five "pure" colors in China, had long connoted emperorship and symbolized the Center. It was the color of the Emperor of the Middle Kingdom, ancestral home of the "descendants of the Yellow Emperor" who were thought to have originated in the valley of the Yellow River. Wang Fuzhi (1619–92), a seventeenth-century loyalist who remained influential until the beginning of this century, entitled one of his more important works the Yellow Book (Huangshu) (1656): the last chapter contrasted the imperial color yellow to "mixed" colors and named China the "yellow centre." On more popular discursive registers, legends circulated about the origins of humans in which noble people (liangmin) were made of yellow mud and ignoble people (jianmin) of vulgar rope—not unlike some Cherokee tales about the shaping of humans from red earth. Huang Zunxian (1848–1905), aged twenty, recorded in his diary that "all people are fashioned out of yellow mud." At fifty-four, as one of the most outstanding reformers of the late imperial period and an important proponent of racial theories, he publicly wondered: "Why is the yellow race not the only race in the world?"

In the case of China—so well documented thanks to the existence of a large literary heritage in the official language—one can find a strong resonance between indigenous social worldviews and racist belief systems at other levels too, patrilineage being a key example. The last dynasty, founded in 1644, was marked by a consolidation of the cult of patrilineal descent, center of a broad movement of social reform that emphasized family and lineage (zu). Considerable friction arose between lineages throughout the nineteenth century in response to heightened competition over natural resources, the need to control market towns, the gradual erosion of social order and organization problems caused by demographic pressures. The militarization of powerful lineages reinforced folk models of kinship solidarity, forcing in turn more loosely organized associations to form a unified descent group under the leadership of the gentry. At court level too, ideologies of descent became increasingly important, in particular with the erosion of a sense of cultural identity among Manchu aristocrats—the founders of the Qing dynasty in 1644. Pamela Crossley has shown how group identity through patrilineal descent became important in the Qianlong period (1736–95), when the court progressively turned towards a rigid taxonomy of distinct descent lines (zu) to distinguish between Han, Manchu, Mongol or Tibetan.[16] Within three distinct social levels—popular

culture, gentry society, and court politics—the common notion of patrilineal descent came to be deployed on a widespread scale in the creation
and maintenance of group boundaries. We will see, in a later section, how
patrilineality was racialized at the end of the nineteenth century.

So far we have indicated that elements of cognitive continuity were crucial to the emergence of new racial vocabularies, which flourished better in
a cultural environment prepared to emphasize real or imagined physical
differences between people. A counter-example might illustrate this point
better: according to Wyatt MacGaffey, the traditional cosmology of the
BaKongo, a population group living in the south of the Congo along the
Angolan border, was based upon a complementary opposition between this
world and the other. In a religion strongly involved with water spirits, it
was believed that the skin of the dead turned white when they crossed the
water to join the spirits in the nether world. When Europeans first arrived
among the BaKongo, it was thought that they had emerged from the water,
where they would return at night to sleep. This integrative worldview, in
which life had no end, prevented the BaKongo from distinguishing population groups in racial terms and impeded the emergence of a sharp
distinction between European culture and BaKongo cosmology. "When the
first Portuguese arrived in Kongo in 1485 they exhibited the principal characteristics of the dead: they were white in color, spoke an unintelligible
language, and possessed technology superior even to that of the local
priestly guild of smiths ... The first Portuguese, like their successors to the
present day, were regarded as visitors from the land of the dead."[17]

The very cross the Portuguese carried was known among the Kongo well
before the arrival of Europeans and understood to represent a link between
spiritual and earthly realms. MacGaffey's emphasis is not on an exotic cosmology far removed from modernity but on the ability of a local religion
to adjust to major upheavals—not least the colonial project under Leopold
II in the Congo to classify the BaKongo as members of a primitive tribe to
be harnessed for colonial labor. Primary education in mission schools, for
instance, was designed to produce a semi-skilled workforce with docile attitudes. While it was successful in transforming the material culture of the
BaKongo, it failed to instill an understanding of the European worldview:
the entire colonial enterprise was understood in the language of witchcraft
as a nocturnal traffic in human beings, schooling being seen as an initiation
camp very similar to pre-colonial cults. As a result, the Congolese symbolic
universe was remarkably resistant to decades of concentrated colonial influence, including the racial panoply bandied around by missionaries and

imperial officers. It also meant that the BaKongo only participated passively in colonial institutions, as two worlds of meaning were segregated without much communication. Admission to the world of understanding, power, and wealth from which they had been excluded would finally come with independence in 1960, or so many believed, as the world would "turn upside down" and ancestors who had been enslaved would return from America along with the secrets of technology. The Congolese might even wake up to find that they had become white.[18]

In stark contrast to the example of the BaKongo, where decades of racial indoctrination failed to displace local cosmologies, complex variables behind the relationship between Hutu and Tutsi created a fertile background on which colonialism could build. When colonialists arrived in Rwanda in the early twentieth century they differentiated not only between Europeans and Africans in racial terms, but they also racialized local differences, describing the minority Tutsi as a tall and elegant race, wearing togas which pointed to a colonial connection with Roman colonies of North Africa. The majority of Hutus, however, were seen as dumb but good-natured, and portrayed as racially inferior to the Tutsi. A system of population registration further consolidated the opposition between Hutu and Tutsi, seen as distinct and internally coherent racial types. The Tutsi exploited these prejudices to their full advantage, using the colonial presence to extend their control over the Hutu. In what Alison Des Forges has ironically called a "great and unsung collaborative enterprise" over many decades, Rwandan intellectuals and European colonialists rewrote a history of the country which fitted foreign assumptions and conformed with Tutsi interests.[19] Administrators, scholars, and missionaries thus helped chiefs, poets, and historians, as Tutsi elitism became racist dogma thanks to the tools of physical anthropology: "Bantu" and "Ethiopoid" came to describe Hutu and Tutsi as social, cultural, and regional differences among each group were ignored in favor of a rigid racial classification based on such methods as the measurement of noses and skull sizes. Even after the 1959 revolution, when the Hutu overthrew the Tutsi, the basic elements of this racial cosmology were used in an ideology of hatred against a once powerful minority now blamed for all evil. Politics as well as a number of conjunctural factors in the early 1990s shifted this vision of radical difference further into an ideology of genocide, underpinning a civil war in 1994 in which eight hundred thousand Tutsi were slaughtered. As Peter Uvin has argued, racist prejudice primarily emanated from the government, but it was also fed by the needs of ordinary people: the seeds planted from above fell on fertile ground, as people explained their misery by scapegoating the Tutsi.[20]

The Politics of Racism

It seems almost trivial to underline that racism is a matter of politics: racist belief systems, like all belief systems, are always linked with issues of power and prestige. The real question is whether we can better specify the political dynamics of racism, despite a wide diversity of global examples. It will be argued here that while it is common to stress the extent to which racism legitimizes social hierarchies and social exclusions, a more precise way of approaching the issue is to emphasize how opposition to the notion of equality often prompts the formulation of a racial discourse. After all, world history is replete with political systems based on strict hierarchy, none of which—up until the very end of the eighteenth century—invoked the notion of race: religion, kinship, language, or culture could all suffice in the formulation of an ideology of radical difference, and Christians had few qualms in dehumanizing and exterminating each other—before slaughtering Americans, Asians and Africans—during the wars of religion between Protestants and Catholics. A theory of political equality is relatively recent in human history—as is the notion of race, and both are dynamically related.

Let us turn briefly to the history of racism in America. As George Fredrickson—a key historian of racial ideologies who has done more than others to relate virulent racism to equalitarian societies[21]—has shown, a social order based on racial distinctions only developed in parts of North America by the late seventeenth century.[22] In the earlier decades free black men were not overtly or significantly discriminated against, and—at least in the case of Massachusetts—they had the same basic rights as others. The situation was less clear elsewhere, in particular in Virginia, although even there free black men could acquire property and exercise an equal right to vote.[23] In most parts of the country, marriages between white servant women and black male slaves were not uncommon. Status—free or slave—rather than race—"white" or "black"—determined social position, a situation which changed with the development of class divisions among free whites, as some managed to acquire land and slaves, relegating others to an inferior position. Both poor whites and wealthy elites increasingly resisted the formation of a social hierarchy with different ranks and privileges, as such a system contravened a widespread ideal of equality. Instead an ostentatious effort was made to push down the most successful free black to a status below that of the poorest white, as "race" became the foundation of what Fredrickson calls a kind of "pseudo-equality" among whites. The contrast made by Fredrickson with South America is illuminating: Spain and Portugal were still feudal societies attuned to a strict social hierarchy of mutually dependent ranks. Slaves were the lowest group in this hierarchy, and freedom simply meant movement up to the next rank, never threatening the elite. Medieval conceptions of hierarchy and social order were adapted to plantation societies, in which the middle ranks were dominated by a range of mixed-blood categories; the bottom was predominantly black and the top was defined as white.

The ideological justification for the division of the colonies in North America into "whites" and "blacks" only came a few centuries later, although tensions mounted with the Declaration of Independence in 1776, which made egalitarian philosophy part of the national creed in the United States. By the 1830s the application of the concept of equal rights to blacks became impossible to ignore. "Before the abolitionists forcefully demanded consistency in the application of egalitarian ideals, it was even possible to subscribe in a general way to an egalitarian philosophy without confronting directly the contradiction between such a creed and the acceptance of slavery and racial discrimination." Once the notion of equality was demanded, apologists of racism could either define blacks as members of a subhuman species or portray equalitarian ideals as a white prerogative only. The view that blacks were inherently inferior to the "master race" hence spread like wildfire, appealing directly to a new biology which emphasized the importance of physical characteristics.

In Europe too the notion of "race," as Michael Banton has argued in his Racial Theories, became widespread not only because of an expansion overseas but more concretely as a consequence of local politics.[24] The novel Ivanhoe, published in 1820 by Walter Scott, popularized the word "race" more than any other work, as relations between Anglo-Saxons and Normans were presented as a struggle between two races. In other European countries the word race came to be used in similar political circumstances. With the French revolution in 1789 and the liberal or republican revolutions of 1848, power was taken from monarchies and vested in the people in the name of equality: but who were "the people" in countries emerging from a feudal system based on sharp hierarchical distinctions of rank and order? Revolutionaries and nationalists attempted to destroy internal boundaries based on birth (royalty, nobility, aristocracy) and to construct instead external boundaries between people defined as nations; this was often done by portraying them as biological units—or "races." Moreover, with the advent of a notion of equality, spread by republican regimes, the exclusion of certain groups of people (blacks, Jews) was increasingly difficult to justify, and here too arguments about permanent, biological inferiority came to the rescue. The most notorious example is probably Germany, as only the Aryans were seen to belong to the nation by the 1930s. Let me turn towards China as a more concrete example, since this essay stresses the global dimensions of racism.

While certain cognitive traditions may have created a fertile terrain for the reception of racial theories in China, a racist belief system appeared only with the reform movement which gained momentum after the country's defeat against Japan in 1894–95. Leading figures like Liang Qichao (1873–1929) and Kang Youwei (1858–1927) selectively appropriated scientific knowledge from foreign discursive repertoires to invent a new sense of group identity. In search of wealth and power in the wake of the country's military rout, in need of a unifying political concept capable of binding all the emperor's subjects together in a powerful nation which could resist the foreign encroachments which had started with the first Opium War (1839–42), the reformers used new evolutionary theories from England to present the world as a battlefield in which different races struggled for survival. They also appealed to patrilineal culture in order to represent all inhabitants of China as the equal descendants of the Yellow Emperor. Extrapolating from an indigenous vision of lineage feuds, which permeated the social landscape of late imperial China, the reformers constructed a racialized worldview in which "yellows" competed with "whites" over degenerate breeds of "browns," "blacks," and "reds." Thriving on its affinity with lineage discourse, the notion of "race" gradually emerged as the most common symbol of national cohesion, as "race" overarched differences of rank, class, lineage, and region to conceptually integrate the country into a powerful community organically linked by blood. Traditional scholars critical of the reformers denounced the use of terms like "yellow race" and "white race," as they implied a degree of relativism that undermined the bases of their sinocentric universe.

Not only did the reformers attempt to destroy existing social hierarchies in favor of a politically integrated concept of race, they also projected internal divisions of rank and status upon the world at large, now seen as a racial hierarchy of "noble" (guizhong) and "ignoble" (jianzhong), "superior" (youzhong) and "inferior" (liezhong), "historical" and "ahistorical races" (youlishi de zhongzu). The formal distinction of rank between "noble

31

people" (liangmin) and "ignoble people" (jianmin), widespread in the empire until the early eighteenth century, found an echo in Tang Caichang (1867–1900), who opposed "noble races" (liangzhong) to "ignoble races" (jianzhong). He phrased it in evenly balanced clauses reminiscent of his classical education: "Yellow and white are wise, red and black are stupid; yellow and white are rulers, red and black are slaves; yellow and white are united, red and black are scattered."

The reformers proposed a form of constitutional monarchy which would include the Manchu emperor: their notion of a "yellow race" (huangzhong) was broad enough to include all the people living in the Middle Kingdom. In the wake of the abortive Hundred Days Reform of 1898, which ended when the empress dowager rescinded all the reform decrees and executed several reformer officials, a number of radical intellectuals started advocating the overthrow of the Qing dynasty: not without resonance to the 1789 and 1848 political revolutions in Europe, the anti-Manchu revolutionaries represented the ruling elites as an inferior "race" which was responsible for the disastrous policies which had led to the decline of the country, while most inhabitants of China were perceived to be part of a homogeneous Han race. The very notion of a Han race emerged in a relational context of opposition both to foreign powers and to the ruling Manchus. For the revolutionaries, the notion of a "yellow race" was not entirely adequate as it included the much-reviled Manchus. Whereas the reformers perceived race (zhongzu) as a biological extension of the lineage, encompassing all people dwelling on the soil of the Yellow Emperor, the revolutionaries excluded the Mongols, Manchus, Tibetans, and other population groups from their definition, which was narrowed down to the Han, who were referred to as a minzu. During the incipient period of 1902 to 1911, when the Qing empire collapsed, minzu as a term was used to promote symbolic boundaries of blood and descent: "nationalities" as political units were equated with "races" as biological units. In the nationalist ideology of the first decade of this century, minzu was thought to be based on a quantifiable number of people called "Han," a group with clear boundaries by virtue of imagined blood and descent. Sun Yatsen (1866–1925) became one of the principal proponents of a Chinese minzu, which he claimed was linked primarily by "common blood." In short, not only was "race" deemed an objective, universal, and scientifically observable given, but it also fulfilled a unifying role in the politics of the nation: it promoted unity against foreign aggressors and suppressed internal divisions. Even the "peasants with weather-beaten faces and mud-caked hands and feet" could be represented as the "descendants of the Yellow Emperor."

As a notion of "equality at birth" spread with new modes of governance which invoked "the people" and "the nation" rather than "estates" or "classes," racial discourse could be used in two distinct but mutually dependent ways: some people could be demonstrated to be inferior at birth, and hence unworthy of equal treatment in the same way that apes were not eligible to vote—blacks in America, Africans in South Africa, Jews in Nazi Germany—while others could be elevated to equal status despite differences of class, culture, or region. This was not only the case with nationalism, as entirely different groups of people came to be represented as political equals within the realm of the nation—from Hong Kong merchants to Hunanese farmers in the case of China—but also with larger political entities, for instance pan-Africanism. As Anthony Appiah showed in a path-breaking study published in 1992,[25] the African nationalism proposed by Alexander Crummell and many of his followers, including Edward Blyden and W.E.B. Du Bois, was based on "race": the most common factor between all Africans was seen to be not merely geography or history but something much deeper and congenital, capable of transcending the continent's many barriers of language and culture: Africa was represented as the land of the black race, as blood, skin, and hair determined negritude. Followers such as Cheikh Anta Diop, a Senegalese physicist, would even see the erosion of the race concept as an ideological assault on Africans, who he portrayed as the superior descendants of "Negroid primacy." Others would develop a theory of melanic superiority according to which people rich in melanin have a better central nervous system and higher sensitivity to other people's magnetic fields.[26]

The Language of Science

Politics is a key component of racism, in particular the modern notion of equality—whether upheld in a vision of racial inclusion or rejected in a effort at racial exclusion—but another core-identifying element is the language of science. Whether proposed by Tutsi historians, Afrocentric politicians, or Chinese reformers, a language grounded in science is shared by global racism, and like all idioms it is rich, flexible, complex, and ever-evolving. The widespread credibility of racial discourse can only be understood when we see how it is harnessed onto science as a system of organized thought about the natural world: if science could produce steamships and predict the movement of celestial objects, surely it was just as powerful in dividing humanity into distinct biological groups? A common mistake made by scholars who expose the scientific fallacy of "race" is to portray "science" as an integrated and uniform body of work rather than as a way of speaking about the natural world. Not only was the prestige of science instrumental in the success of racial discourse, but there was such an abundance of mutually incompatible theories that just about any approach could be justified in the name of science.

It is often stated, for instance, that racism portrays social groups defined as "races" as fixed and immutable entities—hence their permanent exclusion from exercising the vote. The evidence, however, is far more complex. In France, for instance, soft interpretations of heredity were more popular than the hard language of genetics, and they allowed "race" to be portrayed as a flexible rather than a fixed entity, open to change for the better: neo-Lamarckism rather than neo-Darwinism underpinned it. A neo-Lamarckian approach to heredity, in which nature and nurture were seen as mutually interdependent factors while acquired characteristics could be transmitted from parents to their offspring, led to environmental determinism rather than biological determinism. France harbored some of the most outspoken defenders of a neo-Lamarckian approach to eugenics, but the case of Latin America illustrates that soft approaches which combined an emphasis on the environment with hereditarian explanations were far more widespread than had been previously suspected. In three countries examined by Nancy Stepan—Brazil, Argentina, and Mexico—neo-Lamarckian notions were more important than strictly Mendelian explanations of heredity, an emphasis which supported a preventive approach to eugenics in which the environment had to be cleansed of all deleterious factors damaging racial health.[27] In many parts of the world neo-Lamarckism was either prevalent or appeared as a widespread discourse that often mingled with Mendelian and Darwinian accounts in the early decades of the twentieth century in a range of disciplinary and institutional settings. This is not only true for Russia, Brazil, China, and France between the two World Wars,[28] but also for parts of the world where supporters of "hard" inheritance were widespread, for instance the United States. As George Stocking has clearly shown, neo-Lamarckism lingered in American anthropological and social thought even after Mendel's theories had been widely accepted.[29]

A fresh historical appraisal of the available material including countries outside Europe might reveal that the hard Mendelian eugenics familiar from Britain and Germany was not a dominant approach in many developing parts of the world.[30] In China, the reformers mentioned in the previous section selectively appropriated evolutionary theories which supported a soft interpretation of heredity. Rather than appealing to Charles Darwin's emphasis on competition between individuals of the same species, most were inspired by Herbert Spencer's focus on group selection. For reformers like Yan Fu, Liang Qichao and Kang Youwei, processes of evolution were directed by the principle of racial grouping, as individuals of a race should unite in order to survive in the struggle for existence much as each cell contributed to the overall health of a living organism. Apart from the individualistic basis for competition, the reformers also ignored the neo-Darwinian emphasis on the branching process of evolution. They adopted a Neo-Lamarckian theory of linear evolution, which viewed human development as a single line of ascent from the apes: the embryo developed in a purposeful way toward maturity, and this process could be guided by changes to the social and political environment. Neo-Lamarckism offered a flexible vision of evolution which closely suited the political agenda of the reformers, as human progress in the realm of politics was seen as conducive to the racial improvement of the species.

A whole range of possible positions could thus be defended in the name of science—whether appealing to hard genetics to portray "races" as fixed entities or appropriating soft notions derived from Lamarckism to promote "racial improvement" through education. This flexibility is precisely what allowed "race" to connive with other forms of identity. In the case of the Parsees—followers of the religion of ancient Zoroastrians who fled Persia after its conquest and settled in India in the eighth century—notions of religious purity could easily migrate into the realm of science: Sapur Faredun Desai, in a book prefaced by the eugenist Harry H. Laughlin, thus had no difficulty talking about "purity of the blood" and the need to eliminate "inferior" children at birth in order to improve the quality of the race. As the Parsees were confronted with the loss of the "precious germplasm of a distinguished race," the race would be "fast decaying, putting forth the feebleminded, the epileptic, the imbecile, and the insane; the deaf-mutes, the diabetics and the paralytics; the consumptives and the lepers; the cataractual and the blind; the paupers and the degenerated"; the consequence would be that at the time of resurrection all would have to answer for this unconscious behavior.[31] As John Efron has illustrated, some Jewish scholars too were keen to show that Jews were a distinct race: such was the centrality of race in nineteenth-century Europe that they conducted large-scale statistical experiments to determine Jewish skull shape and the prevalence of blue-eyed blond Jews.[32]

As we can see in the case of eugenics, which continued to flourish for decades after World War II, many individuals and institutions operating in the name of science continued to subscribe to the credibility of racial theories even after the collapse of Nazi Germany and the revulsion against race theories it created. Here again the mistake is to see science as an integrated field speaking with a single voice rather than as an ever-evolving constellation of ideas and practices marked by a plurality of views. In Scandinavia, eugenics were implemented for decades after World War II, resulting in tens of thousands of sterilizations. On the basis of recent research, it appears that parts of the world which were on the periphery of scientific research, such as Finland, the Deep South in the United States, and China, harbored strident eugenists who encountered relatively little resistance from either medical experts, government officials, or the general public—although even in mainstream circles eugenics retained its supporters well into the 1960s.[33]

Furthermore, while many scientists in parts of Europe and the United States may have had doubts about the validity of racial classifications, abundant research has shown how politics and ideology shape the outcome of scientific research, whether in Victorian Britain or in the United States today. China, again, is a good example. After the ascent to power of Deng Xiaoping in 1978, the language of science gradually started to replace communist ideology in a number of politically sensitive domains. Palaeoanthropological research illustrates how race and nation have coincided in scientific research since the 1980s.[34] Prominent researchers have represented Beijing Man at Zhoukoudian as the "ancestor" of the "mongoloid race." A great number of hominid teeth, skull fragments, and fossil apes have been discovered from different sites scattered over China since 1949, and these finds have been used to support the view that the "yellow race" today is in a direct line of descent from its hominid ancestor in China. Although palaeoanthropologists in China acknowledge that the evidence from fossil material discovered so far points at Africa as the birthplace of mankind, highly regarded researchers like Jia Lanpo have repeatedly underlined that man's real place of origin should be located in East Asia. Wu Rukang, also one of the most respected palaeoanthropologists in China, came very close to upholding a polygenist thesis (the idea that mankind has different origins) in mapping different geographical spaces for the "yellow race" (China), the "black race" (Africa), and the "white race" (Europe): "The fossils of homo sapiens discovered in China all prominently display the characteristics of the yellow race ... pointing at the continuous nature between them, the yellow race and contemporary Chinese people."

In a similar vein, skulls, hair, eyes, noses, ears, entire bodies, and even penises of thousands of subjects are routinely measured, weighed, and assessed by anthropometrists who attempt to identify the "special characteristics" (tezheng) of minority populations. To take but one example, Zhang Zhenbiao, a notorious anthropometrist writing in the prestigious Acta Anthropologica Sinica, reaches the following conclusion after the measurement of 145 Tibetans: "In conclusion, as demonstrated by the results of an investigation into the special characteristics of the heads and faces of contemporary Tibetans, their heads and faces are fundamentally similar to those of various other nationalities of our country, in particular to those of our country's north and north-west (including the Han and national minorities). It is beyond doubt that the Tibetans and the other nationalities of our country descend from a common origin and belong, from the point of view of physical characteristics, to the same East-Asian type of yellow race [huangzhongren de Dongya leixing]." As a theory of common descent is constructed by scientific knowledge, the dominant Han are represented as the core of a "yellow race" which encompasses in its margins all the minority populations. Within both scientific institutions and government circles, different population groups in China are often represented as one relatively homogeneous descent group with a unique origin and uninterrupted line of descent which can be traced back to the Yellow Emperor.

Finally, while the evidence from China today might be rejected as the product of perverted science produced by a one party-state, recent advances in genomics have rekindled both scientific and popular interest in "race" around the world. As we noted in the introduction, a number of scientists now imply that folk notions about race may actually be scientifically verifiable divisions grounded in DNA: those scholars who denounced race science as fiction only a decade ago may have been too optimistic, if not naive, in proclaiming its demise, as history rarely moves forward in a single, progressive line and science can hardly be seen to operate in isolation from a broader political and ideological context.

Conclusion

This essay has not tried to provide a comprehensive history of how the world was racialized, but has merely suggested that racist belief systems share a common language based on science, that they have a common political tension derived from an egalitarian philosophy, and that they can also diverge considerably according to local cognitive traditions and political agendas: the article contends that an interactive approach alone can take into account how racist belief systems were negotiated, appropriated, and transformed within historically specific contexts. An interactive approach highlights how racism has developed an intensely parasitic relationship with science—itself a historically contingent worldview premised on the systematic study of the "natural world." This is not to say that the many relationships between science and race across the face of the globe have not been complex and changing over the course of the past few centuries, quite the opposite: both have evolved enormously over time, to the point where the biological might even appear to have vanished, but in its weakest form an indirect reference to "nature"—the field of enquiry constructed by science—is rarely absent from racism. Finally, given the continued relevance of both science as a foundation for knowledge and of the notion of equality as a modern political ideology, we should not be surprised at the global dimensions acquired by racism in a relatively short span of time since the late eighteenth century. As distinctions of rank, class, and status became increasingly less formal, concern with "racial" differences expanded, all the more as the movement of people was facilitated by increased openness across the earth—a process still unfolding today. The likelihood of the world moving back to some sort of "color-blindness" is thus extremely unlikely in the near future, as people on all continents express profound interest in the outward appearance of people and are likely to divide humanity along some sort of racial classification—"white" and "black" being poles now adopted almost everywhere, from Latin America to East Asia. However, it is also important to recognize that racism as an organized ideology is only one way among others in which human beings have been classified, marginalized, and demeaned by others in the last couple of centuries: to say that racism has become global does not mean that it is either uniform or universal.

Notes

1. Su Xiaokang, "River elegy," Chinese Sociology and Anthropology 24, no. 2 (1991): 9.
2. Michael Banton, Racial Theories (Cambridge, UK, 1987).
3. On the complex relationship between Volk and Rasse, see Christopher M. Hutton, Race and the Third Reich: Linguistics, Racial Anthropology and Genetics in the Dialectic of Volk (Cambridge, UK, 2005).

4. Marek Kohn, The Race Gallery: The Return of Racial Science (London, 1996).
5. See Elazar Barkan, The Retreat of Scientific Racism: Changing Concepts of Race in Britain and the United States between the two World Wars (Cambridge, UK, 1992).
6. See the overview by Nikolas Rose, "Introduction to the Discussion of Race and Ethnicity in Nature Genetics," BioSocieties 1 (2006): 307–11.
7. Joanna L. Mountain and Neil Risch, "Assessing Genetic Contributions to Phenotypic Differences among 'Racial' and 'Ethnic' Groups," Nature Genetics 36, no. 11 (November 2004): 52.
8. Troy Duster, "Buried Alive: The Concept of Race in Science," in Genetic Nature/Culture: Anthropology and Science Beyond the Two-Culture Divide, edited by Alan H. Goodman, Deborah Heath, and M. Susan Lindee (Berkeley and London, 2003), 258.
9. Niall Ferguson, "We Must Understand Why Racist Belief Systems Persist," The Guardian, July 2006.
10. Percy C. Hintzen, "The Caribbean: Race and Creole Ethnicity," in A Companion to Racial and Ethnic Studies, edited by David Theo Goldberg and John Solomos (Oxford, 2002), 493.
11. Among others, see Eugenia Kaw, "Medicalization of Racial Features: Asian American Women and Cosmetic Surgery," Medical Anthropology Quarterly 7, no. 1 (March 1993): 74–89; Mikiko Ashikari, "Cultivating Japanese Whiteness: The 'Whitening' Cosmetics Boom and the Japanese Identity," Journal of Material Culture 10, no. 1 (2005): 73–91.
12. Unless otherwise indicated, all references in the case of China are to Frank Dikötter, The Discourse of Race in Modern China (Stanford, 1992).
13. On Japan, see Frank Dikötter, ed., The Construction of Racial Identities in China and Japan: Historical and Contemporary Perspectives (Honolulu, 1997); pioneering is John W. Dower, War without Mercy: Race and Power in the Pacific War (New York, 1986).
14. Nancy Shoemaker, "How Indians Got to be Red," American Historical Review 102, no. 3 (June 1997): 624–44.
15. Nancy Shoemaker, A Strange Likeness: Becoming Red and White in Eighteenth-Century North America (Oxford, 2004), 3.
16. Pamela K. Crossley, "Thinking about Ethnicity in Early Modern China," Late Imperial China 11, no. 1 (1990): 1–35.
17. Wyatt MacGaffey, Religion and Society in Central Africa: The BaKongo of Lower Zaire (Chicago, 1986), 199; Wyatt MacGaffey, "The West in Congolese Experience," in Africa and the West: Intellectual responses to European culture, edited by Philip D. Curtin (Madison, 1972), 49–74; see also Suzanne Preston Blier, "Imaging Otherness in Ivory: African Portrayals of the Portuguese, ca. 1492," Art Bulletin 75, no. 3 (September 1993): 375–96.
18. Wyatt MacGaffey, "Education, Religion, and Social Structure in Zaire," Anthropology and Education Quarterly 13, no. 3 (Autumn 1982): 238–50.
19. Alison Des Forges, "The Ideology of Genocide," Issue: A Journal of Opinion 23, no.

2 (1995): 44–47.

20. Peter Uvin, "Prejudice, Crisis, and Genocide in Rwanda," African Studies Review 40, no. 2 (September 1997): 91–115.

21. George M. Fredrickson, Racism: A Short History (Princeton, 2002).

22. George M. Fredrickson, The Arrogance of Race: Historical Perspectives on Slavery, Racism, and Social Inequity (Hanover, NH, 1988), 189–205.

23. The reader should note that there is a substantial literature that disputes the existence of a less racialized first third of the seventeenth century in North America. An excellent overview of the debate and the evidence is presented in Manfred Berg, "Die Ursprünge der Sklaverei in Nordamerika," Zeitschrift für Geschichtswissenschaft 54, no. 9 (2006): 741–60.

24. Michael Banton, Racial theories, 2nd ed. (Cambridge, 1998), 29.

25. Kwame Anthony Appiah, In my Father's House: Africa in the Philosophy of Culture (Oxford, 1992).

26. Kohn, The Race Gallery, 152–59.

27. Nancy Leys Stepan, "The Hour of Eugenics": Race, Gender, and Nation in Latin America (Ithaca, 1991).

28. Mark B. Adams, ed., The Wellborn Science: Eugenics in Germany, France, Brazil and Russia (Oxford, 1990).

29. George W. Stocking, Race, Culture, and Evolution: Essays in the History of Anthropology (Chicago, 1982); see also Jessica Blatt, "'To Bring out the Best that is in their Blood': Race, Reform, and Civilization in the Journal of Race Development (1910-1919)," Ethnic and Racial Studies 27, no. 5 (September 2004): 691–709.

30. Despite the publication of such a pioneering work as Peter J. Bowler, The Non-Darwinian Revolution: Reinterpreting a Historical Myth (Baltimore, 1988).

31. Sapur Faredun Desai, Parsis and Eugenics (Bombay, 1940).

32. John M. Efron, Defenders of the Race: Jewish Doctors and Race Science in fin-de-siecle Europe (New Haven, 1994).

33. See Frank Dikötter, "Race Culture: Recent Perspectives on the History of Eugenics," American Historical Review 103, no. 2 (April 1998): 467–78; and more specifically Edward J. Larson, Sex, Race, and Science: Eugenics in the Deep South (Baltimore, 1996); Gunnar Broberg and Nils Roll-Hansen, eds., Eugenics and the Welfare State: Sterilization Policy in Denmark, Sweden, Norway, and Finland (East Lansing, MI, 1996); Frank Dikötter, Imperfect Conceptions: Medical Knowledge, Birth Defects and Eugenics in China (New York, 1998); Alexandra Minna Stern, Eugenic Nation: Faults and Frontiers of Better Breeding in Modern America (Berkeley, 2005).

34. The following two paragraphs draw on Frank Dikötter, "Reading the Body: Genetic Knowledge and Social Marginalisation in the PRC," China Information 13, no. 2-3 (1998): 1–13.

Chapter 2

How Racism Arose in Europe and Why It Did Not in the Near East

Benjamin Braude

In common usage racism has come to cover a multitude of sins. Racism/racist have frequently become little more than terms of abuse. As a result even in the supposedly precise discourse of the law, race is often confused with practically every other term of collective identity. Nonetheless as a destructive social phenomenon race has functioned in ways that differ significantly from other collectivities. Race is often presumed to have a fixed, more precise, allegedly scientific and objective, biological basis unlike terms—supposedly more cultural or political—such as ethnicity, people, nation, linguistic, or religious group. That race, just as much as these other concepts, is ultimately culturally and socially constructed is of course denied by its true believers.

Discussions of race and racism often ignore a fundamental issue. The division of humanity into various groupings and the essential permanence not only of the groups themselves but also of the criteria that define them are taken for granted. Accordingly the focus has become how and why various forms and degrees of superiority/inferiority or prejudice and oppression against them, i.e., the most conventional definitions of racism, have emerged. Instead one must begin at a more elementary level, the attempt to understand the circumstances that imagined such divisions in the first place, along with the recognition that individuals form ever-changing human groups that rise, merge, separate, fall, disappear, return, and are transformed. Thus understanding racism requires not taking race for granted. More fundamentally one must also establish the context of its construction and then identify, interrogate, and historicize its criteria such as color, continent, language, religion, heredity, biology, physical traits, gender, social-economic role, and so forth. To prove that race is socially constructed, one must examine the construction site and the building blocks.

41

There is a fundamental need for precise definitions and an explanation of why race and racism are so difficult to pin down. Just as nationalism is the belief that there is and, perhaps, should be such a thing as a nation, racism is the belief that there is and, perhaps, should be such a thing as a race. Believers in race and racism are racists. According to racists, a race is one of a fixed number of—typically, about half a dozen—human super-collectivities. Even more essential is the claim that *all* important characteristics of the members of that race are determined by that group's physical heritage. In the racist world-view there is no human individuality. Each individual is merely an inevitable manifestation of the collective to which s/he belongs, with the nature of that collective determined by shared heredity. Racism may succinctly be defined as fixed collective hereditarian over-determinism. As the notorious and prolific anatomist and racist advocate Robert Knox argued in the nineteenth century, "That race in human affairs is everything is simply a fact, the most remarkable, the most comprehensive, which philosophy has ever announced. Race is everything: literature, science, art—in a word, civilization—depend on it."[1] Such a totalitarian view deprives the individual so defined of any moral control or autonomy. Racial stereotyping takes over in such a way that both the stereotyper and the stereotyped are locked into a tight relationship that is inevitable and predetermined, overcoming everything else. A few lines of verse from a classic Hollywood horror film *The Wolf Man* (1941) written by Curt Siodmak, himself a Jewish refugee from Nazi racism, capture this loss of individual will and identity in a quasi-folkloric way: "Even a man who is pure in heart and says his prayers by night may become a wolf when the wolfbane blooms and the Autumn moon is bright."[2]

Racism is often confused with explicitly non-hereditarian forms of cultural prejudice whose markers are, at least in theory, within an individual's control such as religious, linguistic, geographical, economic, and national status. These forms of prejudice may be variously called ethnocentricity, xenophobia, group hatred, class oppression, and simply intolerance. Unfortunately the underdeveloped state of social scientific discussion of prejudice against other, non-racial groups, has left our vocabulary limited and imprecise. Although we all too readily label something as racism or racist, it is awkward to call a similar form of prejudice against a non-racial group, ethnicism or ethnicist. For no reason other than a dearth of semantic imagination, group prejudice becomes racism and the groups so stigmatized, races. All of this is further complicated by the conflicting conventional usages of race in the United States versus Europe. Europeans may call races what Americans call ethnic groups. Ultimately the two fundamental difficulties in understanding racism are first that its core, race, is ultimately a fraud and second, that, whatever reality it might dimly reflect is itself unstable. As Ira Berlin has argued, following E.P. Thompson, race like class is interactive and constantly changing.[3]

The notion of fixed identity and hereditarian determinism has distinguished modern Euro-American racism from other cultures' forms of group construction, past and present. Strikingly evident in most of these notions is the protean element that allows the transformation of the individual from one group to another. These take various guises, be it the grace of conversion, the inheritance of acquired characteristics, the cross-color imagination, the power of place, or the ever-changing curse of Ham. In the pre-Mendelian era the biological was not necessarily hereditarian. Traditional notions common in the classical, ancient near eastern, and medieval Jewish, Christian, and Muslim worlds have long recognized a truth about identity that modern European notions honed over recent centuries have tried to destroy, the principle that identity is ever-changing. The old beliefs may have been wrong about the causes and mechanisms, but they grasped that essential truth. Reputedly, from Hippocrates on, various forms of influence and action could transform physical characteristics within and between generations.[4] Ancient Rabbis, Church Fathers, classical Roman, and Hellenistic thinkers believed that parents of one color could have children of another as a result of a strong image impressed on the imagination of the mother or the father during receptive moments in the creation of a fetus.[5] Medieval Christians not only believed that Jews had a distinct and repulsive stench, but that the grace of conversion would miraculously replace it with the fragrance of the true faith.[6] Almost all who thought about the problem within the Judeo–Christian–Muslim classical tradition believed that if you moved from one climatic zone to another your geo-humoral characteristics would be transformed, in turn changing your physical appearance and psychological make-up. Before the rise of the Atlantic slave trade, the biblical Ham, son of Noah, could be a Mongol, an Indian (in both senses of the word), a Jew, or even a Polish aristocrat, among his many varied identities.[7] Flexibility, openness to change, the possibility of indeterminacy, wonder, and endless transformation distinguished such notions from what developed later. Today such long-abandoned ideas seem so absurd that few students of racism know of them, let alone pay them any heed. If known, they are dismissed as too insignificant to have any social or historical relevance. That would be a mistake. Our inability to take such notions seriously reflects the deep and thorough-going way in which our consciousness has been shaped—distorted is not too strong a term—by a complex and multi-variegated process that rooted racism in modern culture. On the contrary, the longevity, omnipresence, variety, and constancy—to indulge a paradox—of proteanism demand that these notions be integrated into our understanding of the history of collective identity. To do so we must first outline the process that has distorted that long-held understanding.

In modern Europe and the Americas these protean concepts came under attack fundamentally because they conflicted with the demands of the expansionist, initially imperial, and subsequently national, state as well as the accompanying new consciousness of well-ordered collective identities, to borrow Marc Raeff's notion of the well-ordered police state.[8] The attack first emerged in the era of imperial oceanic exploration, expansion, and exploitation beginning in the sixteenth and seventeenth centuries. Across the Spanish-, Portuguese-, and English-speaking oceanic empires, settlers, priests, and propagandists sought to dispel the frightening tradition that horrible consequences attended voyages to the north or the south, that such travelers would "be burned as black as a cole, as the Indians or Black Moores." The source of fear was "the persuasions of certaine Philosophers," who believed that the "Sphere" was divided into "five Zones," only some of which could support human life. On the contrary these advocates of European expansion sought to "proue all partes of the worlde habitable."[9] At this stage none argued for biological explanation of color difference, but preferred divine intervention, a way station on the road to scientific racism. In order to populate these colonies with their own, the expansionists had to attack the earlier forms of flexible identity that had become so threatening, for they challenged the ability of the overseas English, Spaniards, and Portuguese to maintain themselves outside of their homelands. Slavery was essential to this phenomenon, for exploitation supported expansion, creating a complex and pervasive transnational social-economic system with a material interest in firmly establishing racism, but the notion of fixed unchanging identity, a cornerstone of racism, arose for reasons *initially* independent of the slave trade. And this is a point that participants in the historiographical chicken and egg debate about racism and slavery must acknowledge. Continentalism, the belief that Europe, Asia, Africa, etc. were real fixed distinct entities with distinct populations, replaced the ocean-unifying latitudinal permeable zones of the ancient philosophers. The so-called Europeans invented and stabilized themselves and everyone else in the sixteenth and seventeenth centuries in order to promote their worldwide expansion and domination, by maintaining Europeans outside of Europe.

In the eighteenth and nineteenth centuries the attack against indeterminacy drew further sustenance from the peculiar process of European bureaucratic centralization and nation-state invention. The efficient administration of the bureaucratic state required a systematization of individual and collective identity. The medieval common law heritage had accepted the right of individuals to adopt and change their names. The emerging continental bureaucratic convention blocked that flexibility. The invention and imposition of a standard language and uniform linguistic identity reinforced inflexibility.[10] Scientific systemization paralleled that of the political-administrative program. Carl Linnaeus's *Systema Naturae* offered a taxonomy for all life on the planet, animal and vegetable, drawing on the resources created by exploration and expansion and the fashionable impulse for ordering and ranking. Like the state, Linnaeus was obsessed with naming. Building upon Linnaeus, Johann Friedrich Blumenbach perfected the most commonly accepted taxonomy of humanity by adding one race to the Swede's four: Europeans, Ethiopians, Mongolians, Americans, plus Malays.[11] Subsequently, captivated by the reputed beauty of a Georgian female camp-follower's skull, he renamed Europeans, Caucasians, a pseudo-scientific conceit that for reasons that defy commonsense has become a commonplace in the racial lexicon.[12] The absurdity of such a designation is self-evident, but one typical of the delusions that characterize race-science in general. Race à la Russe designates the true Caucasians, that is the Chechnyans, Abkhasians, Azeris, Ossetians, etc. as *Chorniye*, i.e., Blacks. Conflicts between them and Russians become "racial."[13] In Russia, Caucasians are the so-called subaltern, black, dominated group.

On the face of it claiming that so-called Europeans originated at the far edge and indeed over the edge of their own supposedly distinctive land mass, among a swarthy population that by the eighteenth century at least had become mixed Muslim–Christian, practically in Asia, specifically the Near East, seems bizarre. However Blumenbach's alchemic transformation of his own people into Caucasians and its subsequent diffusion in everyday (at least in the United States) pseudo-scientific parlance does reflect a recurring element in Euro-American racial fantasizing, the frequency with which the Near East became its mythical fount. The Near East gained such a role because centuries of Christian speculation about the Bible had placed the final resting place of Noah's ark on Mount Ararat in the Caucasus. Since Ararat is where the repopulating of the world began after the Flood and since the authors of the European-master-of-the-world narrative regarded themselves as the original, default race, calling themselves Caucasian bolstered that arrogation of primacy.

The irony is that Euro-America has attributed so much of its racial vocabulary, conceptions, and justification to the Near East, when in fact that region has been largely alien to the racial project. To be sure many of the currently prevalent tropes of and about prejudice and collective identity may be traced to the Near East. Genealogical systems of identity, the concepts of tribe and peoplehood, multigenerational transmission of collective character, and the most widespread justification for racial slavery in history can all be linked to the scriptural corpus, broadly defined.

But most of these tracings and links are anachronistic mis-re-readings, the chronic disease of imposing holy eternality on ephemeral words. Euro-American study of this region has been handicapped by the barrier of the shared legacy of scripturalism and Hellenism. In fact such false cognates obscure the different original valences that developed in the Near East. We are ill-served by research that fails to acknowledge such divergence. Bernard Lewis, in his pioneering *Race and Slavery in the Middle East*, imprecisely defined race as, "current American usage ... such major divisions as white, black, Mongolian and the like," a version of Linnaeus–Blumenbach-lite.[14] Due to a lack of conceptual clarity, Lewis failed to distinguish between color prejudice as opposed to race/racism. Not only conceptually but also in terms of the critical use of sources, Lewis allowed anachronistic and culturally alien notions to corrupt his evidence. At the very beginning of the book, to prove the deep-rootedness of virulent racial stereotyping in the Muslim East, he cites a tale from the framing chapter of *Thousand and One Nights*. However the version he deployed does not appear in the oldest extant manuscript, dating from the fourteenth century, but only in the later eighteenth- and nineteenth-century versions shaped by Europe. The earlier version indulges in stereotypes that are less repugnant.[15]

Racism did not take hold in the Near East and the Islamic world, and even today it remains a marginal concept for the following reasons, each of which will be addressed below: color-indifference in the ancient Near East, contrasting to Greek color-based identities; klimatism as opposed to continentalism; Quranic quasi-universalism as opposed to Biblical particularism; power of religion and religious identity coupled with a diffused system of religious authority; polygamy and concubinism; weak state bureaucracy; lack of oceanic expansion; and absence of slave societies and economies.

Color-Indifference in the Ancient Near East

In contrast to polarized white–black terms of identity developed in Greek culture, notably in Janiform jug ceramic art[16] and in Greek literature from Herodotus onwards, the Near East had no similar terms of identity, as far as I have been able to tell. In the Bible, as well as the literatures of the Mesopotamian, Nilotic, and Persian empires, the commonest term to designate inhabitants of the Sub-Sahara was Kush, a word whose origins seem to be geographical rather than chromatic. Its common Greek mistranslation, *Aithiopia*, meaning "burnt by the sun" according to its folk etymology, is not the same. None of the other terms for Sub-Saharans, a vocabulary particularly abundant in Egyptian literature, betray any evidence of color-based identity. In the Egyptian visual arts, the same group or individuals could be painted in different colors within the same genre and even within the same work of art. Of course Near Eastern art did offer ethnographically accurate depictions of different people. But there is no literary evidence that they made color *the* marker of identity. The biblical passages that have been so interpreted reflect anachronistic assumptions.[17] In general no societies have been as color-obsessed as the United States and apartheid-era South Africa. Though never reaching such levels, after about 300 BCE Near Eastern society also started to develop notions of color-identity. The spread of Hellenism after the conquests of Alexander the Great introduced Greek black–white terms into the Near East. Conquest creates culture. In this regard the Hellenized addition to the Israelite scriptures (the New Testament), patristic and rabbinic literature, all differ significantly from their ancient inspiration. While color indifference diminished, the ancient legacy did not disappear completely, but did influence subsequent Jewish and Muslim attitudes toward color identity.

Klimatism and Other Pre-Continental Notions of Space

Among the least acknowledged and most ubiquitous distortions of the modern *weltanschauung* is continentalism, the notion that the globe and its inhabitants can be neatly parceled into a varying number of separate and distinct land masses.[18] Just as there is no unanimity about the number and names of races so there is no agreement on the number of continents. In fact continents, rather than being a natural geographic formation extant from time immemorial, are politically inspired notions whose existence has ebbed and flowed over the centuries. The continentalism currently dominant in Euro-America largely reflects early modern imperial political interests.[19] Over the span of history it is merely one of a number of alternative ways of organizing the earth. Previously in Christendom other world-views prevailed, most notably Greek *klimatism*. The traditional Muslim world-view integrated two different systems, the Persian *kishvar* that envisaged the world as containing seven adjoining circles and the Greek *klimata* that divided the world into a similar number of longitudinal zones. As in medieval Christendom, the Greek system dominated. *Klimata* united land and water along with their inhabitants into longitudinally parallel units across the earth's sphere in a way that defied easy political divisions or distinct populations. Since it incorporated the theory that movement across these porous units could change the markers of identity, it represented a remarkably anti-hereditarian impulse. While the *klimata* system did not well survive the needs of the ocean-girding empires, it persisted in the Islamic world well into the nineteenth century. Within so-called Euro-America an element of climatic-determinism has survived, notably in the influential work of Samuel Stanhope Smith, but klimatism has generally been overwhelmed by continentalism.[20] Within the Islamic orbit the traditional geography continued to block the development of racial categories that continentalism permitted and indeed encouraged. One of the reasons why continentalism has prevailed in modern Euro-America, while klimatism survived in the Islamic world, was that each respective meta-geography suited each respective political terrain. Klimatism matched the world-conquering claims of the Islamic community which expanded in a linear direction from the Near East, westward and eastward. Continentalism fitted the world-conquering claims of the Latin Christian community (and its heirs) which expanded in ocean-jumping fashion along both the east–west and north–south axes into a number of different water-divided land masses. The Islamic empire most comfortable with continentalism, the Ottoman realm, incorporated it in imperial sloganeering. Self-consciously aping ancient Rome, the Ottomans expanded on a north–south axis into Europe, beyond the original Islamic base in Afrasia, militarily and conceptually departing from traditional klimatism.

Precise and concrete boundaries represented the distinctly novel characteristic of early modern continentalism. The older systems for defining space (klimatism, kishvar, and the literal antecedents of continentalism itself) were much vaguer. For instance in Latin *continens* meant something quite different from its current meaning, in one respect its exact opposite. Rather than a self-contained and distinct territory, it could mean a great endless land mass; *continens* was synonymous with *continuens*. The standard reference works, the *Oxford Latin Dictionary* and *Thesaurus Linguae Latinae*, inform us that for *continens* a distinctly geographical connotation was secondary to the more common, albeit related, notions of "uninterrupted" and "adjacent." As a spatial noun it had two different meanings: a. "mainland" or "forming a continuous mass"; b. consistent with the base meaning of "adjacent," "the suburbs," that is "those parts of a town outside the city wall, but forming an integral part of it." Roman continents could include not only Hadrian's villa on the outskirts of Rome, but also Caesar's Gaul. The Greek term, *êpeiros*, which is sometimes rendered "continent" in English, at root means "dry land," "land-locked region," or "mainland," that is without access to the sea. The distinctly separate notion of continent in modern usage was not uppermost in Greek minds, rather was its unnatural—or so it seemed to this sea-based people—distance from seaways. Transforming these ancient, vague, and inclusive concepts of space into the neat and distinct continents of the early modern Mercator projection and the modern elementary school geography lesson represented a major though unacknowledged rupture in cosmology.

Inhabitants of medieval Asia, Africa, and Europe constantly intermingled with each other, so much so that these words did not mean what they mean today. The porousness of geographical concepts in the medieval world emerges with mind-boggling clarity in Ulrich von Richental's *Chronicle of the Council of Constance 1414–18*, a compendium of the world on the eve of Europe's expansion. Consistent with its ecumenical pretensions, this church council like the Roman Empire of old claimed to represent the entire world. However its organization, according to Richental, corresponded to no geography familiar to modern conventions. The basic structure of deliberation within the council was organized through the so-called *nacionen* or "nations." The term originated in the residential communities of the major European universities. At Constance there were five: Italian, German, French, Spanish, and English.[21] What was included in each of these categories suggests the degree to which they differed from their modern identities. The Spanish nation comprised, for example, not only most of Iberia, but also "the land called Armenia whence come wayfarers and the best merchants." As for the English they included not only the British Isles but also the kingdoms of "Arabia beyond the sea," the Medes, the Persians, as well as the two Indias, the Great and Lesser, ruled by Prester

John, and the kingdoms of Aithiopia, "where the Moors live," Egypt, and Nineveh. "Wherever Christian people, lay or clergy, live" belong to it. The seeming confusion of such claims notwithstanding, self-evident is an understanding of "nation" which assumes no geographical cohesiveness, territorial identity, blood ties, or imagined ancestry, but rather imagines religion and political control. From Ulrich's perspective nothing could be more alien than the late-twentieth-century assumption of a junction between ethnic identity and politics. However, the contents assigned to each nation were hardly surprising in the quiltwork political consciousness of his own age inspired by the structure of the Holy Roman Empire. They were also consistent with the shifting territorial allegiances which accompanied the rise and fall of dynasties.

As if such notions of nation were not sufficiently disorienting, Richental's concept of the three so-called continents also contradicts what our own age takes for granted: "Africa is Greece and has two empires in it, Constantinople and Athens." Africa also included Wallachia and Turkey, but the Turks also appear in Europe. The languages of Africa were Greek, Turkish, and Armenian, though the latter also appears under Asia. Asia in addition to the standard list of lands and holy places has Carthage and Bulgaria. Hebrew, by the way, was one of the languages of Europe.[22] Richental's consistent statements about African Greece appear too frequently to be dismissed as momentary lapses.

In this age there was no well-ordered tricontinentalism. Nor were there rigid political or geographical borders. More characteristic was the boundary zone rather than the boundary line. The most popular compendium of geographical knowledge in Richental's era was *The Travels of John Mandeville* available in thousands of manuscript and printed copies in almost every language and dialect throughout the length and breadth of Europe. What that authority taught would not have contradicted the essence of what *The Constance Chronicle* claimed. Africa, Asia, and Europe do not play major roles in Mandeville's world view. Africa's chief city was Carthage, Aeneas's rest-stop with Dido on the way from Troy to Rome. As for Europe that is the home of those descended from Noah's son Japhet, who include as well the people of Israel—so perhaps Hebrew is indeed spoken there.[23] Aside from that bit of information Europe is furnished no other identity. Moreover there were several well-established traditions dating back at least to the time of St. Augustine (354–430) that could explain Richental's mental map of Africa. One appeared in an influential work dedicated to Augustine by a disciple, Paulus Orosius, *History against the Pagans*, which reasserted an idea known in ancient Greece and Rome: Europe and Africa were one.[24] Recent research suggests that a wide range of medieval maps transmitted elements of Orosius's world-vision, which in turn influenced every major writer on geography.[25] There were other similar traditions at work. The fifteenth-century illuminated French chronicle, *La fleur des histoires*, which originated in Burgundy, contains an elaborately and carefully drawn picture map on which Africa contains, like Ulrich Richental's account, the city of Athens.[26] Martin Bernal's notion of a black Athena might claim roots far deeper in European consciousness than even he has argued, except that none of the Sons of Noah portrayed on that map were black.

To claim that medieval concepts of continental space were confused is wrong. They simply thought about space very differently from the conventional understanding of the twenty-first century. Porous, fluid, and protean, their notions reflected the very different needs that space might demand, much like Saul Steinberg's famous cartoon of a New Yorker's "View of the World from 9th Avenue." As the cartoon demonstrates we have not lost that sense, but it has been suppressed by the need to define space in a way that responds foremost to the practical considerations of how the state sees and controls the world.

The connection between space and race should be obvious. Defining space is a necessary precondition for defining race. Once space came to be precisely delimited by neat and distinct continental pigeonholes then the denizens therein could be similarly pigeonholed. As discussed above, the initial classifications of races by Linnaeus and Blumenbach were all geographical with a significant continental component: Europeans, Ethiopians, Mongolians, Americans, plus Malays. Subsequently Caucasian came to replace European, but often African took over from Ethiopian. In contemporary usage Mongolian and Malay have largely disappeared, superseded by varieties of Asian, East or Central. However, in earlier centuries as long as Athens lay in Africa and the English "nation" included Arabia, Persia, Egypt, Aithiopia, as well as both Indias (presumably those of south and southeast Asia) it would have been practically impossible to imagine an Aithiopian, European, or Asiatic race. The tools for racial classification had to draw upon clear and precise concepts of space. Otherwise, it would have been very difficult to invent the separate and distinct races, that limited number of human super-collectivities beloved by Robert Knox and his ilk. As the Virginia Circuit Court Judge in Caroline County declared in finding Mildred and Richard Loving guilty of violating the Commonwealth's miscegenation laws in 1959, "Almighty God created the races white, black, yellow, malay and red, and he placed them on separate continents. And but for the interference with his arrangement there would be no cause for such marriages. The fact that he separated the races shows that he did not intend for the races to mix."[27] With the rise of continentalism, Europe not only invented itself, it also broke from its own traditions and separated itself from a geographical heritage previously shared, to a large degree, with the Muslim world. Well into the nineteenth century, Muslim writers from as far apart as Persia and Morocco continued to describe the world in terms of klimata.[28]

Quranic Quasi-Universalism as Opposed to Biblical Particularism

The content of the Quran may very well be the least ethnocentric, the least particularistic, and the most universal sacred text of all the world's great religions. In remarkable contrast to the Jewish and Christian scriptures, there are no genealogies, hardly any place names, no narratives of travel over cherished lands, no ethnically-distinctive divine promises, in other words few markers to explicitly privilege one race or region over any other. The Quran could be described as a deracinated version of the Bible. On the other hand the Quran does display hostility to other religious groups, specifically pagans, Jews, and Christians. Within the chrestomathy of polemic the Quran's attacks are relatively mild, but they are significant. There are other checks on the universalism of the Quran. While Christianity, theologically at least, has accepted the validity of all translations of its scripture—a practical necessity since the original Aramaic of the Gospels has disappeared—Islam has insisted that the Quran can only be fully appreciated in the original Arabic, ideally chanted aloud, a principle embodied in its very name, literally Recitation. As a result Arabic has assumed a role in Islam and Islamic culture worldwide infinitely more important than Latin or Greek in Christianity. Accordingly, and despite the professed universalism of the Quran, Arabs have continuously played a more important role in Islam than Jews, Greeks, or Romans in Christianity, though their dominance does not compare to the role of Jews in Judaism. In addition, although the Quran removed the particularism of the Jewish and Christian scriptural texts, this Jewish–Christian content and interpretation constitutes the essential foundation for understanding the elliptical Quran. So by the back door much of the particularism present in the Bible has been reintroduced into the Quran through exegesis and its popular elaboration. The earliest and most author-itative commentaries on the Quran regularly internalized Jewish and Christian versions of biblical stories that Islam shared.[29] As a result expanded scripture, here defined as the original sacred text and its elaboration, plays a contradictory role with regard to group prejudice in Islam. On the one hand the Quran itself affords a much clearer expression of universalism than can be found in many religions, on the other its interpretation has adopted many of the particularisms of the other children of Abraham and added a few of its own.

Power of Religion, Religious Identity, and Weak Religious Authority

It is a truism that Islam plays a great role in the culture and society of the communities where it predominates. Islam, after all, is a way of life, not a mere faith, that peculiar concept created by the evacuation of the public sphere that much of Christianity in Europe was forced to accept after the wars of religion and the Enlightenment. However while much more pow-erful in one respect, Islam has been much weaker in other, perhaps even more significant ways. Islam has never developed a systematic hierarchy, like a "church" as an autonomous, powerful institution. The Greek Ortho-dox and Roman Catholic Churches are in many respects the successor states of, perhaps, the most powerful empire in history, the Roman. The commonplace that religion and state were one in Islam while separated in Christendom is an oversimplified distortion of a far more complex reality. Islam never had a church-like institution that could be united with a state. Lacking an over-arching administrative structure of its own, institution-ally Islam in fact has been much weaker than Christianity. Within Christianity local churches acted as elementary schools for the develop-ment of local consciousness and political role-playing that eventually led to the rise of movements for particularist nation-states. This worked in dif-ferent ways. While clearly not politically representative, regionally based parishes and bishoprics were closer to the local populace than the institu-tions of the state. They controlled patronage. Exerting local pressure to gain such benefits was a form of public mobilization and consciousness-raising that could offer a model and perhaps foundation for explicitly political and subsequently nation-building activities. The establishment of the Anglican Church in sixteenth-century England, Luther's fight with Rome within Germany, the struggle between "Gallican liberties" and ultramontanism in seventeenth-century France, the rise of linguistically indigenous Slavic and Arabic patriarchates within the Eastern Orthodox Church during that and subsequent centuries, all were early stages in the rise of their respective nation-statist movements. These fights took place because of the existence of a locally powerful institution, the church, which conflicting interests wished to control. By and large such pre-nationalist exercises did not take place within the community of Islam because there were no comparable institutions to fight over. The power and authority of religious institutions were too vague, charismatic, personal, patrimonial, and diffused to justify the struggles that wrecked European Christendom. Without such prior struggles nation-state movements lacked a foundation upon which to build. Therefore nationalism developed much later in the Islamic world, largely as a defensive and derivative response to European imperialism.

What are the implications of these structural differences for the rise of racism? Racism is part of a continuum in the process of creating different forms of collective identity, to which nationalism most closely relates. While elements of racism antedated the rise of nationalism, the nation-state is a necessary precondition for the entrenchment of racism, for the former establishes the utility of large-scale forms of collective identity and encourages the collective ideology of identity that sustains racism.[30] Racism developed in the United States, Germany, and South Africa as an outgrowth of the mass mobilization of the population necessary to establish their respective nation-states.

Polygamy and Concubinism in Contrast to the Monogamous Family

Though inadequately recognized, the family, as invented by the modern European Christian bourgeoisie, has provided the foundation for collective identity and an essential building block in the social construction of nation, race, and racism. However the monogamous nuclear family is a historical anomaly. The historical norm—and even that largely restricted to the few who could afford it—is in fact that the household composed of related and unrelated or not-yet-related elements. The word itself derives from the Latin, *famulus*, "household servant." According to the latest edition of the *Oxford English Dictionary*, family's oldest meaning, dating from about 1400, is "The servants of a house or establishment; the household."

A few centuries later, it was expanded to include, "The body of persons who live in one house or under one head, including parents, children, *servants*, etc. [emphasis added]."[31] Because it was rejected by New Testament morality, European society did not accept the procreative contribution of household servants to the lineage of the master of the household. Their offspring were often illegitimate; the plight of the mothers, banishment. By contrast, ancient Biblical culture as well as most societies, past and present, recognized that procreative and sexual role through the institution of the concubine. Hen-pecked Abraham's dispatch of Hagar to the desert was exceptional. Even God disapproved of it. Perhaps heeding the Almighty, Jacob was not similarly inclined.

Following Abraham's but not Jacob's practice, expelling servants from the family was an important stage in modern European social development, possibly related to the decline of slavery. As slavery reemerged in the plantation system, the exclusion of all servants from the family at least nominally restricted and controlled the biological stock, encouraging monogamy, ultimately causing the servant–slave role in procreation to be ignored and suppressed. The denial of that role made it much easier to invent ideas about pure lines of descent that allowed the family to become the building block for the biologically uniform nation and race.

For a variety of reasons, that process of expulsion and denial took place in Islamic societies much later, and largely under the influence of Euro-Christian social values, beginning only in the late nineteenth century. Concubinage and polygamy have been religiously and socially acceptable in Islamic societies, and for that matter, in most of humanity. Their delegitimization by Christianity is the exception even among the Abrahamic religions. It is necessary to distinguish between acceptance and practice since the expense of maintaining multiple sexual relationships and supporting the resulting offspring could be borne only by a wealthy minority. But as in Euro-America that wealthy minority often determined social norms.

One of the reasons that the Ottoman dynasty and as a consequence its Empire proved longer-lasting and more successful than its many Christian rivals, notably the Habsburgs and Romanovs, was that monogamy and endogamy did not handicap the Ottoman line. The repeated European wars over succession when a dynasty failed to produce a healthy male heir, the cost of inbreeding as evident in the Habsburg chin, and, more fatally, Romanov hemophilia, resulted directly from the religious, ethnic, and class restrictions that limited their variety of breeding partners. Despite European fantasies, the Sultan's harem was not a sex palace, but an extremely efficient system for perpetuating the dynasty with a regular supply of partners for procreation.[32] Since the Empire acquired mates for the Sultan from Eurasia, without further regard to class, religion, or ethnic identity, these greater geo-genetic options created a far healthier gene pool. Since every Sultan had many partners for his bed, sooner or later one was bound to produce a healthy male heir.

Although the Ottoman dynasty had a far more tolerant and open choice of mothers for dynastic succession than its Christian rivals, it also had a significant bias. Potential child-bearers were Muslim, Christian, Central Asian, Caucasian (literally), European etc., but not Sub-Saharan. In this respect as in other ways (discussed above), the Ottomans were the most European of Muslim dynasties. On the other hand the single most important official within the harem, other than the sultan's mother herself, was the so-called black eunuch, a position of great power and influence in the Ottoman court as a whole. Significantly, the highest-ranking individual of Sub-Saharan origin in the administration could not contribute physically to the dynastic line, a revealing example of conditional tolerance.

We know much less about harem life and dynastic reproduction in earlier Muslim states. Any attempt to reconstruct such aspects of medieval Arab society on the basis of the *Arabian Nights* is faulty, as has already been suggested. It is likely that earlier dynasties were more tolerant; though such tolerance can coexist with ethnic slurs and back-biting, as Bernard Lewis has well demonstrated. Arabia, with a history of intimate connections across the Red Sea, had a large Sub-Saharan population integrated in a variety of ways with the rest of society. Traditional Arabian family practice, embraced by early Islam, granted the acknowledged children of concubines the same status as the offspring of a free wife. Coupled with the absence of primogeniture, this polygamous open-family model discouraged the ethnically pure line of descent that came naturally to the linear monogamous servant-*rein* family of modern Christendom and was a precondition for racial thinking.

While the equality of concubine and free offspring had been accepted throughout the Islamic world before the rise of European influence, other aspects of family law lacked uniformity. Twelver Shi'ism, which dominated Persia from the sixteenth century onwards, emphasized a far narrower definition of family, closer to the modern European model, rather than the expansive tribally influenced notion that originated in Arabia and prevailed generally in the Islamic world.[33] This may explain why Persian Shi'ite treatment of non-Muslims included a unique notion of physical impurity and untouchability—verging on the racial—similar to that which has been attributed to the caste system in India, but which is absent in Islam as a whole.

The multi-cultural, multi-religious, multi-hued, polyglot, egalitarian (up to a point) household such as prevailed in the Near East at the center of the Old World contrasts markedly with the dull uniformity of the modern bourgeois family in Christendom, at its edge. The Islamic model by and large was not receptive to the kind of ethnic uniformity that the modern Christian model encouraged. Racism was not an inevitable consequence of monogamy in a parochial social and ethnic setting, but such monogamy could be one element in making racism seem natural.

Weak Bureaucracy and Anonymity

While the Ottoman empire was more oriented to Christendom than any other Islamic state apart from the one first founded by Muhammad and his immediate successors, and while it was arguably the most bureaucratized in the Islamic world, it never practiced the kind of European administrative procedures that helped to fix family identity. An important stage in the development of the narrow nuclear monogamous family—and what could follow from it, as has been argued—was giving it a name. Family names, surnames, had arisen through the patriarchal lineage of the great and wealthy households, but in most of the world apart from that social elite most people did not bear such labels. Most people contented themselves with remembering that they were the son or daughter of their father, with a generation or two added on. Much later, surnames began to be adopted largely as a convenience for the state which found them a useful means of tracking and centralizing the payment of taxes, the drafting of soldiers, and the other varied obligations of commoners.[34] The Ottoman government never ceased to collect taxes, but not until the mid to late nineteenth century did it begin drafting subjects into the army. During the early sixteenth century, a period for which we do have fiscal records, the information listed for each taxable resident was little more than the traditional practice, a first name with a father sometimes thrown in. As the empire developed, its tax collection system tended to be farmed out to local intermediaries who knew their communities and did not require the detailed information necessary for a distant bureaucracy. Neither the Ottomans nor their Muslim predecessors ever forced names on their subjects, further obstructing the construction of a distinctive family identity. Such indifference to surnames survives today. In the Near East last names started to become obligatory only after World War I. Almost a century later, the late ruler of Iraq, Saddam Hussein, is most commonly identified by his first name alone, for a number of reasons including the fact that surnames of the type propagated in Western Europe have still not caught on with the Arab public at large. The concept of kinship has been strong, but the notion of a distinctly named nuclear family unit has not been a historical norm.

Lack of Oceanic Expansion

Islam, like Christendom, produced great expansionist empires, but with a significant difference. Islamic expansion, while not slow—witness the rapid conquests in the two decades after the death of Muhammad—was geographically incremental, that is it moved systematically over adjoining territories, conquering and assimilating regions with familiar peoples and cultures. In this respect the conquests of Muslim empires resembled those of almost all other states. The exception to this universal pattern was of course the unparalleled oceanic expansion of Spain, Portugal, and England, followed by France and Holland. As argued at the outset, this expansion eventually forced a dramatically different way of imagining the world and its peoples. Europeans initially denied the newness of what they encountered, then frantically tried to fit it into their traditional paradigms, the biblical world-view being dominant. Ultimately that failed and the true novelty was finally recognized. Although 1492 has been totemized as the iconic start of this process, it in fact began much earlier in that century. In fathoming the early European responses one should begin not with America but with Africa, not an easy task since Eurocentric periodization and territorialization of human history have consigned that era to the middle ages, thereby reducing its ties to the age of exploration.[35] The Portuguese oceanic explorations of west Africa below the Sahara had shattered Ptolemaic notions of space and scale, creating the first non-incremental imperial expansion. By contrast Muslim expansion in east Africa and the Indian Ocean broke no paradigm since it encountered routes, regions, peoples, and products that had been part of the oecumene for centuries, even millennia, allowing for a certain level of acceptance and integration along the way. European recognition that the western hemisphere fell outside that oecumene, a realization that required nearly two centuries, aroused profound fears. Not only did Latin Christendom leap across the ocean into a new great unknown, it also lacked the intellectual resources to cope with such vast challenges. The most widely read medieval summa of the world's lands and peoples, *The Travels of Sir John Mandeville*, was a fraud mixing a holy pilgrimage with one-legged freaks and other fairy tales of lands further East.[36] By contrast the treatise on the culture and people of India written by the polymath al-Biruni was a well-informed work of great insight and empathy. Biruni was no exception but rather part of a huge library of geographic knowledge (with tall tales of its own), from Ibn Khurradadhbih in the ninth century, through al-Mukaddasi, al-Mas'udi, and of course Ibn Battuta, that in scale and substance dwarfed anything available in Latin Christendom. Wallowing in ignorance, overwhelmed by fear of the unknown, the prospect of contamination by the climes and peoples they encountered horrified the propagandists for Europe's expansion. They invented theories to deny any such possibility. Since nothing they had known earlier prepared them for this novelty, it was not difficult to abandon traditional proteanism, particularly since it immediately threatened their own identity. Islam's very different process of expansion never confronted Muslims with such stark novelty.

Absence of Slave Societies and Economies

The relationship between slavery and racism is an oft-debated question, particularly in early American history. Here it is argued that while it played a significant role in reinforcing the rise of racism, it did not provide the initial impetus. Expansion preceded exploitation. To be sure both reflected material circumstances, so mine is not an argument against the economic basis of racism or for the essentialist assertion that racism has always been present. Rather it is a suggestion that racism arose in the early modern world out of a complex of multiple interrelated factors in which slavery played a prominent, perhaps necessary, but not initially significant role. Obviously slavery in its various guises has been a long-lived and ubiquitous institution in Europe and throughout the world. No one has convincingly argued, however, that racism is as ubiquitous as slavery.

While slavery in and of itself does not automatically lead to racism, its precise nature and circumstances might determine the greater or lesser likelihood of its fostering such a world-view. It is considered that the second of the two closely interrelated major causes (the first being oceanic expansion) for the rise of racism in early modern Euro-America was large scale trans-oceanic agricultural slavery, a phenomenon largely absent in the Islamic world. Even plantation slavery alone, obviously without the trans-oceanic component, was exceptional. Significantly, the one region in which it had been practiced, the marshes of southern Iraq, produced the major slave revolt in Islamic history, the so-called Zanj uprising of the ninth century.[37] After that event Muslims did not embark upon any such enterprises elsewhere. Islam did employ slaves in two other areas, distinctively as soldiers who formed a core military caste, and, not surprisingly as domestic servants. This latter form of slavery was significant and ubiquitous, but because of polygamy and the acceptance of concubinage it could be a device for integration rather than segregation. A color-line existed within the slave system, white slaves generally being higher ranked than black, at least as documented over recent centuries, but it is not clear that these distinctions, notably the rejection of African partners for the ruler's bed, prevailed in earlier periods.

The great historian of the ancient world, Moses Finley, has distinguished between slave societies and societies with slaves.[38] Generally the Islamic world had many societies with slaves, but, in Finley's terms, no slave societies. There is no doubt that invidious prejudice against different groups, variously defined, has existed in the world of Islam, despite the desires of its founders to create a just egalitarian society. However such prejudice, a universal phenomenon in human experience, did not achieve the influence and power that racism achieved in Europe and in the cultures that it spawned elsewhere in the world. Thus the violence that has arisen over the past century in the Near East and more broadly in the Islamic world, e.g., the Armenian and Kurdish conflicts, the Assyrian massacres, civil wars in Lebanon and Iraq, the partition of India, and the Palestine dispute, cannot be blamed on racism. The Islamic world and the Near East has been neither a racist abode nor its opposite. Rather here persecution took other forms, neither worse nor better, simply different.

Notes

1. Robert Knox, *The Races of Men. A Philosophical Enquiry into the Influence of Race over the Destinies of Nations*, 2nd ed. (London, 1862), v.
2. Quoted in BBC online encyclopedia, <http://www.bbc.co.uk/dna/h2g2/A550928>, accessed 24 July 2008.
3. Ira Berlin, *Many Thousands Gone: The First Two Centuries of Slavery in North America* (Cambridge, 1998), 1.

4. "Airs, Waters, Places," in *Hippocrates with an English Translation*, trans. W.H.S. Jones (London, 1923), section 14, 1: 130–33.

5. Benjamin Braude, "Sex and Race in the Eighteenth Century: What Happened to Cross-Color Generation in the Americas?", unpublished paper given at the Conference on Sexuality in Early America, sponsored by the McNeil Center for Early American Studies (University of Pennsylvania) and the Omohundro Institute of Early American History and Culture (Williamsburg, Virginia), Philadelphia, 1–3 June, 2001; and Wendy Doniger, "The Symbolism of Black and White Babies in the Myth of Parental Impression – Critical Essay," *Social Research*, Spring 2003, <http://findarticles.com/p/articles/mi_m2267/is_1_70/ai_102140946/print>.

6. Joshua Trachtenberg, *The Devil and the Jews: The Medieval Conception of the Jew and its Relation to Modern Antisemitism*, 2nd paperback ed. (Philadelphia, 1983), 47–50.

7. See my "The Sons of Noah and the Construction of Ethnic and Geographical Identities in the Medieval and Early Modern Periods," *William and Mary Quarterly* 54, no. 1 (1997): 103–42; "Michelangelo and the Curse of Ham: From a Typology of Jew-Hatred to a Genealogy of Racism," in *Writing Race Across the Atlantic World: Medieval to Modern*, edited by Phillip Beidler and Gary Taylor (New York, 2005), 79–92; and Józef Matuszewski, *Cham* (Łódź: 1991).

8. Marc Raeff, *The Well-Ordered Police State: Social and Institutional Change through Law in the Germanies and Russia, 1600–1800* (New Haven, 1983).

9. In the Anglophone world the best known is George Best's account of Martin Frobisher's search for the Northwest Passage since it was included in Hakluyt paean to exploration and expansion, *Principal Navigations* (London, 1598–1600), 3: 48–69. It was originally published as George Best, *A true discourse of the late voyages of discouerie: for the finding of a passage to Cathaya, by ... Martin Frobisher ... also, there are annexed certayne reasons, to proue all partes of the worlde habitable* ... (London, 1578), 18, 19–20, 28–32. See also Winthrop Jordan, *White over Black: American Attitudes toward the Negro, 1550–1812* (Chapel Hill, 1968), 17, 40, and Alden Vaughan and Virginia Mason Vaughan, "Before *Othello*: Elizabethan Representations of Sub-Saharan Africans," *William and Mary Quarterly* 54, no. 1 (1997): 27. For the Portuguese view, see Ambrósio Fernandes Brandão, (ca. 1555), *Diálogos das grandezas do Brasil (Dialogues of the great things of Brazil)*, trans. and ed., Frederick Holden Hall, William F. Harrison, and Dorothy Winters Welker (Albuquerque, 1987), 91–92. In 1575, just three years before George Best, a Dominican, Francisco de la Cruz, recounted to the inquisitional court in Lima an angelic revelation that "los negros son justamente captivos por justa sentencia de Dios por los pecados de sus padres" ("the blacks are properly enslaved for the sins of their fathers, with the just sentence of God"). Their color comes from God, not from what "Philosophos" claim—Best's favorite boogey-man as well. Marcel Bataillon, "Le 'Clérigo Casas', ci-devant colon, réformateur de la colonisation," *Bulletin Hispanique* 54 (1952): 276–369, particularly 368.

10. Eugen Weber, *Peasants into Frenchmen: The Modernization of Rural France, 1870–1914* (Stanford, 1976) and Pieter M. Judson, *Guardians of the Nation: Activists on the Language Frontiers of Imperial Austria* (Cambridge, MA, 2007).

11. Stephen Jay Gould, "Blumenbach's Racial Geometry," in *The Mismeasure of Man* (New York, 1966).

12. Nell Irvin Painter, "Why White People Are Called 'Caucasian'?," unpublished paper presented at the Conference Collective Degradation: Slavery and the Construction of Race, The Gilder Lehrman Center for the Study of Slavery, Resistance and Abolition, Yale University, 7–8 November 2003.

13. "Racial Riots, Looting Hit Russian Town," *REUTERS*, 3 September 2006, filed at 7:43 a.m. ET; Steven Lee Myers, "In Russian City, a Rampage of Ethnic Violence," *New York Times,* 13 September 2006; Kim Murphy, "Racial Split Seen in Russian Politics, Attacks on minorities are rising. In Moscow, nationalists run an anti-migrant campaign," *Los Angeles Times,* 2 December 2005; Donald G. McNeil, Jr., "Like Politics, All Political Correctness Is Local," *New York Times,* Week in Review, 11 October 1998, 5.

14. Bernard Lewis, *Race and Slavery in the Middle East: An Historical Enquiry* (New York, 1990), 17.

15. *The Book of the Thousand Nights and One Night,* trans., John Payne (London, 1901), 4: 96–97. Lewis, *Race and Slavery,* 111 n. 10 calls attention to Richard Burton's version of the same tale and André Miquel's analysis of its anti-black elements. However it is absent in the definitive edition, Muhsin Mahdi, eds. Alf Layla wa Layla, Leiden, 1984, English trans. Husain Haddawy, *The Arabian Nights, Based on the Text of the Fourteenth-Century Syrian Manuscript Edited by Muhsin Mahdi* (New York, 1990). A systematic comparison of the nineteenth-century English translations by Edward William Lane and Richard Francis Burton to the Haddawy translation has concluded that "issues of race and sex were exaggerated and distorted" in the former, see Kerrin Wood, "Arabian Nights in Comparison," unpublished seminar paper, Boston College, 2000. For the Europeanization of this supposedly Eastern folktale see Raymond Schwab, *L' Auteur des Mille et Une Nuits: vie d'Antoine Galland* (Paris, 1964).

16. For examples of these jugs, *kantharoi* (the precise term) see Jean Vercoutter, et al. *The Image of the Black in Western Art,* vol. 1, *From the Pharaohs to the Fall of the Roman Empire,* trans. William G. Ryan (New York, 1976), 163–66.

17. See my "Black Skin/White Skin: Color Identity and Color Indifference in Ancient Greece and the Near East," *Micrologus: Nature, Sciences and Medieval Societies* 13 (2005): 11–21.

18. Martin Lewis and Kären Wigen, *The Myth of Continents* (Berkeley, 1997).

19. See my "Les contours indécis d'une nouvelle géographie," *Cahiers de Science et Vie* 44 (April 1998): 46–53; and "And That's How Continents Got Invented..." for panel on Revising the History of Space, which I organized for the American Association of Geographers Meeting, Honolulu, 25–28 March 1999.

20. Samuel Stanhope Smith, *Essay on the Causes of the Variety of Complexion and Figure in the Human Species* (1810) ed. Winthrop Jordan (Cambridge, MA, 1965), 9–11, 21, 74, 192–93.

21. *Ulrichs von Richental Chronik des Constanzer Concils 1414 bis 1418*, ed. Michael Buck, 1882, reprint Hildesheim, 1962, 50–52. This edition, based on the oldest of the extant manuscripts is presumptively closer to the original. Accordingly I have used it in preference to the popularized modern abridgement, *Ulrichs von Richental Chronik des Konzils zu Konstanz*, ed. Otto H. Brandt (Leipzig, 1913) and the lavish facsimile edition, based on a later manuscript, Ulrich Richental, *Das Konzil zu Konstanz*, two vols., ed. Otto Feger (Starnberg, 1964). Page references are incorporated in the text.

22. *Ulrichs von Richental Chronik des Constanzer Concils*, 158, 171, 183–84, 203, 206.

23. Eric John Morrall, ed., *Sir John Mandevilles Reisebeschreibung in deutscher Übersetzung von Michel Velser, nach der Stuttgarter Papierhandschrift*, (Berlin, 1974), 20, 29, and 134. Mandeville has many versions, some of which omit the genealogy of Noah, but this version of the ancestry of Israel is the most common as demonstrated in my "The Sons of Noah." That article also contains a discussion of the diffusion and importance of the Mandeville corpus. See also Iain Macleod Higgins, *Writing East: The Travels of Sir John Mandeville* (Philadelphia, 1997).

24. Orosius, 2.1; Latin text and French translation, *Orose Histories (Contre les Païens)*, ed. and trans. Marie-Pierre Arnaud-Lindet (Paris,1990), 1:13, 192. For the unity of Europe and Africa see Patrick Gautier Dalche, "*Situs orbis terre vel regionum*: un traité de géographie inédit du haut moyen âge (Paris B.N. Latin 4841)," *Revue d'Histoire des Textes*, 12–13 (1982–83) : 149–79, particularly 164. More generally for the medieval continuation of the ancient uncertainty about how to divide the world see his "Tradition et renouvellement dans la représentation de l'espace géographique au IXe siècle," *Studi Medievali* 24 (1983): 121–65, particularly 145–47, both photoreproduced in his collection, *Géographie et culture: la représentation de l'espace du VIe au XIIe siècle* (Aldershot, UK, 1997), as articles III and IV respectively.

25. David Woodward, "Medieval *Mappaemundi*," in J.B. Harley and David Woodward, eds. *The History of Cartography*, vol. 1, *Cartography in Prehistoric, Ancient, and Medieval Europe and the Mediterranean* (Chicago, 1987), 300–301.

26. *La fleur des histoires*, 281v–282 r. Brussels, Bibliothèque royale Albert 1er.

27. Loving et ux. v. Virginia, Supreme Court of the United States, 388 U.S. 1, 12 June 1967, <http://www.law.umkc.edu/faculty/projects/ftrials/conlaw/loving.html>, accessed 6 May 2008.

28. Naghmeh Sohrabi, "Signs Taken for Wonder: Nineteenth century Persian Travel Literature to Europe," (Ph.D. diss., Harvard University, 2005) and Muhammad Saffar, *Disorienting Encounters: Travels of a Moroccan Scholar in France in 1845–1846: the Voyage of Muhammad as-Saffar.* trans. Susan Gilson Miller (Berkeley, 1992).

29. This is explored in its complexity and inconsistency in my "Cham et Noé. Race, esclavage et exégèse entre Islam, Judaïsme, et Christianisme," *Annales: Histoire, Sciences Sociales* 57, no. 1 (2002): 93–125.

30. George M. Fredrickson, *Racism: A Short History* (Princeton, 2002) has suggested a related argument for the role of the state in the rise of racism, arguing for the paradox that the creation of the liberal representative egalitarian state necessitated the development of new criteria by which certain groups could be excluded from political life.

31. The Hebrew word for household servant and the word used in the Bible for clan or extended family—there is no biblical equivalent of nuclear family—seem etymologically related, *shifha* and *mishpahah*. The most common Arabic word for family, *ahl*, has a much wider range of meanings, including household, clan, and is etymologically related to *ohel*, "tent."

32. Leslie Peirce, *The Imperial Harem: Women and Sovereignty in the Ottoman Empire* (New York, 1993).

33. J. Schacht, "Law and Justice," in *Cambridge History of Islam,* vol. 2, *The Further Islamic Lands, Islamic Society and Civilization,* eds. Peter M. Holt, Ann K.S. Lambton and Bernard Lewis (Cambridge, 1970), 551.

34. James C. Scott, *Seeing like a State: How Certain Schemes to Improve the Human Condition Have Failed* (New Haven, 1998).

35. Braude, "Sons of Noah," develops this point explicitly.

36. See my "Mandeville's Jews among Others," in *Pilgrims and Travellers to the Holy Land,* eds. Bryan F. LeBeau and Menahem Mor (Omaha, 1996), 141–68, as well as the detailed discussion of Mandeville in "Sons of Noah."

37. Alexandre Popovic, *The Revolt of African Slaves in Iraq in the 3rd/9th Century,* trans. Léon King (Princeton, 1999).

38. Moses I. Finley, *Ancient Slavery and Modern Ideology,* expanded edition, ed. Brent D. Shaw (Princeton, 1998), 135–60.

Chapter 3

Culture's Shadow: "Race" and Postnational Belonging in the Twentieth Century

Christian Geulen

In 1920, the American historian, eugenicist, and racial theorist Lothrop Stoddard published a soon-to-be-famous book, *The Rising Tide of Color against White World-Supremacy*. Along with Madison Grant's *The Passing of the Great Race* (1916) it was the leading work of a widespread racial pessimism in America during the 1920s. Stoddard described a global future that would be overshadowed by various crises and dangers to the supremacy of the white and Nordic races: the competition of the rising yellow races in East Asia, a likely new war in a nationally and racially divided Europe, the uprising of the black races in Africa against colonial rule, triggering global mass migration, and finally the religious fanaticism of what Stoddard called the "brown," mostly Muslim, races of the Near and Middle East.[1]

Looking back at the actual global developments of the twentieth century, it comes as no surprise that today Stoddard's name has gained a new prominence among right-wing theorists and neo-racialist groups that quote him as a prophet of the perils of globalization. In contrast, academic as well as popular history has largely forgotten him, since after 1945 his theories fell into disrepute for being too closely affiliated with Nazi ideology. This affiliation was primarily based upon Stoddard's works on eugenics and racial hygiene, such as his 1922 book, *The Revolt against Civilization: The Menace of the Under Man,* and his two trips to Europe during the 1930s to interview Mussolini, Hitler, and Goebbels. In his reports on these encounters he was quite critical of the military development in Europe, but also fascinated by the racial visions of fascism. Today, however, Stoddard's *The Rising Tide of Color* as well as a second book, *Clashing Tides of Color* (1935), seem to have gained plausibility at least among certain branches of political thought.[2] And even the short article on Stoddard in the "free online encyclopedia" explicitly points to the fascinating, if uncanny, accuracy of his visions, especially his prediction of a rising religious fanaticism among the "brown" races of the Islamic world.

On the one hand, it is quite easy to dismiss such ostensibly accurate prophecies as purely accidental. One might also point out that predicting global crises in the early 1920s was a matter of stating the obvious. On the other hand, such a view tends to disregard the possible long-term impact of such writings throughout the twentieth century by depicting them as examples of a long-overcome exotic zeitgeist. This approach can easily be misleading, however. Works such as Stoddard's and Grant's gained popularity not merely for their specific prophesies but also for the plausibility of their theoretical frameworks and arguments. Oswald Spengler, whose writings fall into the same broad intellectual category, is a case in point. Today it is easy to dismiss most of what Spengler predicted in his *Decline of the West* (1918), yet it seems barely possible to write a history of twentieth century Western political philosophy without Spengler.[3]

The example of Spengler leads to the main subject of this essay: for Spengler did not so much write about race (even though the term does play an important role in his book), but about history and culture. And this emphasis on culture (instead of race) is precisely the reason why Spengler, despite his major contribution to the transnational discourse of decay and degeneration in the early 1920s, has always been accepted as an important and influential, if problematic, visionary of the early twentieth century. Of course, there has long been a debate over the question of how close Spengler's cultural theory was related to concurrent racialist ideologies; but this applies to almost every theory and intellectual current of the 1920s and 1930s. However, this perspective is necessarily one-sided, for it focuses on the entanglement of certain ideas and concepts with the dark powers of racism and fascism—but not vice versa. It takes racism for granted—as being a deterministic ideology of fixed differences and racial hierarchies—and then tries to determine the extent to which certain theories and notions of culture did or did not embrace this ideology. But how does this relationship between race and culture look from the other side? Is it true that racism always ignored culture as being irrelevant or predetermined by racial factors? Why, then, have racial ideologues invested so much energy and time trying to prove this point and reinterpret culture—in all aspects—in racial terms? How entangled was the notion of race with that of culture in the first place? To what extent has racial thinking embraced discourses of culture and history? And what was the long-term contribution of the racial discourse to our understanding of culture? Only by looking at this side of the relationship do we gain a full picture of the role that race and racism played in the intellectual history of the twentieth century.

Thus, instead of defining what we mean, or should mean, when we speak of "race" and/or "culture," this essay looks at the complex development of the terms and their often overlapping semantics throughout the twentieth century. Of course, there have always been certain fixed elements in the meanings of those terms: race has somehow always been linked to the body, to matters of physiology, biology, or at least the outer appearance of human beings. Therefore race (and racism) is usually associated with a supposed "objectivity," with clear-cut lines and differences between races. Culture, in contrast, has always been understood as something created by the human mind, be it material or not. However, today, in the age of genetic engineering when the human mind might be able to create a new species or race, even this basic difference becomes unstable. Moreover, there has never been a concept of race that was exclusively defined in terms of physiology. The term race was always an attempt to connect nature to the non-natural world, to provide culture with a natural or physiological basis. Thus, my essay does not attempt to give a clarification of what race and culture actually are or might be or how they should be understood, but instead prefers to look at selected discourses of race and culture. Historically, these terms share a wide semantic field, including scientific and popular texts and theories, historical and political categories, and, last but not least, the various attempts to define their meaning once and for all.

Obviously, the development of the two concepts in the twentieth century can only be sketched in this essay. Still, one recurring commonality appears to bind the two concepts: both culture and race, especially when used as markers of collective identity, invariably refer to something existing on a subnational as well as on a transnational level. Of course, nation-states have attempted (not very successfully) to harmonize and homogenize their cultural, racial, and national boundaries. But conceptually it was always understood that individuals might change their nationality, but could hardly change their culture or race. Culture and race were always both less and more than what defined the nation state. Still, the twentieth century was certainly an age that was dominated (more than ever before) by the nation state principle. However, it was also the age of the greatest challenges to this principle—represented especially by imperialism, including the classic imperialism of the late nineteenth and early twentieth centuries and its fascist and socialist varieties, and by what we have come to call globalization. Viewed from this perspective, both race and culture, carrying with them a notion of long-term stability independent from political decisions and demarcations, seem to have functioned as two different sides of the same promise: they provide frameworks for postnational forms of collective identity and belonging. This is precisely the reason why they have been quite closely linked to each other in the course of the twentieth century. And even though today many people would like to strictly separate them, by embracing culture and dismissing race, we should be aware of their long-lasting semantic relationship and its effects. After all, it is not the terms themselves that cause harm, but the way we invest them with meaning.

Races and Spaces

To be sure, this essay does not aim to reconstruct and save racial thinking as a forgotten tradition that we should worship or take up again. Nor does it attempt to obscure the differences between race and culture, which are, of course, two distinct concepts of collective identity and belonging.[4] Instead, it focuses on the intricate question of whether or not there is something like an undercurrent of racial thought in the modern discourse of culture. This question has acquired a new significance ever since the end of the Cold War. While crossing and transcending the borders of nation states, cultural claims of belonging and collective identity have become major issues of political conflict. In regard to the challenges of an accelerated globalization, of establishing transnational political orders, of religious fundamentalism, of a still increasing worldwide migration, and of what has been coined as the "clash of civilizations," the twenty-first century appears to be engaged in a desperate search for conceptual as well as practical ways to cope with cultural diversity and conflict, and to create new systems of belonging under postnational conditions.

To some degree these conditions mirror the global constellation of the late nineteenth and early twentieth centuries, when the globalizing dynamics of imperialism and a growing world economy also challenged the principle of the nation state. World War I at first was perceived as a conflict between nation-states, but quickly turned into a global battle of populations and technologies or—in the contemporaries' perspective—between "cultures" and "civilizations." In contrast to the present situation, however, the nation-state system was not openly called into question after 1918. Instead the Wilsonian principle of national self-determination and the Paris Peace Treaties reestablished the nation-state as the only conceivable foundation of world order. Only after the defeat of racist fascism in World War II, with its unimaginable mass destruction, was the nation-state system gradually superseded by the global structure of the Cold War, although the principle itself persisted.[5] Then, immediately after 1989, the nation-state came back with a vengeance, in Europe as elsewhere, leading to a whole range of new European states as well as to a new wave of historical research on nationalism. Today, nation-states are still the major protagonists of global diplomacy. Nevertheless, there is a widespread belief that the "real" conflicts and challenges are simply beyond the control of nation-states, national armies, or national politics; a belief that the coming wars will be, once again, wars between cultures and civilizations, symbolized by the 9/11-image of civilian airplanes deliberately crashing into the World Trade Center.

Thus, even though history never repeats itself, the present-day situation indeed offers striking parallels to the early twentieth century. These parallels quite explicitly inform today's debates on globalization and imperialism, on the constitution of the European Union or on concepts such as Samuel Huntington's "clash of civilizations."[6] In a historical perspective, however, it is important not only to systematically compare global conditions and the role of the nation-state in two different time periods, but also to look at the actual transformations that led from one context to the other and drove forward what could be called the "long goodbye" of national belonging. Moreover, in regard to those historical processes of transformation it is especially important to look at the notion of race and its development through the course of he twentieth century, for at least until the 1960s "race" was a major "third" alternative for conceptualizing collective political belonging, always closely related to, but certainly never completely identical with the concepts of "nation" and "culture."

As Hannah Arendt observed, in the classic imperialist age of the late nineteenth and early twentieth centuries an important function of the notion of race was to harmonize the fundamental contradiction between the structure of the nation-state and that of empire.[7] Race was the key-term of a new language to conceptualize the relationship between the global and the particular along transnational hierarchies and evolutionary models of development. Today, it seems that the concept of culture (or "civilization" or currently also "religion") is increasingly used to understand lines of conflict and forms of collective belonging which transcend and even undermine national borders. The question is if today culture serves as a functional equivalent to race or if it even indicates a historical continuity. To put it more pointedly: what happened to the racial discourse as a form of making sense of an evermore entangled world in the course of the twentieth century?

Before exploring this question through a few selected examples, another look at Stoddard's *Rising Tide of Color* may illustrate the meaning of what was referred to earlier as a possible "undercurrent" of racial thinking in today's view on culture. Stoddard's book contained a colored map depicting the geographical distribution of the major races around the globe: it placed the white races in Europe, North America and Australia, the yellow races in East Asia, the black races in Central Africa, the "Amerindian" races, as Stoddard called them, in Latin America, and the brown races in North Africa and the Middle East. Like other contemporary attempts to visualize a racial world order, Stoddard's map had to either ignore or manipulate controverting facts of the global reality. Regions such as Central America, for instance, are difficult to classify in their multiracial composition. In some cases Stoddard took political borders into account, in other cases he ignored them. Thus, Australia as well as southern Africa were counted as white regions, whereas the United States was clearly divided into a white North and a mixed South. In contrast, such a mixture, according to Stoddard, apparently never happened between the brown and white races of southeastern Europe, where the racial lines—on Stoddard's map—were clear-cut and the "brown territory" began as soon as one crossed the Black Sea.

Today, of course, the global situation of 1920 is depicted historically in a completely different way. Samuel Huntington's *Clash of Civilizations*, for instance, also contains a map of the global situation in the year 1920, dividing the world into countries ruled by the West and those independent from the West, which results in a picture of the globe quite different from Stoddard's. However, two pages further on in Huntington's book we find another map, this time locating the world of civilizations in the post-1990 era. And it is this map that strikingly mirrors, with only a few exceptions, Stoddard's 1920 map of races.[8]

The point here is not to say that Huntington is secretly or unknowingly continuing the racialist discourse of the 1920s. Rather it is to illustrate that throughout the twentieth century "race" as well as "culture" or "civilization" have always been postnational concepts, designed to transcend given political forms of identity by referring to a deeper, supposedly more profound foundation of belonging. In sketching the relationship between race and culture as it developed in the twentieth century, the following paragraphs will focus on the variations of this dual meaning of both terms.

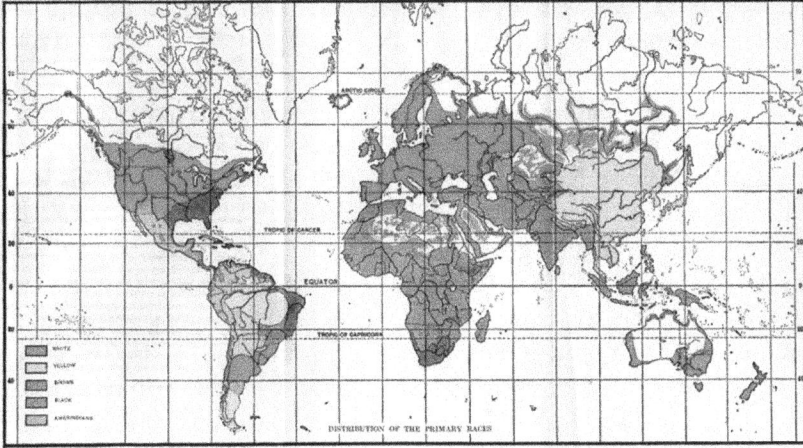

Distribution of the Primary Races in 1920 (L. Stoddard)[9]

Race into Culture

The late nineteenth and early twentieth centuries witnessed a decisive transformation of racial theory from the paradigm of racial war and fixed racial hierarchies to that of race improvement and the production of desired racial compositions. This shift was represented by the emergence and global success of eugenics. But the ideas that this new science put forward had in fact a much broader impact as a popular line of thinking far beyond the dissemination of eugenic concepts. In particular, where the racial discourse took up the Darwinian theory of evolution—and only a few racial thinkers did not—the instrumentalization of Darwinian principles, as a way to artificially mimic nature in order to achieve politically or socially desired results, was a common and almost logical conclusion.[10]

Darwin—despite the title of his major work—had offered a scientific explanation for the development of races that no longer needed "origins," at least not in the sense of placing them in a distant historical past. Instead he had pointed to mechanisms, such as natural selection, that operate and can be observed on a daily basis. It was John Dewey who expressed this implication most clearly in 1911, when he remarked that in the Darwinian logic "interest shifts from ... an intelligence that shaped things once and for all to the particular intelligences which things are even now shaping; shifts from an ultimate goal to the intelligent administration of existent conditions. The Darwinian Logic introduces responsibility into the intellectual life."[11]

71

Of course, Dewey was not the only one to point to this specific aspect of Darwinian evolutionism. Ten years earlier, Karl Pearson, a London professor of applied mathematics, had drawn similar conclusions when he stated that "in the early days, the struggle of race against race was a blind, unconscious struggle of barbaric tribes. But at the present day, in the case of the civilized white man, it has become more and more the conscious, carefully directed attempt of the nation to fit itself to a continuously changing environment." Pearson argued for a scientifically controlled race development in his highly influential essay on "National Life from the Standpoint of Science," which became one of the transnational founding texts of modern eugenics, even though it never mentioned the term.[12]

In Germany, Houston Stewart Chamberlain, arguably the most influential racial thinker of the early twentieth century, repeatedly claimed that races had never been fixed entities, but were products of creative forces operating on a daily basis. In his *Foundations of the Nineteenth Century*, Chamberlain explicitly criticized Arthur Gobineau's theory of races as much too static and fixed to be a sufficient explanation of world history. Against Ernest Renan's famous call for a strict differentiation between race and nation, Chamberlain held that there never was such a thing as an original race. Instead, according to Chamberlain, races were continuously produced through what he called race-building forces such as "marriage, custom, intellectual progress, national politics, scientific discoveries and culture."[13] Chamberlain is an especially interesting case, since his notion of a dynamic and creative race development was among the few ideas of the so-called *völkische* movement that the Nazis explicitly acknowledged as an intellectual forerunner of their own ideological project after 1933.

Four years after the publication of Chamberlain's book, the liberal German historian Otto Hintze, who later became famous for his studies on the history of modern states and bureaucracies, published a review of Chamberlain's book that strongly criticized the notion of race and its usefulness as a historical category. However, in conclusion, he wrote:

> History does not talk about races, but about nations. None of those nations represents a pure race, all grew out of racial mixture. What holds them together is not the same blood, but language and culture. That is especially true for the German nation. In comparison the German nation is still not as fixed and homogeneous as the English or French nations. It still lacks a racial physical foundation. Therefore nothing is more important than to create a strong and fixed national

unity in our homeland. In this sense a strong homeland policy is the precondition of world politics—and here we especially think about our endangered Eastern regions. A kind of racial politics towards the East will be absolutely vital for our future. We have a stock of humans just as fit as in other nations—let us take care to transform it into the German race of the future.[14]

Within one paragraph Hintze shifts from completely dismissing race as a category of historical explanation to envisioning the creation of a new German race (*Germanisierung*) in the eastern provinces of Imperial Germany by and through cultural and political means. Three decades later, the Nazis set out to enact this vision in ways that Hintze, of course, never imagined.

These examples show that at the beginning of the twentieth century racial thinking in the wake of Darwinian evolutionism, in either downright racist or rather liberal forms, turned away from ideas of biological stability and fixed racial hierarchies, and instead embraced the idea that cultural forces and purposeful scientific and political action could produce racial orders. This idea was all the more plausible, since Darwin himself had not considered the fitness of a race as a given, but rather as subject to the test of whether or not it would survive in the struggle for existence. For in the Darwinian view species did not survive because they adapted, they turned out to be well adapted insofar as they survived. Thus, quite ironically, it was the impact of Darwinism itself that, in the long run, undermined deterministic hopes for a stable and fixed racial order, and instead made racial thinkers turn away from nature's "struggle for existence" and hardcore positivist science, and toward the non-natural—that is, in a broad sense, the cultural factors—of racial development.[15]

A very interesting case in this development of racial thinking is the German-American anthropologist Franz Boas, known as one of the key figures in anthropology's early-twentieth-century shift from nature to culture. In 1910 Boas conducted an anthropometric measurement project on the cephalic index and the bodily form of immigrants in New York with the clear intent to disprove claims by anti-immigration activists that the newly immigrating "lower races" from southern and eastern Europe could never become good Americans for biological reasons. Boas intended to study the influence of the American environment on physical characteristics in order to debunk this racial hierarchy of immigrants. For his research he set up a three-stage model in which Ellis Island represented the stage of "zero degree of American influence on immigrants," whereas Manhattan represented some American influence and the rural areas further in the West represented a full-blown "American environment." In addition, Boas compared immigrant children born in their home countries with those born on U.S. soil. The well-known result of this project was that the heads and bodies of the immigrants apparently did change and in most cases toward a more American type. One of the exceptions, however, were the Sicilians, whose heads apparently were not quite as flexible, which is why Boas seriously suggested preventing them from living in New York, instead sending them directly from Ellis Island to the Midwest.[16]

In proposing such measures, Boas arguably used questionable data in order to bolster his political message. Moreover, the project did not rely on a Darwinian but rather on a Lamarckian model of evolution. Still, it is an example of the turn of the scientific notion of race toward cultural factors (here represented in the ominous notion of "environment") resulting from scientific findings. Boas's book on *The Mind of Primitive Man*, which came out immediately after his research on immigrants, is quite rightly celebrated as a fundamental turn of modern anthropology from "race" to "culture." Upon a closer reading, however, it becomes clear how this turn toward culture was very much determined by and came directly out of evolutionary racial thinking.[17] His own anthropometric research project (described in detail in *The Mind of Primitive Man*) had taught Boas that fixed races do not exist and therefore do not matter in the study of human differences. Boas regarded these findings as so crucial that in a letter to a colleague he even went so far as to propose that the entire problem of race prejudice could be solved if it were to become possible to erase racial differences through controlled racial mixing and the systematic relocation of populations to appropriate environments.[18]

Perhaps Boas was not really serious when proposing such a solution, as he never returned to these ideas, dropped the race issue, and went on to study language and culture. Yet it is still important to note that this new interest in culture was prompted by Boas's general insight that races were the physical products rather than the physical precondition of cultures. However, the problematic part of this story was not only that Boas or other liberal anthropologists arrived at this conclusion, but also that eugenicists and pre-fascist promoters of racial hygiene voiced the same ideas. In Germany, for example, Alfred Ploetz and Ludwig Woltmann, who were official advocates of the almighty factor of race, nevertheless published hundreds of articles in their eugenic journals considering the role of culture, politics, and art in the future evolution of the races. Following the course of eugenic thinking from turn-of-the-century Germany to the Nazi period, it becomes clear that eugenicists vociferously called for political action in order to control the racial composition of the nation and adapt it to the cultural norm, i.e., to what the great Germanic culture supposedly once was and would be again for a millennium. This was at the core of works such as Alfred Rosenberg's *Myth of the 20th century*, which its author explicitly conceived as a sequel to Chamberlain's *Foundations of the Nineteenth Century*.[19] In both of these books, culture, understood in a very broad sense as art and philosophy, as social life and collective mentality, and as political power and leadership, figured as a powerful and creative force capable of shaping the world—whereas the "Germanic race" in a biological sense was seen as the ultimate goal.

Across the Atlantic, too, prominent progressives in the turn-of-the-century United States, including the sociologist Lester F. Ward and G. Stanley Hall, publisher of the *Journal of Race Development*, discussed how evolutionary principles could be applied to redesign the global order of the races. In 1911, on the first (and last) "Universal Races Congress" in London, race theorists, eugenicists, progressives, social reformers, and promoters of the international peace movement joined in declaring that the natural laws governing both racial and cultural developments could be and should be instrumentalized by the human mind in order to create a world of mutual understanding and happiness.[20] This belief in scientific control survived the battlefields of World War I almost undamaged, in fact, it was even strengthened by the much more pessimistic view on the racial state of the world that resulted from the war, as described in the works of Stoddard, Grant, and Spengler in the 1920s. In the 1930s, then, the far-reaching identification of political state-building, social control, and population policies was—although connected to very different political ideologies—a transnational phenomenon and a prominent feature of the "Third Reich," of the various European fascist regimes, of Stalinist Russia, and of Franklin D. Roosevelt's "New Deal."[21]

In the early twentieth century, racism shifted its focus from explaining culture and politics through racial differences to producing a new racial order by applying the principles of nature to cultural and political projects. This tendency reached its most fatal form in the National Socialist worldview. The Nazis explicitly conceived of the *Volksgemeinschaft* as something to be forcibly created by exclusion, selection, murder, and genocide.[22] At the same time, National Socialists primarily understood "culture" as the nation's ability and potential to become a master-race. Under Hitler celebrating German history and culture was not a call for the continuation of tradition. Instead, German tradition was perceived as something that had been repeatedly and tragically defeated and betrayed by internal or external evil forces. Only a radical process of self-cleansing and rebuilding, in fact, only the transformation of the German culture into a German race would guarantee a German survival. Thus, the process of merging race and culture that had been going on since the second half of the nineteenth century was brought to its most radical conclusion in Nazi Germany: culture became the determinant of the Germans' potential, a potential insulated by the creation, by all possible means and practices, of a German "race."

Of course, elements of a "classic" racism remained, such as clear-cut racial hierarchies and racial orders. There were stereotypical images of other races in Germanic folklore, for example, but these elements did not play a decisive role in the development of Nazi racial politics. The absence of solidarity that the Jews experienced in everyday life shortly after 1933, the willingness of many Germans to either participate in or ignore the state-organized anti-Semitic violence of the 1930s, the permanent state of emergency that the Nazis quite successfully managed to maintain, and even the bureaucratic aspects of the extermination policies do not primarily indicate a race hatred based on prejudices against the Jews, the slavic races, or the physically and mentally disabled. They more broadly reveal that the logic of racial and biological principles, the logic of the survival of one's own way of life by means of ethnic cleansing, and the logic of identifying biological laws with the political order was widely accepted by Germans in the 1930s and 1940s as the very foundation of their new *Volksgemeinschaft*.[23]

In this sense, even though it sounds paradoxical, Nazi racial politics can be described as racism without race. The race issue was turned into a set of ideological principles and logical mechanisms that centered around the question of what was practically and politically to be done rather than around models of racial hierarchy or racial order. However, at the same time, partly in reaction to the radical forms of racial politics practiced by Nazi Germany, precisely those sciences such as anthropology that had started out by studying race in the nineteenth century, now prepared to dismiss the concept of race once and for all and to replace it with the concept of culture.

Culture into Race

During the last year of World War II, from the Allied invasion of France to the dropping of the atomic bombs on Japan, more people were killed than during the entire period from 1939 to 1944. In the wake of this violent climax, any attempt to make sense of the world, to re-order it and to plan its future required new categories and perspectives. "Reconstruction" after 1945 was a matter of imagining a possible future rather than of rebuilding a shattered past. Thus, words, concepts, and metaphors were made up spontaneously to encapsulate complex situations and quickly became signifiers of the postwar world. For example, Winston Churchill popularized the term "iron curtain" and a French economist invented the concept of the "third world" (in reference to the "tiers état"), not knowing that they had coined metaphors of lasting historical impact.

Following World War II, the new global order of the Cold War (another spontaneously invented term) swiftly replaced the world of nation-states. However, the Cold War also represented a continuation of the ideological conflict between "Western" liberty and "Eastern" equality, which had been simmering since 1917. Obviously, the postwar world needed a new normative framework of collective orientation. Thus, beginning with the founding of the United Nations and the Nuremberg Trials, the emergence of a bipolar political world went hand in glove with efforts to create a new moral order as well. A key issue of this moral reconstruction was racism.

The Nuremberg Trials highlighted the extremes to which racial politics had been taken in the "Third Reich." The Nazi mass murder of European Jews, known as the "final solution," immediately came to epitomize the destructiveness of racist ideologies, even though it took decades of study to fully comprehend its origins and scope. Thus in 1948, in one of its first resolutions, the newly founded United Nations Educational, Scientific and Cultural Organization (UNESCO) suggested an international program for the worldwide dissemination of "scientific facts designed to bring about the disappearance of that which is commonly called race prejudice." As part of this program the well-known anthropologist Claude Levi-Strauss gave a lecture on "Race and History" that was soon internationally received as a kind of founding text of post-1945 anti-racism.[24]

As an anthropologist, Levi-Strauss argued on two levels: on the one hand his task was to dismiss, as convincingly as possible, the notion of "race" as a useful concept for describing differences between human groups. Hence, he put forward the notion of "culture" as being the much more appropriate category. On the other hand, he explicitly refused to embrace a universalism that neglected collective differences. His core idea was to replace the fatal notion of the "inequality of races" with the supposedly liberal idea of the "diversity of cultures." In order to make this twofold argument, Levi-Strauss painted a picture of racism that reduced it to a completely static ideology dividing the world into a small number of discrete and immutable races (dating back to unknown prehistoric origins) whose essential differences meant they should stay as far apart as possible. The notion of a general "inequality of races," Levi-Strauss argued, needed to be abandoned for being false or at least unrealistic and susceptible to ideological instrumentalization. In contrast, he depicted the "diversity of cultures" as a much more complex phenomenon with historical instead of natural origins, one that should by all means be preserved. Even a coming "world civilization" (as it was envisioned by UN officials at the time) could be "no more than a worldwide coalition of cultures, each of which would preserve its own originality," Levi-Strauss insisted.

In his lecture, Levi-Strauss articulated a categorical difference between culture and race, which had a major influence on postwar political thinking and helped to shape what could be called the anti-racist consensus of the Cold War. Soon this consensus helped to put international pressure on downright racist regimes such as in South Africa and the segregationist American South. But there was a price to be paid for this: first, the complex phenomenon of racism, although it had been quite appropriately described and analyzed by intellectuals such as Eric Voegelin and Hannah Arendt,[25] was reduced to a pathological, misanthropic ideology misrepresenting the world as a fixed and ahistorical order of eternal racial differences—a view that a closer look at the history of racism before 1945 would have proved misleading. Second, all ideological tenets of the racial discourse that go beyond the supposedly pathological core ideas of racism, that is to say all the ideas on the evolution of races, racial mixing, the natural perfection and artificial creation of races which had been discussed since Darwin were now relegated to the seemingly innocuous realm of "culture."

Levi-Strauss himself acknowledged as much when he stated at the outset of his essay that "cultural diversity is in no way the outcome of biological differences," but that it should be understood as "simply a parallel phenomenon in a different sphere." A few pages later he explicitly recognized the danger implied in the idea of simply replacing the notion of race with that of culture, namely the danger of providing racial ideologies with a new conceptual framework. In 1952, though, he was willing to ignore his own caveat:

"Last and most important, the nature of the diversity must be investigated even at the risk of allowing the racial prejudices whose ideological foundation has so lately been destroyed to develop again on new grounds." Two decades later, he was convinced that he had made a mistake.

In 1971, again on behalf of the United Nations, Levi-Strauss gave another lecture on the issue, this time entitled "Race and Culture."[26] In this sequel he basically retracted everything he had said earlier about the strict difference between race and culture and about the necessity of seeing them as two distinct conceptual universes. He began by pointing out that geneticists were now discovering a system of biological reproduction far more complex than any simple notion of race would allow—a self-regulating system of genes and selection, characteristics and environments, which Levi-Strauss saw as quite "comparable to the cultural recombination in the evolution of ways of life, techniques, knowledge and beliefs." Furthermore, Levi-Strauss conceded that racism and race hatred had anything but disappeared since UNESCO declared it unscientific. Instead, he pointed to various forms of collective group hatred that were clearly racist in their radical nature and inner logic while at the same time not directed against races in a biological sense, but rather against cultural groups such as the "hippies" and other non-racial communities.

Considering the fact that racist anti-Semitism, compared to hatred of "hippies," is a much more prominent and important example of a form of racism directed against a culture (instead of a pre-supposed racial group— if there ever was one), it becomes clear that in 1971 Levi-Strauss substantially revised his earlier thesis. Now convinced "that cultural and organic evolution are inextricably linked," he acknowledged that the entire issue of racism could not and should not be understood as beginning and ending with a biological race concept. Instead, he wrote, "we must accept the fact" that the actual causes of racism "are much deeper than mere ignorance or prejudice." And in quite a pessimistc tone, he stated that the present course of world history, tending to "level out and nullify" any form of diversity, "is building up tensions to such a degree that racial hatred is a mere foretaste of the greater intolerance that may hold sway tomorrow, without even the pretext of ethnic differences."

Unfortunately Levi-Strauss's second text is his much less prominent contribution to the study of racism. Instead, especially in the 1970s and 1980s, his first essay of 1952 became something like the official Western theory of racism, most often quoted in the post-1968 literature on racism as well as in textbooks. To some degree, it also helped cultural anthropology to become a leading discipline among the humanities, when the social sciences, which had dominated the field since the late 1950s, experienced a crisis of credibility when confronted with what came to be known in the late Cold War era as the "postmodern condition." Because cultural anthropology questioned the logic of modernization and showed a new sensibility to symbolic orders, the concept of culture in the 1980s appeared to be the theoretical key to uncover lost traditions and collective identities that resisted the supposedly inexorable modernization process.

Hence, not before long the preservation of cultural identity became a political issue put forward by the new paradigm of "multiculturalism" and the new interdisciplinary field of Cultural Studies. And Levi-Strauss's ideas from 1952—that cultures are entirely non-natural entities originating in historical change and that they must be preserved in their historical originality—became theoretical cornerstones of the field. Yet after the end of the Cold War, when radical ethnic and racial nationalisms in Eastern Europe and elsewhere flourished, the dark and destructive side of collective cultural identities once again became apparent. Consequently, a more skeptical and critical view on the issue of cultures, cultural difference, and cultural identity was called for.[27] At the same time, intellectuals became aware of the countervailing development of globalization. Arguably this process will further dissolve collective identities and make it very difficult, in the long run, for cultural groups to preserve their "originality."

Thus, today we are confronted with precisely the constellation that Levi-Strauss predicted as the immediate future in his second lecture on racism in 1971: whereas the globalizing forces of the post-Cold War era are about to render the idea of a preservation of cultures obsolete, existing groups—whether conceiving themselves as cultural, national, religious, or social communities—increasingly tend to develop a fundamentalist self-image and an essentialist notion of community. In the post-colonial world, in the United States, in the Middle East, and even in Western Europe people react strongly to the economic and social processes that tend to level out all cultural differences, by reasserting what they perceive as their cultural identities. Thus, "culture" has become the most important and most trusted category for collective identity and belonging in an age in which the structure of the nation-state is increasingly undermined by the globalizing effects of economic relations, mass-migration, and worldwide communication. In such a world, culture can serve as a new foundation of collective identity and belonging, precisely because it is not seen as something given by nature and birth or as something fixed and unchangeable, but as a potent and creative force capable of bringing about a collective order, of producing a collective consciousness, and of articulating a collective will.

This is why today's right-wing nationalists in Germany, for instance, no longer talk about the German *Volk*, let alone a German race. Instead, they talk about German culture as a potential force of collectiveness and identity that is supposedly threatened by strange and uncanny influences undermining its creative power.[28] By the same token, even right-wing ideologies in Germany, France, Great Britain, or the United States no longer refer to natural racial characteristics, but instead insist that fighting for the survival of one's own culture and identity is a basic natural principle.[29] Thus, even in these contexts, the term "race" is conspicuously absent, whereas the ideas that once flourished under this category now tend to gather around the notion of culture. Seen from the other side, it is the notion of culture that—more than any other concept of collective belonging—fits the postnational condition of our current global age, which makes it all the more important to critically rethink both race and culture, not as terms, but in respect to their implications in a given context.

These implications are not just a matter of popular discourses or intellectual debates. In Rwanda and the former Yugoslavia we could directly observe how clearly non-natural boundaries became rapidly transformed into quasi-natural orders of belonging put into practice by ethnic cleansing. Notions such as the global "clash of civilizations" or political agendas such as the global "war on terror" have reintroduced visions of a new world order reminiscent of the racial images of world order so prominent in the imperialist age. And finally, the sciences of physical anthropology, biology, and genetics increasingly tend to compete with the humanities in explaining social and cultural phenomena by referring to genetic predispositions, brain patterns, or natural structures of behavior, implying that the only effective way to change and improve our social and cultural life might be the technological manipulation of our biological life. In all these contexts, racism is present, whereas "race" is not.

Today we are witnessing a transformation of culture into something that once used to be described in terms of race: a notion of collective belonging with deep roots and the creative power to produce long-term collective identities that transcend short-term political constellations. Ostensibly, the world order is made up of different cultures that are involved in a continuous struggle or war with each other. In order to understand the history of this concept, it is necessary to look especially at those forms of racial thinking in the past, which, as early as the beginning of the twentieth century, transformed and widened the concept of race into something much broader than just physiology and bodily appearance. For it was in this context that racism emancipated and detached itself from the notion of race and gained a life of its own. This is one of the reasons why we probably will still witness forms of racism even if we could abandon the idea of race once and for all.

Notes

1. Lothrop Stoddard, *The Rising Tide of Color against White World-Supremacy* (New York, 1920); Madison Grant, *The Passing of the Great Race* (New York, 1916).
2. Lothrop Stoddard, *The Revolt against Civilization: The Menace of the Under Man* (New York, 1922); Lothrop Stoddard, *Clashing Tides of Color* (New York and London, 1935). Stoddard's books are still in print today.
3. See Oswald Spengler, *Der Untergang des Abendlandes* (Wien, 1918); John Farrenkopf, *Prophet of Decline: Spengler on World History and Politics* (Baton Rouge, 2001).
4. See Henry L. Gates Jr. and Dominik LaCapra, eds., *The Bounds of Race* (Ithaca, 1991).
5. See Dan Diner, *Das Jahrhundert verstehen: Eine welthistorische Deutung* (Stuttgart, 1999); Charles S. Maier, "Consigning the 20th Century to History," *American Historical Review* 105, no. 3 (2000): 807–31.
6. Samuel Huntington, *Clash of Civilizations* (New York, 1996).
7. Hannah Arendt, *The Origins of Totalitarianism* (New York, 1950), esp. part II on imperialism.
8. Compare the map "World of Civilizations Post-1990" in: Samuel Huntington, *Clash of Civilizations* (New York, 1996), 26. Some of the differences between the two maps result from the fact that Huntington's notion of civilization (in opposition to Stoddard's concept of race) is closely linked to religious belief-systems. However, this difference simply underlines the primary function of both maps to transform the world into a constellation of a limited number of "entities."
9. Stoddard, *The Rising Tide of Color against White World-Supremacy*. Taken from "wikimedia," scanned from an original. (5 October 2008).
10. See for instance Stefan Kühl, *The Nazi Connection: Eugenics, American Racism, and German National Socialism* (Oxford, 1994).
11. John Dewey, "The Influence of Darwinism on Philosophy," in *The Collected Works, Part II: The Middle Works 1899–1924, Bd. 4: 1907–1909*, edited by J.A. Boydston (1909; London, 1977), 12.
12. Karl Pearson, *National Life from the Standpoint of Science* (London, 1901).
13. Houston Stewart Chamberlain, *Die Grundlagen des 19. Jahrhunderts* (1899, München, 1906).

14. Otto Hintze, "Rasse und Nationalität und ihre Bedeutung für die Geschichte," in *Soziologie und Geschichte: Gesammelte Abhandlungen zur Soziologie, Politik und Theorie der Geschichte*, edited by G. Oestreich, 2nd ed., trans. by the author (1903; Göttingen, 1964), 46–65.

15. See Stephen J. Gould, *The Structure of Evolutionary Theory* (Cambridge, MA, 2002); Peter J. Bowler, *Evolution: The History of an Idea* (Berkeley, 1989).

16. Franz Boas, *Changes in Bodily Form of Descendants of Immigrants* (New York, 1912).

17. Franz Boas, *The Mind of Primitive Man* (New York, 1911).

18. Franz Boas to J.W. Jenks, 31 December 1909, quoted in George W. Stocking, ed., *The Shaping of American Anthropology, 1883–1911: A Franz Boas Reader* (New York, 1974), 213.

19. Alfred Rosenberg, *Mythos des 20. Jahrhunderts* (München, 1930).

20. Gustav Spiller, ed., *Inter-Racial Problems: Papers from the First Universal Races Congress held in London in 1911*, repr. ed. H. Aptheker (1911; New York, 1970).

21. See Wolfgang Schivelbusch, *Three New Deals: Reflections on Roosevelt's America, Mussolini's Italy and Hitler's Germany* (New York, 2006).

22. See Michael Wildt, *Volksgemeinschaft als Selbstermächtigung: Gewalt gegen Juden in der deutschen Provinz, 1919–1939* (Hamburg, 2007); Saul Friedländer, *Das Dritte Reich und die Juden: Verfolgung und Vernichtung, 1933–1945* (München, 2007).

23. See esp. Wildt, *Volksgemeinschaft*.

24. Claude Levi-Strauss, "Race and History," public lecture (UNESCO, 1952).

25. Eric Voegelin, *Rasse und Staat* (Tübingen, 1933); Hannah Arendt, *The Origins of Totalitaranism* (New York, 1950).

26. Claude Levi-Strauss, "Race and Culture," public lecture (UNESCO, 1972).

27. Two important critiques of the paradigm of "culture" in the 1990s can be found in Walter B. Michaels, *Our America: Nativism, Modernism, and Pluralism* (Durham, 1995); Robert J.C. Young, *Colonial Desire: Hybridity in Theory, Culture and Race* (London, 1995).

28. See Mark Terkessidis, *Kulturkampf: Volk, Nation, der Westen und die Neue Rechte* (Köln, 1996).

29. See Pierre-André Taguieff, *Die Macht des Vorurteils: Der Rassismus und sein Double* (Hamburg, 2000); Etienne Balibar, Immanuel Wallerstein, *Rasse, Klasse, Nation: Ambivalente Identitäten* (Hamburg, 1990).

Chapter 4

Racism and Genocide

Boris Barth

The Problem of Definitions

Racism and genocide are global phenomena that require global analytical concepts. Racism did not appear in one single context or in a clearly definable period of time. However, controversies about the sense of more or less extended concepts of racism do not affect the general *communis opinio* that racism has something to do with social hierarchies, interpretation of differences, power, genetic origins, or economic exploitation. According to Albert Memmi's famous definition, people from different regions of the globe look different, but racism starts with the interpretation of these differences.[1] Racism can be interpreted as the hierarchization of human beings according to their skin color, outlook, ancestry, or—in modern terms— their genetic origins. Especially since the end of the nineteenth century racism means the biologization of the social sphere. Within this general framework many other and more specific definitions are used for the classification of cases of racism in different societies.[2] The definition of genocide, however, is a highly controversial subject, because no basic consensus exists among historians, sociologists, political scientists, and scholars of international law.

Each concept and each attempt to define a historical phenomenon has its own history. Especially if one focuses on genocide, it is not possible to avoid a general debate about definitions. Most of the recent and often fierce controversies about the problem of "what is genocide" are only the result of conceptual and terminological confusion arising from rather different national research traditions. This is also the result of some vague formulations in the famous UN "Convention on the Prevention and Punishment of the Crime of Genocide" and the subsequent debates in contemporary international law. In 1948 it was clear for nearly all members of the newly founded United Nations that the National Socialist mass murder and the Auschwitz gas chambers represented a completely new type of crime which was committed by a state and which had to be punished by the international community by new means as well. Inspired by the Polish lawyer Raphael Lemkin, who coined the word "genocide" in his book "Axis Rule in Occupied Europe," the so called genocide convention became international law after complicated debates among the UN's new member nations.[3]

In several respects the genocide convention contained no precise definitions. During the negotiations different interests of the respective states had to be taken into account. According to the convention national, racial, ethnic, and religious groups could become the object of genocide and need special protection. In view of the Holocaust the inclusion of racial and ethnic groups in the convention in 1948 seemed to be obvious and did not need more detailed explanation, but today the definition of a racial group is much more difficult, if not impossible. Many scholars even refuse to use the term "racial" group, because this would mean indirectly accepting some kind of racist interpretation of differences between human beings.

Both the United States and the Soviet Union pressed successfully for the exclusion of political groups. The Soviet motivation was obvious, because otherwise the Stalinist terror of the 1930s and the policies toward the different nationalities within the Soviet Union could have been suspected of being genocidal. The U.S. position was less clear, but obviously it was designed to prevent topics like the former racial slavery, the displacements of the native Americans or other dark chapters of American history becoming subjects of international discussion. The exclusion of political groups has therefore often been the subject of harsh criticism, but despite the respective interests that led to this decision, it made sense in the long run. The definition of ethnic or religious groups is extremely difficult in many cases; the proper definition of political groups is impossible and would only provoke endless propaganda battles in the context of conflicts and wars. Helen Fein points out that the Khmer Rouge, the SS, the NKVD and other organizations were also without doubt political groups or political organizations that did not need any special international protection—on the contrary.[4] A single person can become a member of a political group and leave it voluntarily. Leaving an ethnic group that is threatened by a potential perpetrator, however, is nearly impossible.

For the creators of the convention it was obvious that genocide meant the killing and annihilation of a certain group of human beings, especially a group like the millions of Jews in Europe under Nazi-German rule. But it was not clear how many members of such a group had to be killed before the convention should come into force. The main goal of the convention was not a scientific definition but the prevention of genocide, if necessary by an international military intervention organized and led by the United Nation's Security Council. Such an intervention only makes sense before any mass killings have ended or while a genocide is still about to develop. The Norwegian delegation suggested that not only the destruction of a group "as a whole" but also "in part" already constituted genocide, because otherwise the aim of prevention would not be achievable. What "in part" exactly meant, however, was never defined, and—as the subsequent debates showed—it is indeed impossible to give a clear definition. If, for example, the murdering of 10 percent or more of a special group or of a population was defined as genocide "in part," the Security Council would grant potential perpetrators the right to kill, let us say, 5 or 8 percent of that group. The result would not be the prevention of genocide but the encouragement of massacres on a smaller scale.[5]

Since the 1980s one more aspect has caused confusion because of other vague formulations in the genocide convention. According to Article II. e., the transfer of children from one group into another by force is regarded as genocide. This article was introduced into the convention as a reaction to the National Socialist racial policy in occupied Poland between 1939 and 1944. Some parts of the Polish population in the annexed territories were classified, according to racial criteria, by SS commissions and race theorists. An unknown number of very small children who were regarded as "Aryan" were taken away from their parents and brought up in special orphanages and later at specially chosen schools, which were run by the SS or by comparable National Socialist organizations. These children acquired a completely new identity and became German native speakers, while their parents were usually murdered in concentration camps. Despite much historical scrutiny it will never become clear how many Polish children were taken away, because shortly before the end of World War II nearly all the relevant SS files were destroyed. Today an unknown number of German citizens are still living in Germany without having any knowledge of their real ancestry or identity.[6] The stealing of children in this case was part of a gigantic technocratic project to reorganize the mixed populations in the conquered East according to racist criteria and it was directly linked with the Holocaust, the displacement of populations, and radical eugenic measures.

Today two ways of dealing with the convention in regard to the stealing of children and other comparable questions can be imagined. The first one is to interpret the convention literally. This would have very far-reaching consequences, because in this case the stealing of children could be already interpreted as genocide, even if no one was killed and even if there was no intention to destroy a group or a people. The stealing of children has happened rather often in history, as is illustrated by the transatlantic slave trade or by the well-known policies of early modern Turkey of stealing Christian children and raising them as the new military elite of Janissaries. The second way of interpreting the convention would involve translating its meaning at the time into modern terms. If one accepts a literal interpretation of the convention, the logical consequence would be to deny an important difference. Probably several tens of thousands of Greek children were brought into communist states (mainly to Yugoslavia and Albania), against their parents' wills, at the end of the Greek Civil War in 1948/49. Even if no one was killed, this was of course a crime that reached international dimensions. If one classifies these children as victims of genocide, however, there is hardly any conceptual difference between them and the victims of an annihilation camp like Treblinka. Most historians in the Western world would probably refuse to draw this far-reaching conclusion.

The very different ways of reading the genocide convention are also the result of rather different national traditions. After 1948 the genocide convention was almost forgotten for several decades. As a result of the lack of scientific international debate about the topic, rather different national traditions developed, starting with the United States. When the problem of genocide was rediscovered, mainly by American anthropologists and sociologists in the 1980s, not by historians or by scholars of international law, many cases of genocide were identified. Frank Chalk, who has found more than thirty suspected cases of genocide in history, Kurt Jonassohn, and many other authors plead for a more extensive definition.[7] Alexander Hinton uses a comparable approach and identifies a huge number of genocide cases as well. Other authors found even more cases, starting with the destruction of ancient Carthage by the Romans. From today's point of view, no specific definition was used for these theoretical approaches: nearly every big massacre and many cases of mass killings were simply classified as genocidal and terms like mass-murder, big destructions, and genocide are used as synonyms.[8] Other authors have criticized the influential and extended definition by Israel W. Charny, because for him genocide is not a concept but a moral evaluation.[9] His approach is so general that the special character of an extreme form of state crime is completely lost. Again the question remains: should one not make a clear distinction between the Tiananmen massacre in Beijing and Auschwitz? Last but not least, one important point that characterizes genocide when compared with other state crimes is overlooked as well: if one uses a narrower definition, genocide in the twentieth century always had an ethnic dimension or was based on racist ideas.

Other authors from the English-speaking community are using narrower concepts, and they are taking the specific ethnic dimension into account. Mark Levine, for example, makes no conceptual difference between ethnic cleansing and genocide. For him some regions of the Near East, especially Eastern Anatolia, can be classified as a "modern zone of genocide," because massacres and mass killings of civilians took place several times during the late nineteenth and the twentieth centuries, starting with the Ottoman massacres in 1878, followed by the Armenian genocide and ending with the gas attacks on Kurds under Saddam Hussein. Levine asserts a direct connection between nation building and state formation on the one hand and ethnic cleansing and huge massacres of minorities on the other.[10]

In Germany and to some extent in France as well until the end of the 1990s the field was dominated by historians who used a very strict definition, due to the fact that the annihilation of the European Jews during World War II was regarded as the ultimate and only case of real genocide. Especially in Germany every attempt to start comparative genocide research at an international level was faced with the suspicion of playing down the meaning of the Holocaust. This attitude was partly the result of the long and very difficult process of coming to terms with one's own past, which was a major preoccupation of German public opinion for several decades. Again at the end of the 1980s a very small number of German nationalist historians and political right-wing organizations tried to minimize the Shoah but did not succeed in the long run.[11] As a result of these internal German debates, however, serious comparative genocide research did not start until the end of the 1990s. Additionally, in the German language, the term genocide is normally used as a synonym for *Völkermord* (murder of peoples) or for final solutions, and this fact already limits the use of other concepts of genocide.

Since the end of the 1990s two rather different developments have brought completely new attempts into the international debate on defining genocide: the cases of Ukraine and of Australia. After the breakdown of the Soviet Union, history became a kind of a raw material in some of the new states. It was regarded as an extremely important basis for the creation of new national states and for the refusal of imagined or real new Russian imperialism. Not only historians but also parts of the new national elites tried to find and construct new identities of their own by the rediscovery of past suffering. Especially in Ukraine the *holodomor* (Ukrainian for hunger catastrophe) served and serves exactly in that way. Only few Ukrainian historians do not share the opinion that the great hunger catastrophe of 1932/33, which led to the deaths of more than three million victims at least, should be classified as genocide. However, even if no serious historian in the West doubts the number of casualties, which perhaps was even much higher, until today not one single document has been been found which can prove any genocidal intention of the Soviet leaders in the 1930s. In 1929 Stalin initiated a war against the villages, which until then were hardly controlled by party organizations, and against the strong national Ukrainian identities, which existed even in the regional Ukrainian Communist party. Furthermore, in the countryside the collectivization was accompanied by the attempt to build up a national Soviet heavy industry at almost any price. Stalin simply did not care about the number of victims resulting from the utopian objectives of the first Five-Year Plan, which was introduced for the modernization of the country in a precipitate way. However, the aspect of race and ethnicity is almost entirely missing during the time of starvation. Not only Ukraine but also many other Asiatic republics of the Soviet Union were hit hard by the hunger catastrophe. The terror against the Ukrainian peasants was also organized by Ukrainian party cadres and by troops that consisted of ethnic Ukrainians. These armed forces prevented the peasants from escaping from the regions of starvation. The *holodomor* remains one of the most horrible Stalinist crimes, but it is doubtful whether it makes sense to use the genocide terminology.[12]

A rather different debate started in Australia after some historians showed growing interest in the Aborigines' history and in the history of the so called "stolen generation." No doubt, white settlers killed many Aborigines while conquering the country in the nineteenth century. In the twentieth century many "mixed-race" children of Aborigines were taken away from their mothers by the Australian state authorities. The most extreme research position is taken by Tony Barta, who compares the treatment of the Aborigines with the Nazi policy towards the Jews. According to Barta, the colonization of Australia went hand in hand with the economic exploitation and the virtual annihilation of the Aborigines. Colin Tatz is also convinced that Australia was a genocidal society and Dirk Moses regards the settlers' frontier violence as identical with genocide.[13] The genocide argument is based on two very different facts, and again it is doubtful whether it makes sense to use it in this context. First, despite all the cruelties that happened during the colonization of Australia, most of the deaths among Aborigines were not caused by white settlers but by European diseases such as smallpox. About twenty thousand Aborigines were killed by settlers and there is no doubt that these murders were barbarous. But these crimes were not committed by the government or by state authorities, which often tried to introduce protective measures for the indigenous population. Second, the case of the stolen generation is more difficult. During the twentieth century about 10 percent of the "mixed-race" children of Aborigines were separated from their mothers in the hope that they could be offered a better future if they were brought up by white parents or by white institutions. The intention was not to kill children or mothers but to improve these children's social chances. At that time this behavior was completely in accordance with widely accepted Western norms. In the democratic world white children were also taken away from their mothers and given to their richer fathers or to state authorities if their chances there were regarded as being better. In the Australian case, certainly latent or open racism may have contributed to the governmental attitude towards the Aborigines, who were regarded as primitive and needed to be given the benefits of civilization, but any murderous intention is missing. The literal interpretation of the genocide convention leads to the paradoxical result that some Australian historians accuse their government of having committed genocide, even if no one was killed.

Since the 1990s a general feeling of discontent with the genocide definition in the UN convention has arisen among many scholars from different disciplines. Horrible massacres were obviously not genocide, and the Communist crimes in Stalinist Russia and Mao's China are excluded from the concept. For some authors the existing genocide terminology is too narrow to integrate other brutal forms of suppression and mass murder, for others it is too far reaching. As a result, an inflation of new concepts has appeared. Alongside genocide one finds terms like genocidal massacres, ethnocide, politicide, democide, feminizide, ecocide, economicide, etc. The inflation of new concepts—whether useful or not—is always a certain indicator that the extension of an older concept does not work properly anymore. Apart from this inflation, the term genocide has been in public use for a huge variety of different cases that have nothing to do with extreme forms of mass killings, sometimes not even with mass violence. To give only a few examples, mixture of races, the misuse of drugs, methadone programs, birth control, medical treatment of fundamentalist Catholics, the closing of synagogues in the Soviet Union, and the abortion of children in the United

States have all been regarded as genocidal in the past. In the words of Helen Fein: "If this is awful it must be genocide."[14]

Because of this growing conceptual confusion, some historians suggest that only a strict and narrow definition makes sense because fortunately genocide is a very rare and rather special crime, which, as some colleagues agree, did not appear before the twentieth century. The following three points are crucial for a clear definition and might form a basic consensus among scholars from different disciplines.

First: the most important point is "intention." In the past many peoples have died out or have disappeared from the earth like, for example, the Caribbean Indians. But the early modern Spaniards never had the intention of murdering them all. Although it may sound cynical, killing was a by-product of the general colonial situation. Despite many cases of brutal treatment the Indians in some cases were needed for slave labor or, in other cases, even as Spanish allies. Most of them died from diseases such as small-pox or measles—the killers were microbes which had previously been unknown in the Caribbean. The crucial point for the definition of genocide is not the number of victims (which may even be small in theory), nor the brutality of the killings and massacres, but the intention of the perpetrator. In the tradition of Hannah Arendt's famous analysis[15] of Adolf Eichmann's behavior in Jerusalem one should ask first: was or is there a government which decided to annihilate a large and self-defined group of human beings without exception and without giving pardon because it did not wish to share the face of the earth with them? Genocide without intention should be excluded per definition.

Second: the aim of the perpetrator is to kill a self-defined religious, eth-nic, or national group—without exception and without leaving open any path to surrender. Using this definition means that the concepts of geno-cide and final solutions are identical. At the same time cases like Hiroshima or the bombing of Dresden, which sometimes have been classified as geno-cidal, are also excluded with good reasons. One can ask whether these bombing attacks were necessary from the military point of view or whether it is possible to justify them in moral terms against the contemporary back-ground. However, they were part of a great and total war. At no time did the Americans think of killing all Japanese or German civilians. On the con-trary, had Germany or Japan surrendered earlier, no such bombings would have taken place.

Third: genocide is a crime committed by a state. In theory it is possible to imagine powerful criminal groups or mafia organizations killing large groups of people. However, until today only states have had the necessary means and power to organize mass killings on a large scale. The number of perpetrators who plan and carry out a final solution can be relatively small, and also in concentration or death camps only some hundreds of men are necessary for the killing itself. But only a state has the necessary infrastructure to organize the whole complicated killing process. Behind the paramilitary troops a large bureaucracy is needed for the classification and the selection of the victims, and huge transport capacities must be organized as well.

This narrow definition of genocide includes the following cases, even if many details still remain controversial: the Young Turkish crimes against the Armenians in 1915–16 or 1915–23; of course the National Socialist politics of annihilation against the Jews since 1941; the destruction of the Gypsies and some of the Slavic nations; and the case of Rwanda in 1994. Beyond these four cases of undoubted genocide there are still three or four more which can be classified as genocidal—or not—again only depending on the definition. These cases are the German war of annihilation against the Herero in 1904 in the colony of German South West Africa, the Communist crimes in Stalinist Russia and in China under Mao Tsedong (although it is very doubtful that the concept of genocide can help in any way to understand what was going on in the Soviet Union in the 1930s), and the Khmer Rouge's killing fields in Cambodia.

The enormous difficulties in distinguishing between killings for political or racist reasons can be demonstrated by the crimes of the Khmer Rouge. I do not agree with the thesis that Cambodia between 1975 and 1978 was ruled by a Communist regime. Too many aspects that have been typical of Communism elsewhere were missing: the cult of the worker, the state's double structure with old bureaucracy and new political party, and the general belief in history as progress. Instead, the ideology of the Khmer Rouge was an amalgam of very different ideological sources, of which communism was only one among others, e.g., indigenous Khmer racism. Such ideological mixtures of indigenous ideas and different European influences are typical of East Asia, but normally not with comparably destructive results. After coming to power the Khmer Rouge started at once to kill systematically not only the Vietnamese and Chinese minorities but also the Cham, a small Muslim people of Polynesian origin.[16] Until today the regime's racism has been grossly underestimated.

This is not the place to discuss all of the pro and contra arguments for each single case mentioned above. This has been done several times, and a great number of controversies remain unresolved.[17] In this context it is more interesting to analyze the connection between racism, the ideologies of genocidal regimes and the ideas of genocidal perpetrators and to ask whether one can imagine genocide without racism.

Genocide and the Factor of "Race"

Racism is a global phenomenon that appeared in the early modern European context at different times and in many different societies. Genocide in its narrow definition mentioned above, however, is very rare and is limited to the history of the twentieth century. In the twentieth century a strong connection arose between some new forms of racism and the decisions of governments to annihilate self-defined groups by final solutions.

Racism on the one hand does not automatically lead to murderous ideologies or to genocidal fantasies, but on the other hand some kind of racism was always a necessary precondition for developments which in the worst cases led to genocide. The motivation of all genocidal regimes was deeply rooted in modern racist convictions. All of the following four points were necessary for the radicalization of racist ideas in the twentieth century and all were responsible for the escalation in the direction of genocidal situations which had been unknown in centuries and societies before.

1. Ethnic Cleansing

Ethnic definitions of populations and dreams of ethnic cleansing are a necessary but not a sufficient precondition for genocide. The term "ethnic cleansing" was introduced as late as 1992 in most of the Western languages as a result of the civil wars in former Yugoslavia, but cleansing even in its genocidal form had started already during and after World War I. Andrew Bell-Fialkoff defines cleansing as follows: "Population cleansing is a planned, deliberate removal from a certain territory of an undesirable population distinguished by one or more characteristics such as ethnicity, religion, race, class, or sexual preference. These characteristics must serve as the basis for removal for it to qualify as cleansing." With this broad definition Bell-Fialkoff already finds cleansing in classical antiquity.[18] Population cleansing is a phenomenon that is indeed rather old, but at the beginning of the twentieth century the new concept of the "ethnic" classification of populations had disastrous effects especially in multi-ethnic Europe. Ethnic cleansing could happen in a huge variety of forms, starting with relatively peaceful bureaucratic measures and ending as "final solutions" with murderous consequences.[19]

In the European context, new interpretations of ethnicity and race were products of the early twentieth century and especially of World War I. A relatively small population exchange according to ethnic criteria already took place in 1913 in the Mediterranean and it foreshadowed the following events. After the end of the second Balkan War, the Ottoman Empire and Greece on the one hand and Bulgaria and the Ottoman Empire on the other, signed two international contracts to organize an exchange of civil populations. Because of the outbreak of World War I, these treaties remained on paper, but for the first time in European history the map of Europe was actively redrawn from an ethnic point of view.[20] Not during but after the Great War more than ten million people in Europe became refugees, mainly for ethnic reasons.

The idea of ethnic cleansing and of creating racially "pure" societies by force was introduced in the twentieth century but had several preludes already in the early nineteenth century. There are many examples, but three will be mentioned here. From time to time the white North American society was concerned with the problem of how to get rid of its "free negroes," who were regarded as being unfit for the white Protestant American civilization for racist reasons. The idea of sending them all back to Africa and of creating the state of Liberia as a new home for free black Americans can be interpreted as an early concept of cleansing according to ethnic criteria. However, the idea did not work because at that time the white American society was not prepared to use violence to the necessary extent, i.e., to force free blacks to leave the country. The very few black emigrants to Liberia went voluntarily, while most of the freed black slaves preferred to remain in North America. Much more radical fantasies appeared in the American South after the end of the American Civil War. Ideas of genocidal dreamlands could be found among many white lynch mobs, not to speak of white terrorist organizations such as the Ku Klux Klan. Individual cases of murder and even small-scale massacres like the Arkansas Riot of 1919 and the Tulsa Riot of 1921 were widely accepted in the American society of the South, and the social degradation of "negroes" was even welcomed. Massacres on a genocidal level, however, would have been opposed by huge parts of liberal public opinion. Violence stopped before the step towards cleansing was even taken into consideration.

Genocidal fantasies also arose during the American Civil War during the guerrilla conflict in Missouri, especially on the part of Confederacy partisans, an example which has been analysed by Michael Fellman. Even though an enormous potential for violence existed, this conflict did not lead to the killing of innocent women and children. Only males were murdered indiscriminately. According to Fellman, both of the conflicting parties accepted a special code of honor, which was responsible for the limitation of the killings.[21] Both sides were white and mostly Protestant; they shared the same culture and social classes. The concept of race and ethnicity was missing—from our point of view the most important fact. The same units which had problems with killing white women and children behaved in quite a different and much more violent way if they were used against native Americans during and after the Civil War.

It was the Young Turkish government that went from theory to practice in the spring of 1915. Armenians represented the perfect internal enemy for the Young Turks and were regarded as a fundamental threat to the regime. The idea of getting rid of all Armenians in some way had already come to the minds of the Young Turks before the outbreak of World War I, and the Young Turk's revolution in 1908/09 was already accompanied by huge massacres in Adana. Young Turkish thinking was strongly influenced by the Western liberal perception that modern states should be dominated and inhabited by only one single nation, i.e., the Turks. When Turkey entered the war the diffuse mixture of anti-Armenian prejudices, dreams of Turkish racial superiority, the dream of creating a new pan-Turanian empire, including all Turkish and Mongolian races, and unfounded rumors of an Armenian conspiracy led to radicalization, which reached a peak during the Galipoli crisis in spring 1915. Despite all the facts that ran counter to the Young Turks perception, all Armenians were regarded as a security risk, which had to be wiped out by all means. What started as some kind of ethnic cleansing ended up as genocide.[22]

2. Pan-Ideologies

If older nineteenth century racist ideas came together with newer imperialist thoughts and pan-ideologies of the twentieth century, the sudden danger of mass murder and genocide grew enormously. Pan-ideologies are so dangerous because they propagate unlimited imperialism without definable objects. Most of the multi-ethnic and multi-religious empires in world history are based on some kind of pan-thinking, but normally the aspect of race is missing. If a pan-ideology was connected with twentieth-century racism, however, the results were disastrous. Many of the Young Turks were dreaming of a pan-Turanian empire from Constantinople to Mongolia, including all Turkish races and annihilating those who could not be integrated. This ideology, which also contained some "blood and soil" elements, opened the door for the Armenian genocide. The Nazi pan-ideology used other but similar stereotypes. The anti-Jewish prejudices in Germany came into being rather differently from the Armenian case in the Ottoman Empire, but Nazi ideologues never doubted that the Jews had to disappear in some way or another and that they were responsible for all kinds of political and economic evil which threatened the Aryan races and the German people. National Socialist anti-Semitism was even more vague than the Young Turkish pan-ideology, because the Nazis were never able to develop a clear or concise definition of a Jewish race.[23]

The conquest of the "Ostraum" meant imperialism without objects and the declaration of a racial war. Today most historians are convinced that a close connection existed between the Holocaust and the war in the East from summer 1941.The early plans for the attack on the Soviet Union after spring 1941 followed exactly the National Socialist race ideology. Some administrative conceptions for the Barbarossa plan included the killing of at least thirty-one million people who were regarded as superfluous or dangerous for racist reasons. The Jews, who in the eyes of the Nazi leaders were the most "dangerous" enemy, were only the first race to be annihilated systematically, first by special units using machine guns, then by mobile gas-commandos and at last by gas chambers in annihilation camps. The killing of Russians and other Slavic populations, which came next in the National Socialist racial hierarchy, was already organized in a much less systematic way in the first months of the war, but also with a rather deadly consequence. Leningrad was not conquered, although in autumn 1941 this would have been possible and reasonable from a military point of view, because the population of the city was condemned to death by hunger. Also in many other occupied places hunger was used as a weapon against the Russian civilian population. In 1941 most of the Russian prisoners of war died of starvation in the German POW camps.[24]

Recently some German authors have tried to find some economic rationality in the planning for the war in the East and in the killing of millions of people. Susanne Heim and Götz Aly point out that the word "race" is missing in most of the annihilation plans. Christian Gerlach argues that the German hunger plans were dictated by the need to avoid a food crisis in Central Europe as a long-term effect of the British blockade, which is comparable to the situation in World War I. Gerlach has found a huge number of new sources concerning the German occupation policy in Russia and has analyzed many hitherto unknown massacres that took place in 1941 and 1942.[25] However, his conclusions about the German motivations are not shared by most German and international historians. The perception of a coming hunger crisis in Germany had no basis in reality, since the general food situation in 1941 was acceptable and—taking the objective data into account—no crisis was in the offing. Christopher Browning and others also do not accept an idea of any economic rationality in the German planning for occupied Russia. Who should live and who should starve was a political decision. In the words of Christopher Browning, it was "racism gone berserk."[26]

Although many sources concerning Rwanda are still missing or have not been published, Hutu Power no doubt was an extremist and racist movement, too. The "Ten Commandments" of the Hutu were a manifesto of open racism, and combined with hate messages in the popular radio programs "Mille Collines" created an atmosphere of uninhibited violence, which had already been established in Rwandan society since 1990. Since the end of World War II hardly any regime has propagated such an open and violent kind of racism. The decision for genocide was made by a modern and technocratic elite, whose position was endangered and who tried to secure it by the proclamation of hate and violence.[27] The question of racism is not controversial, but it is debatable whether Hutu Power can be classified as a pan-ideology. William A. Schabas doubts it, because the Hutu extremists did not think about the annihilation of Tutsi outside Rwanda.[28] Other authors are not so sure about the case. Massacres with ethnic backgrounds were not limited to Rwanda but also took place between Hutu and Tutsi in the neighboring countries from 1972 on at the latest, and the ideology of Hutu Power did not stop at the border of Rwanda.[29]

3. Classical Conservatism and Liberalism in Crisis

Together with extreme forms of racism and a pan-ideology a third precondition is necessary for the development of a racist genocidal regime. Classical conservatism and liberalism in the Western world sometimes went hand in hand with racist ideas, but never with genocidal mass murder. A fundamental crisis of old, conservative elite structures and of bourgeois liberalism is necessary for the radicalization of racism towards final solutions. All Fascist regimes despised Western liberalism because of its universal attitude, the proclamation of human rights, and the general idea of civil societies.

Both conservatism and liberalism could become extremely aggressive in foreign affairs and were open to imperialist ideas, but they offered protection against genocidal racism. Before 1908/09 the Islamic Ottoman bureaucracy was conservative in the literal sense of the word, i.e., it wanted to preserve both its power position and the empire without radical reforms, but at the same time it was immune to new racist classifications of the population. It ruled the country in a strictly autocratic way but had no religious or ethnic barriers for the recruiting of even very high officials: every Muslim who spoke Turkish could start a career no matter where he came from or what his ethnic background was. The breakdown of Ottoman conservatism was a direct result of the growing threat of Western imperialism and the rising Turkish nationalism in the Ottoman Empire. The Sultan and his conservative bureaucrats were partly swept away when the nationalist Young Turks took over. Hitler's rise in Germany can only be understood against the background of the loss of World War I and the extreme crises of both German conservatism and liberalism. Aristocratic conservatism lost much of its power in the new democratic Weimar Republic after 1918/19, and the threatened conservatives turned towards the extreme right during the 1920s, although many of them still showed a certain distance toward the Nazi Party, which was regarded as being much too proletarian. In 1930, when the rise of the Nazi Party began, the left-wing liberal German party (DDP) had almost ceased to exist and the right-wing liberals (DVP) were fighting for their survival.

While we should be hesitant to idealize the autocratic Wilhelmine German state, it is certain that within its intact conservative and liberal elite structure the rise of Nazi desperados would have been impossible. World War I marked the watershed between aristocratic conservatism and liberal bourgeois societies on the one hand and the rise of genocidal racist fanatics on the other. The liberal protection against the radicalization of racist ideas broke down at last in the final crisis of Weimar Germany.

4. Social Darwinism

The new racism of the twentieth century is mainly based on popular forms of Social Darwinism and on the idea that societies could be improved by way of technocratic measures. Contemporary Social Darwinism in an almost classical form was put in a nutshell by the British Prime Minister, Lord Robert A. Salisbury, in a famous speech in 1898: "You can roughly divide the nations of the world in the living and the dying."[30] Of course Salisbury's world views were far from any genocidal thoughts but they were fully in accordance with modern imperialism at the end of the nineteenth century. He was interested in the question of who would later have the right or the power to cure or to annex the poor patients, whom he called dying nations. However, the notion that some peoples were inevitably about to die in the figurative sense and that the reason for this had something to do with their racial or ethnic quality was already widespread among the European elites before World War I.

There is only scant research on the Young Turks' relation toward Social Darwinism. However, they were strongly influenced by modern Western European technocratic thinking, which was concerned about topics such as the rise and decline of nations. To stop the obvious decline of their country and to rebuild it in accordance with past glory it was necessary—in their opinion—to define a new Turkish national state. They introduced the West European liberal idea of a homogenous national state to a multi-ethnic and multi-religious empire in which the Turks themselves were only a small minority. This went hand in hand with the belief that societies could be ethnically developed, organized in a technocratic way, and improved by modern measures of population planning. In the Ottoman Empire these concepts were to have disastrous consequences.[31]

National Socialism in Germany combined radical Social Darwinism with the twentieth century's most extreme forms of eugenics from the very beginning. Only the strong had the right to live, the weak had to disappear to improve the quality of one's own race. The first victims of systematic mass killings in Germany were not the Jews or other unwanted minorities, but handicapped and mentally disabled Germans, no matter whether they belonged to what the Nazis called the Aryan race or not.[32]

Technocrats of very different origins shared the general belief in violent social technologies. Talat Pascha, the Young Turkish Minister of the Interior, who organized the Armenian genocide, was a fanatic technocrat like Heinrich Himmler, the German architect of genocide, and—although we still do not have all the necessary sources to support the assertion—Colonel Theoneste Bagasora might be called Rwanda's Himmler. The modern racism of the twentieth century combined with dreams of ethnic cleansing and the belief in violent social technologies such as popular Social Darwinism provide the necessary preconditions for genocide.

Conclusion: Genocide, Racism, and Democratic Societies

One last aspect of the relation between racism and genocide should be mentioned briefly: the fiercely debated problem of racism, genocide, and democracy. According to Michael Mann and other authors, extreme forms of racism and ethnic cleansing are part of the dark side of democracy.[33] Historically, there was no contradiction between democratic systems and racism, and a freely elected parliament offered no guarantees against the rise of racist ideas. In some cases, especially in white settler societies like the USA, Australia or the Boer republics in South Africa, democratic ideas even promoted the rise of racism. A democratic society is even able to favor population cleansing, as many examples in European and in American history demonstrate. However, as historical experience shows to this day, genocide in its narrow definition is impossible in democracies and in relatively free societies. The reasons for this fact are controversial, but the most likely explanation is that extreme atrocities and mass killings would have been debated at once in the free press, in parliaments, in churches, and in other comparable institutions. Democratic public or published opinion made the last step towards genocidal killing nearly impossible—even in openly racist societies.

This can be shown by the example of the notorious German colonial war in the settler colony of German South East Africa in 1905/06. General v. Trotha, a well-known hardcore racist, started his war of annihilation against the Herero people after their uprising against German colonial rule. It may be debatable whether his intention was ethnic cleansing or genocide, but there are no doubts about the extreme atrocities committed by the German colonial army. There is also no doubt about the racist motivation of the army leadership, and probably German public opinion would have accepted a very harsh treatment of the indigenous population after the end of the war. However, it did not accept large-scale massacres of civilians. Much has been written about the killing of innocent Herero civilians and the brutal treatment of prisoners in camps. Much less research has been done on the massive resistance in German society, in many parties, in the churches, in the press, in the imperial parliament and even within the Conservative government. This massive internal resistance forced the army and the emperor to stop the open killings after only a few weeks and to change the whole colonial policy towards a more effective and less violent regime. Perhaps one may define General v. Trotha's war against the Herero as genocidal, but the crucial point here is that it was impossible to lead such a war in a relatively open society with some democratically elected institutions, a free press and a hardly censored public opinion.

A democracy is able to accept massive killings of self-defined enemies, as shown by the experiences of the two world wars and many colonial wars and several conflicts. No doubt democracies can also be extremely racist and may tolerate Apartheid and other comparable "separate but equal" regimes. Genocide in its narrow sense, however, was never accepted, as the so-called scapegoat argument shows.[34] Racism often worked in the direction of constructing groups of enemies, which were used as scapegoats in internal struggles, but genocide was never popular and always prepared in great secrecy. If a final solution had been a popular undertaking a regime would have started to kill its self-defined enemies as openly as possible, but the contrary was always the case. Even in Nazi Germany, the most extreme case of a totalitarian dictatorship with absolute control over the press and other media, the Holocaust and other forms of massacre were planned and organized under cover even at a time when the regime was sure it would win World War II and no external resistance could prevent it from doing what it wanted.

Notes

1. See Albert Memmi, *Rassismus* (Frankfurt, 1987), 103.
2. For a conceptualization of racism and racial discourse see John Solomos and Les Beck, *Racism and Society* (London, 1996), 25–29. For an overview and a discussion of the most important theories of race and racism, see John Solomos, *Race and Racism in Contemporary Britain* (London, 1989), 1–23.
3. On the history and the interpretation of the UN genocide convention, see William A. Schabas, *Genocide in International Law: The Crime of Crimes* (Cambridge, 2000). For the new concept of genocide, see Raffael Lemkin, *Axis Rule in Occupied Europe: Laws of Occupation, Analysis of Governments, Proposals for Redress* (Washington, 1944).
4. On this argument, see Helen Fein, "Definition and Discontent: Labelling, Detecting, and Explaining Genocide in the Twentieth Century", in *Genozid in der modernen Geschichte*, edited by Stig Förster and Gerhard Hirschfeld (Münster, 1999), 13 (11–21).
5. See Lawrence LeBlanc, *The United States and the Genocide Convention* (Durham, 1991), 36.
6. See Georg Lilienthal, *Der Lebensborn e.V.: Ein Instrument nationalsozialistischer Rassenpolitik* (Stuttgart, 1985).
7. See Frank Chalk, "Redefining Genocide," in *Genocide: Conceptual and Historical Dimensions*, edited by George J. Andreopoulos (Philadelphia, 1994), 52 (47–63);

Kurt Jonassohn, "What is Genocide?" in *Genocide Watch*, edited by Helen Fein (Yale, 1992), 18 (17–26).

8. See Alexander Laban Hinton, ed., *Annihilating Difference* (Berkeley, 2002); Samuel Totten, William S. Parsons, and Israel W. Charney, eds., *Genocide in the Twentieth Century: Critical Essays and Eyewitness Accounts* (New York, 1995).

9. See Helen Fein, "Genocide, Terror, Life Integrity, and War Crimes: The Case for Discrimination," in *Genocide*, 100.

10. See Marc Levine, "Creating a modern 'Zone of Genocide': The Impact of Nation- and State-Formation on Eastern Anatolia, 1878–1923," *Holocaust and Genocide Studies* 12 (1998): 393–433.

11. See the documents in *"Historikerstreit": Die Dokumentation der Kontroverse über die Einzigartigkeit der nationalsozialistischen Judenvernichtung* (München, 1987).

12. On the *Holodomor*, see Robert Conquest, *The Harvest of Sorrow: Soviet Collectivisation and the Terror-Famine* (London, 1986); Gerhard Simon, "Holodomor als Waffe: Stalinismus, Hunger und der ukrainische Nationalismus," *Osteuropa* 14 (2004): 44 (37–56); Jörg Baberowski, "Wandel und Terror: Die Sowjetunion unter Stalin, Ein Literaturbericht," *Jahrbücher für Geschichte Osteuropas* 43 (1995): 97–129. Other authors use the genocide terminology, believing that communism and genocide are nearly identical concepts. See Rudolph J. Rummel, *Lethal Politics: Soviet Genocide and Mass Murder since 1917* (New Brunswick, 1996); James E. Mace, "Soviet Man-Made Famine in Ukraine," in *Genocide in the Twentieth Century*, edited by Samuel Totten, William S. Parsons, and Israel W. Charney (New York, 1995), 97–138.

13. See for example Tony Barta, "Relations of Genocide: Land and Lives in the Colonization of Australia," in *Genocide and the Modern Age*, edited by Isidor Wallmann and Michael N. Dobkowski (New York, 1987), 237–51; Colin Tatz, *With Intent to Destroy: Reflecting on Genocide* (London, 2003); A. Dirk Moses, ed., *Genocide and Settler Society: Frontier Violence and Stolen Indigenous Children in Australian History* (New York, 2005).

14. See Fein, *Genocide, Life Integrity, and War Crimes*, 95.

15. See Hannah Arendt, *Eichmann in Jerusalem: Ein Bericht von der Banalität des Bösen* (München, 1986), 328.

16. On the ideological sources of the Khmer Rouge, see Karl D. Jackson, ed., *Cambodia, 1975–1978: Rendezvous with Death* (Princeton, 1989); David P. Chandler, *Brother Number One: A Political Biography of Pol Pot*, rev. ed. (Boulder, 1999); Ben Kiernan, *The Pol Pot Regime: Race, Power, and Genocide in Cambodia under the Khmer Rouge, 1975–79* (New Haven, 1996).

17. See for example Boris Barth, *Genozid: Völkermord im 20. Jahrhundert, Geschichte, Theorien, Kontroversen* (München, 2006); Eric D. Weitz, *A Century of Genocide: Utopias of Race and Nation* (Princeton, 2003); Benjamin A. Valentino, *Final Solutions: Mass Killing and Genocide in the Twentieth Century* (Ithaca, 2004); William D. Rubinstein, *Genocide: A History* (Harlow, 2004).

18. See Andrew Bell-Fialkoff, *Ethnic Cleansing* (Basingstoke, 1996), 3, 7.

19. On the history of ethnic cleansing, see Norman Naimark, *Fires of Hatred: Ethnic Cleansing in Twentieth-Century Europe* (Cambridge, MA, 2001).

20. See Rubinstein, *Genocide*, 142; Rolf Hosfeld, *Operation Nemesis: Die Türkei, Deutschland und der Völkermord an den Armeniern* (Köln, 2005), 114.

21. See Michael Fellman, *Inside War: The Guerrilla Conflict in Missouri during the American Civil War* (New York, 1990); Boris Barth, "Partisan und Partisanenkrieg in Theorie und Geschichte: Zur historischen Dimension der Entstaatlichung von Kriegen," *Militärgeschichtliche Zeitschrift* 64 (2005): 69–100.

22. See Gerard J. Libaridian, "The Ultimate Repression: The Genocide of the Armenians, 1915–1917," in *Genocide and the Modern Age: Etiology and Case Studies of Mass Death*, edited by Isidor Waliman and Michael N. Dobkowski (New York, 1987), 203–35; Donald Bloxham, "The Armenian Genocide of 1915–1916: Cumulative Radicalization and the Development of a Destruction Policy," *Past and Present* 181 (2003): 141–91; David Bloxham, *The Great Game of Genocide: Imperialism, Nationalism and the Destruction of the Ottoman Armenians* (Oxford, 2005).

23. On the meaning of pan-ideologies, see Barth, *Genozid*, 184–96.

24. See the still classic study of Christian Streit, *Keine Kameraden: Die Wehrmacht und die sowjetischen Kriegsgefangenen, 1941–1945* (Stuttgart, 1978).

25. See Christian Gerlach, *Krieg, Ernährung, Völkermord: Forschungen zur deutschen Vernichtungspolitik im Zweiten Weltkrieg* (Hamburg, 1998); Christian Gerlach, *Kalkulierte Morde: Die deutsche Wirtschafts- und Vernichtungspolitik in Weißrußland, 1941 bis 1944* (Hamburg, 1999); Susanne Heim and Götz Aly, "Sozialplanung und Völkermord: Thesen zur Herrschaftsrationalität der nationalsozialistischen Vernichtungspolitik," in *"Vernichtungspolitik": Eine Debatte über den Zusammenhang von Sozialpolitik und Genozid im nationalsozialistischen Deutschland*, edited by Wolfgang Schneider (Hamburg, 1991), 11–23.

26. See Christopher Browning, *The Path to Genocide: Essays on Launching the Final Solution* (Cambridge, 1992), 85; Ulrich Herbert, "Rassismus und rationales Kalkül: Zum Stellenwert utilitaristisch verbrämter Legitimationsstrategien in der nationalsozialistischen Weltanschauung," in *"Vernichtungspolitik,"* 31 (25–35).

27. See Alison Des Forges, *Kein Zeuge darf überleben: Der Genozid in Ruanda* (Hamburg, 2002), 16, 21, 24; Christian P. Scherer, *Ethnisierung und Völkermord in Zentralafrika: Genozid in Rwanda, Bürgerkrieg in Burundi und die Rolle der Weltgemeinschaft* (Frankfurt, 1997).

28. Schabas, *Genozid im Völkerrecht*, 320.

29. Scherrer, *Ethnisierung und Völkermord*, 121.

30. The "dying nation" speech was first published in *The Times*, 5 May 1898.

31. On the Young Turks' concepts of a liberal nation-state and their general ideas, see David Kushner, *The Rise of Turkish Nationalism, 1876–1908* (London, 1977); Masami Arai, *Turkish Nationalism in the Young Turk Era* (Leiden, 1992); Sükrü Hanioglu, *Preparation for a Revolution: The Young Turks, 1902–1908* (Oxford, 2001).

32. See Ernst Klee, *Euthanasie im NS-Staat: Die "Vernichtung lebensunwerten Lebens"* (Frankfurt, 1985); Karl A. Schleunes, "Nationalsozialistische Entschlußbildung und die Aktion T 4," in *Der Mord an den Juden im Zweiten Weltkrieg*, edited by Eberhard Jäckel and Jürgen Rohwer (Frankfurt, 1987), 70–83; Hugh Gregory Gallagher, "Holocaust: The Genocide of Disabled Peoples," in *Genocide in the Twentieth Century*, 265–98.

33. See especially Michael Mann, *The Dark Side of Democracy: Explaining Ethnic Cleansing* (Cambridge, 2005).

34. For the scapegoat argument see: Valentino, *Final Solutions*, 23, 31.

Chapter 5

Slavery and Racism in Nineteenth-Century Cuba

Michael Zeuske

In recent years, historians have paid much attention to slavery and race in the Americas and in world history. Their work has produced a stimulating new picture.[1] This chapter will take a closer look at race-making and racial discourse in a society other than that of the much-studied antebellum United States, namely nineteenth-century Cuba. However, before turning to this subject, we should first briefly consider the broader historical context in which Cuban slavery developed.

In the "big picture" of Atlantic or "Western" slavery we find three main stages of slavery that have implications for the process of race-making.[2] The first stage roughly dates from 1440 to 1650. At the beginning of this period, the *sclavus nigrus* (*black Slav*) in Sicily in 1430 established the initial link between slavery and blackness. The slavery practiced on the Atlantic Islands prepared the stage for introducing Africans as agricultural slaves to the Americas. Finally, the point of no return in linking "African" origins, including the construction of blackness, to slavery as a labor system in the Americas appears to have come by the mid seventeenth century.[3]

The second stage stretches from the mid seventeenth century to the first wave of abolition, including the revolution in Saint Domingue (modern-day Haiti) in 1791, the end of slavery in the new Latin American republics, and emancipation in the British colonies in 1833. A third stage that was characterized by expanding slavery into new territories, as it happened, for example, in the American South and in Cuba, began around 1800 and lasted until slavery was finally abolished in the southern United States (1865), Cuba (1886) and Brazil (1888).

Upon closer examination, it is clear that slavery as a system of labor, especially the so-called "second slavery," did not require extensive race-marking.[4] Slaves were brought to the Americas to perform labor on the plantations. It was the work they did that marked them.[5] Working either as field hands or house servants, they could be readily identified as bound residents of the plantations. With a history of up to three hundred years of African enslavement in the American plantation regions, slavery had become linked to race almost by definition. Nearly everywhere, the class of field workers was overwhelmingly black. Thus the black population of the "second slavery" regions, including the southern United States, Brazil, and Cuba, was always in danger of being identified as slaves.[6]

With regard to analyzing race and racism in Cuban history, there are several key issues that have implications for the spread of racism in the Atlantic World. First, we need to separate the development of racial thinking from slavery.[7] While slavery was a key factor in the process of the Iberian expansion, we need to ask whether it makes sense to apply the terms "race" and "racism" to an age that had not yet developed a clear concept of race, despite an intense cultural stereotyping of Africans.[8] Does racism adequately describe the hierarchical order between roughly 1450 and 1780, which was based primarily on religious distinctions (skin color and other phenotypical traits did play a role as social markers, but were not based on a theoretical framework)?[9] Or should we rather confine this term to the modern period? Should racism be exclusively defined by those theories that explicitly relied on "scientific" and "anthropological" concepts of race? In this chapter, it will be argued that, beginning at the end of the eighteenth century, Cuban Creole elites developed a peculiar biological theory of slavery that amounted to some kind of functional racism without a clear concept of race. Although they used the word *raza*, the central concept was *clase negra* (negro class).[10]

The second point is the enormous significance of African slavery for Cuba's economic and demographic development in the nineteenth century. Until 1810, Cuba was formally part of the Spanish Empire in America. The port of Havana was a major commercial hub linking "plantation America" to Europe. By the time Spain's continental colonies in the Americas had gained their independence (1830), the Cuban elites agreed to remain under the rather weak Spanish rule. Following the breakdown of Saint Domingue in the 1790s, Cuban planters had established a booming sugar production based on mass slavery. By the 1830s, western Cuba and the roaring port cities of Havana and Matanzas had become the richest agricultural region in the Atlantic basin. This "Cuba A" or *Cuba grande* represented the most advanced export-oriented agricultural economy in the world. Its highly efficient slave-based *ingenios* (factories in the fields) focused on the mass production of white sugar and its by-products, while the island was industrializing more rapidly than Spain itself. For example, the first railroad in Latin America was constructed on Cuba as early as 1837–39.[11]

Moreover, despite the outlawing of the Atlantic slave trade by Great Britain and the United States in 1808, Cuba maintained a large illicit African slave trade until 1870.[12] The smuggling of slaves sustained the Cuban commercial boom that generated one of the highest per capita incomes worldwide. Mostly because of the African slave trade, the Cuban population skyrocketed from one hundred and seventy thousand inhabitants in 1774, the year of the first official census, to one million in 1841. Sixty percent of the population were African slaves or free people of color. As a consequence, the island had the most diverse slave cultures in the entire New World, including the Lucumí-Yoruba, the Congo-Angola-Macuá (Bantu), the Arará-Mina-Fon, the Carabalí-Ibo, the Mandinga-Senegalese and the Gangá.[13] These slave communities had their own languages (*habla bozal*), secret warrior societies (*abakuá, ogboni*), religions (*santería, palo monte, vudú, tumba francesa, maní*, etc.) as well as their own musical styles.[14]

Yet there was also "Cuba B," *Cuba pequeña* or "little Cuba," inhabited by local white elites, free black and colored farmers, and the fugitive slaves known as *cimarrones* (maroons). Among these groups, racial hierarchies were less pronounced and they claimed to be the "real Cubans." In fact, until the nineteenth century the term "Cuban" referred specifically to "people from Santiago de Cuba." It was in "little Cuba," first in the mountainous Eastern province of Oriente, that the interracial army of *mambises* (a Congo word for ghost warrior) arose in the 1860s to challenge Spanish colonial rule. From 1868 to 1898, Cuba underwent sweeping changes, the most important of which were the wars of independence, the restructuring of the sugar industry according to the needs of the U.S. market, and gradual emancipation, resulting in the abolition of slavery in 1886. After this transformation, slaves disappeared from public discourse but reappeared in three different roles: first, as *libertadores* who had participated in the struggle against Spain and who became icons of an empty and pompous nationalism; second, as *negros brujos* and *hampa afro-cubana*, black sorcerers and criminals, who became the objects of anthropological science; and third, as the masses of the black urban and rural underclasses who were stigmatized by their surnames identifying them as former slaves.[15]

Since the end of the eighteenth century, the "racialization of Cuba," that is the construction of a biological concept of race, developed along different lines. Three elite groups in particular were instrumental in transforming religious concepts of social hierarchy into biological and racist ideas, namely the imperial elite of Spain, the urban Creole oligarchy of slave owners, and Creole anticolonial thinkers and activists. The latter group, although it founded an anticolonial and anti-slavery tradition, did not have much success and is therefore neglected in this essay.

The Spanish state intended to impose a new juridical order on its Caribbean sugar colonies, partly based on descent and skin color. In 1785 and 1789 Spain imposed new slave codes that laid the conceptual groundwork for the legal and intellectual establishment of a *clase negra* as a separate racialized group. In the "Código Negro Carolino" for the Island of Santo Domingo, the crown and the imperial bureaucracy tried to codify a fundamental hierarchy of *clases* (classes) defined by an elaborate scheme of colors. The "negro class" of slaves formed a separate class. The free colored population was divided into *morenos* (blacks), *mulattos* (offspring of one white and one black parent), and *pardos* (colored). Assuming that dark-skinned women had children with light-skinned men, the Código created six ranks (*rangos*) of color ranging from black to light-skinned mulatto and dividing the offspring into *secundones, tercerones, cuarterones*, etc. Those in the sixth rank were classified as "white," provided that the paternal ancestors had all been white.[16] While the Códigos established a *clase negra* and took pains to separate that class from the other groups (*castas*) of colonial society, the Spanish crown opened channels of social mobility for wealthy *morenos, pardos,* and *mulattos*. The 1795 *Real Cédula del Gracias al Sacar*, a royal decree granting permission to change social ranks, allowed them to buy symbols of whiteness, including the title "don" and, for example, admission to the university or to the guild of lawyers. However, the local elites of slave owners in the Spanish colonial empire successfully rejected the reform project of the slave codes, including the goal of the *Real Cédula de Gracias al Sacar* to commercialize the color question. Nevertheless, they embraced the racialization project of the codes, particularly the concept of *clase negra*.[17]

The racialization of slavery dovetailed with the slave owners' interest in promoting the sugar boom. In order to produce more sugar, they needed more slaves. The Haitian Revolution (1791–1803), made by slaves and free blacks, added political momentum to the issue of race. On the one hand, the breakdown of Saint Domingue/Haiti opened up new markets for Cuban sugar and coffee. On the other hand, the Haitian Revolution raised the question of liberty and equality throughout the entire Caribbean and Atlantic world.[18] Slave owners successfully employed racialization as a means of controlling their slaves on the sugar or coffee estates (*ingenios, cafetales*) and their house slaves in the cities. In adopting racial concepts, they incorporated the latest developments of racial theory and science.[19]

A key figure among Cuban elite intellectuals was Francisco de Arango y Parreño (1765–1837), the secretary of the organization of Cuban planters, the *Real Consulado de Agricultura y Comercio* (Royal Consulate of Agriculture and Commerce). Arango strongly advocated the importation of more female slaves in order to create a more balanced gender ratio among Cuban slaves. He was a friend of Alexander von Humboldt and is considered one of the first cultural biologists in the Americas.[20] The Haitian Revolution had a major impact on Arango. In 1808, he still remembered how "on 20th November, 1791, the news of the rebellion in Guarico [an old Spanish name for Le Cap in Haiti] arrived in Madrid."[21] On the same day, Arango wrote a letter to the King in which he compared sugar production in Saint Domingue and Cuba and made proposals how to improve production methods and control of the slaves in both regions.[22] One year later, in his renowned *Discurso sobre la agricultura de la Habana y medios de fomentarla* (A lecture on agriculture in Havana and the means for developing it) of 1792, a kind of Adam Smith-like program of modernization for colonial capitalism based on mass slavery, Arango admitted: "The insurrection of the Negroes of Guarico enlarged the horizon of my ideas." Employing the comparative method, he also gave rise to the myth that slavery was more humane in the Spanish colonies than in the French: "The fate of our freedmen and slaves has been better and they have been happier than the slaves and freedmen in the French colony [of Saint Domingue]. Their numbers are smaller than those of the white population and, aside from that, they could never take over the important garrison of Havana." But Arango envisioned a future when a prosperous Cuba would have five to six hundred thousand African slaves. But he stressed that precautions would have to be taken right away to forestall slave rebellions like the one in Saint Domingue.[23]

In his *Representación* of 1811, Arango articulated the main elements of the Cuban racial project, which was embraced by the slaveholding elite of Havana.[24] In the aftermath of Napoleon's occupation of the Iberian Peninsula in 1808, the territories remaining under Spanish control embarked on a liberal constitutional process. In a protest (representation) of the Havana elite against a uniform code of rights for all citizens of the Spanish empire, as it was discussed in the Constitutional Assembly of the liberal Cortes in Cádiz between 1810 and 1812, Arango employed the divisions of caste and color that had been ordained by the mother country in the 1780s. In his plea against the abolition of slavery and the slave trade, he relied on the distinction between the slaves of ancient Rome on the one hand and the "modern slaves" of the Americas on the other. While the former were as white as their masters, and sometimes more competent, Arango defined the latter in racial terms, using phenotype and culture as his criteria. Modern slaves were "of black color, kinky hair, crude facial features and savage customs … Nature has made the black man different from the white man." To emphasize this difference, he devised an early version of the so-called "one-drop rule," according to which everybody with a known or visible trace of African ancestry must be classified as a "Negro." "All cultured nations," Arango wrote, "persist in the view that it is politically advantageous to treat the liberated *bozal* and the *cuarterón* equally, even though the latter might be the son or grandson of very commendable people." Because he believed that one drop of "Negro blood" infected the blood lines of whites for generations, regardless of visible signs or personal memory, Arango demanded that all Africans and their descendents be forever set apart as a social group. "Once the doors are closed to our slaves and their offspring to ever identify with us," he concluded, "it follows that the doors to civil liberty must also be closed." Consequently, hierarchies of skin color, *clases*, had to be established covering "the many different classes of people living in Cuba who fall between the two extremes of whites and *bozales*."[25]

Arango then goes on to discuss the negative consequences of the relatively easy manumission of slaves in Cuba. In his view the most disquieting result was the emergence of "corrupt swarms of bees of urban negroes and mulattos" who formed a large group of free people of color in the *barrios*, ports, and streets of the Cuban towns and who refused to work either on the sugar plantations or take the poorly paid jobs as house servants of the elite.[26] Obviously, Arango's key objective was to diminish the status of free men and women of color in order to press them into agricultural work. As early as in his 1792 *Discurso sobre la Agricultura*, he had demanded the disbanding of the black and mulatto militias, the *batallones de pardos y morenos*, which had a long tradition in Spanish America. "All of them are negroes," Arango insisted, "they more or less share the same grievances and bear the same grudges against us."[27] In his *Representación*, Arango also reminded his readers of the religious legitimization of slavery, which had traditionally played a key role in the Spanish Empire, namely that it was a Christian duty to save the souls of the slaves. As a good liberal he could not resist blaming the Catholic Church for its negligence in discharging its mission.[28]

By constructing a stark contrast between "white" and "black" as *clases* and *castas* and by linking skin color to slave status, including free blacks and *pardos* whose ancestors had been manumitted generations ago, Arango established a Cuban version of the one-drop rule that linked modern racial arguments to older concepts of the purity of blood, the *limpieza de sangre*, and religion in general. In the vein of an Adam Smith of the American plantation economy, Arango marked the economic *clase* of field slaves as *negra*. By evoking the notion of a indelible racial stigma, he tried to lock all descendents of slaves for generations into a cultural prison of blackness. And when he served as the Cuban envoy to the Cortes from 1812 to 1814 his arguments did not fall on deaf ears. Reflecting the pressures from the planters of Havana and the Captain General of Cuba, the liberal Spanish constitution of 1812 denied the *castas pardas* (colored castes), that is free people of African ancestry, citizenship and voting rights.

It is certainly true that Arango was one of the fathers of the concept of a *raza negra*.[29] For him, however, as for many other members of the Cuban elite, the term *clase* was more important than *raza* in facilitating social and political exclusion. For the most part, *raza* served as a unifying concept to categorize those 70 percent of the Cuban population with colored or black ancestors. Nevertheless, Arango, perhaps the greatest thinker among the planter elites of the Americas, initiated one of the most important racial projects in the history of Cuba and, possibly, of the Atlantic world.

Yet this does not mean that he was a racist. Under the changing historical conditions after 1815, Arango understood much earlier than the rest of the Cuban elite that in a colonial situation race could be used as a flexible and inclusive concept beyond slavery. Thus he progressively metamorphosed from a propagandist of slavery and black inferiority into an advocate of abolition and racial equality. In 1817, Arango collaborated with Spain in signing a treaty with Great Britain to officially end the Atlantic slave trade.[30] Subsequently, he began to write on improving slavery, for example, by importing more female slaves to create a more equal gender balance. More importantly, against the backdrop of the wars for independence waged by Spain's continental colonies and the skyrocketing prices for slaves, Arango also began pondering the abolition of slavery and envisioning a future when the time would come "to delete the memory of slavery."[31]

However, the language of his proposals reads like modern racist theories of breeding. Arango speculated that large-scale racial mixing between whites and blacks would eventually "bleach" the latter. "Nature itself," he wrote, "shows us the easiest and the safest way to achieve this end. She teaches us that black skin color gives way to white skin color and that the former will disappear if the mixture of both races is continued long enough.

The offspring of such mixtures, we may observe, distinctly leans toward the white." Thus, Arango proposed, in racist terms, a seemingly anti-racist program of political *cubanidad* (Cubanness), albeit one that was grounded in racist ideas about regulating interracial procreation. His main motivation behind this project was to gradually remove the menace of black slave rebellions that continued to haunt the Cuban elites. "Let us try, then, this bold method," he called upon his fellow white Cubans, "let us promote these half-breeds rather than try to prevent them and let us employ the fruits of such mixtures for the benefit of civil virtue." "This approach," he wrote in 1816, "deserves more attention than all other proposals for the present and future safety of Cuba. It will quickly reduce the numbers of our born enemies, it will unite us with the mulattos and, in the long run, it will whiten all our negroes."[32] Thus, Arango, against the backdrop of an extremely dynamic slave society, devised a protonationalist program of racial reform. In order to create a "new man" without the "prejudice of color," he promoted miscegenation and in effect became an "anti-racist racialist."

In many ways, Arango's ideas anticipated the ambiguities of race that would later become typical for Cuban society. Of course, it would have been impossible to enact his proposals. To begin with, they were completely at odds with the marriage patters of the Cuban elites who considered marriage as a way to form alliances among themselves. Moreover, the "prejudice of color" had emerged during centuries of slavery and could not easily be eradicated. The work in the sugar fields was regarded as "slave labor" and therefore as "black labor."[33]

By 1832, five years before his death, Arango had changed again and turned into an opponent not only of the slave trade and of sharp racial divisions but also of slavery itself. That year, he wrote his last great treatise, entitled "Representación al rey sobre la extinction del tráfico de negros y medios de mejorar la suerte de los esclavos coloniales" (Representation to the King on the extinction of the negro trade and remedies to improve the fate of the colonial slaves). Among his proposals, he listed both the effective abolition of the slave trade and the deletion of color prejudice. To implement his project of racial mixing he suggested establishing separate colonies of colored females and white males, who he thought should be agricultural workers and recent immigrants from Europe.

In trying to bolster his proposals, Arango tackled the "notorious question of the *natural inferiority of this race* [blacks] in comparison to the white race."[34] He did not believe that it deserved much attention since debating that question seemed outdated and ridiculous. The inferiority of blacks,

Arango pointed out, was often justified by their different physical appearance, particularly the "color of their skin, their kinky hair, and the thickness of their lips." "But I do not know," he continued, "why and how one can possibly infer from such bodily features any differences in the development of their intellectual and moral faculties." Obviously there was an infinite variety of skin color between the extremes of white and black, including copper and yellow. The different skin colors among humankind, Arango reasoned, were most likely created by differences in the ability to absorb sunlight. Neither color nor hair texture nor the shape of the skull had any conceivable relationship to human intelligence, "this noble emanation of the Divine." Moreover, neither all whites nor all blacks were identical in their bodily features.[35]

These arguments indicate that there were intense debates on racial and biological questions among the Cuban sugar elite. Contesting the racial justifications of slavery that were popular within his social class, Arango developed a kind of liberal historical materialism that subordinated race to utilitarian considerations of economic prosperity and social tranquility. Basically, his 1832 plea to abolish slavery and discard racial inequality was predicated upon the same overall goals as his 1811 *Representación* in which he had defended slavery based on racial difference. In fact, from his *Primer Papel Sobre el Comercio de Negros* (*First Paper about the Negro Trade*) of 1789 down to his last great *Representación* of 1832 Arango was primarily concerned with the economic and financial dynamics of slavery and the slave trade. However, he was only successful as a racist defender of slavery. Once he turned into an opponent of both slavery and "color prejudice," his appeals fell on deaf ears.[36]

This should not be surprising, given the economic development of Cuba in the nineteenth century. The system of Atlantic slavery, including the slave raids and the trade in Africa, the infamous middle passage across the Atlantic, and the plantation economies of the Americas, made Cuba a model of mass slavery and technological modernity.[37] Even though the Atlantic slave trade was officially outlawed in 1820 and continued only as an illicit business, the process of commodification and accumulation connected to the slave economy continued unabated. The rise of *Cuba grande* between 1790 and 1840 was made possible by the break-up of the large colonial *haciendas,* known as the "demolición de las haciendas comuneras," and their transformation into smaller yet more efficient production units called *ingenios.* Former slave traders reinvested their profits into new technologies and modern forms of organizing labor on the plantations.[38]

Because the sugar boom was predicated on mass slavery, racism—reflected in the concept of the "negro class" and in pervasive "color prejudice"—served an evidently ideological function, namely to subdue the religious and humanitarian opposition to slavery that came from groups of Cuban intellectuals who were not tied to the sugar industry. Arango himself lost his influence when the new "negrero" capitalists, many of whom were engaged in the smuggling of slaves, seized control of Cuban politics and the economy between 1830 and 1840 and began to displace the old Creole elites of Havana.[39]

During this period, Cuban and Spanish intellectuals such as the Catholic priest Félix Varela (1788–1853) who dared to advocate the abolition of slavery were rare exceptions. Opponents of slavery mostly represented the *Cuba pequeña* and hoped to break the domination of the planter class by promoting the immigration of poor immigrants from Spain to replace black slaves.[40] In general, however, the racial ideology of slavery prevailed. Its adherents not only included the class of slave traders and slaveholding planters but also those groups that were economically dependent on or socially tied to the system of slavery such as guards, slave drivers, the operators of the sugar mills, shopkeepers, doctors, notaries, priests, mayors etc., not to speak of the great majority of petty slave owners in the towns along the island. Their view of slavery focused on what Arango called "the famous question of the *natural inferiority of this race.*" The reception of new European race theories further reinforced this ideology.[41]

Incrementally these new theories began to contaminate the writings of Cuban intellectuals. José Antonio Saco, who wrote the first important modern history of world slavery, carried further the ideas of the Cuban elite about the *raza africana*. When the first signs of a genuine Cuban nationalism began to emerge, he insisted that only white men could form the Cuban nation. Saco can rightly be called an open racist. He wanted to maintain slavery but not the slave trade, which kept bringing even more blacks to Cuba. He blamed all of the island's social evils on the presence of Africans and confessed that he wished for a "reduction, even extinction of the black race, if it were possible."[42]

However, the ideology of slavery and racial ideas did not play a major role in the terror campaign, known as *La Escalera* (The Ladder), which the Spanish colonial authorities waged against the free colored and black populations of Cuba in the wake of the 1843 slave revolt southeast of Matanzas. The military proconsuls of the Crown had become deeply troubled by the incipient Cuban nationalism, the growing influence of British abolitionism, the ongoing smuggling of slaves that threatened Spain's relations with Great Britain, and the frequent uprisings among Cuban slaves. Spanish authorities worried they were losing control and decided to reassert their power with an iron fist. They brutally crushed the slave rebellion near Matanzas, killing hundreds of blacks, both slave and free. The immediate purpose of the massacre was to forestall a slave revolution as it had occurred in Haiti in 1791. But the colonial masters went further and exploited the incident to launch a campaign of state terror and oppression that amounted to a quasi-military dictatorship. Although the terror mainly targeted the conspiratorial networks among free blacks and slaves, its larger motive was to demonstrate to the Creole elite that it needed imperial protection. Still, the terror also reinforced racial hierarchies and had a profound impact on the black population. Most importantly, the masses of the free coloreds, the *mulattos* or *pardos*, who so far had been loyal supporters of both the Spanish crown and the slave system, were all made a part of the dangerous *clase negra*. In cultural representations, everyday life, and official documents, they were stigmatized. They had to carry a passport that identified them by explicit racial markers as, for example, in "Francisco, *pardo*," or "José de la Cruz, *moreno*." In everyday parlance they would be called "*pardo* Francisco" or "*moreno* José," respectively.[43] Moreover, in the wake of the *Escalara* terror, the Spanish proconsuls banned the "Milicias de Pardos y Morenos" which outnumbered Spanish colonial troops ten to one. Ten years later, however, the imperial General Captain had to reinstate the "colored militias" in order create a military counterweight against a group of slave-holding planters who played with the idea of seeking annexation by the United States.[44]

However, in the second half of the nineteenth century Spain inexorably lost its hold on Cuba. In the late 1860s, the crisis escalated into the wars of independence that lasted until 1898. During the same period Cuba modernized its sugar production to meet the demands of the U.S. market and began the process of abolition, emancipation, and post-emancipation that did not end until the early twentieth century. Simultaneously, the peculiar duality of racism and anti-racism, which had taken roots since the late eighteenth century, continued and gave rise to new contradictions.

The principles of color-blindness and anti-racism, which Arango had espoused later in his life, played an important role among the so-called *Cabildos de nación*. These were councils representing "African nations" as, for example, the *Cabildos de Congos*, *Cabildos de Minas*, *Cabildos de Lucumiés*, and the *Cabildos de Mandingas*. Mutual aid societies, the *Sociedades de Ayuda Mutúa*, were organized according to the same principle.[45] More-over, the interracial workforce of the sugar economy and the docklands, which included ex-slaves, free people of color as well as "white Spaniards" who had immigrated to Cuba from the Canary Islands and Galicia, were also committed to racial egalitarianism. At least officially, race was not an issue among the labor movement. During the Cuban wars of independence between 1868 and 1898 the independence movement created the largest and most powerful interracial army of the entire western hemisphere. For ex-ample, the *pardo* Antonio Maceo—as he was called in the racialized language of the colonial era—was second in command of this army. Maceo was a free person of color who had risen through one of the *Cabildos de Congos*. Other strongholds of anti-racist thought and sentiment were the schools and civic organizations led by blacks and mulattos. One of the most salient achievements of the egalitarian wing of the anticolonial movement was a decree by the Spanish colonial authorities that the titles of honor *don* and *doña* were to be included in the official documents of all Cubans.

In contrast, the racist tradition established by the early Arango was con-tinued by elite thinkers such as José Antonio Saco who advocated banning the slave trade but would have preferred to deport all free blacks to Africa. According to Saco, the "Cuban nation" should only include Cuban-born white males. Furthermore, when abolition took shape between 1870 and 1890, the planters and colonial bureaucrats invented new methods of race-marking, albeit without openly using racial language. The law mandated that the emancipated slaves, upon becoming "new citizens," had to adopt one of the two surnames of their former master. Thus, their status as ex-slaves was clearly marked in everyday life. In the Castilian tradition all persons of legitimate birth have two surnames, one paternal and one ma-ternal. Slaves, however, were usually given only a single first name, for example Maria or José. Moreover, most former slaves and free blacks had never been officially married and hence their children were, as far as the law was concerned, born out of wedlock. As a consequence, official documents, by explicitly pointing out that the bearer had no second surname—*sin otro appellido* or s.o.a.—identified persons with only one surname as former slaves without using an explicitly racial marker. Although illegitimate birth also pertained to some poor whites, the practices of naming primarily served to continue the stigma of slavery which coincided with race.[46]

On the surface, however, the Cuban nationalism that emerged in the an-ticolonial struggles of the late nineteenth century was predicated upon a color-blind and "race-blind" discourse. In order to secure the loyalty of the rural black and colored population, the white nationalist revolutionary José Martí called upon all Cubans to forget slavery. For Martí, a Cuban was more than a white man or a black man, he was a "man without color."[47] This official ideal continues to this today.

Notes

1. Ivan Hannaford, *Race: The History of an Idea in the West* (Baltimore, 1996); Consuelo Naranjo Orovio & Armando García González, *Racismo e Inmigración en Cuba en el siglo XIX* (Madrid, 1996); Peter Wade, *Race and Ethnicity in Latin America* (London, 1997); Naranjo Orovio and Miguel Ángel Puig-Samper, "Delincuencia y racismo en Cuba: Israel Castellanos versus Fernando Ortiz," in *Ciencia y facismo*, edited by Rafael Huertos and Carmen Ortiz (Aranjuez, 1998), 12–23.

2. David Brion Davis, "Looking at Slavery from Broader Perspectives," *American Historical Review* 105, no. 2 (2000): 452–84.

3. Charles Verlinden, "Encore sur les origines de sclavus = esclave," *L'esclavage dans l'Europe médiévale*, Vol. II: *Italie-Colonies italiennes du Levant. Levant latin - Empire byzantin* (Gent, 1977), 999–1010; J. Phillips, and D. William, *La esclavitud desde la época romana hasta los inicios del comercio transatlántico* (Madrid, 1989), 85; Jacques Heers, *Esclavos y sirvientes en las sociedades mediterráneas durante la Edad Media* (Valencia, 1995).

4. Dale W. Tomich, "The 'Second Slavery': Bonded Labor and the Transformations of the Nineteenth-century World Economy," in *Rethinking the Nineteenth Century*, edited by F.O. Ramírez (Stanford, CA, 1988), 103–17; Tomich, *Through the Prism of Slavery: Labor, Capital and the World Economy* (Boulder, CO, 2004).

5. Ira Berlin, *Many Thousands Gone: The First Two Centuries of Slavery in North America* (Cambridge, MA, 1998), 1–14.

6. Michael Zeuske, "Comparing or Interlinking? Economic Comparisons of Early Nineteenth-Century Slave Systems in the Americas in Historical Perspective," in *Slave Systems: Ancient and Modern*, edited by Enrico Dal Lago and Constantina Katsari (Cambridge, 2008), 148–83.

7. Joseph C. Miller, "Slaving as Historical Process: Examples from the Ancient Mediterranean and the Modern Atlantic," in *Slave Systems: Ancient and Modern* , edited by Enrico Dal Lago, Enrico and Constantina Katsari (Cambridge, 2008), 70–102, especially 96.

8. James H. Sweet, "The Iberian Roots of American Racist Thought," *William and Mary Quarterly* 54, no. 1 (January 1997): 143–66.

9. Trevor Burnard, *Mastery, Tyranny, and Desire: Thomas Thistlewood and His Slaves in the Anglo-Jamaican World* (Chapel Hill, 2004); Olwyn Blouet, "Bryan Edwards and the Haitian Revolution," in *The Impact of the Haitian Revolution in the Atlantic World*, edited by David P. Geggus, (Columbia, 2001), 44–57; Hering Torres, Max

Sebastián, *Rassismus in der Vormoderne: Die 'Reinheit des Blutes' im Spanien der Frühen Neuzeit* (Frankfurt, 2006).

10. The word *raza* (race) in American Spanish and in local variants of Spanish could have, until the twenty-first century, many meanings; it was really a very "slippery concept." See for example Nancy P. Appelbaum, *Muddied Waters: Race, Region, and Local History in Colombia, 1846–1948* (Durham, 2003), 9–11.

11. Joseph Fradera, *Colonias para después de un imperio* (Barcelona, 2005).

12. Michael Zeuske and García Martínez, "La Amistad del Caribe," *Caribbean Studies* (Puerto Rico), forthcoming.

13. David Richardson Eltis and Stephan Behrendt, "Patterns in the Transatlantic Slave Trade, 1662–1867: New Indications of African Origins of Slaves Arriving in the Americas," in *Black Imagination of the Middle Passage*, edited by Maria Diedrich, Henry Louis Gates Jr., and Carl Pedersen (Oxford, 1999).

14. Michael Zeuske, "Afrokuba und die schwarze Karibik," in *Schwarze Karibik: Sklaven, Sklavereikultur und Emanzipation*, edited by Michael Zeuske (Zürich, 2004), 247–336.

15. Fernando Ortiz, *Hampa Afro-Cubana: Los negros brujos (Apuntes para un estudio de etnología criminal)* (Madrid, 1906); Fernando Ortiz, *Hampa afro-cubana: Los negros esclavos* (La Habana, 1916) [reprinted as: *Los negros esclavos*, La Habana: Ed. de Ciencias Sociales, 1975]; Fernando Ortiz, *Contrapunteo cubano del tabaco y del azúcar* (La Habana, 1940), Fernando Ortiz, "El fenómeno social de la transculturación y su importancia en Cuba," in *Revista Bimestre Cubana*, 46 (Julio–Dic. 1940): 273–78; Enrique Beldarraín Chaple, *Los médicos y los inicios de la antropología en Cuba*, (La Habana, 2006), 28; Michael Zeuske, "Hidden Markers, Open Secrets: On Naming, Race Marking and Race Making in Cuba," in *New West Indian Guide* 76, nos. 3 & 4 (2002): 235–66; Michael Zeuske, "Legados de la esclavitud en Cuba," in *Cuba: De colonia a república*, edited by Martín Rodrigo y Alharilla (Madrid, 2006), 99–116.

16. Código Negro Carolino, "Extracto del Código Negro Carolino, formado por la Audiencia de Santo Domingo ... para el gobierno moral, político y económico de los negros," Santo Domingo, 14 de marzo de 1785, in Konetzke, *Colección de documentos para la historia de la formación social de Hispanoamérica* (Madrid 1959/62, III/2, 553–73 (Doc. No. 280); Código Negro Español, "R. Instrucción sobre educación, trato y ocupación de los esclavos," Aranjuez, 31 de mayo de 1789, in Ibid., 643–52 (Doc. No. 308).

17. Félix Varela, "Proyecto de decreto sobre abolición de la esclavitud en la Isla de Cuba y sobre los medios de evitar los daños que puedan ocasionarse a la población blanca y a la agricultura," in *Varela, Escritos políticos*, edited by de Ciencias Sociales (La Habana, 1977), 268–76.

18. David P. Geggus, ed., *The Impact of the Haitian Revolution in the Atlantic World* (Columbia, 2001); Zeuske, "Comparing or Interlinking?," 148–83.

19. González-Ripoll Navarro and María Dolores, "La oligarquía criolla y peninsular: hombres y mujeres del azúcar," in González-Ripoll Navarro, *Cuba, la isla de los ensayos: Cultura y sociedad, 1790–1815* (Madrid, 1999), 127–38; Consuelo Naranjo, Garcia Gloria, Ada Ferrer, and Josef Opartný, eds., *El rumor de Haiti en Cuba: Temor, raza y rebeldia, 1789–1844* (Madrid, 2005).

20. Amores Carredano, "Las élites cubanas y la estrategia imperial borbónica en la segunda mitad del siglo XVIII," in *Elites urbanas en Hispanoamérica*, edited by Luis Navarro García (Sevilla, 2004), 189–96; Gonzalez-Ripoll Navarro, "El proyecto de Arango y Parreño," in *Cuba, la isla de los ensayos ...* Ed. González-Ripoll Navarro, 198–205; Dale W. Tomich, "The Wealth of the Empire: Francisco de Arango y Parreño, Political Economy, and the Second Slavery in Cuba," in *Comparative Studies in Society and History*, No. 1 (2003), 4–28; Gloria García, "El otro Discurso sobre la agricultura," in *Arango y Parreño*, Francisco, Obras. Ensayo introductorio, compilación y notas García Rodríguez, (La Habana, 2005), Bd. I, 1–56. Zeuske, "Comparing or Interlinking? Economic Comparisons of Early 19th-Century Slave Systems in the Americas in Historical Perspective," 148–83.

21. Francisco Arango y Parreño, *Obras de D. Francisco de Arango y Parreño*, 2 vols., (La Habana, 1952), I: 55.

22. Arango, „Representación hecha a S.M. con motivo de la sublevación de los esclavos en los dominios de la Isla de Santo Domingo" (20 November 1791), in *Obras,* I, 111–12.

23. Arango, "Discurso sobre la Agricultura de la Habana y medios de fomentarla" (1792), in *Obras*, I, 114–62, esp. 148–49; see also Sybille Fischer, *Modernity Disavowed: Haiti and the Culture of Slavery in Age of Revolution* (Durham, 2004).

24. Arango y Parreño, "Representación de la Ciudad de la Habana a las Cortes, el 20 de julio de 1811, con motivo de las proposiciones hechas por D. José Miguel Guridi Alcocer y D. Agustín de Argüelles, sobre el tráfico y esclavitud de los negros; extendida por el Alférez Mayor de la Ciudad, D. Francisco de Arango, por encargo del Ayuntamiento, Consulado y Sociedad Patriótica de la Habana," in *Obras*, II, 145–89; see also "Documentos anexos a la Representación del 20 de julio de 1811," in Ibíd., 188–223 and "Documentos que atañen a la Representación de 20 de julio de 1811," in Ibíd., 224–37.

25. Arango, *Representación de la Ciudad de la Habana a las Cortes, el 20 de julio de 1811*, 158–60.

26. Ibid., 166.

27. Arango, "Discurso sobre la Agricultura de la Habana y medios de fomentarla" (1792), 114–62.

28. Arango, *Representación de la Ciudad de la Habana a las Cortes, el 20 de julio de 1811*, 167.

29. Aline Helg, *Our Rightful Share: The Afro-Cuban Struggle for Equality, 1886–1912* (Chapel Hill, 1995) 3.

30. "Voto particular de varios consejeros de Indias sobre la abolición del tráfico de negros. Redactado por el cuban Francisco de Arango y Parreño, 15 de febrero de

1816," in *Obras*, II, 274–81; "Real cédula circular a Indias sobre prohibisión de la trata (19 de diciembre de 1817)," in Fernando Ortiz, *Los negros esclavos*, ed. de Ciencias Sociales (La Habana, 1975), 424–26.

31. Arango, "Ideas sobre los medios de establecer el libre comercio de Cuba y de realizar un empréstito de veinte millones de pesos," in *Obras*, II, 292–308, here 307.

32. Ibid.

33. Ibid.

34. Arango, "Representación al rey sobre la extinction del tráfico de negros y medios de mejorar la suerte de los esclavos coloniales," in *Obras*, II, 529–614.

35. Ibid., esp. 530–33; 556–57.

36. Arango, "Primer papel sobre el comercio de negros," in *Obras*, I, 79–84; Francisco Ponte Domínguez, "Su testamento político," in Ponte Domínguez, *Arango y Parreño. Estadista Colonial Cubano* (La Habana,1937) 222–29; Gloria García, "Ensayo introductorio. Tradición y modernidad en Arango y Parreño," in Arango y Parreño, *Obras*. Ensayo introductorio, compilación y notas García Rodríguez, 2 vols., (La Habana, 2005), 1–56; for the perspective of the slaves, see Gloria García, *La esclavitud desde la esclavitud. La visión de los siervos* (México, 1996); Michael Zeuske, *Geschichte der Sklaven und der Sklaverei auf Kuba* (forthcoming).

37. Michael Zeuske, "Sklavenbilder: Visualisierungen, Texte und Vergleich im atlantischen Raum (19. Jahrhundert, Brasilien, Kuba und USA)," in *Zeitenblicke* 7, No. 2 (10.11.2008): URL: <www.zeitenblicke.de/2008/2/zeuske>.

38. Javier Laviña and Michael Zeuske, "Failures of Atlantization: First Slaveries in Venezuela and Nueva Granada," *Review* 31, no. 3 (2008): 297-343.

39. See Zeuske, *Geschichte der Sklaven und der Sklaverei auf Kuba*.

40. Félix Varela, "Proyecto de decreto sobre abolición de la esclavitud en la Isla de Cuba y sobre los medios de evitar los daños que puedan ocasionarse a la población blanca y a la agricultura" in Varela, *Escritos políticos* (La Habana, 1977) 268–76; Ibarra, "El abolicionismo de Varela. Cambio sin ruptura," in Félix Varela, *Ética y anticipación del pensamiento de la emancipación cubana* (La Habana, 1999), 120–27; *Félix Varela y la prosperidad de la patria criolla. Introducción y selección documental de Piqueras, José Antonio*, (Madrid, 2007); Naranjo Orovio, Consuelo & Armando García González, *Racismo e Inmigración en Cuba en el siglo XIX* (Madrid, 1996); Peter Wade, *Race and Ethnicity in Latin America* (London, 1997); Naranjo Orovio and Miguel Ángel Puig-Samper, "Delincuencia y racismo en Cuba: Israel Castellanos versus Fernando Ortiz," in *Ciencia y facismo*, edited by Rafael Huertos and Carmen Ortiz (Aranjuez, 1998), 12–23.

41. Naranjo Orovio, Consuelo, and Armando García González, *Racismo e Inmigración en Cuba en el siglo XIX* (Madrid, 1996); Peter Wade, *Race and Ethnicity in Latin America* (London, 1997); Naranjo Orovio and Miguel Ángel Puig-Samper, "Delincuencia y racismo en Cuba: Israel Castellanos versus Fernando Ortiz," in *Ciencia y facismo*, edited by Rafael Huertos and Carmen Ortiz (Aranjuez, 1998), 12–23.

42. José Antonio Saco, *Contra la anexión, recopilación de sus papeles con prólogo y ultílogo por Fernando Ortiz*, vol. 1 (La Habana,1928), 82; José Antonio Saco, *Historia de la esclavitud de la raza africana en el Nuevo Mundo y en especial en los países Americo-Hispanos* (La Habana, 1893); Francisco J. Ponte Domínguez, "Saco historiador máximo de la esclavitud, pero abolicionista sólo de la trata," in Ponte Domínguez, *La personalidad política de José Antonio Saco* (La Habana, 1931), 191–99.

43. Robert L. Paquette, *Sugar Is Made With Blood: The Conspiracy of La Escalera and the Conflict between Empires over Slavery in Cuba* (Middletown, CT, 1988); Robert L. Paquette, "Revolutionary Saint Domingue in the Making of Territorial Louisiana," in *A Turbulent Time: The French Revolution and the Greater Caribbean*, edited by Barry D. Gaspar and David P. Geggus, (Bloomington, 1997), 51–75.

44. Michael Zeuske, "Deutsche Emigranten in Amerika und das Schicksal Kubas: Eine Geschichte des Schweigens (1848–1851)," *Zeitschrift für Geschichtswissenschaft* 42, no. 3 (1994): 217–37.

45. Matt D. Childs, "'The Defects of Being a Black Creole': The Degrees of African Ethnicity in the Cuban Cabildos de Nación," in *Slaves, Subjects, and Subversives: Blacks in Colonial Latin America*, edited by Jane G. Landers and Barry M. Robinson (Albuquerque, 2007), 209–45.

46. Michael Zeuske, "Hidden Markers, Open Secrets: On Naming, Race Marking and Race Making in Cuba," 235–66; Zeuske, "Legados de la esclavitud en Cuba," 99–116.

47. Ada Ferrer, "The Silence of Patriots: Race and Nationalism in Martí's Cuba," in *José Martí's 'Our America': From National to Hemispheric Cultural Studies*, edited by Jeffrey Belnap y Raúl Fernández (Durham, 1998), 228–49; Alejandro de la Fuente, *"A Nation for All": Race, Inequality, and Politics in Twentieth-Century Cuba* (Chapel Hill, 2001).

Chapter 6

Toward a Transnational History of Racism: Wilhelm Marr and the Interrelationships between Colonial Racism and German Anti-Semitism

Claudia Bruns

For obvious reasons, research on racism in Germany has traditionally focused on anti-Semitism in general and the Holocaust in particular. Historians tended to explain German anti-Semitism as part of the country's separate path, or *sonderweg*, toward nationhood in the nineteenth century.[1] According to Christian Geulen, anti-Semitism in Germany represented a central "medium in the process of bourgeois-national self-understanding."[2] Despite a few attempts to go beyond this nation-centered perspective by comparing racist atrocities in Nazi Germany and the Soviet Union, the German public as well as German historians tended to be skeptical of such endeavors. Above all, critics charged that historical comparisons harbored the danger of calling into question the "uniqueness" of and thus trivialize the Holocaust.[3] The last two decades have witnessed attempts to internationalize the Holocaust, however—a development that introduced new comparative and transnational perspectives to the historical analysis of racism. Nevertheless, this new scholarship continues to examine anti-Semitism in isolation, neglecting other forms of racist ideologies and practices.[4]

Although historians have recently begun to examine possible connections between anti-Semitism and colonial racism, they continue to focus on the Holocaust and tend to confine their research to ideological (usually linear) continuities between white colonial racism and "radical" (eliminatory) anti-Semitism.[5] This new line of interpretation aroused considerable opposition among German historians. Jürgen Zimmerer's theses concerning the continuities between the colonial crimes of the German Empire in Southwest Africa and the Nazi war of extermination in Eastern Europe[6] have been subject to particularly harsh criticism.[7] Jeffrey Herf, for instance, argued that "radical anti-Semitism" could not be compared with anti-black racism, since in each case the perpetrators' aims, declared intentions, and ideological–pathological personality traits differed considerably.[8] Even though Herf rightly emphasizes certain unique aspects of the Holocaust, privileging the Shoah and the murderous intent of the perpetrators that led to it, he appears to diminish the deadly consequences of centuries of capitalist exploitation of black slaves.[9] Such a concentration on the uniqueness of the Holocaust tends to obscure our view of "the dynamic historical relations between the Holocaust and preceding genocides"[10] as Dirk Moses has pointed out, and, more importantly, of the various connections, interrelationships and transnational interactions between different racist discourses such as colonial and anti-Semitic racisms.

The debates about the connections between colonial racism and anti-Semitism reflect a long-established dichotomy between anti-black racism and racial anti-Semitism in the historiography of racism. Incidentally, this is true not only for German scholars, but also for U.S. historians, who tend to neglect anti-Semitism or consider it marginal. Influenced by these binaries, scholars of colonialism and anti-Semitism saw no need to develop a comparative and interdiscursive approach because of the general assumption that the two forms of racism, which were believed to differ fundamentally, were not suitable for comparison.

As Neil MacMaster and Robert Miles have pointed out, however, both anti-black racism and anti-Semitism are generally regarded as forms of racism, and should therefore be included in any conceptual framework that aims to analyze the development of modern racism.[11] MacMaster is highly critical of the argument of George Mosse and others that these two forms of racism were distinct from one another and geographically unconnected. Mosse argues that anti-black racism emerged only in Western European societies that came into contact with Africans within the context of imperial colonialism, while anti-Semitism was confined to Central and Eastern Europe, where Jews constituted a larger proportion of the population.[12] According to MacMaster, Mosse's analytic division of Europe into two zones of racial discrimination is flawed, since there was little empirical evidence for a correlation between societies' contact with minorities and the emergence of certain forms of racism in those societies. In Britain and France, for instance, powerful anti-Semitic movements emerged in the late nineteenth century, even though Jews constituted less than 1 percent of the two countries' populations. Similarly, racialized, anti-black stereotypes permeated public discourse in Central and Eastern European societies, which had little or no part in colonial ventures.[13]

As suggested by MacMaster, comparative and transnational perspectives promise to shed new light on the complexities of the history of racist ideologies and practices in Europe. Of course, comparing colonial and anti-Jewish racism harbors certain dangers, including the likelihood of being confronted with debates about hierarchies of suffering and competing notions of victimhood among blacks and Jews. Ultimately, however, historians will have to transcend questions of "uniqueness" to fully comprehend the history of this phenomenon. Future research ought to explore how the threads of colonial racism spread throughout Europe, how they were adopted and transformed within different national and regional settings and constellations, and whether and how they were interrelated with early anti-Jewish discourses in the period 1700–1900. Clearly, such approaches must go beyond comparisons and analyze transfers, network constellations, and intersectionalities.[14] Conceptually, this transfer-centered perspective would have to distinguish between a *trans-European* dimension (transfers between European countries and their colonies), a *transnational* dimension (transfers within Europe), and an *interdiscursive* dimension (cross-fertilization of various racist discourses). Rather than narrowly focusing on the exchange of ideas, economic networks, or political institutional interdependence, this approach would have to explore the complex interplay of all these dimensions.

The following paragraphs seek to put this approach into practice, focusing on Wilhelm Marr, the "founding father" of German racial anti-Semitism. Marr's story suggests that transfers of colonial racism into anti-Jewish discourses played a significant role in the development of German anti-Semitism. Until now, scholars of anti-Semitism have failed to consider the significance of Marr's travels in former colonial countries in North and South America. A close reading of his papers reveals that his experience with slavery, racial segregation, and indentured servitude contributed to the transformation of Marr's beliefs about race and politics. In fact, Marr's "colonial experience" became a decisive factor in his metamorphosis from a radical democrat and religious anti-Judaist to a racial anti-Semite.[15]

Wilhelm Marr was born in 1819 in Magdeburg and died in 1904 in Hamburg, having been a citizen of the German Reich for about a generation. A trained merchant, journalist, and political activist, Marr was not only one of the central founding figures of modern anti-Semitism in Germany, but he was also a radical democrat and revolutionary of 1848. Like Heinrich Heine and Ludwig Börne, he was part of the revolutionary "Young Germany" movement, which advocated Republican ideas resembling those of the French Revolution. Despite being an adherent of the cult of individualism, Marr frequently corresponded with Wilhelm Weitling, one of the fathers of German Socialism, and used communist idioms when addressing such issues as class and property.[16] His book *Young Germany in Switzerland: The History of Secret Associations in Our Days*, which was published in 1846, became a bestseller and made Marr a well-known personality in Germany and Europe.[17] In 1852, disappointed with the failure of the 1848 revolution, Marr migrated to Central America, where he lived, with only a short interruption, until 1860.[18]

A few years after his return to Germany, Wilhelm Marr publicly renounced his democratic ideals and presented himself to a surprised public as a radical anti-Semite. Looking back, he rightly called himself the "patriarch of anti-Semitism," having coined the term that later became the sine qua non of international vocabulary. Interestingly, the neologism "Antisemitismus" (anti-Semitism) first appeared on 2 September 1879, in the *Allgemeine Zeitung des deutschen Judentums* (General Newspaper of German Jewry), which mentioned an advertisement published by Marr for an "anti-Semitic weekly."[19] Even though he has been considered the creator of the term anti-Semitism ever since, Marr had actually announced the publication of a "social policy" or "anti-Jewish" weekly, not an "anti-Semitic" one. It was apparently the newspaper's editors who switched the terms. At the end of September 1879, Marr, having adopted the term, called for the founding of an *"Antisemiten-Liga"* (League of Anti-Semites). This organization contributed significantly to the popularity of the term anti-Semitism, which was used in countless pamphlets and became a staple of public discourse.[20]

Two main factors appear to have contributed to Marr's evolution into an anti-Semitic racist. On the one hand, Marr was influenced by various late-nineteenth-century philosophers that sought to undermine Christianity, Christian society, and the conservative social order, the most prominent of whom were materialist philosopher Ludwig A. Feuerbach and German theologian Bruno Bauer. Feuerbach's *The Essence of Christianity* (1841), for instance, attacked Judaism along with Christianity. He demanded that both religions, which he regarded as backward, be abandoned in the name of emancipation.[21] Feuerbach maintained that materialism and egoism were the main flaws of Judaism, a critique that would play a critical role in Marr's anti-Jewish and anti-Semitic writings.

On the other hand, Marr was influenced by his travels in North and South America, which contributed to the fusion of religious anti-Semitism and colonial racism in his modern anti-Semitic ideology. Biographers of Marr, including Moshe Zimmermann and Paul Lawrence Rose, largely ignore this formative period or downplay its significance later in his life.[22]

By contrast, Marr's contemporaries acknowledged these connections from the very beginning. Each time he published a new anti-Jewish pamphlet, for instance, he was officially accused of having been engaged in slave trading. In reality, Marr, having resumed his merchant career, brought German indentured servants to Costa Rica. These immigrants, who planned to settle permanently in the country, were first committed by contract to work ten hours per day for a period of two years. However, the conditions offered by Costa Rica, a country that had gained independence only five years earlier and sought white workers from Europe, were apparently criticized by the *Berlin Central Society for Colonialization*. This criticism led to the later accusation of Marr being a "slave trader," charges he repeatedly denied.[23]

In 1863 Marr published his two-volume *Journey to Central America* (*Reise nach Central-America*) as part of his memoirs dealing with the years of 1852–1860. Marr's travelogue is written in the typical form of a chronological report based on personal experience, which, as the author implies to his reader, is derived from a letter to a prematurely departed friend, a narrative strategy used to attest to the impartiality, naturalness, and authenticity of the narrated impressions.[24]

A presentation of his first encounter with the African-American population in New York is followed by the detailed description of the voyage. Marr's text fits the common pattern in numerous popular cultural texts on the role and social status of the black population, which gives an overriding impression of America.[25] "Seeing black men for the first time," African-American writer James Baldwin observed, can be considered a primordial scene of trans-cultural contact, which is subject to a kind of cultural adaptation already in the travelogues by constructing a relation between "the self" and "the other."[26] The portrayal of blacks in travel literature is thus directly related to the "self-reflexive description of a new [own] identity."[27] Codifications of "the self" and "the other" are embedded in a process of narrative negotiation, which often undergoes changes, shifts and re-codifications within the individual texts. This is also true with regard to Marr's work, which compares Germany's white lower classes with African-Americans:

Fare well, poor compatriot! But here, there is a class of people whose
fate is not preferable to yours … They are the coloured. With moral
indignation I read the words 'coloured people admitted' on a carriage
of Harlem-Rail-Road. For I have learned by heart the 'Déclaration des
droits de l'homme' during confirmation classes, and the thermome-
ter of my admiration for the freest people on Earth decreased by some
degree when I read the caste-like etiquette stated on the rail car.[28]

Marr viewed the "coloured" as being on a par with the white proletarians
in Germany. He integrated them into his previous worldview as equals
within the context of his socialist fight for the liberation of the working
class. Noticing the strict segregation of "races" in public transportation,
Marr changed his view of American society, which from then on appeared
as the radical other. Having formerly perceived the North Americans as the
"freest people on Earth," he now shows his disappointment about the
openly practiced violation of African-Americans' civil rights (*droits de
citoyen*).[29] In his narrative, Marr emphasized his commitment to different
ideals, which, according to him, were a consequence of his German socialist background: "I had learned from books that there is a clear
borderline between the coloured and the white in the South, in Louisiana
and other states, but here, in enlightened New York, that every Negro is a
free person even if he is not allowed to be a free person: such conventions
directly violate the droits de citoyen—I had not expected this!"[30]

In order to prove his commitment to full equality, Marr describes how
he enters the railroad carriage reserved for "coloured ladies and gentlemen."
He responds to the disapproving look of the driver by calling out the revolutionary slogan of fraternity. At the same time, Marr questions his own
act of civil disobedience, later dismissing the ideals of fraternity as being
pure "philosophizing" and finally calling the initiative a "false investment."
Marr's ideals appear to be shattered in the face of what he perceives as insurmountable physical disparities. He ascribes the smell "of ten muskrats"
to the "Blacks" sitting opposite him, a situation that resolves the author to
"stay put in this philanthropic situation only until the next street corner"
and, in the end, to walk the rest of the way on foot. "If you love your fellow
human beings," Marr explains his decision, "it does not mean that you have
to smell them; my heart beats for everyone, but my nose is my property,
despite Proudhon."[31] Later, however, "With the fresh air," his "philanthrop-
ism returned, of course," and Marr prepared a speech "on the equality of all
human beings" that he presented to friends on the same day.[32]

Some four or five months later, Marr traveled to Central America. By the time he arrived in Nicaragua, his emphatic support of equality and fraternity had given way to an ideology that drew radical distinction between various groups of people and relied on "racial" lineages to classify them. For example, Marr described people whose ancestry was equally divided between Native American and African-American in an extremely negative way, exclusively characterizing them with animal analogies: "One third tiger, one third monkey and the last third pig formed the deformed human shape of the Nicaraguan Zambo."[33] His initial fear of these people first evolves into curiousness before giving way to a feeling of disgust. Marr now explicitly questions "the fraternal elective affinity [*Wahlverwandtschaft*] put forward by our European ideologists."[34] Abjuring his socialist ideals, Marr concludes in his narrative: "It would really be a pity … if it were true that *all human beings are brothers*."[35] Obviously Marr's narrating alter ego has undergone a fundamental change, which is directly linked with his immersion in a racialized society and categories of colonial hierarchical formation.[36]

The necessity of finding one's own position in this social context clearly contributed to a modification of Marr's former democratic and egalitarian attitude. The reader can observe the German immigrant's integration into American society particularly on account of his disregard and debasement of the Afro-American (and "mixed") population, as Toni Morrison and others have stated. This contributed to the creation and the perpetuation of a racist hierarchy as a consensus of society as a whole, not only in America but also in the country to which Marr brought his experiences: Germany of the 1860s. Contact with the system of colonial racist discourse contributed greatly to Marr's transformation from a radical democrat to a racial anti-Semite.[37]

In order to understand fully the evolution of Marr's thinking, however, we need to consider the processes of adaptation that fused racist and religious anti-Jewish discourses. Marr's first anti-Jewish pamphlet, which appeared before his memoirs, was not published by himself but by a former friend and fellow democrat, Friedrich August Hobelmann, a supporter of Jewish emancipation. Hobelmann sought Marr's support for a law that would have granted equal rights to the Jews of Bremen, but Marr's response of 4 June 1862 dashed Hobelmann's hopes. Apparently, Marr anticipated a strong reaction, and the text suggests that he deliberately provoked it, since he mentioned at the very beginning of his letter that he would not object to Hobelmann using or even publishing his remarks to spark a debate "among honest men."[38] Hobelmann was indeed outraged and published Marr's response only nine days later. It appeared in the form of an open letter in the supplement of the German newspaper *Courier an der Weser* and marked the beginning of Marr's career as an anti-Semitic ideologue.

In his letter, Marr's anticlerical approach reveals implicit anti-Jewish dimensions. Marr claimed that as long as the Church was not separated from the state, Jewish emancipation would only be a component of the distorted and unenlightened system of church–state relations.[39] This view appears to have been influenced by Bruno Bauer, who wrote in one of his essays: "We must be free ourselves before we think of inviting others [Jews] also to take part in freedom."[40] But Marr faced a dilemma. His attacks on religion did not provide sufficient justification for his increasingly radical distinctions between Jews and non-Jews in his writings.[41] Marr, in the words of Zimmerman, therefore used "a better method for distinguishing between being a Jew and non-Jew, a method relating to *race*."[42] He began to fuse his anticlerical approach with racial categories. For the first time, Marr invoked racial arguments to deny that Jews were capable of integration: "I believe that Judaism, because of its racial particularity [*Stammeseigentümlichkeit*], is incompatible with our political and social life. It must, because of its inner nature, seek to build a state within a state."[43]

From the outset Marr's racializing of the Jews is interwoven with anti-black categories. One quite obvious example can be found in his comparison of the granting of rights to the Jews in Bremen to the granting of rights to apes: "You would not permit ten thousand monkeys to settle in Bremen," Marr claimed in the letter to Hobelmann. Categories of colonial racism were thus adopted and transferred into a (newly created) discourse of modern anti-Semitism. Tellingly, in the same letter no other pair of opposites seems to express the radicalism of the chasm between "orientalized" Jews and his own racial group better than the contrast between black and white: "The oriental element [of Judaism] is politically and socially incompatible with ours, just as black and white will never produce a color other than gray."[44]

In the aftermath of the public outcry that his letter had provoked in Germany, Marr elaborated on his anti-Jewish ideas in *Der Judenspiegel* (The Mirror of the Jews).[45] In this hastily written book, which was published in June 1862, he drew an even more explicit connection between "Jews" and "Blacks," claiming that "Negro blood" could also be found within the Jewish body.[46] This argument extended the strong European tradition, dating back to the Middle Ages or even Hellenistic times, that Jews were "black" or at least swarthy[47]—while simultaneously indicating a significant shift from the color of the (outer) skin to the color of the inner nature: the blood.[48] "Inner blackness" is a construction that appears to have made the invisible differences of the (highly integrated) German Jews more plausible. According to MacMaster, "Blacks" functioned as the "basic model of the inferior racial Other," which was used to "blacken" and racialize the Jews from 1860 onwards[49]—not unlike and interrelated with the "essentializing" strategies of gender describing the Jews as effeminate. The formation of anti-Semitic discourse was thereby not only accompanied by a growing tendency to define national identity in racial terms[50] (in which the Jews were defined as the internal Other), but also—as MacMaster pointed out— by a simultaneous shift within the colonial anti-black discourse, which followed the violent partition of the "Dark Continent" at the end of the nineteenth century and the American Civil War.[51]

Marr's long article "Toward an understanding of the Events in North America"[52] also addressed the issue of "Blacks," this time with reference to slavery. The text appeared in the newspaper *Freischütz* in February 1863, a few months after the publication of *Der Judenspiegel*, and after the outbreak of the American Civil War in 1861. Marr's interpretation of U.S. society was understood by the German public as a defense of slavery. According to Jacob Audorf, an activist of the international labor movement, Marr claimed that "the Negroes are closer to beasts than to human beings."[53] Following an almost identical structure of composition, Marr also ascribed inferior physical characteristics to Jews and quoted from *The Jews and the German State* (1859), a book written by the well-known anti-Semitic author Heinrich Naudh (a.k.a. Heinrich Nordmann).[54]

The ways in which Marr addressed the "racial issue" led his critics to compare him to white supremacists in the American South. One anonymous liberal stated: "Marr despises the 'race' of the Jews … just as a pure-blooded Southern Yankee despises the colored race, and any person in whose veins flows even one drop of African blood."[55] As a self-confident liberal, he asserted that "Marr's attempt to find supporters for the American South's Yankeeism here, in Germany, is doomed to failure … [and that] we have already gone beyond the stage of fine distinctions between humans on the basis of 'races' and 'religions.'"[56] Marr finally lost the respect he had enjoyed among the democratic-radical community in his adopted home Hamburg and gave up his political posts.[57]

This complex shift toward racial anti-Semitism becomes condensed in the figure of the "black" Jew, who stands for the system of racial hierarchy itself. For Marr, Jews now not only became something akin to "primitive black tribes" and primates; he also criticized them as the inventors of slavery and mass executions (a reference to the Old Testament), in order to legitimate depriving them of their civil rights in a new (non-religious) manner: "That race which under Joseph's ministry introduced slavery, which under Mordechai's ministry committed mass slaughter of men, which even to this day celebrates the memory of these horrors in the political Purim festival, is not entitled … as Jews to equal civil rights."[58]

In his early anti-Semitic texts Marr's arguments made reference to several other discourses, including religious, biological, and cultural ones.[59] The simultaneous "racialization" and combination of traditionally religious, ethnological, and politico-economical critical strands of argumentation reveals the multilayered process of construction of racial anti-Semitism *in nuce*. Consequently, Marr's texts should not be read as confused and contradictory, but can be regarded as an obvious effort to unite and transform diverse discursive strands into one single anti-Semitic discourse. It is above all this process of transformation that makes Marr's work so instructive for studying the shift toward racial anti-Semitism. In these texts he inscribes both the "racial knowledge" he acquired overseas and the virulently anti-Semitic discourses of his immediate environment.

This becomes evident when we examine Marr's justification for his resistance to Jews in Bremen. He cites traditionally religious arguments, while refuting them at the same time.[60] Then he goes on to claim that Jews are simply a social rather than a religious group, only to remark later that Jews were a type of "tribe" (*Stamm*) with specific traits, which he describes earlier in the text as "racial" characteristics. But when Marr claims that "the Jews" are solely interested in maximizing their own profits, he uses religious, social, *and* political arguments. He regards religion as both cultural product and social (racial) nature, inextricably intertwined in the political realm, a combination that Marr regarded as extremely dangerous: "Religiously they are commanded to do so, socially this is their nature, politically this is a consequence of both."[61]

Of course, one did not have to travel to America in order to encounter colonial racism and racial theories. In other parts of Europe, people also worked intensively on similar processes of adapting colonial racism to different discursive and social fields. For example, the British race theorist Robert Knox claimed that the concept of "race" should not only be seen as connected to "Negroes, Hottentots, Red Indians and savages," but as detached from the colonial setting and thus part of inner-European contexts.[62] Racial differences between European nations were, according to Knox, just as important as colonial race distinctions.[63]

Categories of colonial racisms were thus increasingly transferred into inner-European processes of group formation, be it the nation as a whole or other social and ethnic groups inside the nation such as workers, anti-socials, homosexuals, or Jews. The real difference distinguishing the time after 1860 from the preceding period is not biologization, even if it became much more dominant, but the trend toward the multiplication of *one* European race into numerous inner-white racisms. To analyze the relationships between these different forms of race discourses (each with their complex net of intertwined patterns of legitimization) remains a future task for further academic research to tackle.

Notes

1. See Jürgen Kocka, "Asymmetric Historical Comparison: The Case of the German Sonderweg," *History and Theory* 38 (1999): 40–50.
2. Christian Geulen, *Geschichte des Rassismus* (Munich, 2007), 88.
3. See Rudolf Augstein, ed., *Historikerstreit: Die Dokumentation der Kontroverse um die Einzigartigkeit der nationalsozialistischen Judenvernichtung* (München, Zürich, 1987); Dan Diner, ed., *Ist der Nationalsozialismus Geschichte? Zu Historisierung und Historikerstreit* (Frankfurt am Main, 1987).
4. For a review of the comparative research on Fascism during the last 15 years, see Roger Griffin and Matthew Feldman, *Fascism: Critical Concepts in Political Science*, 5 vols. (London and New York, 2004); Aristotle A. Kallis, ed., *The Fascism Reader* (London and New York, 2003). See also Sven Reichardt's recent essay "Neue Wege der vergleichenden Faschismusforschung," *Mittelweg* 36, no. 1 (2007): 9–25, which traces the "third wave" of comparative research on fascism that emerged in the early 1990s in Great Britain and the United States but has only recently enriched discussions in Germany.
5. The study of German colonial history began around the same time. Formerly this episode of German history was considered largely irrelevant and inconsequential, a view that has fundamentally changed in the past decade. This change resulted from a growing impact of Anglo-American postcolonial studies and confrontation with the issues of globalization, which encouraged the academic study of the subject and awakened public interest in the topic. See Sebastian Conrad and Shalini Randeria, eds., *Jenseits des Eurozentrismus: Postkoloniale Perspektiven in den Geschichts- und Kulturwissenschaften* (Frankfurt, 2002). In the context of dealing with the German colonial past, anti-black (or -white) racism also became the focus of attention. An increasing number of studies on colonial racist discourses and practices have been published in the past few years, focusing specifically on the period of the German Kaiserreich and the first half of the twentieth century. See

Frank Becker, *Rassenmischehen–Mischlinge–Rassentrennung: Zur Politik der Rasse im deutschen Kolonialreich* (Stuttgart, 2004); Anette Dietrich, *Weiße Weiblichkeiten: Konstruktion von 'Rasse' und Geschlecht im deutschen Kolonialismus* (Bielefeld, 2007); Sara Friedrichsmayer et al., eds., *Imperialist Imagination: German Colonialism and its Legacy* (Ann Arbor, MI, 1998); Pascal Grosse, *Kolonialismus, Eugenik und bürgerliche Gesellschaft in Deutschland 1850–1918* (Frankfurt, 2000); Gudrun Hentges, *Die Schattenseiten der Aufklärung: Die Darstellung von Juden und "Wilden" in den philosophischen Schriften des 18. und 19. Jahrhunderts* (Schwalbach/Ts., 1999); Birthe Kundrus, ed., *Phantasiereiche: Zur Kulturgeschichte des deutschen Kolonialismus* (Frankfurt, 2003); Frank Oliver Sobich, *"Schwarze Bestien, rote Gefahr:" Rassismus und Antisozialismus im deutschen Kaiserreich* (Frankfurt am Main, 2006). In the meantime, the first results of substantial research on the history of Afro-Germans and "blacks" in Germany and Europe have become available. See Fatima El-Tayeb, *Schwarze Deutsche: Der Diskurs um "Rasse" und nationale Identität, 1890–1933* (Frankfurt, 2001). Peter Martin, *Schwarze Teufel, edle Mohren: Afrikaner in Geschichte und Bewusstsein der Deutschen* (Hamburg, 2001); Sandra Maß, *Weiße Helden, schwarze Krieger: Zur Geschichte kolonialer Männlichkeit in Deutschland, 1918–1964* (Köln, 2006).

6. Jürgen Zimmerer, "Die Geburt des 'Ostlandes' aus dem Geiste des Kolonialismus. Die nationalsozialistische Eroberungs- und Beherrschungspolitik in (post-)kolonialer Perspektive," *Sozial.Geschichte* 19, no. 1 (February 2004); Jürgen Zimmerer, "Holocaust und Kolonialismus: Beitrag zu einer Archäologie des genozidalen Gedankens," *Zeitschrift für Geschichtswissenschaft* 51 (2003): 1098–119; see also Philipp Ther, "Imperial Instead of National History: Positioning Modern German History on the Map of European Empires," in *Imperial Rule,* edited by Alexei Miller and Alfred Rieber (Budapest, 2004): 47–68; David Blackbourn, "Das Kaiserreich transnational: Eine Skizze," in *Das Kaiserreich transnational: Deutschland in der Welt 1871–1914,* edited by Sebastian Conrad and Jürgen Osterhammel (Göttingen, 2004), 302–24; Janntje Böhlke-Itzen, *Kolonialschuld und Entschädigung: Der deutsche Völkermord an den Hereros, 1904–1907* (Frankfurt, 2004).

7. See Robert Gerwarth and Stephan Malinowski, "Der Holocaust als „kolonialer Genozid"? Europäische Kolonialgewalt und nationalsozialistischer Vernichtungskrieg," *Geschichte und Gesellschaft* 33 (2007): 439–66; Pascal Grosse, "What Does German Colonialism Have to Do with National Socialism? A Conceptual Framework," in *Germany's Colonial Pasts,* edited by Eric Ames et al. (Lincoln, 2005): 115–34; Birthe Kundrus, "Kontinuitäten, Parallelen, Rezeptionen: Überlegungen zur 'Kolonialisierung' des Nationalsozialismus," *Werkstattgeschichte* 43 (2006): 45–62; Birthe Kundrus, "Von den Herero zum Holocaust? Einige Bemerkungen zur aktuellen Debatte," *Mittelweg* (2005): 82–91; Birthe Kundrus, "Von Windhoek nach Nürnberg? Koloniale 'Mischehenverbote' und die nationalsozialistische Rassengesetzbebung," in *"Phantasiereiche": Der deutsche Kolonialismus aus kulturgeschichtlicher Perspektive,* edited by Birthe Kundrus (Frankfurt, 2003), 110–

31; Gesine Krüger, "Coming to Terms with the Past," *GHI Bulletin* 37 (2005): 45–49; Gesine Krüger, *Kriegsbewältigung und Geschichtsbewusstsein: Realität, Deutung und Verarbeitung des deutschen Kolonialkrieges in Namibia, 1904–1907* (Göttingen, 1999): 62–69.

8. In the one case, according to Herf, we find the "mere" will to exploit, and in the other, a "paranoid" will to exterminate. Jeffrey Herf, "Comparative Perspectives on Anti-Semitism: Radical Anti-Semitism in the Holocaust and American White Racism," *Journal of Genocide Research* 9, no. 4 (2007): 575–600.

9. See Dirk Moses, "The Fate of Blacks and Jews: A Response to Jeffrey Herf," *Journal of Genocide Research* 10, no. 2 (2008): 1–19.

10. Dirk Moses, "Conceptual Blockages and Definitional Dilemmas in the 'Racial Century': Genocides of Indigenous Peoples and the Holocaust," *Patterns of Prejudice* 36, no. 4 (2002): 19.

11. Neil MacMaster, *Racism in Europe, 1870–2000* (Houndmills, 2001): 1–12; Neil MacMaster, "'Black Jew–White Negro': Anti-Semitism and the Construction of Cross-Racial Stereotypes," *Nationalism and Ethnic Politics* 6, no. 4 (2000): 65–82; Robert Miles, *Race after "Race Relations"* (London, 1993); Robert Miles, "Explaining Racism in Contemporary Europe," in *Racism: Modernity and Identity on the Western Front*, edited by Ali Rattansi and Sally Westwood (Cambridge, 1993), 189–221; See also Paul Gilroy, *The Black Atlantic: Modernity and Double Consciousness* (London, 1996): 205–23; Bryan Cheyette, "White Skin, Black Masks: Jews and Jewishness in the Writings of George Eliot and Frantz Fanon," in *Cultural Readings of Imperialism: Edward Said and the Gravity of History*, edited by Keith Ansell-Pearson, Benita Parry, Judith Squires (London, 1997), 106–9.

12. George Mosse, *Towards the Final Solution: A History of European Racism* (London, 1978), 56, 70; MacMaster, *Racism in Europe*, 5.

13. MacMaster, *Racism in Europe*, 5.

14. For examples of this type of scholarship, see Gunilla Budde, Sebastian Conrad ,and Oliver Janz, eds., *Transnationale Geschichte: Themen, Tendenzen und Theorien* (Göttingen, 2006); Sebastian Conrad and Jürgen Osterhammel, *Das Kaiserreich transnational: Deutschland in der Welt, 1871–1914* (Göttingen, 2004); Kimberlé Crenshaw, "Mapping the Margins: Intersectionality, Identity Politics, and Violence against Women of Color," *Stanford Law Review* 43, no. 6 (1991): 1241–99; Elsa Dorlin, *La matrice de la race: Généalogie sexuelle et coloniale de la nation française* (Paris, 2006); Heinz-Gerhard Haupt, "Die Geschichte Europas als vergleichende Geschichtsschreibung," *Comparativ* 14, no. 3 (2004): 83–97; Heinz-Gerhard Haupt and Jürgen Kocka, eds., *Geschichte und Vergleich: Ansätze und Ergebnisse international vergleichender Geschichtsschreibung* (Frankfurt, 1996); Hartmut Kaelble and Jürgen Schriewer, eds., *Vergleich und Transfer: Komparatistik in den Geschichts-, Sozial- und Kulturwissenschaften* (Frankfurt, 2003); Michael Kearney, "The Local and the Global: The Anthropology of Globalization and Transnationalism," *Annual Review of Anthropology* 24 (1995): 547–65; Cornelia Klinger and

Gudrun-Axeli Knapp, "Achsen der Ungleichheit–Achsen der Differenz: Verhält-nisbestimmungen von Klasse, Geschlecht, 'Rasse'/Ethnizität," *Transit. Europäische Revue* 29 (2005): 72–96; Matthias Middell, "Kulturtransfer und Historische Komparatistik: Thesen zu ihrem Verhältnis," *Comparativ* 10 (2000): 7–41; Francesca Miller "Feminisms and Transnationalism," *Gender & History* 10 (1998): 569–80; Jürgen Osterhammel, "Transnationale Gesellschaftsgeschichte: Erweiterung oder Alternative?" *Geschichte und Gesellschaft* 27 (2001): 464–79; Kiran Klaus Patel, *Nach der Nationalfixiertheit. Perspektiven einer transnationalen Geschichte* (Berlin, 2004); Philipp Ther, "Beyond the Nation: The Relation Basis of a Comparative History of Germany and Europe," *Central European History* 36 (2003): 45–73. For a review of relevant previous work, see Deborah Cohen and Maura O'Connor, eds., *Comparison and History: Europe in Cross-National Perspective* (New York, 2003), 181–97; Peter Mandler, *History and National Life* (London, 2002); Donald R. Kelly, "Grounds for Comparison," *Storia della Storiografia* 39 (2001): 3–16.

15. See Susanne Zantop, *Kolonialphantasien im vorkolonialen Deutschland (1770–1870)* (Berlin, 1999).

16. Moshe Zimmermann, *Wilhelm Marr: The Patriarch of Anti-Semitism* (New York, 1986), 15; Paul Lawrence Rose, *Revolutionary Antisemitism in Germany From Kant To Wagner* (Princeton, 1990), 278.

17. Wilhelm Marr, *Das Junge Deutschland in der Schweiz: Ein Beitrag zur Geschichte der geheimen Verbindungen unserer Tage* (Leipzig, 1846).

18. A Germany with a monarch such as Frederick William IV, the Prussian king, would be, according to Marr, a monarchical-barbaric Germany, which led him to temporary particularism; a republic not embracing all Germany would be preferable to a Germany without a republic. Zimmermann, *Wilhelm Marr*, 27.

19. When exactly the catchphrase "anti-Semite" arose remains controversial. While the majority of scholars attribute the popularization of the term to Wilhelm Marr or his circle (See Werner Bergmann, *Geschichte des Antisemitismus,* 3rd ed. (Munich, 2006), 6; Peter G.J. Pulzer, *Die Entstehung des politischen Antisemitismus in Deutschland und Österreich, 1867–1914* (Göttingen, 2004), 19; Sven Brömsel, "Antisemitismus," in *Nietzsche Handbuch. Leben–Werk–Wirkung,* edited by Henning Ottmann (Stuttgart, 2000), 184; Annette Hein, *"Es ist viel 'Hitler' in Wagner": Rassismus und antisemitische Deutschtumsideologie in den Bayreuther Blättern (1878–1938)* (Tübingen, 1996), 123; Otto Ladendorf, *Historisches Schlagwörterbuch: Ein Versuch* (Strasbourg and Berlin, 1906), 7.), Cornelia Schmitz-Berning dates the first appearance of the word "Antisemit" to the year 1822 and Hein to 1860, while the *Deutsches Fremdwörterbuch* (1913–1988) dates it to 1875. The word "antisemitisch" could be found in the 1865 *Staatslexikon* by Rotteck and Welcker. This was an isolated instance, however, which had no lasting impact, much like the appearance of the word "unsemitisch" that same year in the *Staatswörterbuch* by Bluntschli and Berater. The Jewish scholar Moritz Steinschneider had already called the French historian and philologist Ernest Renan to task for his "anti-Se-

mitic prejudices" in 1860. Also see Rose, *Revolutionary Antisemitism in Germany*, 288; Zimmermann, *Wilhelm Marr*, X.

20. The young Berlin secondary school teacher Ernst Henrici, in turn, was the first politician to popularize Marr's racially orientated propaganda and the "Anti-semiten-Liga." Together with Bernhard Förster, a fellow teacher and Nietzsche's brother-in-law, and Max Liebermann von Sonnenberg, he organized the *Anti-semiten-Petition*, which was submitted to Otto von Bismarck in April 1882 and bore two hundred and twenty-five thousand signatures, mainly from northern and eastern Prussia. See Pulzer, *Die Entstehung des politischen Antisemitismus in Deutschland und Österreich*,140–41.

21. Ludwig A. Feuerbach, *Das Wesen des Christentums* (Leipzig 1841), new ed. by Erich Thies. Feuerbach's collected writings in 6 vols.; vol. 4 (Frankfurt: Suhrkamp, 1971) (English: The Essence of Christianity, 1855).

22. Both Zimmermann and Rose extensively discuss Marr's political conflicts with liberal Jews but only briefly mention his stay in Costa Rica and ignore the connections between Marr's time spent abroad and his turn toward racism. See Zimmermann, *Wilhelm Marr*; Rose, *Revolutionary Antisemitism in Germany*. See also Pulzer, *Die Entstehung des politischen Antisemitismus in Deutschland und Österreich*,105–6. He cites "economic conditions and the political climate" as the central reasons for Marr's rebirth as an anti-Semite. In addition, Marr's decision "to shift the fight against the Jews from the religious to the racial field" was, as Pulzer elucidates, a "clever move: … [G]iven the growing indifference towards religion among the middle and working classes, an appeal to rally in defense of Christianity was unlikely to evoke an enthusiastic reaction. The element of the pseudo-scientific, the topical and seemingly objective and dialectical sides of this tinpot Darwin rendered this new approach attractive to those who believed they had outgrown the childish trappings of traditional Christianity. Marr deliberately rejected all motifs of religious intolerance." Zimmermann, apart from his otherwise lucid political contextualization of Marr's biography, prefers speculating on the role played by Jewish and "half-Jewish" women in forming Marr's immense hatred of the Jews. According to Zimmermann, Marr drew from one of his marriages, which ended in divorce in 1877, "the insurmountable central point of his racism: that pure racial characteristics (his second wife) were preferable to mixed race (his first and third wives)." See Zimmermann, *Wilhelm Marr*, 46, 70–73, quote on 71.

23. Zimmermann, *Wilhelm Marr*, 35.

24. The report avoids specific dates but, according to the author, it refers mainly to Marr's experiences during the first year of his stay in America in the early 1850s.

25. Heike Paul, *Kulturkontakt und Racial Presences: Afro-Amerikaner und die deutsche Amerika-Literatur, 1815–1914* (Heidelberg, 2005), 30.

26. Ibid., 2.

27. Ibid., 8; Ulla Haselstein, *Die Gabe der Zivilisation: Kultureller Austausch und literarische Textpraxis in Amerika, 1682–1861* (Munich, 2000), 19.

28. Wilhelm Marr, *Reise nach Central-America*, vol 1., 2nd ed. (1863; Hamburg, 1870): 117.

29. The motto chosen for his 1846 book *Young Germany in Switzerland* was "Freiheit, Gleichheit, Humanität!" (Freedom, Equality, Humanity!).

30. Ibid., 118.

31. Ibid., 118.

32. Ibid., 119.

33. Ibid., 168.

34. Ibid., 168. Whilst communicating with the "colored population," identified by the narrator as "Jamaican Mulattos" and "Haitian Negroes," political conversations arose in which the narrator finds that the "colored" talked "reasonably about the politics of their countries." However, the apparent closeness between the black people's bloody fight for liberation and Marr's political revolutionary past in Germany is not underlined. In fact, in the next moment, the narrator believes he has found proof of a general disability to "actually autonomously produce ideas," a thought directly connected to Euro-American discourses on race and gender.

35. Marr, *Reise nach Central-Amerika*, vol. 1, 169.

36. In the second volume of his travelog we can also read: "As it is, in these countries reason forces thoughts into my mind that I would have condemned only six months ago. *Species* and *degeneration, autonomy* and *reflection*[.]" Marr, *Reise nach Central-Amerika*, vol. 1, 47.

37. Toni Morrison, "On the Backs of Blacks," in *Arguing Immigration*, edited by Nicholaus Mills (New York, 1994), 97–100; Paul, *Kulturkontakt und Racial Presences*, 2.

38. Wilhelm Marr to [Friedrich August?] Hobelmann, 4 June 1862, published by Hobelmann in the Supplement of the *Courier an der Weser* 161 (13 June 1862) reprinted and trans. Zimmermann, *Wilhelm Marr*, 116–18.

39. Ibid., 118.

40. Bruno Bauer, *Die Judenfrage* (Braunschweig, 1843), trans. Zimmermann, *Wilhelm Marr*, 44.

41. Ibid.

42. Ibid.

43. Emphasis added. Marr to Hobelmann, reprinted and trans. Zimmermann, *Wilhelm Marr*, 117; Moshe Zimmermann, "Gabriel Riesser und Wilhelm Marr im Meinungsstreit: Die Judenfrage als Gegenstand der Auseinandersetzung zwischen Liberalen und Radikalen in Hamburg (1848–1862)," *Zeitschrift des Vereins für Hamburgische Geschichte* 61 (1975): 59–84; Rose, *Revolutionary Antisemitism in Germany*, 282.

44. Marr to Hobelmann, reprinted and trans. Zimmermann, *Wilhelm Marr*, 117.

45. The letter caused an enormous debate in Hamburg and a fierce attack on Marr. The Berlin satirist Julius Stettenheim, Marr's former disciple, wrote a manifesto, which represented Marr as a "Jew-eater [*Judenfresser*]." A play was also performed in which Marr was portrayed as the evil Haman. Zimmermann, *Wilhelm Marr*, 46.

46. Wilhelm Marr, *Der Judenspiegel* (Hamburg, 1862), 51.

47. "Since Satan was identified as black and the Jews were perceived as his allies, they were also depicted as black. … As early as Hellenistic times," anti-Jewish literature "maintained that the Jews were lepers (having defective skin) who were expelled from Egypt (which made them black)." See Abraham Melamed, *The Image of the Black in Jewish Culture: A History of the Other* (London, 2002), 31. In contrast to Melamed, Neil MacMaster points out that the earlier negative marker was "not a form of racism in the modern sense," but a common symbol in "an almost universal system of meanings through which the symbolism of blackness denoted all that was most feared (the devil, Hell, the night, pollution, magic, etc.)." MacMaster "Black Jew–White Negro," 67. See also Jana Husmann-Kastein, "Schwarz-Weiß. Farb- und Geschlechtssymbolik in den Anfängen der Rassenkonstruktionen," in *Weiß-Weißsein-Whiteness*, edited by Martina Tißberger et al. (Frankfurt, 2006), 43–60. For a psychoanalytic perspective on the "black Jew," see Sander Gilman, *Difference and Pathology: Stereotypes of Sexuality, Race and Madness* (Ithaca, 1985); Sander Gilman, *Freud, Race, and Gender* (Princeton, 1993), 19–22, 158–59, 163–64.

48. This resembled the structural development of white racism in the United States after the Civil War, which manifested itself in the "one-drop rule."

49. The image of the "black Jew" symbolized not only a "synthesis of two projections of Otherness within the same code," as Sander Gilman put it, but signified, according to MacMaster, a peculiar change in the mid-nineteenth century, when Jews were not only described as "black," but were specifically racialized as "black Negroes," "black Africans," or even as "white Negroes." MacMaster, "Black Jew–White Negro," 67; Gilman, *Difference and Pathology*, 31.

50. While the Jew was "Africanized," the very idea of Western culture with its roots in Greek civilization was "whitened," not least through the systematic denegation of Afro-Asiatic cultures as being the sources of Greek learning. Martin Bernal, *Black Athena: The Afroasiatic Roots of Classical Civilisation* (London, 1991).

51. MacMaster, "Black Jew–White Negro," 71.

52. Wilhelm Marr, "Zum Verständnis der Nordamerikanischen Wirren," *Der Freischütz. Politik, Unterhaltung, Lokal-Zeitung* (Hamburg, 1863).

53. Jacob Audorf, *Herr Marr und die Arbeiterfrage, nebst einem Wort an Deutschlands Arbeiter* (Hamburg, 1863), 14.

54. H[einrich] Naudh, *Die Juden und der Deutsche Staat*, 3rd rev. ed. (Berlin, 1861).

55. Quoted in Zimmermann, *Wilhelm Marr*, 49.

56. Ibid.

57. Zimmermann, *Wilhelm Marr*, 49.

58. Marr to Hobelmann, reprinted and trans. Zimmermann, *Wilhelm Marr*, 117.

59. See the work of Colin Kidd, which shows how strongly racial and religious discourses were intertwined, and how the racial discourse began as a theological construct. Colin Kidd, *The Forging of Races: Race and Scripture in the Protestant Atlantic World, 1600–2000* (Cambridge, UK, 2006).

60. He notes, for example, "You would not permit [them] to settle in Bremen. Not for religious reasons, oh no! But because monasticism endangers the common weal." Marr to Hobelmann, reprinted and trans. Zimmermann, *Wilhelm Marr,* 117 .
61. Ibid.
62. Robert Knox, *The Races of Men: A Fragment* (1850; Miami, 1969), 39.
63. Ibid., 24–35.

Chapter 7

Transatlantic Anthropological Dialogue and "the Other": Felix von Luschan's Research in America, 1914–1915

John David Smith

Today historians agree that the Atlantic world of the nineteenth and early twentieth centuries was an interconnected "transcultural space," one that reconciled a rich exchange of cultural influences and selective appropriations between Germany and the United States.[1]

Writing recently historian Christof Mauch remarked that "At the turn of the twentieth century, the Atlantic was still a geographic obstacle to frequent cross-continental encounters and a barrier to communication. … Only a few of the more prominent German scholars and none of the leading German politicians or members of the ruling nobility visited the United States." While yes, direct transatlantic contacts were rare, Mauch notes correctly that "the cultural and intellectual exchange between Germans and Americans was nevertheless intense." He describes this "intercultural transfer" as "a multilayered and far-reaching process." Many Germans came to the United States "to encounter 'the other': everything that their country was not."[2] This chapter focuses on Austrian anthropologist Felix von Luschan (1854–1924) who came to America to research "the other." In doing so, however, he may in fact have found himself.

In July 1914 Luschan, then professor of anthropology at the University of Berlin and curator of the anthropological collection at Berlin's Royal Ethnological Museum, traveled to Australia for an extended research trip. Luschan sought to gather evidence to support monogenism, to examine the Tulgai skull, and to measure indigenous peoples in order to collect anthropometric data. Understanding the development of Luschan's views regarding "race" is essential to explaining what appear to be contradictions in his ideas regarding "inferior" peoples worldwide.[3]

Luschan became Imperial Germany's leading physical anthropologist following Rudolf Virchow's death in 1902. With an ambitious research agenda ahead of him, Luschan traveled to the Pacific, planning fieldwork in Australia, New Zealand, New Guinea, India, Indonesia, and Southern Babylonia. The prestigious British Association for the Advancement of Science met in Sydney that year and its members invited Luschan to present a lecture on eugenics. In his lecture "Culture and Degeneration," Luschan identified four serious phenomena that he believed were leading to the degeneration of "civilized" societies worldwide: the increase of mental disorder, the increase of crime, the breakup of urban families, and the deliberate restriction of birthrates.[4] Adding luster to his Australian invitation, Luschan received an honorary doctorate of science from the University of Adelaide where, he recalled, the audience cheered (*gecheert*) him more enthusiastically than he had ever been before.[5]

Luschan's visit to Australia ended on a decidedly negative note, however. It was the only unlucky journey of his lifetime, he later recalled bitterly. On 4 August 1914, Great Britain declared war on Germany, and the Australians' warmth toward Luschan soon turned to ice. An Austrian, Luschan gradually felt the sting of xenophobia as his Australian hosts grew suspicious of nationals from the Central Powers.[6] On 2 September, Luschan informed his colleagues at the Berlin museum that the outbreak of the war had forced him to abandon his research trip: the Australians had revoked his invitation to work at their national museum; they also forbade his travel to New Zealand. Fearful of possible internment by the Australians, Luschan and his wife left Australia aboard an American ship, the SS *Ventura*, en route to a neutral port. The United States had not yet entered World War I (it declared war on the Central Powers in April 1917) and Luschan expected to make his way back to Germany via the United States.[7]

As he steamed toward Samoa and Hawaii, Luschan's thoughts gravitated toward Germany. He craved information on the situation back in his adopted home. He wanted to support the German war effort. He worried about his specimens at the museum. He needed to communicate with one of his students at the university. He wondered about the condition of his Berlin flat. And he worried about his finances.

Despite his concerns, Luschan took a detour that delayed his return to Germany, added data to his scientific research, and enriched his life. In mid-September he disembarked the SS *Ventura* in Hawaii to conduct anthropological field work. Though Luschan realized that Hawaii, then an American territory, could prove to be dangerous if war broke out between the United States and Japan, he nevertheless concluded that Honolulu should provide opportunities for him to conduct academic work and to earn some much needed money. Fortuitously, Luschan's old friend William T. Brigham (1841–1926), director of the Bernice P. Bishop Museum of Ethnology in Honolulu, offered him hospitality, a small grant, and help lining up subjects for his anthropometric research.[8] Luschan planned to spend a week in Honolulu and then make his way to San Francisco.[9]

The hard-working Luschan "found so delightful anthropological work in Honolulu" that he ultimately remained in the city for four weeks and put his time in Hawaii to good use.[10] He organized the anthropological collection of the Bishop Museum, classifying and measuring eighty-three human remains and four associated funerary objects of Lanai's first inhabitants. He also measured contemporary adult males. Luschan, who justified increased military and naval expenditures because he believed that war served as an engine for human progress, applauded American efforts to fortify Hawaii.[11] "The military facilities and the preparations made by the Americans in Honolulu," he wrote in 1915, "especially the heavy artillery, made a great and lasting impression on me." He later recalled that the Luschans' four weeks in Honolulu "were the best time we ever had."[12]

On 15 October Luschan finally arrived in San Francisco. Over the next two and a half months he and his wife traveled eastward, visiting museums and sightseeing (including "two wonderful days at the Grand Canyon" where, much to Luschan's delight, they observed "Indians"). "Von Luschan is in Chicago now," Luschan's friend Franz Boas of Columbia University wrote late in the month, "and we hope to see him here shortly. You can imagine that the whole situation of Germany keeps us in a constant state of excitement and worry."[13] While Luschan shared Boas's pro-German sympathies about the war, he nevertheless took advantage of the opportunity to travel in America. Perhaps to his surprise, Luschan found museum collections in Chicago, New York, and Washington comparable to the best museums in Europe, even his prized museum in Berlin.

In order to help finance his trip, Luschan delivered many illustrated lectures at American universities, including Johns Hopkins, Cornell, Chicago, and the Universities of California, Wisconsin, Illinois, and Pennsylvania, and at German-American societies in several major cities. Having prepared to lecture in Australia, New Zealand, and India, Luschan traveled with what he described as "a large quantity of my very best slides."[14] In the United States he received the standard speaker's fee of $50 per lecture. Luschan also addressed the American Anthropological Association in Philadelphia on "Convergency," arguing that physical and cultural characteristics were related, not independent variables.[15] Summarizing his American activities in 1914, Luschan recalled: "We were especially delighted with the University of Illinois, Urbana, where I gave seven lectures, attended by most of the Professors and many hundreds of students."[16]

Luschan had first inquired about the possibility of lecturing at Illinois while still in Honolulu, contacting James H. Breasted, the renowned Egyptologist and director of the University of Chicago's Haskell Oriental Museum. Breasted wrote to University of Illinois President, Edmund J. James, proposing that Luschan lecture at Illinois. "Von Luschan holds the greatest post in his line in Europe," Breasted informed James, "and easily ranks among the leading three or four anthropologists of the world. Indeed I should put him at the head of the list. He speaks and writes perfect English."[17] Impressed by Luschan's credentials, James agreed to have Luschan present a series of lectures, "if they do not cost us too much."[18]

Luschan accepted James's terms. During his busy week at the university Luschan presented several formal lectures, gave an informal talk before the faculty, and attended numerous receptions and dinners.[19] The *Champaign Daily-Gazette* reported that in his lecture on "Excavations of a Hittite Capital," Luschan underscored the relation between biblical history and recent discoveries of archaeological exploration.[20] The *Daily Illini* published that Luschan based his lecture on "Anthropology of Western Asia" on his extensive fieldwork in Asia Minor, and that in his talk he traced the evolution of Arabs, Greeks, and Turks from Syrian origins.[21] In his lecture on "Culture and Degeneration," the newspaper explained, Luschan employed charts to emphasize his points concerning the deleterious effects of alcoholism and physical degeneration on a nation's well-being. "The great excess of urban mortality," he concluded, "both in Europe and in America is due to drink and public conscience must insist on absolute isolation of both criminals and drunkards as the only remedy for this evil." In his lecture Luschan also implored administrators at American colleges and universities to establish professorships for anthropologists. These scholars, he insisted, were essential to remedy social evils.[22]

In his lecture on "Polygenism or Unity of Mankind" Luschan ridiculed the state of contemporary European ethnological scholarship. There was, he explained,

a learned modern Anthropologist, Prof. Klaatsch in Breslau [who] pretends, that from two paleolithic human skeletons found in France and now in the Berlin prehistoric museum[,] one is to be connected with gorilla, the other with orangutan. Much farer [sic] go some of his students, who connect the tall Negroes with the gorilla, and the African Pygmies with the chimpanzee, the Chinese with the orang[utan] and the Japanese with the Gibbon. An Austrian Dilettante, Lanz Liebenfels even connects the white races—as far as they have blue eyes and light hair—with the angels and pretends that the colored races were originating from some diabolic incest between these angels and the apes. He finds the proof for this theory in some dark passages of the Bible and on the Monolith of Salmanassar, where soldiers bring some small long-tailed macacus to the king.

Nonetheless, Luschan insisted that Europeans were conducting serious anthropological research. After his discussion of "the various primitive races of mankind," Luschan announced: "The great question is, if these races are related to one another like the different races of horses, or if some of them are so distant from one another, as horse is from ass."[23]

In his lecture Luschan criticized American polygenists for justifying slavery and other forms of racial discrimination. He explained:

The old view in the Southern States went to the latter side; one called mulattos the children of white men and Negroes as one calls mules the hybrid between horse and ass. And as these mules are as a rule not fertile, those old southern anthropologists made it their first aim, to show, that also the offspring of mulattos became sterile in a few generations. And up to now there are some so-called anthropologists sticking to the old telltale of the inheritability of quadroons or octoroon women. We others know now, that there is equal absolute and unlimited fertility between all human races and that casual sterility of some octoroon women is only due to their having been abused in their early childhood.

In the Old South, Luschan argued, "The colored man was considered to be like cattle and … anthropology was wanted to show and demonstrate how Negroes were not men but only a sort of speaking apes."[24]

In his Illinois lectures Luschan carefully differentiated between two powerful and often confused forces—environment and heredity—and their effects on human development. Environment, Luschan maintained, determined the peculiar condition and progress of races. "Wherever environment is favorable, favorable before all to the *mutual exchange* of individual and carnal *mental and technical achievements*—then progress is quick so quick as we saw with the Races of the Mediterranean. When environment is unfavorable, we see *men* remaining nearly unaltered for an untold number of thousands of years, as is shown with the aboriginals of Australia, that have retained till now most of the qualities of early paleolithic man in Europe." Luschan went on to warn the University of Illinois students that "[t]he great problem for the future [was] if and *how quick* human groups, that had been under [un]favorable circumstances for long periods and had suffered by their environment can recover and reach our own lives when brought under favorable circumstances." Playing to the patriotism of his American audience, and ignoring the rigid racial segregation of schools throughout much of the United States, Luschan added: "[h]ere, *under the stars and stripes* more than in any other country in the world public instruction is equally open to the white and to the colored races. I feel sure, the results will be a splendid one."[25]

Heredity, Luschan explained in another of his Illinois lectures, not environment, held the key to understanding mental and bodily qualities, mental diseases, and criminality. Convinced that most people were ignorant of the "dark and mysterious" science of inherited traits, whether in plant, animal, or human species, he praised the work of agricultural experimental stations attached to American "land grant" universities. He considered these "perhaps the most perfect institutions … [of] their kind all over the world and would pay a visit from the old Continent."[26]

Heredity was more than a "scientific sport" of collecting data, Luschan said. For twenty years scientists had distinguished between the transmittance of what he termed "normal" racial and other bodily and mental characteristics, and the transmittance of "abnormal," pathological qualities such as mental and physical diseases. In his lecture Luschan cited examples from the human, plant, and animal worlds to illustrate "recessive and dominant characters" and how certain characteristics recurred over time. "Miscegenation," he said, "very often leads to a re-establishment of a more or less pure type," making it hard "to know, why a man is dark, [has] colored blood[,] or is he on the dark end of the range of variation." But whereas plants and animals could be bred, Luschan explained, "unhappily" man could not be bred.

Paraphrasing the British geneticist William Bateson (1861–1926), Luschan joked that if people could be bred, the world would be very boring—populated only with George Washingtons and King Solomons.

Seriously, he said, the "budding of mankind would prove highly inefficient as to real progress," yet Luschan obviously favored some form of selective breeding among humans. "There are *good* germ cells," he argued, "and to them mankind has to thank for the progress it has made till now, and for the progress it will make in the time to come." He admonished the students in his audience in Urbana to control the destinies of their future offspring by careful selection of their mates. "Indeed," Luschan lectured, "you must make Eugenic doctrines part of your religious creed[.] Take with you from here the conviction of the supreme and paramount Duty of Health and be not careless in choosing a husband or a wife."[27]

Despite his eugenic creed, Luschan admitted in another lecture that scientists really knew little about genetics and suggested the vague implications for racial mixing. "If two different races, a native one and strange invaders intermarry, the final result never corresponds to the arithmetical means, as has been so often said and believed. Above all we should be aware, that somatic type and language—the two principal features of the human races[—]are not influenced equally by such an intermarriage." Luschan recognized that science aside, much of the discourse on "race" was socially constructed, referring to the "social meaning of pigmentation," and noting the "impossibility of giving a scientific definition of the *white* race." There still was much to learn about racial mixing and black culture, he said. Before his arrival in the United States, Luschan had wondered whether Africans had transported their language and culture to America. "I am very unknowledgeable on these topics," he admitted to Hugo Schuchardt (1842–1927), an Austrian linguist.[28]

In order to become more "knowledgeable" about race and the transference of so-called racial characteristics, Luschan used his sojourn in the United States not only to sightsee and lecture, but also to study what his American colleagues termed the "race problem." The Austrian scholar generally considered American racial scientists (Luschan dubbed them "so-called anthropologists") to be rank amateurs. For example, he judged the writings of William Benjamin Smith (1850–1934) and Robert W. Shufeldt (1850–1934) to be anachronistic and embarrassingly inadequate. Smith's blatantly racist *The Color Line* (1905), Luschan wrote in a draft of a book review, contained "next to nothing" of value on the race question, "and of real science less than nothing." Luschan insisted that humans shared innumerable characteristics with one another and were "absolutely deficient with their very next relations in the animal kingdom, even with the anthropoid apes." He informed Americans that the "unity of mankind" eliminated race as a factor in social relations. His point was that people of various races had more in common genetically than the contemporary meaning of "race" implied. All kinds of "blood" then, including African "blood," pulsed through the veins of white southerners.[29]

Luschan hammered home these arguments and others in a book review of Shufeldt's *America's Greatest Problem: The Negro* (1915), published in the *American Anthropologist*, America's most prestigious ethnology journal. Based on dog-eared "sentimental phrases and boundless exaggerations," not empirical research, Shufeldt's Negrophobic book condemned African-Americans as immoral criminals and espoused their forced deportation. According to Luschan, the book offered not "one single new or interesting statement." He considered Shufeldt's observations on Negro hair, crania, and physiognomy to be anachronistic—evidence "of the author's entire lack of scientific training and discernment." While mindful that "the colored man is a serious problem for the United States," Luschan nevertheless urged calmness, patience, scientific inquiry, and tolerance. Eventually, he predicted, "the problem will be solved, just as well, as sooner or later modern society will be forced, in Europe no less than in America, to revise its old social ideas and its old criminal laws. Certainly there are criminals and persons with inferior morality and inferior intellect in every human group, white and colored; but we shall sooner or later learn to eliminate them. This *can* be done and *will* be done, but certainly not in the way Dr. Shufeldt tries to suggest to us."[30]

To educate himself, and to take advantage of the "laboratory" that the United States provided for a study of race, during his stay in America Luschan decided to gather empirical data on African-Americans. In 1911 he complained that reliable statistics on American blacks, especially mulattoes, were impossible to obtain; his trip to America thus offered a tremendous opportunity to compile scientific evidence.[31] "I would like to study some Problems of Heredity," he informed Booker T. Washington in December 1914. "I would like to study the exact pedigree of some hundred colored families for 3 or if possible 4 generations and to note some anthropometric and other data on bodily and mental qualities of every single available member of these families." Luschan had conducted similar research on 320 Greek families on the Island of Crete.[32] "I think," Luschan wrote to the eugenicist Charles B. Davenport (1866–1944), "this might give quite good results for some Heredity Questions and might perhaps be useful also for some questions connected with the great Negro-Problem."[33]

Washington (1856–1915), who had read "The Anthropological View of Race," Luschan's controversial lecture at the 1911 Universal Races Congress in London, volunteered to help him find several generations of African-American families that were appropriate for longitudinal research.[34] He suggested that the Luschans visit Baltimore, Washington, New York, Boston, Charleston, Savannah, Mobile, and New Orleans. "At Hampton Institute and Tuskegee Institute," Washington explained, "it would be difficult to find such families for the family ties in these particular sections were broken up by the slavery system, whereas, in Savannah and the other cities … there were in the days of slavery a considerable free Negro population which, if I understand the purpose of your study, have the elements as to heredity, race mixture, etc., which you desire to get hold of." Luschan accepted Washington's invitation to visit his famous school at Tuskegee, Alabama.[35]

In January 1915 Luschan finalized plans for his field research. He explained to readers of Berlin's *Vossische Zeitung* that he and his wife had decided to

> visit Alabama, Virginia, Baltimore, and Washington to study several hundred black families, record their family trees, and examine them all from an anthropological standpoint; we thereby hope to gather rich material for the study of heredity questions, as well as to contribute to the elucidation of the great mulatto problem. I consider this the most important social problem facing the United States today, yet one on which most people in the United States are not completely clear. Official statistics leave much to be desired; no great distinction is made between the very dark Africans and the much lighter-skinned mulattos, usually they are all labeled "colored." Naturally it is impossible to determine what the future of these over ten million coloreds is going to be, at least not before knowing how much white blood is mixed in with theirs, and whether or not the number of light-skinned mulattos is increasing or decreasing within the total number of colored peoples.[36]

A month later Luschan informed President James of Illinois that he and his wife were in the South "to study the Negro problem" (*zum Studium des Neger-Problems*). They had already conducted fieldwork for two weeks in St. Louis, Missouri, and were embarking for Memphis, Tennessee; Greenville, Mississippi; New Orleans, Louisiana; Mobile, Alabama; and Tuskegee. The Luschans would return to New York by way of Hampton, Virginia. Their mission was "to study the family trees of colored families everywhere along our trip, and exactly measure and register every available member of those families. We also hope to gather material for general hereditary problems this way."[37]

With this research strategy in mind, Luschan contacted a broad range of southerners hoping to obtain access to willing "subjects" for his research. Ironically, in January 1915 he approached William Benjamin Smith, the Tulane University mathematics professor whose *The Color Line* he had judged so unscientific. Flattered "that a scholar of such renown" would write to him, Smith explained that his book "was the inspiration of the moment, a deviation at right angle from the paths of my serious activities." Smith explained that several years earlier a colleague had attempted to assist Charles B. Davenport in measuring blacks and identifying racial pedigrees. The research, however, proved "difficult because of the reticence, suspiciousness, and general untrustworthiness of the subjects." Nonetheless, Smith believed that "such studies as you have in hand should certainly lead to exceedingly instructive and illuminative results." Smith also hoped to disarm Luschan's fears that he would encounter anti-German sentiment in New Orleans. While, Smith maintained, most Americans held Austro-Hungarian militarists responsible for the war, "there seems to be little feeling against the Germans, whom all admire not merely for their extraordinary intellectual endowments and cultural achievements, but also no less for the many signal moral, social, and emotional qualities et al. on the national and social character."[38]

Luschan also sought assistance for his research from another Tulane University faculty member: Robert Bennett Bean (1874–1944) of the university's medical school. Bean published widely on comparative anatomy and heredity, including the highly influential 1906 article "Some Racial Peculiarities of the Negro Brain" published in the *American Journal of Anatomy*. Bean concluded that on average Negro brains were smaller than Caucasian brains; that Negro brains were distinguishable from Caucasian brains "according to the amount of admixture of white blood"; and that the anterior half of the frontal lobes in Negro brains were relatively smaller than in Caucasian brains. Negroes, Bean thus asserted, were "objective"; Caucasians were "subjective." Negroes had well developed lower mental faculties (smell, sight, handcraftsmanship, body-sense, melody) while Caucasians possessed more highly developed mental faculties (self-control, willpower, ethical and aesthetic sense and reason).[39] White supremacists of the day cited Bean's findings as proof of the backwardness and degeneracy of African-Americans.[40]

Bean, not surprisingly, welcomed Luschan, who also held an MD degree, as a colleague interested in the heredity (Luschan often referred to it as "pedigree") and alleged racial traits of African-Americans. In April 1915 Bean agreed to ship Luschan various anatomical specimens of Negroes. These included "the nipple region of the breast, the ears, hyper, meso, and hypo, the heads and brains." Luschan welcomed these specimens. His museum in Berlin held perhaps the world's largest and foremost collections of skulls and skeletons.[41]

Aside from providing him with anatomical specimens, Bean also encouraged Luschan's research and eagerly awaited the results of his work on the heredity of American blacks. Years before, Bean had investigated this subject, he informed Luschan, "but gave up in despair because I could not in a single case be sure of the child's father. In many cases there was such striking similarity between the child and the neighbor's father and knowing the personal history of the families and the natural habits of the negro I believe the father in many cases was a neighbor. What value would such records have?" Luschan nevertheless proceeded enthusiastically with his research project on black southerners.[42]

Luschan very much hoped that a visit to "Dunleith," Alfred Holt Stone's large cotton plantation near Greenville, Mississippi, would reap insightful data for his research project. Stone (1870–1955) published *Studies in the American Race Problem* (1908), according to Luschan "a remarkable book on the Negro question (*die Negerfrage*)."[43] Contemporaries considered Stone, though neither a trained sociologist nor an anthropologist, one of America's foremost authorities on the "Negro problem." Luschan judged Stone a lay scholar who "studied the social aspect of the whole problem better than most other historians above the 'Color-Line.'"[44] Luschan described himself as "the very warmest admirer of" Stone's book, "which I take to be the best, if not the only good book on the Negro Problem."[45]

Luschan approached Stone in February 1915 to ask for his help. "We want to study about 100 pedigrees and to measure exactly every single available [member] of such families." He hoped that Stone would assist him in identifying "*intelligent* coloured families on your plantation or in your neighborhood" that would allow the Luschans to record their family histories and take their measurements. "We would also be interested," Luschan added, "in coloured families with more or less white blood, as we want to study some problems of heredity in Negro-White crosses. Mrs. v. Luschan and myself ... can work about 8 hours a day and can do the measurements of 3 to 5 men or women per hour, so that we could manage to study 30 or 40 every day."[46]

Stone promised to help Luschan meet "subjects" for his research by introducing him to both "an intelligent colored physician" and a white doctor in Greenville. He suspected that the Luschans would fare better in lining up black families in the city than in the country. "At any rate," Stone explained, "they are likely to be more easily approached there, through a negro doctor, than out here." At "Dunleith" Luschan would "be free to prosecute your investigations among our plantation negroes, or not, just as you may determine after reaching here." Stone suspected that Memphis, with its large black population, might be a fruitful location for the Luschans' research. The black community there, Stone explained, was "made up of recruits from all parts of the cotton south, and offering, I believe, more nearly a typical average of our negroes than does the same population in New Orleans."[47]

Luschan also sought the assistance of other southerners in identifying black "subjects" for his research. Bolton Smith of Memphis, a banker and trustee for the Carnegie Foundation of Washington, DC, befriended the Luschans. He recommended that upon reaching his city, Luschan should consult the German-trained Dr. Marcus Haase, a leading dermatologist. Haase reportedly would provide Luschan access to African-Americans at the Memphis hospital and clinic. Smith also introduced Luschan to Rabbi William H. Fineshriber of the Memphis synagogue who in turn put Luschan in touch with contacts in New Orleans. Smith went so far trying to assist Luschan that he even provided him access to his postman's daughter who, according to Smith, had Indian, Samoan, and Hawaiian lineage; she reportedly represented "that hyperextension in other colored people."[48]

While Smith assisted Luschan in Memphis, the influential German-American antiquarian John Max Wulfing (1859–1929) hosted the Luschans in St. Louis, Missouri, and helped them make contact with black schoolteachers. During their southern fieldwork Wulfing forwarded the Luschans' mail and kept in close contact with them. "I am under the impression that there are not many Germans in the South," Wulfing wrote in March 1915, "and that hence you may not have an opportunity to see German newspapers. ... The account of your work in Memphis and meeting the Negro Millionare [sic]," Wulfing wrote, "was most interesting, and I am very glad to know that you have met with such success." Another contact in St. Louis, Edward S. Williams, principal of the Banneker School, arranged for Luschan to examine an elderly African-American woman.[49]

The Luschans also received considerable help in identifying black "subjects" in Louisiana. The Reverend John A. Rice of Forth Worth, Texas, introduced Luschan to two New Orleans clergymen, the Reverends R.E.

Jones, editor of the influential *Southwestern Christian Advocate*, and Professor M.S. Aldrich, president of New Orleans University. Both had many contacts within the African-American community. Rice also introduced him to the Reverend W.C. Gaynor, a Benedictine priest at St. Joseph's Abbey, located in St. Tammany Parish about seventy miles north of New Orleans. Gaynor instructed Luschan to seek subjects for his anthropometric research beyond the city of New Orleans, "where the pure negro can hardly now be found and is too sophisticated and insolent when found." Interior towns, places such as Lafayette or Opelousas, were preferable because they possessed "a large colored population more or less untouched by the spread of modern manners." Gaynor was confident that clergy in both towns would assist Luschan in identifying suitable black families for his research.[50]

Gaynor cautioned Luschan, however, to be prepared before commencing his field research for what he considered the peculiarities of the contemporary African-American. "The modern negro is fast getting away from the ancient type. He is sophisticated, aims at being equal to the white man, resents the imputation of inferiority, and in his heart nourishes a growing hatred of the white man's condescension. Your approach to him, therefore, would have to be cautious and rather through those whom he knows and respects." Perhaps, Gaynor suggested, a local clergyman could serve as an intermediary between Luschan and his black subjects, "for the negro is naturally polite and obliging." Nevertheless, Gaynor continued, "when it comes to measuring his head or introducing the project of tracing his ancestry back to the jungle, I should not care to guarantee you a good reception from him. Like all young Americans he wishes to be known as American and not African."[51]

Notwithstanding Gaynor's warnings, during their stay in the United States the Luschans found many willing black subjects. In Memphis they met Josiah T. Settle (1850–1915), a prominent African-American attorney who promised to help them obtain information on "our so called colored people." "Do you mean their ancestry only?" asked Settle, "or in addition what they have accomplished in their professions, business enterprises &c?" Settle promised to send the Luschans a photograph of himself as well as of other blacks. "As soon as you will inform me as to the scope of the information you desire upon pedigree &c. I will send you that also."[52]

Throughout their travels the Luschans measured African-Americans, including "hundreds of school children [who] individually march[ed] by us."[53] They recorded the length of their fingers and the size and form of their nostrils. They coded skin colors and analyzed photographs of black youth and adults.[54] At Virginia's Hampton Institute the Luschans tested black students from within the same families to measure the influence of heredity and presented an illustrated lecture on heredity.[55] George P. Phenix (1864–1930), Hampton's vice principal, thanked the Luschans for their visit to his school. "We have had no guests here in a long time who have given us more pleasure than you and your good wife. We should have been glad if you could have made your stay with us longer." Phenix enclosed information on the Wilkinson family for Luschan's research files. "I am astonished at the completeness of the record but I presume there were grandparents who remembered clearly their grandparents."[56]

Luschan collected ethnological and anthropometric data on black schoolchildren in Memphis, Greenville, St. Louis, Tuskegee, and New Orleans, ultimately gathering statistics on 814 black pupils. As the Luschans traveled throughout the South they distributed questionnaires to schoolteachers about their students' ethnicity.[57] Eager to please Luschan, E.E. Bass, superintendent of the Greenville Public Schools, agreed to send him photographs of what Bass described as "negro-chinese children." Luschan apparently sought to use these photographs as evidence for his research. Bass reported, however, that the children's parents failed to cooperate. "They put me off and off," Bass reported, "with some trivial excuse," leading Bass to conclude that the parents "were apprehensive of some ulterior motives on our part." Finally, after talking to one of the mothers, Bass determined that she feared that he and Luschan were conspiring to take her children away from her. "I assured her that such an idea was entirely without foundation," Bass explained, and the woman agreed to have her children photographed.[58]

In March 1915 Luschan informed Franz Boas that his field research in the South was progressing smoothly. Both blacks and whites had greeted the Luschans warmly and they were compiling valuable data. Luschan was surprised, however, that what he termed "multiple 'colored' families closely resembled Europeans; some had even become millionaires" (*mehrere 'farbige' Familien die absolut rein europäisch aussehen. Einige von diesen sind Millionäre*). He wondered why affluent blacks remained in Jim Crow America, where they were, according to Luschan, de-classed (*declassiert*), when they could move to Europe where they would be treated as equals.[59] A month later Luschan reported enthusiastically on his findings to Charles B. Davenport: "We did very good work and brought back the pedigrees of about 100 families and the exact measurements etc. of about 350 persons. We saw also a good many Indians and Persons with mixed Indian and

Negro blood."[60] "We hope," Luschan explained to Edward S. Morse, director of the Peabody Museum of Salem, Massachusetts, "that with this material we shall be able to find some laws in heredity; principally we want to learn, how many single traits are transmitted by heredity *independently* from one another."[61]

Having completed their research in March 1915, the Luschans sought passage back to Germany.[62] Though evidence disproves Luschan's later rhetorical and politically motivated assertion that Americans held him for seven months "against his will," transatlantic travel posed serious risks during World War I.[63] In April the Luschans sailed on a neutral vessel, a ship of the Scandinavian American Line, from New York to Germany via Norway. Luschan wrote to an American colleague, anthropologist Robert H. Lowie (1883–1957), that the voyage was perilous both because of thick fog and "lurking English warships."[64] When he finally arrived in Berlin on 15 May, members of the city's academic community greeted Luschan not as a returning hero, but rather with accusations that he had stayed away from his adopted country too long, that he was too friendly toward Britain, and that he was disloyal. Luschan responded quickly, defending his loyalty and establishing his patriotic support of the German war effort by celebrating German nationalism and militarism in articles and speeches.[65]

Luschan also rushed to publish his findings on American blacks. They were not dying off due to competition with whites; black men posed no sexual threat to white women; Jim Crow segregated the races in public but the races obviously mingled privately—the skyrocketing mulatto population attested to that. Based on his admittedly unscientific research method (but "still a whole lot better than everything I know in this field in America," he quipped), Luschan concluded that more than 75 percent of the four thousand schoolchildren he studied came from mixed African–European ancestry. White Americans' arbitrary racial classifications based on "'a drop' of colored blood" thus was "rather amusing to non-prejudiced Europeans." Luschan considered racial mixing commonplace: "for thousands of years [people] have been carrying Negro blood in their genes without seriously damaging their moral, intelligence, and social value." Though Luschan believed that American Negroes and Africans in Germany's colonies benefited from the infusion of "good white blood," he urged Germans "to protect our home from the penetration of significant quantities of African blood."[66]

Luschan insisted that while there was nothing inherently "inferior" about American Negroes or mulattos, there nonetheless were "inferior" Negroes and mulattos, much as there were "inferior" whites. All races, he said, had "inferior elements" or, as he preferred to label them, "negative variables." Committed fully to eugenics, Luschan emphasized "the necessity to fight and eliminate the inferior people" among American Negroes by isolating them and preventing them from reproducing. Defining "racial hygiene" broadly, he favored elevating "inferior" blacks "at all costs in terms of health, morals, and intellect." Once "inferior" elements in America's black population had been improved, he predicted that "the coloreds will stop being a danger to the whites." Most blacks could be educated and would become useful citizens, he wrote, and they deserved equality with whites. Luschan admired the vocational school model introduced at Hampton Institute and perfected at Tuskegee Institute, comparing these institutions favorably to German technical schools. In them blacks received necessary skills and lessons in morality. All in all, Luschan commended "the admirable energy [with which] the colored people … in the last five decades have worked on their social and moral development."[67]

In 1919 Luschan complained to Boas that his work on American blacks had largely been ignored, assuming his findings too "Negro friendly" (*negerfreundlich*) for conservative Americans and Germans. Three years later, in *Völker, Rassen, Sprachen*, Luschan again commented favorably on American blacks. Though Negroes had made great strides educationally and contrasted positively with whites in morals and public health, anti-Negro prejudice remained rampant; fears of miscegenation haunted white southerners. Luschan predicted that whites would segregate blacks, isolating them in a "pure Negro Republic" and "freeing the rest of the Union of this unwanted element." He considered the "Negro question" America's most troubling issue, one with no answer in sight.[68]

At least one contemporary scholar, however, the renowned American anthropologist Melville J. Herskovits (1895–1963), paid close attention to Luschan's American field research. In 1930, upon the request of Mrs Luschan (Felix von Luschan died in February 1924) and Boas, Herskovits published compilations of Luschan's 1915 measurements of American blacks then deposited at the American Museum of Natural History in New York. The data comprised two sets from the Luschans' fieldwork in St. Louis, Memphis, Greenville, New Orleans, Tuskegee, and Hampton. One set comprised 349 individuals—the total of all measurements that they recorded during their American research. The other set consisted of measurements of 155 persons—men (52) and women (103) between the ages of twenty and seventy.

According to Herskovits's summary, in their research the Luschans measured certain characteristics (*die Merkmale*) of African-Americans that they considered statistically significant in drawing anthropological con-clusions. These included head length, head width, length–width index, nose height, nose width, upper facial height, whole facial height, ear height, ear width, thickness of the lip, zygomatic arch width, and body size. Based on the Luschans' data, Herskovits extrapolated three conclusions.

First, males on average had a larger mean value for each characteristic. In other words, men generally had longer heads, longer noses, and larger bodies than women. The one exception was lips. Women on average had thicker lips than men. Second, the data identified relatively "few pure Ne-groes"; "most of the individuals measured by Luschan descended from whites and Negroes, Indians and Negroes, or from whites, Indians, and Ne-groes." Third, because Luschan gathered his data from several locations and then combined the statistics, the variations from the average tended to be larger than they would have been had he sorted his data by individ-ual location.[69] While Herskovits unfortunately provided little analysis of Luschan's American research, his lectures and field research nevertheless underscored the Austrian scholar's commitment to a non-racialist vision of the human species.

Like Boas and some other early German physical anthropologists, Luschan espoused cultural relativism and challenged longstanding notions of "superior" and "inferior" peoples based on race. People differed, Luschan said, because of environmental, historical, social and, less significantly, bi-ological forces. He moved in his work from empirical measurements (craniometry) to its seemingly natural successor, anthropometrics tied to genetics. Like other German scientists, by the early twentieth century he embraced Gregor Mendel on inheritance and Charles Darwin on evolu-tion and adaptation by natural selection. But Luschan's old-fashioned linguistic and anthropometric analyses had convinced him of the "absolute singularity of the human race"—that differences within the so-called races were superficial compared to the unity of species traits. As troubling as Luschan's language of "racial hygiene" is today, in his day eugenics appealed to a diverse range of physicians, scientists, and intellectuals on both sides of the Atlantic. They sought to improve humankind by treating and pre-venting diseases that transcended races and nationalities. Trained in medicine, Luschan favored medicalizing "race," endorsing social measures to increase the number of "competent" persons in Germany and, in his words, "restrict the fecundity of the incompetent."[70]

Yet for all his appreciation and celebration of people of color and their complex cultures, Luschan remained an elitist, a zealous nationalist whose hierarchical, paternalistic approach to social change reflected the *Weltan-schauung* of the colonizers, not the colonized. Luschan thus offers an interesting case study of what historian H. Glenn Penny identifies as the persistent ambiguity that lay at the heart of many German anthropologists' relationships with their subjects.[71]

Much like the white supremacists he criticized in America, Luschan also defined American blacks as a "problem." Sociologist Malgorzata Irek, the modern scholar largely responsible for rescuing Luschan from scholarly oblivion, goes so far as to assert that he rationalized lynching of African-Americans "as a healthy reaction of society against too liberal ... [legislation]." Her undocumented allegation is doubtful, if not spurious, however, because acts of racial violence would have dramatically contradicted Luschan's liberal nineteenth-century beliefs, his anti-racism, his bureaucratic mentality, and his commitment to law and order. While Luschan did identify "inferior" persons of color, he also identified "inferior" whites. He based such classifications on culture and behavior, not genetic make-up.[72]

Still, Luschan was unwilling to share his "good white blood" with "inferior" folk, black, white, red, or whatever. No social activist, Luschan's anti-racism always was theoretical and, after 1900, biologism, heredity, and eugenics increasingly dominated his thinking. In 1911, for example, Luschan shocked the audience (including W.E.B. Du Bois) at London's Universal Races Congress when he espoused the natural inequality between races, racial separation, Social Darwinism, and militarism, praising "our splendid [German] soldiers and our glorious ironclads," and dismissing "small-minded people [who] whine about the horrid cost of Dreadnaughts." Luschan assured those in attendance that research on "the so-called colored peoples" would promote "mutual sympathy," but nonetheless insisted that "*racial barriers will never cease to exist*, and if ever they should show a tendency to disappear, it will certainly be better to preserve than to obliterate them."[73] Before Luschan ventured to America in 1914, he and other leading German scientists had already begun abandoning liberal, anti-racist anthropology.[74]

By the time that Luschan traveled to Australia, and then researched, lectured, and collected data in Hawaii and in the United States, he had shifted significantly to an emphasis on Darwinian struggle and, as Luschan exhibited to students at the University of Illinois, espoused both hereditarianism and environmentalism.[75] Contemporary hereditarians and environmentalists, according to anthropologist George W. Stocking, interpreted "race as an integrated physical, linguistic and cultural totality."[76] Clearly, during the World War I period Luschan opposed racism in theory, yet in practice he zealously supported racial theories that justified German colonialism, eugenics, militarism, and nationalism.

Ironically, instead of refining his conclusions and reconciling his contradictions, Luschan's field research in the United States exacerbated them. Recording the racial characteristics of hundreds of African-American subjects brought him no closer to clarifying his racial and social thought. For example, in a glaring contradiction Luschan maintained on the one hand that heredity, not environment, controlled physical and intellectual traits. But on the other hand he argued that so-called "inferior" peoples could be educated to become law-abiding, useful citizens. Luschan left America ambivalent about and ambiguous on the meaning of racial inferiority, on the status of mixed-race peoples, on the importance of racial differences—in short, on the significance of "race."

While his American fieldwork convinced Luschan of the significant progress African-Americans had made since emancipation, like white conservatives in the United States, he nonetheless judged American blacks to be at the crux of an unsolvable "race problem." Though generally anti-racist toward individual African-Americans, Luschan's experiences and observations in America, and with America's so-called "race problem," nevertheless failed to deflect his shift away from cosmopolitanism and towards militaristic German nationalism, racial hierarchies, and Social Darwinism. Luschan may have encountered "the other" in America, but he fell short of understanding "everything that [his] country was not."

Notes

1. See Christiane Harzig, "Gender, Transatlantic Space, and the Presence of German-Speaking People in North America," in *Traveling between Worlds: German-American Encounters*, edited by Thomas Adam and Ruth Gross (College Station, TX, 2006), 147.
2. Christof Mauch, "Oceans Apart? Paradigms in German-American History and Historiography," in ibid., 5, 6, 8.
3. On these contradictions, see John David Smith, "W.E.B. Du Bois, Felix von Luschan, and Racial Reform at the *Fin de Siecle*," *Amerikastudien* 47 (2002): 23–38.
4. Felix von Luschan, "Culture and Degeneration" [typed speech, August 1914], Nachlass Luschan. Handschriftenabteilung, Staatsbibliothek zu Berlin, Germany (hereafter cited Nachlass Luschan).

5. Charles R. Hodge to Felix von Luschan, 29 July 1914, Nachlass Luschan; Felix von Luschan, "In Australien und Amerika," *Berlin Vossische Zeitung*, 31 January 1915, clipping in Königliches Museum für Völkerkunde, Acta betreffend Verschiedene Angelegenheiten der ethnologischen Abteilung, vol. 21.

6. In the *Berlin Vossische Zeitung* citation above Luschan referred to himself and his wife as "us Germans" (*uns Deutsche*) when in fact they were Austrians.

7. Luschan, "In Australien und Amerika;" Felix von Luschan to Edward S. Morse, 9 September 1914, E.S. Morse Collection, Phillips Library, Peabody Essex Museum, Salem, Massachusetts.

8. Felix von Luschan to Herr Rechnungsrath continued, 7 September 1914, Königliches Museum für Völkerkunde, Acta betreffend Verschiedene Angelegenheiten der ethnologischen Abteilung, vol. 21; Luschan to the Königliches Museum für Völkerkunde, 13 September 1914, Königliches Museum für Völkerkunde, Acta betreffend Verschiedene Angelegenheiten der ethnologischen Abteilung, vol. 21; Luschan to Herr Rechnungsrath, am Sedan-Tage 1914; Herbert E. Gregory to Luschan, 31 March 1920, Nachlass Luschan.

9. Luschan to Morse, 9 September 1914, Morse Collection.

10. Felix von Luschan to Edward S. Morse, 15 October 1914, Morse Collection.

11. Felix von Luschan, "Der Rassen-Kongreß in London 1911," *Koloniale Rundschau* 3 (1911): 600.

12. "Nord-Amerikas Vernegerung. Bericht aus der Anthropologischen Gesellschaft," *Berlin Vossische Zeitung*, 19 July 1915, clipping in Nachlass Luschan; US Department of the Interior, National Park Service, *Federal Register* 60, no. 125 (29 June 1995): 33846; Felix von Luschan, *Anthropological View of Race*, 2nd ed. (New York: published on board the "*Vaterland*," 1915), 1; Felix von Luschan to William T. Brigham, 17 February 1920, William T. Brigham Papers, Bernice P. Bishop Museum, Honolulu, Hawaii.

13. Felix von Luschan to Alfred L. Kroeber, 26 October 1914, Alfred L. Kroeber Papers, Bancroft Library, University of California, Berkeley; Franz Boas to Eduard Seler, 30 October 1914, Königliches Museum für Völkerkunde, Acta betreffend Verschiedene Angelegenheiten der ethnologischen Abteilung, vol. 38.

14. Luschan to Morse, 9 September 1914, Morse Collection.

15. See Robert H. Lowie, "The Philadelphia Meeting of the American Anthropological Association," *Science*, New Ser., 41 (5 February 1915): 221.

16. Luschan to Brigham, 2 December 1914, Brigham Papers.

17. James H. Breasted to Edmund J. James, 23 September 1914, Liberal Arts and Sciences' Department and Subject File, University Archives, University of Illinois at Urbana-Champaign (hereafter Liberal Arts and Sciences' Subject File).

18. James to Breasted, 26 September 1914; Breasted to James, 2 October 1914, Liberal Arts and Sciences' Subject File.

19. Kendrick C. Babcock to Breasted, 2 November 1914; Luschan to Babcock, 4 November 1914; E.O. Hayes to President [Edmund J.] James, 7 November 1914,

Edmund J. James Papers, University Archives, University of Illinois at Urbana-Champaign (hereafter James Papers).

20. "Felix von Luschan Comes to Lecture," *Champaign Daily-Gazette*, 7 November 1914, 3.

21. "Berlin Professor Lectures on Evolution in Asia," *Daily Illini*, 10 November 1914, 1.

22. "German Anthropologist Condemns Drink as Fatal," ibid., 11 November 1914, 1.

23. Felix von Luschan, "Unity of Mankind" (unpublished lecture manuscript), Nachlass Luschan. Luschan referred to Hermann Klaatsch (1863–1916) and Lanz von Liebenfels (1874–1954).

24. Luschan, "Unity of Mankind"; Malgorzata Irek, *The European Roots of the Harlem Renaissance*, Berliner Beiträge zur Amerikanistik 1 (Berlin, 1994), 54–55.

25. Luschan, "Unity of Mankind."

26. Felix von Luschan, "Heredity" (unpublished lecture manuscript), Nachlass Luschan.

27. Luschan, "Heredity."

28. Felix von Luschan miscellaneous lecture notes, n.d., Nachlass Luschan; Luschan, "Unity of Mankind"; Irek, *The European Roots of the Harlem Renaissance*, 54–55; Felix von Luschan, book review draft manuscript of William B. Smith, *The Color Line*, and Felix von Luschan, "Sociology," manuscript lecture notes, 6 January 1915, 5, Nachlass Luschan; Felix von Luschan to Hugo Schuchardt, 16 January 1914, Hugo Schuchardt Papers, Karl-Franzens-Universität, Graz, Austria.

29. Luschan, draft manuscript of book review of Smith, *The Color Line*, Nachlass Luschan.

30. Felix von Luschan, review of R.W. Shufeldt, *America's Greatest Problem: The Negro*, in *American Anthropologist* 17 (July–September 1915): 573–74.

31. Luschan, "Der Rassen-Kongreß in London 1911," 607.

32. Felix von Luschan to Booker T. Washington, 23 December 1914, in *The Booker T. Washington Papers*, ed. Louis R. Harlan, 14 vols. (Urbana, 1972–1989), 13: 202–3.

33. Felix von Luschan to Charles B. Davenport, 21 December 1914, Charles B. Davenport Papers, American Philosophical Society Library, Philadelphia.

34. See Felix von Luschan, "Anthropological View of Race," in *Papers on Inter-Racial Problems Communicated to the First Universal Races Congress held at the University of London, 26–29 July 1911*, ed. Gustav Spiller (1911; New York, 1970), 13–24.

35. Washington to Luschan, 2, 12 January 1915, Nachlass Luschan.

36. William R. Shepherd to Felix von Luschan, 26 January 1915, Nachlass Luschan; Luschan, "In Australien und Amerika."

37. Luschan to James, 28 February 1915, James Papers.

38. William Benjamin Smith to Felix von Luschan, 31 January 1915, Nachlass Luschan.

39. Robert Bennett Bean, "Some Racial Peculiarities of the Negro Brain," *American Journal of Anatomy* 4 (September 1906): 354–431.

40. See I.A. Newby, *Jim Crow's Defense: Anti-Negro Thought in America, 1900–1930* (Baton Rouge, 1965), 31, 39, 50, 193, and David W. Southern, *The Progressive Era and Race: Reaction and Reform, 1900–1917* (Wheeling, IL, 2005), 50.

41. Robert Bennett Bean to Felix von Luschan, 7 April 1915, Nachlass Luschan.

42. Ibid.

43. On Stone, see John David Smith, "High Authority or Failed Prophet? Alfred Holt Stone and Racial Thought in Jim Crow America," *Journal of Mississippi History* 68 (Fall 2006): 195–212.

44. Luschan to James, 28 February 1915, James Papers.

45. Felix von Luschan to Alfred Holt Stone, 11 February 1915, Nachlass Luschan.

46. Ibid.

47. Stone to Luschan, 15 February 1915, Nachlass Luschan.

48. Bolton Smith to Luschan, 1, 29 March, 10 April 1915, Nachlass Luschan.

49. Felix von Luschan to Franz Boas, 17 February 1915, Franz Boas Papers, American Philosophical Society, Philadelphia; John Max Wulfing to Felix von Luschan, 15 March 1915; Edward S. Williams to Felix von Luschan, 19 February 1915, Nachlass Luschan.

50. John A. Rice to Felix von Luschan, 3 March 1915; W.C. Gaynor to Luschan, 24 January 1915, Nachlass Luschan. On St. Joseph's Abbey, see John R. Kemp, "Art Has a Prayer at this Abbey Near Covington," *Louisiana Life* 24 (Winter 2004/05): 32–35.

51. Gaynor to Luschan, 24 January 1915.

52. Josiah T. Settle to Felix von Luschan, 14 April 1915, Nachlass Luschan.

53. Felix von Luschan, "Die Neger in den Vereinigten Staaten," *Koloniale Rundschau* 7 (1915): 521.

54. Luschan to Boas, 17 February 1915, Nachlass Luschan.

55. "Visitors," *The Southern Workman* 44 (May 1915): 317.

56. George P. Phenix to Felix von Luschan, 5 April 1915, Nachlass Luschan.

57. For sample responses, see Questionary, 9–22, Nachlass Luschan; T.J. Graham to Felix von Luschan, 5 April 1915, and enclosed forms, Felix von Luschan Papers, Division of Anthropology Archives, American Museum of Natural History, New York, New York.

58. E.E. Bass to Felix von Luschan [April 1915], and enclosed forms, Nachlass Luschan.

59. Felix von Luschan to Franz Boas, 5 March 1915, Boas Papers.

60. Luschan to Davenport, 5 April 1915, Davenport Papers.

61. Luschan to Morse, 5 April 1915, Morse Collection.

62. Ibid.

63. Felix von Luschan, *Rassen und Völker: Deutsche Reden in Schwerer Zeit Nr. 33* (Berlin, 1915), 20.

64. Felix von Luschan to Robert H. Lowie, 6 May 1915, Robert H. Lowie Papers, Bancroft Library, University of California, Berkeley; note from Böddinghaus, 18 May 1915, Königliches Museum für Völkerkunde, Acta betreffend Verschiedene Angelegenheiten der ethnologischen Abteilung, vol. 21.

65. Andrew David Evans, "Anthropology at War: World War I and the Science of Race in Germany" (Ph.D. diss., Indiana University, 2002), 166–69.

66. "Nord-Amerikas Vernegerung: Bericht aus der Anthropologischen Gesellschaft," *Berlin Vossische Zeitung*, 19 July 1915, clipping in Nachlass Luschan; Luschan, "Die Neger in den Vereinigten Staaten," 522, 518, 519, 532, 537.

67. Luschan, *Rassen und Völker*, 19; Luschan, "Die Neger in den Vereinigten Staaten," 535, 536, 508; Luschan notes on Hampton Institute, no date, Nachlass Luschan. Luschan was active in the German eugenics movement as early as 1905. In 1912 he served on Germany's Consultative Committee at the First International Eugenics Congress. See *Problems in Eugenics: Papers Communicated to the First International Eugenics Congress held at the University of London, July 24th to 30th, 1912* (London, 1912), xiii.

68. Luschan to Boas, 22 November 1919, Boas Papers; Luschan, *Völker, Rassen, Sprachen* (Berlin, 1922), 24–25, 27–28; Walter Rusch, "Der Beitrag Felix von Luschans für die Ethnographie," *Ethnographisch-Archäologische Zeitschrift* 27 (1986): 451.

69. Melville J. Herskovits, "Felix von Luschans Messungen Amerikanischer Neger," *Zeitschrift für Ethnologie* 61 (1930): 337–63.

70. Luschan, *Rassen und Völker*, 9–10; Hans Grimm, "Felix von Luschan als Anthropologe: Von der Kraniologie zur Humanbiologie," *Ethnographisch-Archäologische Zeitschrift* 27 (1986): 420; Andrew Zimmerman, *Anthropology and Antihumanism in Imperial Germany* (Chicago, 2001), 215; Benoit Massin, "From Virchow to Fischer: Physical Anthropology and 'Modern Race Theories' in Wilhelmine Germany," in *Volksgeist as Method and Ethic: Essays on Boasian Ethnography and the German Anthropological Tradition*, edited by George W. Stocking, Jr. (Madison, 1996), 136, 137n, 140; Felix von Luschan quoted in Ursula Zängl-Kumpf, "Luschan, Felix (Ritter Edler) von (1854–1924)," in *History of Physical Anthropology*, edited by Frank Spencer, 2 vols. (New York, 1997) 1: 623.

71. W.E.B. Du Bois, *The World and Africa: An Inquiry into the Part Which Africa has Played in World History* (1946; New York, 1965), 5; Luschan, "Anthropological View of Race," 23–24; Benoît Massin, "De L' Anthropologie Physique Libérale à la Biologie Raciale Eugénico-Nordiciste en Allemagne (1870–1914): Virchow–Luschan–Fischer," *Revue d'Allemagne et des Pays de Langue Allemande* 25 (1993): 396; H. Glenn Penny, "Practicing Anthropology in a Conradian Universe: The Question of Ambiguity and the Case of Alberti Vojtûch Friä" (unpublished paper in author's possession), 5.

72. Malgorzata Irek, *From Spree to Harlem: German 19th Century Anti-Racist Ethnology and the Cultural Revival of American Blacks*, FU Berlin Institut für Ethnologie Schwerpunkt Sozialanthropologie Sozialanthropologische Arbeitspapiere Nr. 27 (Berlin, 1990), 22; Rusch, "Der Beitrag Felix von Luschans für die Ethnographie," 452; Massin, "From Virchow to Fischer," 80, 142–43, 102.

73. Luschan, "Anthropological View of Race," 22, 21, 23.

74. Zimmerman's revisionist *Anthropology and Antihumanism in Imperial Germany* challenges the liberalism-to-racism interpretation and identifies racism deeply embedded in Imperial Germany's liberal anthropology.

75. See Richard Weikart, *From Darwin to Hitler: Evolutionary Ethics, Eugenics, and Racism in Germany* (New York, 2004), 17.

76. George W. Stocking, "The Turn-of-the-Century Concept of Race," *MODERNISM\modernity* 1 (January 1994): 15, 16.

Chapter 8

Transits of Race: Empire and Difference in Philippine-American Colonial History

Paul A. Kramer

It remains unclear at exactly what point in his 1902 travels David P. Barrows decided that Filipinos were not Indians. An anthropologist and newly-appointed chief of the Philippine-American colonial government's Bureau of Non-Christian Tribes, Barrows had in late 1901 been sent on a six-month-long tour of Indian reservations, schools and academies in the United States. The mission itself was unsurprising. Barrows was a scholar of Native American culture, having earned a PhD in 1898 from the University of Chicago for research on the ethno-botany of the Cahuilla Indians of California.[1] Following a year's service as the superintendent of Manila's schools, he had been appointed to the new Bureau, which was tasked with conducting ethnological research among the Islands' animists and Muslims in order to recommend policy for their governance and "assimilation"; Barrows's appointment itself seemed to suggest the official commensurability of Native American and Philippine "tribes."[2] His survey of Indian schools and reservations in both the eastern and western parts of the country and meetings with Washington-based officials at the Bureau of Indian Affairs, it was hoped, would gather for the Philippine colonial regime "information as to the results obtained by the present administration of Indian affairs."[34]

More striking, then, perhaps, were Barrows's conclusions: that the U.S. government's policy toward Indians was unsuitable for export to the Philippines, that the old empire, in a sense, had virtually nothing to teach the new.[4] Barrows did express his enthusiasm for reservation schools, and Supreme Court decisions which expansively defined legislative power over Indian tribes.[5] But Indian education in general had been "unsuitable and disappointing in its results."[6] Barrows similarly emptied his satchel of both reservation policies that recognized tribes and "assimilation" policies that sought to dismantle them; the latter, despite what Barrows considered the good intentions of reformers, had "not brought forth satisfactory results, and in a thousand cases has not done justice to the Indian."[7] Nor did reservation policing and justice have much to teach Philippine proconsuls. While Barrows believed that Native Americans' "democratic" culture allowed them to be safely empowered in courts and police forces, Malayan society's "aristocratic" traditions precluded this possibility.[8] Whether because of their abject failures on the North American continent—often due to white predation—or the "ethnological" differences between Native Americans and "Malayans," Indian policy for Barrows had little to offer. "My belief," he wrote to his superior, "is that we will not find in the policy of the Government in treating with Indians a model which can be generally followed in handling the wild tribes of the Philippines."[9]

Upon a second, sharper glance, Barrows's perspective is not, in fact, so surprising. At the turn of the twentieth century, the federal government's Indian policy was widely discredited as both corrupt and insufficiently "civilizing," hardly the starting point for a fledgling overseas colonialism eager to prove its "uplifting" character.[10] Barrows may have also had a professional investment in emphasizing his specifically Philippine expertise in ways that would downplay easy equivalences: how many other U.S. anthropologists, after all, could speak authoritatively about "Malayan" peoples? But while Barrows returned relatively empty-handed from the Bureau of Indian Affairs, he did not entirely reject Indian–Philippine linkages in anthropological or policy terms, either. He does not appear, for example, to have resisted the idea of the survey itself as impractical or absurd. And his sense that the Philippine-American colonial regime ought to encourage the "admixture" of "Malayan tribes" with "the Christian Filipino" through the "assignment of individual holdings ... leaving superfluous land open to settlement from outside," sounded much like assimilationist Indian policy, however unselfconsciously.[11] But Barrows would read Indian policy through a Philippine-American colonial lens, applying a highly selective filter to potential policy transits between old and new empires. He had broken up Indian policy into discrete, manageable parts—law, land-tenure, and schools, for example—determined for himself which if any of these elements fitted ongoing Philippine agendas, and translated these components into Philippine terms. Native Americans and Philippine "non-Christians" were alike enough to be compared, in other words, but they and their situations were different enough to persuade Barrows away from simplistic ethnological or policy projections. While Indian policy had been significant enough to be consulted, its application abroad—the actual difference it would make in helping Americans interpret Philippine realities—would be determined according to colonial logics and patterns.

This essay attempts to carry out a transnational history of race-making in Philippine-American colonial histories of the early twentieth century.[12] In doing so, it participates in a rich, emerging literature on racial and gendered difference and U.S. empire in this period.[13] But it also seeks to push beyond perspectives that focus only on the perceptions and agency of U.S.-based actors, or that comprehend U.S. colonial racial formations as involving either the "export" of "domestic" racial discourses, practices and institutions, or the installation of generic "colonial discourses" that emerge organically from the colonial situation itself.[14] It aspires instead to a perspective that is attuned to dynamics unfolding in both the United States and the Philippines, to the syncopated timelines of Philippine and U.S. histories as they collided and interwove, and to Filipino and U.S. perceptions, voices and actions. In historiographic terms, it hopes to address the impact—necessarily asymmetrical—of Philippine-American colonialism on both U.S. and Philippine nationalisms.[15]

If Barrows had been ambivalent about exactly how much of U.S. racial politics to export, historians of the U.S. empire have traditionally been far more confident that turn-of-the-century Americans projected their racial visions overseas. Sometimes contemporary racial idioms, especially "Social Darwinism" or "Anglo-Saxonism" are identified as partial "causes" of turn-of-the-century U.S. colonialism itself, especially as elements of broader cultural "crises."[16] In other cases, Americans are said to have run their new overseas empire more or less automatically from Indian-policy and/or Jim Crow rule books. The most elaborated argument along these lines is a 1980 essay by Walter Williams which argues that Indian policy "served as a precedent for imperialist domination over the Philippines and other islands occupied during the Spanish–American War."[17] At first glance, Williams marshals a wealth of evidence linking Indian and Philippine policy: Congressional debates, legal terminology, conference deliberations and career trajectories that appear to situate nineteenth-century Indian policy as the "origin" of Philippine colonial policy after 1898. But upon closer examination, much of Williams's evidence erodes. His attempt to link the two contexts through the legal categories used to characterize Native Americans and Filipinos, for example, hinges on the conflation of "ward" and "domestic dependent nation" on the one hand—central legal categories of nineteenth-century Indian policy—and the post-1898 term "national" applied to the U.S. Caribbean and Philippine sub-jects. While these concepts all represent diverse instruments of legal colonialism, Williams does not provide any actual legal evidence that the terms themselves, let alone broader analogies or comparisons, crossed be-tween legal settings.[18] Indeed, in one footnote, Williams observes with a certain puzzlement that "[e]xplicit comparisons with Indians were not made by the Supreme Court opinions in the Insular Cases," even though, from his perspective (if not, perhaps, from the Justices') "these opinions were directly parallel to Indian cases." One possible reason for this "omission," for Williams, was the Justices' recognition of "the extreme complexity of Indian case his-tory," and their desire not "to complicate the Insular Cases by bringing in decisions relating to Native Americans."[19]

In the absence of other kinds of evidence of policy connections, Williams places more than ideal faith in correlations: tabulating Congressional votes, he finds that a hand-chosen group of "Indian policy leaders" was roughly twice as likely to vote for "the imperialist position," an overlap that he is certain was "not coincidental, but represented to some degree a similar worldview."[20] He argues from career trajectory: the fact that 87 percent of the United States' generals in the Philippines "had experience with Indians in the West" suggests "a remarkably high exposure" to what Williams calls, somewhat vaguely, "the military ramifications of United States Indian pol-icy among the army leadership in the Philippines."[21] Finally, the "similarity in the administration of the Philippines to Indian affairs" is illustrated by a presumed relationship between the Bureau of Indian Affairs and the Bu-reau of Insular Affairs. Assuming that the bureaus were redundant—that, by definition, their tasks should have been channeled into a single agency—Williams feels compelled to explain their "separation," which he attributes to "organizational jealousy" and what he here calls the "low reputation" of the Bureau of Indian Affairs.[22] Evidence for policy similarities teased from the two BIAs, however, is thin. Both had been transferred from the War Department to the Interior Department, ninety years apart. "Even the bu-reau names were similar," he observes.[23]

Williams does show compellingly that, as Americans debated the new overseas colonialism, the white conquest of the West and the Native Amer-ican presence mattered. What remains unexplored are the diverse and sometimes conflicting ways that they mattered, how much they mattered relative to other discourses and practices, and what the fact that they mat-tered actually means.[24] Much of the problem derives from Williams's collapsing together of different kinds of linkage (models, analogies, precedents, and origins, for example, each of which operates differently) and his shifting criteria for what constitutes "connection" (similarity, simultaneity, correlation and causation, among them.) Historians approaching these themes might go further by asking what these invocations of Native Americans were meant to do; who used them (and who did not, or opposed their use); at what moment and in what context they were employed (and in which settings they were not); how the references themselves worked rhetorically and conceptually; what other surrounding discourses they built upon, or were impinged upon by; what, if any, relationship they had to larger practices, policies and institutions; and whether those who used them accomplished their goals in doing so and/or faced unintended consequences. Two broad inquiries may help to reframe the connection between race and empire in a less schematic way.

First, what questions was race being mobilized to answer? Williams shows that, for the proponents of overseas colonialism, at least, the image of Native Americans had been enlisted as an answer, if a highly charged and contested one, to at least one moral–historical question (what made colonial empire something other than an illegitimate break with U.S. traditions?) and one question of legislative power (what if anything allowed Congress to govern a people without their consent?). Beyond those arenas, however, the enlistment of Indian-white history in debates over actual Philippine colonial policy was uneven, the absences as telling as the presences. Americans would not, for the most part, use Native Americans to make sense of a war against a uniformed Philippine army, although some would imagine guerrilla combat in the Islands as "Indian warfare." Native Americans would not often be invoked to explain what criteria should be employed to determine which Hispanicized Filipinos should be permitted to serve in the colonial bureaucracy, although, as Barrows's survey suggested, they would appear in discussions about "non-Christian" policy. So when Americans invoked images of Native Americans, African-Americans or other Asians and Asian-Americans in discussing the Philippines, they would sometimes do so in an attempt to "annex" the new colony to older racial questions. But they would do so just as frequently in order to answer questions that emerged from the peculiarities of the colonial situation itself. And in many cases they would not refer to these other racial contexts, present or past, at all. Transfer, export, and projection—the Philippines as seen through Indian territory—were not reflexive or default responses, but strategies in particular contests whose terrain, combatants, and stakes merit historical inquiry.

Secondly, who got to pose the questions in the first place? Traditional literature on race and U.S. empire places its exclusive focus on the metropolitan United States in terms of sources, voices, agents, and analytical categories. Whether they are politicians, journalists, missionaries, academics, or activists, Americans raise the critical questions, which they then answer employing exclusively "domestic" idioms, revealed in U.S.-based sources, from the *Congressional Record* to political cartoons. In the most extreme cases, the "world" is merely a "mirror" upon which "domestic" idioms and anxieties are projected. Pushed far to the background are ways in which U.S. responses—even where they took "domestic" form—were prompted by the actions of agents located outside the United States. As it is hoped to show in the present case, for example, the devolution of Filipino leader Emilio Aguinaldo in American imagery from a heroic statesman to an "Oriental despot," had everything to do with Philippine resistance to U.S. invasion. Non-U.S. actors shaped the questions that Americans asked themselves about their empire in myriad other ways. Filipino advocates and opponents of colonialism saw their arguments circulated before the American public. And even before the conquest of the Islands was fully over, Filipino elites themselves emerged as a critical audience for U.S. colonial discourse; Filipinos' knowledge (and American translations of it) and Filipinos' political pressure (and American reactions to it), would play central roles in shaping U.S. racial-imperial discourse and practice. American references to all Filipinos as "Indians," for example, thin out the closer they got to Filipino audiences. At the same time, Filipinos would prove resourceful in selectively importing imagery of U.S. racial politics in making their claims; they would, for example, have their own uses for imagery of Native Americans. Any full account of race and U.S. empire requires a careful attention to the multiple, competing and sometimes unanticipated publics and authors of Philippine-American racial discourse.

In this essay, four contexts are explored that played defining roles in rebuilding race in Philippine-American colonial history, contexts that shaped particular intersections and configurations of race and power whose contours cannot easily be reduced to either "exports," or to generic "colonial discourses." It was these contexts, it will be argued, that determined the underlying logics which would, after 1898, filter the importation and non-importation of U.S. racial discourses and practices to the Philippines. The first context was a Spanish colonial racial state in the Philippines which distributed rights and powers on the basis of an interlaced set of hierarchies, within and against which Filipino elites would struggle in the late nineteenth century in their search for reform and, eventually, national independence. The second was the war that violently interrupted that search, brought about by a U.S. invasion of the Islands after 1898; U.S. racial understandings of the Islands' peoples would be propelled by and intertwined with the process of colonial war-making itself. Third was the process of colonial state-building, in which Filipino–American collaboration provided both the necessity and occasion for new racial idioms, practices, and institutions that might organize and justify a colonial administration which partially included elite Filipinos in colonial politics. Fourth and finally was the question of migration: when large-scale Filipino migration to the continental United States began in the late 1920s, it forced colonial officials to defend the occupation against racial nativists and economic protectionists who, once again, redrew the Filipinos' racial place on the map, this time in the interests of insulating the United States from its colony.

Spanish Colonial Legacies

The Philippines that Americans encountered at the turn of the century had been wrought by the forces of race and empire for centuries. By the late nineteenth century, Spanish colonial society in the Islands was predicated on a multi-layered racial system which placed the European-born (*peninsulares*) over the Philippine-born (*criollos* or *espanoles filipinos*); the racially pure above those "mixed" (*mestizo*) with Chinese or *indios* (natives); and Hispanicized Catholic groups above the unconverted (*infieles*) of all kinds: the Chinese, animists, and Muslims.[25] As the Philippines became more fully integrated into the world economy in the nineteenth century, the process gave rise to an urban elite in the Islands which came to call itself *ilustrado* (enlightened) on the basis of its intellectual and cultural sophistication.[26] Many influential *ilustrados* were Chinese *mestizos*, descendents of Chinese and *indio* parents, with ties to both commercial and landed wealth.[27] This elite became increasingly frustrated with the educational and political restraints of colonial society, particularly where they themselves were targeted by reactionary Spanish officials as actual or potential *filibusteros* (subversives). Among the *ilustrados*, a literary and intellectual effort which came to be known as the Propaganda movement campaigned for reforms that would open greater space in Spanish colonial society and politics for "natives"; when these efforts failed, revolution would break out in the Islands, first, abortively, in 1896, and with more decisive results in 1898.[28]

Activists in the Propaganda campaign, among other efforts, challenged the racial rationales that Spanish colonialists had deployed to explain why the Islands' inhabitants could not be trusted with either "self-government" or representation in the Spanish legislature. They ridiculed the sheer inconsistency and arbitrariness of Spanish racial criteria. As *ilustrado* essayist and novelist José Rizal wrote in 1887, when the Spanish government "has to ask us for something, it puts a human nature in our bodies, and takes it away when we ask for representation in the Cortes, freedom of press, rights, etc."[29] They countered Spanish evidence of the Islanders' inherent "indolence" with narratives of politico-economic exploitation; "superstition" was laid at the feet of the natives' indoctrination by Spanish friars. The most cosmopolitan *ilustrados*, able to witness Europe at first hand during their studies or travels abroad, noted with satisfaction that Spanish workers and peasants exhibited many of the same traits. At the same time, the Propaganda movement sought to promote *ilustrado* "civilization" measured in educational and artistic achievement, Spanish-language ability and bourgeois sophistication, before Spanish and broader European audiences. In their attempts to deracialize "civilization" by making it a "native" possession and feature, propagandists mitigated among themselves some of the racial divisions between *criollos*, *mestizos* and *indios*. Especially in the expatriate *ilustrado* community in Europe, a new term—"Filipino"—was used to cut across these racial divisions.[30]

But the *ilustrado* category of "civilization" as a resource for claims-making was itself highly bounded: by tying "civilization" closely to European (if not always explicitly Spanish) roots and diffusions, the *ilustrados* drew tight lines around a still-prospective "Filipino" polity that closely followed the edges of Spain's power, with Muslims and animists—undefeated and unassimilated by Spain—outside of the emerging, imagined polity and society. In their efforts to reconstruct the Islands' history in their self-defense, the *ilustrados* drew upon a theory of "wave migration," which explained the Islands' diversity through an ethno-historical account of progressively more "civilized" invasions, each one of which had driven its more "savage" predecessor further into the mountains. The most recent, and "civilized" of these waves, from which they believed their ancestors derived, had proven most amenable to the "civilizing" influences of Christianity.[31] When Spanish colonialists denigrated Filipino "civilization" through the holding up of animists and Muslims, *ilustrados* would often reinforce this standard by charging that these groups did not properly represent Filipinos' "civilized" character.[32]

Filipino struggles within, and adaptations of, these Spanish colonial racial forms would have a lasting impact on subsequent Philippine-American colonial history. They explained why, when the Philippine Revolution under Emilio Aguinaldo succeeded in defeating Spanish land forces in Spring 1898 and Aguinaldo declared an independent Philippines, he would lay claim to international recognition on the basis of Filipino "civilization." As U.S. colonial officials would soon learn, Filipino elites were highly sensitized to, and prepared to challenge, overtly "racial" attempts to denigrate their abilities—particularly where they were associated with animists and Muslims—and often eager to demonstrate their "capacities" for self-government.

War and Colonial Race-Making

The crucible in which Philippine-American racial politics would be forged would be fired initially, and with searing effect, by imperial war. Until February 1899, the racial angle of U.S. imperial politics had largely pointed "inward," towards Americans' "Anglo-Saxon" historical destiny and political capacity for overseas colonial conquest and rule.[33] Where this racial vision faced outward, its target was Spain, the United States' recent antagonist, whose violence against civilians in Cuba had been melded with its Catholicism into an enmity based on a vision of "medieval" corruption, decadence and cruelty. The primary question that race answered in mid-1898 was what resided so deeply in American nature that it permitted, indeed, required Americans to deploy their military against the Spanish colonial empire. From May 1898, when Dewey's cannons introduced most Americans to the Philippines, Spain's largest remaining colony, through the December signing of the Treaty of Paris, in which Spain ceded the Islands to the United States in exchange for a $20 million payment, American visions of Filipinos were unfocused, with far more press and public attention directed toward the U.S. campaigns in Cuba. But in mid-1898, at least some U.S. coverage had depicted Emilio Aguinaldo, who had declared Philippine independence in June following his return to the Islands by Dewey, as a heroic patriot whose aspirations—not unlike those that had inspired American revolt against the British—Americans ought to recognize.

When the U.S. army occupied Manila in August 1898, insisting that Aguinaldo's forces remain outside the capital, it set in motion a machinery of mutual suspicion. While U.S. diplomats pried the Islands from Spain's delegates in Paris, U.S. army officials on the ground issued public assurances that the Americans presence was meant to free and protect the Islands' people. While Aguinaldo had earlier urged his followers to see the United States as the Islands' liberators, he and his officials now suspected imperial designs.[34] Flashpoints between U.S. and Filipino sovereignty—when U.S. officers sent their troops just across Filipino lines outside Manila, where American soldiers did not feel Manila's sidewalks were big enough to share with Filipinos, or sensed they had been cheated by adept Filipino bargaining—had a way of focusing U.S. racial imaginations on Filipinos in new ways. Older terms of hatred and disgust, like "nigger," would be retooled with increasing intensity by many U.S. soldiers in their letters and diaries. But even as tensions rose in late 1898 and early 1899, Filipino hospitality won many friends among U.S. soldiers, who often reported favorably to their families of their Filipino hosts' nobility, heroism, and "civilization," and the legitimacy of their dreams for national independence.[35]

When fighting broke out between U.S. and Filipino troops in early February 1899, it threw up a new question: what kind of enemy were Filipinos? On the one hand, this was a juridical issue, the question of whether the United States was fighting a "war" against another nation-state or merely suppressing an "insurrection" against its legitimate authority. A *New York Times* editorial urging the ratification of the Treaty of Paris had put it simply: if the Senate did not confirm the Treaty, Americans might "look with leniency" on combatants who "had been persuaded to consider themselves an independent nation resisting a foreign foe." The signing of the Treaty, by contrast, and the attendant refusal to tolerate "the fiction of an independent Government at Malolos," would make Filipino fighters "insurgents against their own Government."[36] On 6 February, the Senate heeded the advice from the *Times*, inventing in the process what Americans would call, for at least a century, the "Philippine insurrection." But if Filipino fighters did not represent a nation-state, what kind of political entity were they?[37] It was in this context that U.S. colonialists discovered the Philippines' "tribes": enlisting an evolutionist discourse that cast the nation-state as the highest stage of political development, they reduced Aguinaldo's government to the will-to-power of a single, Tagalog "tribe" over an impossible plurality of others. (The U.S. colonial official Dean C. Worcester, a zoologist by training, conveniently tabulated eighty-four of them.)[38]

The tribalization of Philippine society recast the United States' short-term goal as the "protection" and "liberation" of the majority of Islanders from Aguinaldo's sinister hegemony, with the longer-term prospect of "assimilating" the Islands' tribal diversities into a unified nation-state. But it did not go uncontested. In 1900, the New England Anti-Imperialist League asked Filipino nationalist Sixto Lopez to produce a "brief statement of the facts" on the "tribes"; Lopez's account skewered official U.S. figures, arguing that the figure of eighty-four had been the result of "imagination, bad spelling, translation, subdivision, and multiplication." But the "tribes" were not entirely fictional, either. It was just that the term "tribe," for Lopez, only pertained to "non-Christian" groups, not to the lowland Catholic majority. Here Lopez imported the image of Native Americans to make his point. The "so-called 'tribes'" in the Philippines were, he wrote, a small minority, analogous to "the uncivilized or semi-civilized remnants of the Indian tribes still inhabiting certain parts of the United States." Filipinos could not be Indians, in other words, because they had "their own" Indians.[39]

In a context of war, the character of the enemy also spoke powerfully through the manner in which it fought. Here, during the first nine months of the war, Aguinaldo confounded those who would denigrate the Philippine Republic by engaging U.S. troops in "civilized" warfare, defined in terms of open combat in formations and uniformed troops. Indeed, despite the persistent failure of this strategy, it appears that Aguinaldo hesitated to break with it for fear that, were his soldiers to adopt guerrilla tactics, they might win militarily, but surrender their broader claims to "civilization."

These fears were realized when, after November 1899, Aguinaldo finally ordered his forces to scatter into the countryside, dissolve into peasant villages, and rely on deception, concealment, and hit-and-run attacks. Even as the Philippine "enemy" became harder to actually identify on the ground, the American sense of the character of that enemy sharpened. U.S. soldiers, tracking "insurgents" onto entirely unfamiliar social and geographic terrain, found this kind of warfare nerve-racking; boredom, frustration, and rage gathered around a sense of the insurgents as cowardly and treacherous. What darkness in the essence of Filipinos, Americans asked, made them fight the way they did? This was "savage" combat; it followed that those who practiced it were "savages." In their efforts to comprehend the guerrilla war, some observers would apply a language of "Indian warfare," while others employed more generic evolutionary criteria. "The war on the part of the Filipinos," wrote Secretary of War Elihu Root, "has been conducted with the barbarous cruelty common among uncivilized races."[40] Furthermore, widespread Filipino peasant support for the fighters, through the supply of provisions and the gathering of intelligence on U.S. forces, suggested to U.S. soldiers and commanders that there was little meaningful distinction between those engaged in actual fighting and the villagers who sustained them. "The whole population has been rank insurrectos from hide to heart," complained General Hughes, a fact that General Arthur MacArthur attributed to what he called "ethnological homogeneity."[41]

As U.S. efforts stalled, a growing number of soldiers and officers came to understand themselves as engaged in a war not against an army or even an insurgency, but against a "savage" population. This meant that the restraints on tactics and targets that characterized "civilized" warfare no longer applied in the Philippines. Following McKinley's re-election in November 1900, General Arthur MacArthur issued a proclamation that broadened both the official definition of the Filipino "enemy" and of acceptable tactics against it.[42] While Filipinos had not had enough "ethnological homogeneity" to be self-governing, they did, apparently, possess enough to be made war upon as a whole. Following MacArthur's order, the boundary between civilians and combatants, already fragile, collapsed in many places, giving rise to a racial-exterminist warfare against Filipino society. U.S. soldiers destroyed Filipino homes, food supplies and animals, tortured captives and killed prisoners and civilians, their actions often animated by highly charged racial language.[43] In some areas of continuing resistance, U.S. officers ordered a war on rural society through the "reconcentration" of village populations into crowded, and soon disease-ridden, camps. While anti-imperialists had been unable to defeat colonialist forces in 1900, they did successfully politicize U.S. troop conduct, forcing the administration and the army onto the defensive.[44] Against mounting evidence, the war's advocates asserted that American "cruelties" were isolated, exaggerated and punished. But they also argued that they were justified by the exceptional character of the enemy and the war. When, during a Senate investigation in 1902, Senator Rawlins asked General Hughes whether the burning of entire towns by advancing U.S. troops was "within the ordinary rules of civilized warfare," Hughes replied succinctly, "These people are not civilized."[45]

Collaboration, State-Building and Inclusion

While the U.S. military was reluctant to admit it, it was impossible to rule an empire through perpetual war. The provinces that U.S. officials chose to call "pacified," sometimes implausibly, had often been subjected to extreme violence, but they were also places whose elites had, over a long and uneven timeframe, broken with the Philippine army and extended their loyalty and services to the Americans. A fragile and self-conscious "postwar" regime would grow from these initial contacts and collaborations, as the second

Philippine Commission, under the leadership of William Howard Taft, traveled the countryside establishing provincial governments, accompanied by members of a U.S.-backed Federalista Party. The Philippine-American colonial state, chartered by Congress in the 1902 Organic Act, would be partly U.S.-appointed, and partly elected by a highly restricted Filipino electorate consisting of literate males who either possessed property or had held office previously, and would thereby be permitted to vote in municipal and provincial elections. By 1907, these voters were allowed to select the representatives to an archipelago-wide Philippine Assembly, the lower house of the legislature, beneath the U.S.-appointed Philippine Commission. This "colonial democracy" would be sustained and bounded by a new apparatus of repression and surveillance, in the form of the Philippine Constabulary and the Philippine Scouts, which would fight the remnants of the residual, internalized war.[46]

The process of colonial state-building, in the midst of ongoing warfare, raised new and thorny questions: having (mostly) conquered the Philippines, how should the United States govern them? And what kind of "subjects" were Filipinos? These questions were taken up by the newly-arriving civilian officials of a consolidating colonial regime, in dialog with select Filipino interlocutors; they were also hotly debated in the United States among social scientists, legal thinkers, and journalists. Attempts to answer these questions by civilian officials in the Islands were crushed between two competing realities: the U.S. military's racialization of Filipinos as permanently "savage" others, reflected in much U.S. press coverage, and the mandate to justify civilian rule itself (as opposed to either continued military rule or outright withdrawal).[47] As subjects of a prospective, interventionist civilian state, Filipino nature would need to be malleable enough to be transformable, but intractable enough to require extensive political and financial resources, and patience. "Assimilation" would need to be necessary, possible, and difficult. The question was what primordial, but still-changeable, Filipino flaws required alteration, and how to plausibly connect these failings to the still-developing capacities of a colonial regime very much in the making.

In answering these questions, civilian officials constructed an alternative account of Philippine reality: where the U.S. military had increasingly fused the Philippine populace into one sinister whole, they asserted, successful colonial governance meant making the right distinctions. The hearings of the Philippine Commission, alongside government-sponsored ethnography and survey work, established the framework within which these new forms of "local" knowledge would develop.⁴⁸ The racial system that emerged from these spaces owed much to conservative *ilustrado* accounts of Philippine society and history, but the U.S. colonial regime would also transform and governmentalize these frameworks in unprecedented ways.

On the one hand, the new racial formation consisted of an essentialized class critique of lowland society, based on an understanding of the relationship between a corrupt and all-powerful "cacique" class—the very figures the U.S. regime itself was cultivating and empowering—and a superstitious, irrational and powerless peasantry.⁴⁹ But on the other hand, it was based on an "optimistic" anthropological assessment of individual Filipinos' "capacity" for "progress." Under long-term colonial "tutelage," Filipinos could "mature" and "assimilate" U.S. customs and loyalties; as they did so, American officials would recognize and reward their accomplishments through the gradual devolution of power. The enlightened masses might even, for some, overturn "cacique" authority itself. This elastic, inclusionary racial formation relied upon a double reading of Spanish Catholicism and its legacies. On the one hand, the Spanish had "pre-civilized" the lowland population; on the other, they had tutored Filipinos in "feudal" social institutions and habits of mind that would have to be patiently eradicated. By inviting but also delimiting Filipino participation, it proved highly effective in making the case for the colonial presence before skeptical Filipinos and Americans. For Filipino elites, it held out promises of progress, recognition and power that the *ilustrados* had pursued since the days of the Propaganda movement; directed at Americans, it asserted that Filipino transformation was both necessary and possible, and posed no threat to the United States itself.⁵⁰ Where the U.S. aim was depicted as the imperial mitigation or interruption of primordial forms of oppression, it lent U.S. colonialism a distinctly "progressive" political and moral cast.⁵¹

If one key axis of the new racial formation, developed in the context of lowland state-building, was "cacique" politics, the other, which corresponded to the new state's encounters with its territorial limits, was Christianity. The theory of "wave migration," communicated from the *ilustrados* to the Americans, corresponded to, and helped Americans make sense of, the U.S. colonial state's own ragged geographic and cultural frontiers. The Philippine-American War had left the forbidding highlands of Luzon, inhabited by animist communities, and the Muslim South, unconquered. Rather than attempting to fold the inhabitants of these regions into the rest of the archipelago's semi-electoral political system, U.S. officials established distinct forms of politico-military rule which were justified by, and in turn helped to give life to, "ethnological" differences among low-land, animist and Moro peoples. "Non-Christians," as animists and Muslims would be classified (in an awkward translation of the Spanish *infiel*), were too "savage" to be granted even limited "self-government," and merited only "paternal" leadership, the only kind their civilizational state prepared them to respect. In highland Luzon, governance would be placed in the hands of militarized governors under civilian rule, while in the South, the U.S. military would resist civilian rule and attempt to isolate the region from central authorities. This bifurcated racial state, divided at the edges of Hispanicization and Catholic evangelization, would, quite literally, be put on the map with the inauguration of two "special" provinces, Mountain Province in the North and Moro Province in the South. In both, American rulers seeking to establish their authority found themselves compelled to negotiate with chieftains who sought to enlist the newcomers in their rivalries, and whose actions the Americans could neither fully comprehend nor control; as a result of these alliances and of their breakdown, violence remained close to the surface of politics in "non-Christian" regions.[52]

If the ideologies of the colonial state were organized around narratives of assimilation, evolution and maturation, they were also driven towards a peculiar, new goal: the self-conscious cultivation of a Filipino "nation." While American colonial officials often traded expertise with other Southeast Asian colonial powers, an American willingness to work through other peoples' nation-states (especially those under their construction) set the U.S. colonial empire somewhat apart. "Nationality" as collective aspiration was not in itself dangerous as long as it was sheared from "illegitimate" notions of sovereignty or self-government. From early in the U.S. colonial period, American officials lauded Filipinos' desires for "nationality," a status that they believed lay far into a hopeful future. They seized hold of the martyred figure of José Rizal, whom peasant and working-class radicals had placed at the center of a millenarian politics, and promoted him as a conservative "national" hero, his call for Filipino self-reform pressed forward and his anti-imperialism trimmed back. Following the initial suppression of publications advocating "independence," U.S. colonial officials developed close ties with an emerging generation of elite Filipino politicians, exemplified by Manuel Quezon and Sergio Osmena, who had come of age during the Revolution. They would propel themselves through election cycles and enlarge their power within the colonial state by using highly popular (and not always containable) nationalistic rhetoric. It was telling that their home, the dominant force in Filipino-American colonial politics for most of the U.S. period, was called the Nacionalista Party. While this nationalist-colonialist regime was not without significant tensions—particularly, in the 1920s, over the boundary between Filipino legislative and U.S. executive power—Filipino political elites and their American patrons could agree on much, from the centrality of sugar and export-oriented development and the need for open access to U.S. markets, to the suppression of "banditry" and other perceived threats to social order, to the settler-colonization of Mindanao by landless Hispanicized Filipinos, to the need for U.S. military protection of the Islands, especially from Japan.[53]

It was, perhaps, the breadth of inter-elite consensus between Americans and Filipinos in the present of the early twentieth century that charged questions of futurity. From relatively early on, U.S. officials had (when compelled) measured the prospective duration of the occupation in loose decades although it was always, importantly, to be finite—a permanently temporary presence. This fact made the future a versatile playground for colonial politics: Filipino nationalists could and did achieve popular support by pressing for and achieving less delayed and more defined transitions of sovereignty, without having to demand forms of independence that might threaten their own monopolistic political power which was, after all, lodged deep in the colonial state itself. The exemplary transition here was the 1916 Jones Act: advocated by Filipino nationalists and U.S. anti-imperialists when they had been presented with the political opening of "anti-imperialist" Democratic rule after the 1912 elections, it was hailed by Quezon, one of its chief architects, as a major shift in the terms of Philippine-American colonialism. The Jones Act did, in fact, replace the appointed, American-dominated, Philippine Commission as the Islands' legislative upper house with an elected Philippine Senate, while formalizing in a preamble "ultimate independence" as the narrative endpoint of the colonial regime, when "stable" government was achieved. But this dialectic of promise and deferral proved a powerful way to anchor a nation-building colonialism: measured in years, the Jones Act would be marginally more successful in perpetuating colonial rule than the original Organic Act of 1902.

U.S. colonialists' nation-building project in the Philippines, in a context of aggressive, ongoing retentionist politics, produced a new and potentially self-perpetuating question: what remained wrong with Filipino nationalism as it was? Why was it still incapable of securing the intangible condition of "stability"? The question surfaced most pointedly during periods when the existing terms of U.S. colonialism were being challenged. At such moments, colonialists told the story of their spotless intentions and heroic efforts at nation-building tragically striking the deep bedrock of Filipino failings that, by definition, had nothing to do with the U.S. presence itself: venal, autocratic "caciques" who exploited the rural masses, self-seeking politicians who plundered public coffers, incompetent bureaucrats, irrational, "hysterical" agitators, and a passive and superstitious populace. That Philippine-American colonialism had generated new forms of corrupt "cacique" rule and a bifurcated racial state was certain, but here retentionists carefully drew a *cordon sanitaire* through their moral accounting of the colonial state, externalizing its positive achievements, especially in health and education, as American gifts, and racializing its failures as expressions of an intractable Filipino essence. Some Filipino authors sought to actively expose and challenge this flexible racial-colonial form. In his 1916 *The Case for the Filipinos*, for example, Maximo Kalaw criticized retentionists for justifying U.S. control by claiming exclusive credit for the regime's accomplishments, while painting Filipinos in "the darkest colors … exaggerating, if not entirely creating new, native vices and shortcomings."[54]

In discrediting the prospects for "stability" under Filipino nationalist self-government, few ideological resources proved more useful than a racial politics of divide-and-rule that essentialized the volatile boundary between Christian and "non-Christian" in need of prolonged, perhaps indefinite, U.S. policing. Left to themselves, retentionists maintained, the Islands' peoples would rend themselves apart along racial lines, as lowland Filipinos attempted to seize the land, labor and resources of "non-Christians" and, in turn, faced "barbaric" resistance. U.S. officials cast themselves in the role of protectors, defending "non-Christians" in the North from exploitation by lowlanders, and Catholics in the South from Muslim warfare and enslavement.[55] In an October 1910 address, for example, Dean Worcester had apparently predicted, to the outrage of nationalist editors, that if the United States were to withdraw from the Islands, the result would be an inevitable Christian–Muslim race war in which Muslims would triumph by virtue of their superior valor; he also implied that the Negritos of Northern Luzon had a greater claim to the "original property" of the Philippines than did lowlanders (as well as superior hygiene).[56]

Filipino nationalist responses to Worcester's speech reflected common approaches to the racial politics of divide-and-rule. An "Anti-Worcester Committee" was formed; the Philippine Assembly passed a resolution condemning his statements as "false, slanderous, and offensive to the Philippine people."[57] But respondents were more likely to charge Worcester with getting his civilizational hierarchies wrong than with dividing the Philippines against itself.[58] One sardonic cartoon imported imagery of Native Americans to assert Filipino nationalist claims. It featured Worcester in Washington, DC, standing next to a stereotyped Native American in a feather head-dress. "Mr Red Skin" says to him: "You have said in Manila that the Negritos, as the earlier inhabitants of the country, are the only ones with territorial rights in the Philippines. My friend, apply this story to America. When are you all leaving?"[59] Here the critique of divide-and-rule naturalized white-settler colonialism in North America in order to express Philippine civilizational hierarchies that owed something to the theory of "wave migration." The lowland Catholic claim to the Philippine Islands— as opposed to the Negritos'—was, for the cartoonist, as irrefutable as the white claim to the United States. Here a vision of Native Americans helped at least some Filipino nationalists accommodate themselves to the role of settler-colonialists.

Migration, Decolonization, and Exclusion

According to predictions that were at the core of the Philippine-American colonial racial state, Filipinos would eventually earn complete "self-government" through a protracted process of tutelage and assimilation, at the end of which the mysterious condition of "stability" would be achieved and demonstrated to the American public. But formal Philippine independence would not, in fact, arrive in this way. The decade and a half after the Jones Act saw Filipino nationalists attempting to defend their grip on the colonial state against Republican efforts to reassert U.S. executive authority; assertions of Filipino "progress" and "capacity" would be countered by an increasingly aggressive retentionism, exemplified in Katherine Mayo's 1925 *Isles of Fear*, a harrowing survey of partial Filipino self-government as unbridled "cacique" rule.[60] Ultimately, decisive pressure for formal Philippine independence in the metropole came not as the fulfillment of a promise but as the recognition of the Islands as a threat: specifically, threats supposedly posed by Philippine agricultural products to domestic producers and Filipino migrants to white racial purity. Ultimately, an aversive anti-colonialism would prove far more successful in generating Philippine "self-government" than assimilationist colonialism had.

At the turn of the century, U.S. colonialists had exhibited little enthusiasm for the prospect that colonialism might forcibly attach vast new supplies of Filipino labor to what were, at that moment, virtually insatiable continental demands. If anything, the prospect of large-scale Philippine-American labor migration was a huge liability. In seeking arguments, anti-colonialists had, in effect, "annexed" the Philippines to decades of politically successful anti-Chinese, nativist mobilization. The result was what can be called an aversive anti-colonialism: envisioning empire as an interconnected, borderless body. Anti-colonialists anticipated with horror that, if the United States were to occupy the Philippines, Filipinos would inevitably come to occupy the United States, a reverse colonization with dire political, moral and racial implications. "If the Philippines are annexed ... " enquired Samuel Gompers, "[c]an we hope to close the flood-gates of immigration from the hordes of Chinese and the semi-savage races coming from what will then by part of our own country?"[61] For Gompers and others, the threat was one of racialized political economy: by effectively nullifying "Asiatic" exclusion, colonial empire in the Philippines would undermine "white" metropolitan labor markets whose standards were already buckling under "Asiatic" competition.

But metropoles and colonies were often sharply at odds over the imperial politics of migration, particularly where, as in the British case, metropolitan officials preoccupied with capitalist development and treaty obligations to the states of actual or would-be migrants clashed with colonial settlers who defined their power in exclusionary, racial-territorial terms.[62] The Philippine-American case saw this dynamic somewhat reversed: colonial authorities in the Islands, who saw the need to promote and organize certain Asian migrations in the interests of colonial politics and development, were being governed by a metropole in which a "white" settler-colonial politics had increasing national-imperial purchase. Nonetheless in two distinct arenas Philippine-American colonial officials either actively cultivated or permitted Asian migrations that cut against a strictly exclusionary logic. The first was pursued in the interests of colonial politics: observing that other imperial powers often attempted to secure the loyalty of local elites by attracting them to the metropole for purposes of an intimidating process of political and cultural "assimilation," the colonial regime established the *pensionado* program, which would eventually sponsor the college educations of approximately three hundred Filipino students in the United States in exchange for subsequent service in the colonial state as teachers, engineers, and civil servants.[63]

A second, and more fraught, issue involved the question of Chinese emigration to the Philippines. In conquering the Philippines, the United States had projected itself into a dense, centuries-old Chinese commercial-migrant empire whose capital and trade fastened the Philippine economy to the rest of the region and whose family networks reached far into the Philippine elite.[64] For the Philippine Commission, as well as many U.S. merchants based in Manila, colonial prosperity and tax revenue depended upon this ongoing mobility of Chinese migrants to and from the Islands. For U.S.-based nativists like California Republican Julius Kahn, however, it was better to "retard exploitation" and "allow the natives ultimately to participate in the development of their own land," than to crush them by "opening the gates" to Chinese merchants.[65] (Here, interestingly, non-Chinese Filipinos were placed in the rhetorical position of West Coast whites, as prospective victims of "Asiatic" invasion.) In April 1902, Congress did extend Chinese exclusion to the Islands, but the law's actual enforcement by Philippine authorities was, perhaps structurally, haphazard.[66]

Perhaps the most decisive way that Philippine-American migration shaped the imperial politics of race was by helping to bring formal Philippine-American colonialism to a close. Aversive anti-colonialism notwithstanding, policy-makers initially passed no specifically anti-Filipino exclusion laws, apart from those directed at Chinese-descended Filipinos. For this reason most Filipinos, legally categorized as U.S. "nationals," retained open migration rights to U.S. territory. If continental nativists feared the advent of Filipino migrant laborers, it did not take long for another imperial power to take an interest: the Hawaiian Sugar Planters' Association (HSPA), which, beginning in 1907, brought rising numbers of Filipinos to the Islands' plantations. Filipinos, in the meantime, perceived their rights to migrate to U.S. territory as integral to their status as U.S. nationals, one of the political claims that they, as colonial subjects, could make on the metropole. One force that would propel Filipinos to the continental United States was the rising, but still selective, wall of exclusionist legislation. The Asiatic Barred Zone, inaugurated in 1917 and extended in the 1924 Immigration Restriction Act, closed off the existing supply of agricultural laborers to West Coast planters.[67] This funneled the imperial search for labor power towards Mexico, through a hemispheric exemption, and towards the Philippines, deliberately gerrymandered outside of "Asia" when it came to exclusion. The result, by the late 1920s, was the sudden advent of large, predominantly male working-class Filipino communities on the West Coast; whereas U.S. imperialists had seen the Philippines as a commercial "stepping stone" to China, Hawaii had turned into a Filipino migratory stepping stone to California.[68]

By the late 1920s, West Coast exclusionists flushed with victory turned their attention to Filipino migrants.[69] They found themselves compelled to answer a new racial question: what was so intractably dangerous about Filipinos that it warranted altering nearly three decades of "assimilating" migration policy? They answered it by countering colonial narratives of transformation with visions of a new "Asiatic" threat: Filipinos as unassimilable, mongrelizing labor competition. Meanwhile powerful U.S. agricultural interests, the Philippines' U.S. competitors in sugar and oils, sought to raise tariffs against Philippine imports. By the early years of the Depression, nativists and protectionists had discovered Philippine independence as a possible solution: decolonization—or at least the formal detachment of the United States from the Philippines in matters of migration rights and tariffs—could simultaneously promote both racial purification and agricultural price supports. Filipino independence activists resisted the exclusionist terms of their would-be allies. "Do not exclude Filipinos from the United States," stated Manuel Roxas pointedly during Senate hearings in 1930, "before you have placed us in a position to exclude Americans from the Philippine Islands."[70] Congress did not, however, heed Roxas's call: the 1935 Tydings-McDuffie Act, which inaugurated a transitional "Commonwealth" government, retained U.S. sovereignty while restricting Filipino migration to fifty persons per year. Where nativists had called for the Islands "complete independence," as one California Congressman had in 1932, "[f]or the sake of our social and economic welfare," decolonization had been an expression of racial insularity.[71]

As historians attempt to move beyond traditional, nation-state scales, whether in the name of "imperial" histories, or attempts to "internationalize" accounts of the past, they run the risk of annexing these "worlds" to their prior, national canons and conventions. Imperial history in this mode would be nothing more than the history of a powerful nation-state writ larger; international histories would simply "nationalize" the global.[72] One cautionary sign of such annexations would be summons to international history as a way of "enriching" the national past, rather than as a possible means to new, multi-national or non-national frames. Another would be historical accounts that describe the uncomplicated "diffusion" outward from national histories of discourses, practices, and institutions. A third would be "reflexive" analysis that moves in the other direction, emphasizing the importance of the transnational only insofar as it illuminates the making of the national, often through unmediated processes of "import." Accounts of U.S. history that reduce its racial-imperial politics to the wholesale "export" of other racial forms, with which this essay began, fall prey to this annexationist impulse, by rendering the United States' new overseas empire significant—and legible—only through its reflection of other racial pasts and presents. It is not, of course, that other histories of race-making—of Indian conquest and removal, Jim Crow segregation and disenfranchisement, and Chinese exclusion especially—played no role in the way Americans came to understand and govern their overseas empire in the twentieth century. It was that the transport of these histories was subject to complex and shifting filters whose openings and closures were determined by myriad and contending actors, and whose patterns were often not reducible to metropolitan formulas. Rather than speeding from Philippine references to African-Americans, Native Americans or Chinese migrants to presumptions about a widespread "export" or outward "projection" of race, historians might linger over the question of why, when, and how these references appear, and their depth and significance with respect to other forms of difference. In pursuing global and imperial histories of race, the historian's task may be to track the contingent process by which forms of essentialized difference were made, contested, transformed, and undermined, keeping in mind both the baggage that historical actors chose to carry (selected, at least in part, in anticipation of new climates and necessities) and the customs regulations that circumstances imposed on them.

Notes

1. On Barrows, see Kenton Clymer, "Humanitarian Imperialism: David Prescott Barrows and the White Man's Burden in the Philippines," *Pacific Historical Review* 45, no. 4 (November 1976): 495–518. Barrows presents his recollections of the trip in his memoirs: *Memoirs of David Prescott Barrows, 1873–1954* (1954), chapter 8, microfilm at the Bancroft Library, Berkeley, California.

2. On the Bureau of Non-Christian Tribes, see Paul A. Kramer, "The Pragmatic Empire: U.S. Anthropology and Colonial Politics in the Occupied Philippines, 1898–1916" (Ph.D. diss., Princeton University, 1998), esp. chapter 3; Karl Hutterer, "Dean Worcester and Philippine Anthropology," *Philippine Quarterly of Culture and Society* 6 (1978): 125–36.

3. Report of the Chief of the Bureau of Non-Christian Tribes, in *Report of the Philippine Commission* (Washington, DC: 1902), Vol. 1, 683. Barrows was given leave in November 1901 and left the Philippines on 11 December, arriving in Pomona, California on 11 January. His itinerary remains unclear, but based on his letters before departing East, he intended to visit the Pimas at Sacaton reservation, the Apaches at San Carlos reservation, Indian Territory, the Carlisle and Lawrence Indian schools, and the Bureau of Indian Affairs. While in Washington, he testified before the hearings of the Senate Committee on the Philippines on 12–13 March 1902: *Af-*

fairs in the Philippine Islands, Senate Document 331, 57th Congress, 679–704. Having returned to Pomona in early April, he wrote to his superior, Dean C. Worcester, of his findings and departed for the Islands again in May.

4. This is especially striking in light of Barrows's earlier willingness to draw equivalences. "In my opinion we will have to extend to much of the islands a reservation system similar to the Indian service here at home," he wrote to his mentor, the anthropologist Frederick Starr, in August 1900, shortly before his arrival in the Islands. This may have been driven by Barrows's own ambitions: "I shall at any rate try to get transferred into the organization of a system controlling the wild tribes," he wrote in the same letter. Barrows to Starr, 16 August 1900, Folder "June 1892–Dec. 1900," Box 1: "Letters by Barrows, 1892–1910," Barrows Papers, Bancroft Library, Berkeley, California (hereafter cited as Barrows Papers).

5. Report of the Chief of the Bureau of Non-Christian Tribes, in *Report of the Philippine Commission*, 684.

6. Report of the Chief of the Bureau of Non-Christian Tribes, 684.

7. Ibid.

8. Barrows's willingness to draw distinctions between Indians and Philippine "non-Christians" appears to have increased as he conducted his fieldwork in the Islands. In an "Outline of Monograph: 'Social Organization of the Igorrote Community,'" Barrows observed: "It is amazing to find in a people just emerging from lower barbarism such a development of the unscrupulous commercial instinct." He then wrote, and crossed out, the following phrase: "The warrior, the leader of natural gifts, the prophet, all those leaders for example who dominate in a tribe of American Indians, has gone before the man who is powerful through wealth." Folder: "Vol. 17, Field Notes - Benguet and the Cordillera of Luzon/June to August 1902," Carton 2, Barrows Papers.

9. Barrows to Dean C. Worcester, 7 April 1902, Folder: "Jan.–Sept. 1902," Box 1: "Letters by Barrows, 1892–1910," Barrows Papers.

10. For critiques of the reservation system and the emergence of an "assimilationist" Indian policy, see Frederick E. Hoxie, *A Final Promise: The Campaign to Assimilate the Indians* (Lincoln, 1984).

11. Report of the Chief of the Bureau of Non-Christian Tribes, 684.

12. For the purposes of this essay, I define race as a system of power and knowledge predicated on the notion of a hierarchical relationship between essentialized communities of difference and affiliation. For a classic formulation of "racial formations" theory, see Michael Omi and Howard Winant, *Racial Formation in the United States: From the 1960s to the 1980s* (New York, 1986).

13. See, especially, Kristin Hoganson, *Fighting for American Manhood: How Gender Politics Provoked the Spanish-American and Philippine-American Wars* (New Haven, 1998); Matthew F. Jacobson, *Barbarian Virtues: The United States Encounters Foreign Peoples at Home and Abroad, 1876–1917* (New York, 2000); Laura Wexler, *Tender Violence: Domestic Visions in an Age of US Imperialism* (Chapel

Hill, 2000); Mary A. Renda, *Taking Haiti: Military Occupation and the Culture of US Imperialism, 1915–1940* (Chapel Hill, 2001); Laura Briggs, *Reproducing Empire: Race, Sex, Science, and US Imperialism in Puerto Rico* (Berkeley, 2002); Warwick Anderson, *Colonial Pathologies: American Tropical Medicine, Race, and Hygiene in the Philippines* (Durham, NC, 2006).

14. For a highly useful critique of the "colonial discourse" framework that emphasizes the need to study race-making within specific and variable colonial contexts, see Nicholas Thomas, *Colonialism's Culture: Anthropology, Travel and Government* (Princeton, 1994). For an excellent discussion of the varieties of both colonial state-building and racial formation in the U.S. colonial empire, see Lanny Thompson, "The Imperial Republic: A Comparison of the Insular Territories under U.S. Dominion after 1898," *Pacific Historical Review* 74, no. 4 (2002): 535–74.

15. On the historiography of U.S. empire in the late nineteenth and early twentieth centuries, see Joseph Fry, "Imperialism, American Style, 1890–1916," in *American Foreign Relations, 1890–1993*, edited by Gordon Martel (London, New York, 1994), 52–70; Louis A. Pérez, *The War of 1898: The United States and Cuba in History and Historiography* (Chapel Hill, 1998). On Philippine historiography, see Reynaldo Ileto, "Outlines of a Nonlinear Emplotment of Philippine History," in *The Politics of Culture in the Shadow of Capital*, edited by David Lloyd and Lisa Lowe (Durham, NC, 1997); Glenn May, "The Unfathomable Other: Historical Studies of U.S.–Philippine Relations," in *Pacific Passage: The Study of American–East Asian Relations on the Eve of the Twenty-First Century*, ed. Warren Cohen (New York, 1996), 279–312. On the historiography of the U.S. colonial period, and the importance of situating it in a global field, see Julian Go, "Introduction: Global Perspectives on the U.S. Colonial State in the Philippines," in *The American Colonial State in the Philippines: Global Perspectives*, edited by Julian Go and Anne L. Foster (Durham, NC, 2003), 148–81.

16. For the classic statement, see Richard Hofstader, "Cuba, the Philippines, and Manifest Destiny," in *The Paranoid Style in American Politics and Other Essays* (New York, 1965), 145–87.

17. Walter L. Williams, "United States Indian Policy and the Debate over Philippine Annexation: Implications for the Origins of American Imperialism," *Journal of American History* 66, no. 4 (1980): 810–31. For more recent elaboration, which argues primarily through homology and juxtaposition, see Anne Paulet, "To Change the World: The Use of American Indian Education in the Philippines," *History of Education Quarterly* 47, no. 2 (2007): 173–202.

18. Williams claims that Native peoples were defined as "nationals," "[p]recisely the same status was conferred upon island subjects after the Spanish–American War." (813) He also argues from simultaneity: "By 1898, while the United States was conquering overseas territories, the Court was characterizing Indians as dependent wards under the 'paramount authority' of Congress … " (813) footnote 17.

19. Williams, "United States Indian Policy," 813, footnote 17.
20. Ibid., 824.
21. Ibid., 828. This is not to suggest that military officers did not make direct connections in their own minds, and in policy terms, but that these linkages cannot be proven, as Williams claims, on the basis of career trajectory alone.
22. Ibid., 828–29.
23. Ibid., 828.
24. Williams suggests that his larger effort in linking these two cases is to demonstrate that the Indian-white situation is "colonial" by connecting it causally to what he presumes is an unequivocal "colonial" case in the Philippines.
25. On the racial structure of Spanish colonial society, see Marya Camacho, "Race and Culture in Spanish and American Colonial Policies," in *Mixed Blessing: The Impact of the American Colonial Experience on Politics and Society in the Philippines*, edited by Hazel M. McFerson (Westport, CT, 2002), 43–74. For the urban dimensions of this social structure, see Ronald R. Reed, "Hispanic Urbanism in the Philippines: A Study of the Impact of Church and State," *University of Manila Journal of East Asiatic Studies* 11 (1967): 1–222.
26. On the *ilustrados*, see Vicente L. Rafael, *The Promise of the Foreign: Nationalism and the Technics of Translation in the Spanish Philippines* (Durham, NC, 2005); Cesar Majul, "*Principales, Ilustrados*, Intellectuals and the Original Concept of a Filipino National Community," *Asian Studies* 15 (1977): 1–20.
27. On the Chinese *mestizos*, see Edgar Wickberg, "The Chinese Mestizo in Philippine History," *Journal of Southeast Asian History* 5, no. 1 (1964): 62–99.
28. On the Propaganda movement, see John N. Schumacher, *The Propaganda Movement, 1880–1895: The Creation of a Filipino Consciousness, the Makers of Revolution* (Manila, 1973).
29. Rizal, quoted in Schumacher, *The Propaganda Movement*, 71–72. On Rizal's anti-racism, see Paul A. Dumol, "Rizal Contra European Racism: An Autobiography of José Rizal Embedded in Blumentritt's Obituary of Rizal," in *European Studies: Essays by Filipino Scholars*, ed. Vyva Victoria Aguirre (Quezon City, Philippines, 1999).
30. For a more detailed treatment of anti-racial arguments launched by the Propaganda movement, see Kramer, *The Blood of Government*, 52–66.
31. On "wave migration" as an element of *ilustrado* historical ideology, see Filomeno V. Aguilar, Jr., "Tracing Origins: Ilustrado Nationalism and the Racial Science of Migration Waves," *Journal of Asian Studies* 64, no. 3 (August 2005).
32. The exemplary moment here was the 1887 Madrid Exposition, when many *ilustrados* charged that the Spanish organizers' display of the "uncivilized" was a deliberate effort to discredit Filipino "civilization." See, especially, Luis-Angel Sánchez-Gómez, *Un Imperio en la Vitrina: El Colonialismo Español en el Pacífico y la Exposición de Filipinas de 1887* (Madrid, 2003).
33. On the reinvention of "Anglo-Saxonism" as a defense of U.S. overseas colonialism, see Paul A. Kramer, "Empires, Exceptions and Anglo-Saxons: Race and Rule be-

tween the British and United States Empires, 1880–1910," *Journal of American History* 88, no. 4 (2002): 1315–53.

34. On Philippine-American tensions in this period, see Teodoro A. Agoncillo, *Malolos: The Crisis of the Republic* (Quezon City, Philippines, 1960).

35. For a more extended discussion of this complex moment in Philippine-American interactions in and around Manila, see Kramer, *The Blood of Government*, 102–11.

36. "The Status of the Filipinos," *New York Times*, 9 February 1899, 6.

37. This question was posed in a context of political contestation over the war itself, prompted by an "anti-imperialist" movement. For the U.S. debate on the Philippine-American War, see Richard E. Welch, *Response to Imperialism: The United States and the Philippine-American War, 1899–1902* (Chapel Hill, 1979). For an overview of the anti-imperialist movement, see Jim Zwick, "The Anti-Imperialist Movement, 1898–1921," in *Whose America? 1898 and the Battles to Define the Nation,* edited by V.M. Bouvier (Westport, CT, 2001), 171–92.

38. As Secretary of the Interior, Worcester would play a disproportionate and, eventually, notorious role in the shaping of imagery surrounding "non-Christian" peoples. On Worcester, see Rodney J. Sullivan, *Exemplar of Americanism: The Philippine Career of Dean C. Worcester* (Ann Arbor, 1991).

39. Sixto Lopez, *The "Tribes" in the Philippines* (Boston, 1900).

40. Root, in "Charges of Cruelty, etc., to the Natives of the Philippines," Senate Document 205, 57th Congress, 17 February 1902, pt. 1, 2.

41. Hughes, "Diary of Events from December 14 to December 29, received by the War Department February 9, 1901," quoted in *Facts about the Filipinos* 1, no. 10 (15 September 1901): 33; MacArthur, Report to Adjutant General of the Army, 1 Oct. 1900, in *Annual Report of Major General Arthur MacArthur, US Volunteers, Commanding Division of the Philippines*, vol. 1 (Manila, 1900), 6.

42. MacArthur, "Proclamation," in Annual Report of the Secretary of War, 1901, 57th Congress, 1st session, House Doc. 2, Vol. 1, pt. 4, 91–96.

43. Stuart Creighton Miller emphasizes the role of racism in U.S. troop conduct in *"Benevolent Assimilation": The American Conquest of the Philippines, 1899–1903* (New Haven, 1982).

44. On the investigation of atrocities, see Richard E. Welch, Jr., "American Atrocities in the Philippines: The Indictment and the Response," *Pacific Historical Review* 43, no. 2 (1974): 233–53.

45. Rawlins and Hughes, quoted in "Affairs in the Philippine Islands," Senate Document 331, 57th Congress, 1st Session, pt. 1, 559.

46. On Filipino-American collaboration politics, see Paul D. Hutchcroft, "Colonial Masters, National Politicos, and Provincial Lords: Central Authority and Local Autonomy in the American Philippines, 1900–1913," *Journal of Asian Studies* 59, no. 2 (2000): 277–306; Michael Cullinane, *Ilustrado Politics: Filipino Elite Responses to American Rule, 1898–1908* (Quezon City, Philippines, 2003); Ruby Paredes, ed., *Philippine Colonial Democracy* (Quezon City, Philippines, 1989); Norman Owen,

ed., *Compadre Colonialism: Studies of the Philippines Under American Rule* (Ann Arbor, 1971).

47. These struggles over race informed broader tensions over military–civilian transition at the uncertain "end" of the Philippine-American War. See R.E. Minger, "Taft, MacArthur, and the Establishment of Civil Government in the Philippines," *Ohio Historical Quarterly* 70, no. 4 (1961): 308–31.

48. On the Philippine Commission, and the work of the colonial state more generally, see Glenn Anthony May, *Social Engineering in the Philippines: The Aims, Execution, and Impact of American Colonial Policy, 1900-1913* (Westport, CT, 1980).

49. For reflections on the legacies of this interpretation in scholarship on Philippine politics, see Reynaldo Ileto, "Orientalism and the Study of Philippine Politics," in *Knowing America's Colony* (Manoa, HI, 1999).

50. For an account of one key Filipino enthusiast of U.S.-led "assimilation," see Barbara Gaerlan, "The Pursuit of Modernity: Trinidad H. Pardo de Tavera and the Educational Legacy of the Philippine Revolution," *Amerasia Journal* 24, no. 2 (1998): 87–108.

51. For a more extended account of this "inclusionary" racial formation, see Kramer, The *Blood of Government*, chapter 3.

52. On U.S. military rule in Mindanao and Sulu as an effort to construct a distinct colonial regime within the U.S. colonial state, see Patricio Abinales's highly insightful "An American Colonial State: Authority and Structure in Southern Mindanao," in *Images of State Power: Essays on Philippine Politics from the Margins* (Diliman, Philippines, 1998), 1–52. For an overview of U.S. military rule in the South, see Peter G. Gowing, *Mandate in Moroland: The American Government of Muslim Filipinos, 1899-1920* (Quezon City, Philippines, 1983). On the establishment of Mountain Province, see Howard T. Fry, *A History of the Mountain Province* (Quezon City, Philippines, 1983). On the impact of U.S. colonial structures in Northern Luzon on highlander identity, see Gerard A. Finin, *The Making of the Igorot: Contours of Cordillera Consciousness* (Quezon City, Philippines, 2005). On the colonial census as an instrument of division between "savage" and "civilized" Filipinos, see Vicente Rafael's pioneering "White Love: Surveillance and Nationalist Resistance in the U.S. Colonization of the Philippines," in *Cultures of United States Imperialism*, edited by Amy Kaplan and Donald Pease (Durham, NC, 1993), 185–218.

53. On the linkages between Filipino nationalism and U.S. colonialism, see the essays in Paredes, ed., *Colonial Democracy*. It appears that white-Native American history may have played an important role in U.S. officials' and Filipino approaches to the settler-colonization of Mindanao; this is an extremely promising avenue for future research.

54. Maximo Kalaw, *The Case for the Filipinos* (New York, 1916), xi–xii.

55. On the politics of "slavery" in this context, see Michael Salman, *The Embarrassment of Slavery: Controversies over Bondage and Nationalism in the American Colonial Philippines* (Berkeley, 2001).

56. The original text of the speech does not appear to exist. For nationalist press clippings in response, see "Los Infieles y Worcester," El Ideal, 11 Oct. 1910, in Folder: "Lecture, 1910, given at the YMCA," Box 2, Dean C. Worcester Papers, Bentley Library, University of Michigan (hereafter cited as Worcester Papers).

57. Resolution quoted in James H. Blount, *The American Occupation of the Philippines, 1898–1912* (New York, 1912), 584.

58. Elite Filipinos also accused U.S. officials of deliberately foregrounding "non-Christians" at the St. Louis World's Fair of 1904 as an argument for U.S. imperial retention. On the construction of the Philippine exhibit at the fair, and contestation over it, see Kramer, *The Blood of Government*, chapter 4.

59. "Worcester en Washington" (cartoon), *Alipatos*, 9 Nov. 1910, in Folder: Lecture, 1910, given at the YMCA," Box 2, Worcester Papers.

60. Katherine Mayo, *The Isles of Fear: The Truth about the Philippines* (New York, 1925).

61. Samuel Gompers, "Imperialism—Its Dangers and Wrongs," in *Republic or Empire?: The Philippine Question*, William Jennings Bryan, et al. (Chicago, 1899), 209–10. On racism among anti-imperialists more generally, see Christopher Lasch, "The Anti-Imperialists, the Philippines, and the Inequality of Man," *Journal of Southern History* 24, no. 3 (1958): 319–31.

62. See, esp., Robert A. Huttenback, *Racism and Empire: White Settlers and Colored Immigrants in the British Self-Governing Colonies, 1830–1910* (Ithaca, 1976).

63. On the *pensionado* program, seen through students' publications, see Emily Lawsin, "Pensionados, Paisanos, and Pinoys: An Analysis of the Filipino Student Bulletin, 1922–1939," *Filipino American National Historical Society Journal* 4 (1996).

64. On the Chinese in the nineteenth-century Philippines, see Edgar Wickberg, *The Chinese in Philippine Life, 1850–1898* (New Haven, 1965).

65. Julius Kahn, 57th Congress, 1st Session, 1902, *Congressional Record*, vol. 35, 3692.

66. On the U.S. policy towards Chinese immigration in the Philippines, see Irene Jensen, *The Chinese in the Philippines during the American Regime, 1898–1946* (San Francisco, 1975).

67. On the 1924 exclusion act, see Mae Ngai, *Impossible Subjects: Illegal Aliens and the Making of Modern America* (Princeton, 2004).

68. On Filipino migration to the United States during the early twentieth century, see Bruno Lasker, *Filipino Immigration to the Continental United States and to Hawaii* (Chicago, 1931). Alongside political mobilization, anti-Filipino violence became common during this period. On the most extensive incident of this violence, see Howard A. DeWitt, "The Watsonville Anti-Filipino Riot of 1930: A Case Study of the Great Depression and Ethnic Conflict in California," *Southern California Quarterly* 61, no. 3 (1979): 291–302.

69. On this movement, see the essays in Josefa M. Saniel, ed., *The Filipino Exclusion Movement, 1927–1935* (Quezon City, Philippines, 1967).

70. Roxas, in House Committee on Immigration and Naturalization, *Exclusion of Im-*

migration from the Philippine Islands, 71st Congress, 2nd Session, 1930, 106.

71. Richard Welch, in House Committee on Insular Affairs, *Independence for the Philippine Islands*, 72nd Congress, 1st session, 1931, 378–79.

72. For a thoughtful critique of the "internationalizing" turn within U.S. history along these lines, see Louis A. Pérez, Jr., "We are the World: Internationalizing the National, Nationalizing the International," *Journal of American History* 89, no. 2 (September 2002).

Chapter 9

Interrogating Caste and Race
in South Asia

Gita Dharampal-Frick and Katja Götzen

"Treating caste as a form of race is politically mischievous and scientifically nonsensical."[1] This contentious statement by André Béteille, a
renowned Indian anthropologist, was formulated in anticipation of the
United Nations sponsored "World Conference against Racism, Racial Discrimination, Xenophobia and Related Intolerance" (WCAR),[2] held in
Durban, South Africa, in August 2001. As a prelude to this international
event, the issues of caste and race in India and the contested nature of their
shared affinities sparked an intense debate. The controversy itself was cat-
apulted to center stage by the demand of Dalit[3] (or so-called untouchable)
spokesmen for the inclusion of caste, and by implication, the discriminatory practice of untouchability within the wider Western discourse on
racism, as part and parcel of the agenda of this conference. Presumably the
ulterior aim of "interested" parties was for an international campaign to be
launched against caste discrimination under the aegis of the world organization. This demand, however, was vehemently opposed by the Indian
government, as well as by some sections of civil society,[4] partially as a knee-
jerk reaction, and partially as a matter of principle, in opposition to the
engrained "colonial mentality of attempting to understand Indian reality
through western categories of analysis" as averred by D.L. Sheth,[5] an Indian political sociologist and senior research fellow at the Delhi Centre for
the Study of Developing Societies. The ensuing altercation, with different
stands taken by representatives of the media, academia, and the NGO sector, generated voluminous literature which was admittedly more politically
motivated than guided by strictly academic concerns.[6]

To obtain a meaningful understanding of these heated debates of crucial
contemporary socio-political importance, addressing issues related to caste,
race, national cultural identity[7] and, more pertinently, to practices of dis-

crimination and social inequality, this essay aims to trace and deconstruct, in the first instance, the historical genealogy of the category "caste" as used in the subcontinent from the early modern period onwards. In doing so, the focus will, secondly, be on the entangled history of the caste–race discourse. An endeavor will be made to foreground how this ideological inter-linkage was instrumentalized from the latter half of the nineteenth century, both to legitimize as well as to resist systems of domination and socio-political discrimination.

Caste, like race, constitutes not only a discursive but also an extremely loaded concept, especially since the discriminatory categories of casteism and racism are implied in these designations, respectively. Needless to say, the inter-linkage of both terms has been a subject of contention which long predates the Durban conference.[8] Hence, by looking at race in the mirror of caste, our intention is to view the global dimensions of racism from the periphery. Yet, with the focus being on India, caste will be at the heart of this essay, as underscored by the following succinct quote from Susan Bayly's seminal study on historical developments in Indian society and politics:

> Of all the topics that have fascinated and divided scholars of South Asia, caste is probably the most contentious. Defined by many specialists as a system of elaborately stratified social hierarchy that distinguishes India from all other societies, caste has achieved much the same significance in social, political and academic debate as race in the United States, class in Britain and faction in Italy. It has, thus, been widely thought of as the paramount fact of life in the subcontinent, and for some, as the very core or essence of South Asian civilisation.[9]

This passage highlights the significance of academic discourse on caste, albeit with due caution: by mentioning the "stratified social hierarchy"[10] Bayly refers to the scaled ordering of the four varnas (Brahmins, Kshatriyas, Vaishyas and Shudras) which, though primarily conceptual categories, have been interpreted as constituting actual social strata. They have been defined as representing four broad occupational groupings, namely the priests (or Brahmins), warriors and kings (Kshatriyas), merchants and craftsmen (Vaishyas) and laborers and peasants (Shudras); the most influential and yet increasingly controversial interpretation of the fourfold varna hierarchical system has been elaborated by Louis Dumont.[11] The conventional definition of caste would also include the practice of endogamy, the high status of the Brahmins, and the marginalization of the Dalits. Furthermore, as elucidated by Ronald Inden in his postmodern critique of "orientalist" scholarship on India,[12] caste has been construed, from the colonial period onwards, as representing the "substantialised agent of Indian society and history"; according to this essentialized reading, caste is castigated for excelling other systems of stratified discrimination. Thus, caste society has been decried not only as setting India apart from the West (as well as from other Asian civilizations), but also for being responsible, notably in colonial discourse, for the former's arrested civilization, economic stagnation, and political fragmentation. This essentialization of difference is in itself most intriguing and constitutes a trend that dates from the nineteenth century.[13] Our intention in this essay is to unravel this transcultural discursive entanglement by contending that the discourse on race has impinged on our understanding of caste, albeit with varying degrees of intensity, and that thereby "caste" as a hermeneutic phenomenon has to a certain extent been racialized. Whilst elucidating the epistemology of the caste–race discourse, and thereby deconstructing the process by which our knowledge about the concept of caste has been produced, we shall endeavor to highlight the transformations (determined by differing historical-political contexts) that have taken place over the past five hundred years.

Quite tellingly, in like manner to "race,"[14] the term "caste" itself, was first introduced into India by the Portuguese at the beginning of the sixteenth century and had similar broad semantic connotations: the Portuguese *casta* not only embraced several meanings such as "family," "stock," "kind," "strain," "clan," "tribe," and "race," but consequently was also used to designate various kinds of social groups, besides Hindu ones, such as the "caste of Moors," the "caste of Christians," etc.[15] Hence, it must be emphasized that the early Portuguese usage was very non-uniform. Moreover, the much-discussed nineteenth-century "racist" notion of "purity of blood," deduced from the etymological derivation of the word from the Latin *castus*, meaning "chaste" or "pure," was by no means foregrounded in the early sixteenth century, but only latently implicit, if at all.[16] This inherent semantic polyvalency of the term caste, including as only one of its meanings the category of race,[17] constituted an instrument employed by external observers to describe the socio-cultural heterogeneity confronted on the western (or Malabar) coast of India.[18] How bewildering this polyphony of social codes must have appeared to an early modern European observer is apparent from the following brief remark, made in 1516 by Duarte Barbosa, the famous proto-ethnographer of maritime India: "This King (of

Calicut) keeps 1000 women, to whom he gives regular maintenance, and they always go to his court to act as the sweepers of his palace … these are ladies, and of good family (*estas saom fidalgos e de boa casta*)."[19] What apparently struck the Portuguese observer were not merely the numerous women in the King's retinue, but rather the incongruous nature of their lowly occupation.[20] Indeed, social stratification being defined along the axis of purity/impurity à la Dumont[21] does not seem applicable here. Furthermore, Barbosa's remark by no means constitutes an odd anomaly, for early modern European accounts are replete with such disconcerting *aperçus* which, nonetheless, help to underscore the multidimensional forms of social organization in the different regions of India.[22] Yet, despite this focus on empirical heterogeneity, there is an underlying tendency even in these descriptive reports to categorize or conceptually straitjacket the observed polyvalence.[23] For instance, in early German reports dating from the early sixteenth century, rather than recourse being taken to the linguistically foreign Portuguese *casta*, a variety of other more familiar terms were referred to, such as "estate," "family," "guild," "nation," etc., representing sociological concepts commonly employed in the early modern European-German context. This terminological usage, whilst constituting a cognitive semantic imposition, is simultaneously indicative of the fact that the distinctive societal ordering perceived in Indian society was being brought in line with similar European social divisions; India was thus being drawn closer to Europe, albeit on the latter's terms, rather than being distinguished from it, as would be the case later, when India became conquered territory. This implicit acknowledgement of a coeval relationship[24] between India and Europe in pre-colonial times constitutes a striking contrast to late-nineteenth- and early-twentieth-century Western attitudes.

Admittedly, when observing the ethnically diverse Indian population, physical "racial" differences were perceived, as is apparent from references made to nuances of differing skin pigmentation; however, these phenotypical differences were not yet categorized and discriminated against according to a "racist" hierarchy. Everyday social life in the different Indian regions was viewed basically from a non-Brahmanical angle, whereby the multi-dimensionality and plurivalency of social formations were highlighted, as in a case study of Tamil society with its ninety-eight groupings, described by a German missionary at the beginning of the eighteenth century.[25] In these early modern proto-ethnographies, with stress laid on the occupational variety in the general populace, stereotypical notions about the so-called caste society which later achieved hegemonic status—such as linear hierarchy, rigid occupational specialization, the racial implications of group endogamy,[26] and last but not least, the preeminent status of the Brahmins—were not yet an issue in European perceptions of Indian regional societal formations.

By the late eighteenth century, this non-dogmatic and less ideologically weighted understanding of the plurality and contextually contingent nature of Indian communitarian society was radically transformed due to a complex cluster of intertwined historical developments. Prominent among them were factors emanating from the colonial situation (and its ideologies of legitimacy);[27] these included, for instance, relationships of increasingly pronounced political asymmetry between Europeans and Indians,[28] concomitant drastic changes in the Indian socio-political order as a result of political subjugation,[29] economic disruption and impoverishment of wide sections of the population leading to demographic and cultural upheavals,[30] new intellectual concerns of the colonial administrator-cum-scholars influenced by ethno-religious theories formulated in Europe,[31] and last but not least, the so-called "Orientalist" appropriation of selected Indian scriptural traditions,[32] which also involved a certain measure of collaboration on the part of indigenous Brahmin scholars. To understand the tangible repercussions of this complex scenario not only on Indian societal formations but also on the perceptions of colonial administrators and scholars we need to briefly look into specific aspects of "oriental" knowledge production whose "findings" significantly influenced the subsequent streamlining or pigeonholing of the plethora of Indian social groups.[33]

After the British conquest of Bengal (subsequent to the battle of Plassey in 1757),[34] in order to gain a secure political foothold as well as to construct a legalistic administrative framework,[35] strategic importance was given to the selective appropriation of the region's cultural heritage. Towards these ends, British scholars were employed at the Royal Asiatic Society in Calcutta,[36] founded in 1784 under the auspices of the first Governor-General, Warren Hastings.[37] With an aim to classify and codify Bengali (and by extension Indian) society, these orientalist scholars[38] endeavored to discover or reconstruct the origins of Indian societal order based on scriptural Brahmanical explanations. This approach was in line with the ongoing European preoccupation with civilizational origins and the belief in the authoritative nature of ancient scriptural traditions.[39] Accordingly, it was no coincidence that the *Manusmriti*,[40] also known as the *Manavadharmashastra,* was translated by the founding father of Indology, William Jones, in 1794.[41] This ancient scripture, rendered into English as the Laws of Manu,[42] attracted

Jones's attention since it represented an orthodox Brahmanical defense of social status, listing as it did, from a Brahmanical perspective, the social obligations and duties of the four stratified varnas. Paradigmatically, these varnas which (as mentioned above) constitute conceptual social categories were understood as representing actual social groups. Furthermore, erroneously viewed as a generally accepted Indian legal code, this text was endowed with canonic importance, not least because it was seen as providing trans-cultural and meta-historical modes of understanding Indian society which in turn were amenable to British colonial interests of codifying the multivalent social relations into a single (Brahmanic) hierarchical register.[43] This re-appropriation by means of a quasi re-invention of tradition was further amplified by the collaboration of Brahmin scholars who rightly hoped not only to maintain but to further extend their social influence and heighten their ritual standing by assisting in attributing hegemonic preeminence to specific Brahmanical scriptural treatises.[44]

Significantly, on an etiological level, Manu, who in the ancient scripture exemplifies not merely the ancient law-giver but also the progenitor of mankind, was identified by Jones, steeped in Biblical mythology, with Adam in the Book of Genesis.[45] This constructed identification supposedly emphasized the universal truth of the biblical origin myth, echoes or remnants of which, according to Jones's (mis)interpretation, could be found in ancient Brahmanical scriptures. Yet even prior to his translation of the Manusmriti, another biblical myth denoting racial origins was brought to bear in a more significant discovery also attributed to Jones: this was the identification of the philological kinship between Sanskrit, Greek, Latin, Gothic, Celtic, and Old Persian, ancient languages which were all shown to originate from a primordial, yet "lost" *Ursprache*—later to be termed proto-Indo-European.[46] Thus, Jones was held in esteem for having laid the groundwork for the subsequent elaboration of the Indo-European language family. This apparently modern comparative philological appraisal was, however, as already elucidated by Trautmann and others, rooted in, or at least connected with, another much more traditionally oriented project, namely that of defending the Old Testament biblical narrative.

Indeed, in defense of Mosaic ethnology[47] and against Voltaire's construction of a pre-Mosaic deism, Jones categorized the speakers of these so-called Indo-European languages as being the descendants of one of Noah's three sons, namely Ham. As for the other two, Shem was designated as the forefather of the Arabs, while Japhet was believed to be the progenitor of the Tartars. This categorization, needless to say, gave a completely different rendering to the later more common interpretation of Japhet being designated as the forefather of the Indo-Europeans, Shem of the Semites, and Ham—the cursed son—as ancestor of the (black) Africans. What is even more significant for our topic is that it was Jones's application of Mosaic ethnology to explain the philological pedigree of Sanskrit that eventually constituted the theoretical basis for conflating the origins of language with those of race.[48] On the one hand, it sewed the seeds that germinated and grew into the Indo-European or Aryan family tree; at the same time, however, it laid the foundations for the advancement of the Aryan theory of race, which would inspire Max Müller[49] several decades later to emphasize with rhetorical flourish that the British and Indians were in fact distant cousins. After having turned once more to the Manusmriti and its origin myth of the four varnas, we will pick up this thread again.

As already indicated, the Laws of Manu did not have any real empirical validity in pre-colonial times. From the nineteenth century onwards, however, the structured hierarchical ordinance elaborated in this ancient treatise was increasingly viewed (due its obvious cognitive, cultural, and ideological appeal) as defining and indeed constituting the Indian caste system: in short, the Brahmanical ritualistic and prescriptive *varnashramadharma*[50] (or social ethical code) was interpreted as the organizing principle par excellence, representing a cohesive albeit primitive form of Indian social order.

In addition, yet another Brahmanical etiological myth substantiating the Manu scenario was given canonical status, namely the Purusha narrative from the Rigveda.[51] This ancient vedic text details the ritual origin of the four varnas from the sacrificial body of the Purusha (presumed to be an Indian equivalent of the Greek Prometheus): from his head the Brahmin or priests emanated, from his shoulders the Kshatriyas or kings, from his thighs the Vaishyas or merchants and craftsmen, and from his feet the Shudras or peasants. This integrative ritual scenario in which Hinduism abounds, signifying from an emic perspective the single racial origin of all social groups, represented primarily the embodiment of a holistic, organic vision of human community. Yet this metaphorical conceptualization was taken literally by the early orientalists as designating the ranked functional and religiously sanctioned hierarchy of the Hindu body-politic.

Needless to say, it was this canonization by British and later European orientalists of ancient Brahmanical scriptural lore, dating from the first or second millennium BC, that increasingly served as a blueprint for understanding early-nineteenth-century Indian society—despite (or perhaps because of) the latter's obvious plurivalency and multidimensionality; and it was this canonization that, conjoined with the Portuguese term *casta,* not only defined caste organization as Brahmanically hierarchical and discriminatory, but also projected it as stultifyingly ritualized.[52] This, in turn, opened the floodgates of admonitions from evangelical missionaries and Utilitarian-minded administrator-scholars alike. The Baptist missionary William Ward, for instance, made the following statement in 1822:

> Like all other attempts to cramp the human intellect, and forcibly to restrain men within bounds which nature scorns to keep, this system, however specious in theory, has operated like the Chinese national shoe, it has rendered the whole nation crippled. Under the fatal influence of this abominable system, the bramhuns have sunk into ignorance, without abating an atom of their claims to superiority; the kshutriyus became almost extinct before their country fell into the hands of the Musulmans; the voishyus are no where to be found in Bengal; almost all have fallen into the class of shoodrus, and shoodrus have sunk to the level of their own cattle.[53]

The missionary's denunciation was due in part to the fact that the empirical reality of thousands of social communities or *jatis* did not by any means conform to the stratified linear hierarchy of the fourfold varna scheme. This was especially true of Bengali society in which the varnas of the Shudras and the Brahmins predominated almost exclusively; the situation was further compounded by the socio-cultural upheaval and economic impoverishment in the aftermath of the Bengal famine of 1770, which resulted in the death of one-third of the region's population.[54] Another reason for Ward's condemnation of so-called caste-ridden Indian society, however, can be attributed to the proselytizer's exasperation, for the cohesive caste community stubbornly resisted Christian conversion. Another missionary, William Carey,[55] despairingly wrote that: "All are bound to their present state by caste, in breaking whose chains a man must endure to be renounced and abhorred by his wife, children and friends."[56] Furthermore, Carey describes caste as "a prison which immures many innocent beings," thus, using a far more forceful metaphor than Ward's "Chinese shoe." Also in line with the French missionary Abbé Dubois, he condemned caste as "a system that brooked neither individual dissent nor any form of freedom of movement." In accordance with Christian polemics, caste was declared the "most cursed invention of the Devil that ever existed,"[57] and had already induced Charles Grant to demand a Christian crusade against the system.[58] This proselytizing zeal compares, in the European context, to contemporary abolitionists' calls for anti-slavery legislation. Indeed, the equation of caste and slavery was by no means uncommon among Christian missionaries of the time, as underscored by William Wilberforce,[59] one of the staunchest abolitionists, whose harsh critique of the perceived inhuman character of caste society induced the British government to endorse full-scale missionary activity on the subcontinent. He articulated this position in a speech before the British Parliament in 1813:

> Why need I, in this country, insist on the evils which arise merely out of the institution of Caste itself; a system which ... must truly appear to every heart of true British temper to be a system at war with truth and nature; a detestable expedient for keeping the lower orders of the community bowed down in an abject state of hopeless and irremediable vassalage. ... Christianity ... has been acknowledged even by avowed sceptics, to be, beyond all other institutions that ever existed, favourable to the temporal interests and happiness of man: and never was there a country where there is greater need than in India for the diffusion of its genial influence. ... Our religion is sublime, pure and beneficent. Theirs is mean, licentious, and cruel. ... Equality is the vital essence and the very glory of our English laws. Of theirs, the essential and universal pervading character is inequality; despotism in the higher classes, degradation and oppression in the lower.[60]

Similarly, for James Mill, the arch utilitarian and author of the hegemonic *History of British India*[61] (who, never having been to India himself, relied on orientalist research), the brahmanicized projection of Indian society represented: "a system of priestcraft, built upon the most enormous and tormenting superstition that ever harassed and degraded any portion of mankind, their minds were enchained more intolerably than their bodies; in short that, despotism and priestcraft taken together, the Hindus, in mind and body, were the most enslaved portion of the human race."[62] In line with utilitarian reasoning whilst proclaiming that "the priesthood holds the greatest authority in the lowest state of society,"[63] Mill proceeded to fix the binary distinction between enlightened Britain, the civilized nation-state, and caste-ridden Indian society. Mill and like-minded colonial administrators in dire need of Britain's civilizing mission declared that the latter, branded a primitive society *par excellence*, would be freed from the slavery of caste.

Paradoxically, in the aftermath of the Great Rebellion of 1857,[64] the importance of "Brahmanized caste" as a classificatory category and an analytical lens through which Indian society was perceived grew significantly. This was mainly due to the colonial administration's preoccupation with reinforcing political control. To achieve this goal, not only was Manu's rigidly defined hierarchical ordering instrumentalized most efficiently to establish social order (abetted by the philological assistance of reputed Indologists such as the eminent Max Müller), but also, and more importantly, the new science of race was given a significant role in refurbishing the British Raj.[65] Subsequently, caste metamorphosed into a racialized avatar, a transformation assisted by various nineteenth-century scientific developments. Firstly, misconstrued translations through supposed philological expertise, for instance, of the crucial term *varna* (that in Sanskrit signifies "category" or "quality," and "color" only in a symbolic, ritualistic context), gave rise to an influential rendering (which still holds sway), interpreting it as denoting skin color or pigmentation, so that the fourfold conceptual hierarchy could be explained as with racial categories.[66] Similarly other Sanskrit words describing descent groups and kinship relations such as *vamsa, kula, jati,* and *gotra* were translated as "race."[67]

Anthropological knowledge in support of the imperialist project soon empirically complemented such racially oriented philological scholarship.[68] Besides being applied in revamping the army with new recruits from communities originating from northwest India, designated as "martial races," and in branding oppositional forces as criminal tribes or castes,[69] the new science of anthropology was crucial to the subcontinental decennial census operation initiated in 1871. Apart from policing society and controlling labor migration, the overarching aim of the undertaking was clearly to inventory India's caste society like a "cadastral survey of the land."[70] The exercise was intended not so much to list the number of people belonging to individual castes, but rather to determine and fix the relative status of different castes with the aim of providing a pan-Indian operational hierarchy—in line with the Brahmanical varna scheme—to serve as a controlling adjunct to colonial authority.[71]

On the one hand, this social engineering turned out to be an almost impossible undertaking, due to the strong sense of prestige and status manifested by most individual castes whose resistance to being pigeonholed into specific hierarchically defined varna categories led to endless disputes, counterclaims, and petitions. On the other hand, due to the rigorous nature of the exercise (testifying to the authoritarian modus operandi of the colonial bureaucratic state) and its reliance on indigenous sociological categories which, though disputed and theoretical in nature, were nevertheless familiar and commanded a certain authority,[72] the varna hierarchical scheme soon gained recognition as a pan-Indian model of social organization—at least by the Westernized classes who hoped through their compliance would yield political and economic gains. In this gigantic subcontinental census operation further assistance was sought from the new racial science of anthropometry.[73] Scholar-administrators on the census commission zealously adopted the theories and methods of the French race theorists Broca[74] and Topinard,[75] and the criminologist Bertillon,[76] for measuring and categorizing different bodily features as race markers. In the forefront of these officials were Herbert Risley[77] and Edgar Thurston,[78] who hoped to refine and expand European theories of race by applying them to specimens of Indian endogamous caste society, which seemed like an ideal laboratory for late-nineteenth-century race science.[79] Through the application of the infamous nasal index, for instance, Risley hoped to demonstrate that "the social status of the members of a particular group varies in inverse ratio to the mean relative width of their noses";[80] his colleague, Thurston, surmised that "intelligence is in inverse proportion to the breadth of the nose."[81] The latter is said to have remarked that "no one with a nasal index exceeding 78 need apply" for the advertised position of clerkship in his office.[82]

Risley's obsession with race as the defining feature of caste led him to proclaim: "The remarkable correspondence between gradations of (social) type as brought out by certain indices and the gradations of social precedence further enables us to conclude that *community of race*, and not, as has frequently been argued, *community of function*, is the real determining principle, the true *causa causans*, of the caste system."[83] Risley persisted in upholding racial indices despite innumerable discrepancies in concrete scientific findings, indicative of the fact that measurable biological differences between higher and lower castes were insignificant. However, given that the science of racial anthropology, often employing an *ex ante* deductive methodology, was driven by its own logic and impetus, setbacks, such as difficulties in providing accurate measurements, did little to dampen the census commissioner's enthusiasm. Further, the census project aimed not merely to fix Indian social hierarchy, defined according to racial categories, but even more significantly, to determine the racial origins of the disparate Indian populations; indeed, ascertaining their rank within a typology of races was the crux of the matter.[84]

We shall now briefly review the implications of the Aryan theory of race[85] that had since the era of William Jones derived academic sanction from the work of comparative philologists such as Max Müller and Christian Lassen, ideological sanction from Joseph Arthur de Gobineau, and political sanction by the end of nineteenth century from the imperialist project.[86] The basis of the theory, as mentioned earlier, was the equation of language and race, and its genesis lay in the philological relationships noticed between Sanskrit and Greek, Latin, and other European languages. Yet, it is indeed paradoxical how this theoretical proposition of trans-culturality, implicit in Jones's universal language family as well as in the averred racial unity of Aryans from the West and the East as posited by Max Müller (and subscribed to enthusiastically by Westernized Indians, who wanted to be considered on a par with the colonial strata), eventually became the basis for underscoring racial difference on the subcontinent in an almost irrevocable manner. Pivotal to this transformation was the European dichotomy between Aryan and Semitic which served as a conceptual fulcrum facilitating the construction of its Indian counterpart in the Aryan/Dravidian divide.[87]

How this transposition could gain forceful legitimacy is enigmatic to say the least, since the very terminology on which it was founded seems contestable, given that the crucial term *arya*—derived from Sanskrit and denoting nobility[88]—did not necessarily possess any racial or ethnic connotations in the Vedic context of origin. For race science, however, this was of little consequence, for the multi-ethnic Indian scenario was far too interesting to be dismissed. To unravel the ethnic puzzle, the following explanation was construed: in the second millennium BC, the Aryans, as civilizing tribes who supposedly originated from Central Asia, spread westward to Europe and eastward to the Indian subcontinent.[89] There they came into close contact with an unequivocally black race, the Dravidians, who due to their skin pigmentation and snub noses (apparently indicative of racial inferiority), were conquered by the white aquiline-nosed Aryan race.[90] *Summa summarum*: it was supposedly the antagonism between diametrically opposed races, the Aryan and Dravidian, which distinguished the racial history of India from elsewhere and accounted for the rise of its peculiar institution of caste. With great panache, Risley, the main propagator of this contrived theory, explicated the origins of caste:

The principle upon which the system rests is the sense of distinctions of race indicated by differences of colour: a sense which, while too weak to preclude the men of the dominant race from intercourse with

the women whom they have captured, is still strong enough to make
it out of question that they should admit the men whom they have
conquered to equal rights in the matter of marriage.[91]

Hence, as a result of the strict adherence to caste endogamy, the upper
castes were deduced to be the descendants of the Aryans or arya-varna, as
constituted by the Brahmins, Kshatriyas, and Vaishyas, while the lower
castes or Shudras were categorized as the conquered non-Aryans or dasa-
varna. Further explaining that all social differences were reducible to racial
differences, Risley delineated the following all-embracing explanation:

Once started in India, the principle was strengthened, perpetuated,
extended to all ranks of society by the fiction that people who speak
a different language, dwell in a different district, worship different
gods, eat different food, observe different social customs, follow a different profession, or practise the same profession in a slightly different
way must be so unmistakably aliens by blood that intermarriage with
them is a thing not to be thought of.[92]

Needless to say, this racialized interpretation of caste, though criticized for
its pseudo-scientific claims,[93] was instrumentalized extensively in colonial
discourse, and subsequently greatly influenced the self-perceptions of educated Indians. Furthermore, caste, reified as a rigid Brahmanical system,
was held responsible, by Risley and others, for rendering Indians politically
impotent, making them the pliable subjects of conquerors. Due to its frag-
mentary tendencies resulting from racial animosities, caste was considered
antithetical to the development of a strong nation-state and inimical to national unity.[94] On the one hand, this latter fissiparous characteristic was
borne out to a certain extent by nineteenth- and early-twentieth-century
movements of self-assertive resistance, entangled as they were in the net of
colonialist rhetoric; led by low-caste or non-Brahmin spokesmen in various regions of India, such movements proactively applied the racist theories,
in inverse order, to resist systems of economic and political domination[95]
On the other hand, nationalist politicians, such as Mahatma Gandhi, in an
attempt to disprove the colonialist verdict, attempted to reform caste society, also by providing more integrative understandings of Indian social
ordering.[96] Interestingly, B.R. Ambedkar, leader of the "untouchables" and
one of India's most vehement opponents of the caste system, castigated in no
uncertain terms the racist interpretation of its origins.[97]

Yet the racist virus continued to breed: after Independence, despite the fact that the Indian constitution of 1950 outlawed caste discrimination, the influence of a racialized caste discourse persists into the present day, with Dalits and human rights activists campaigning to brand caste discrimination and the practice of untouchability internationally as racism or India's "hidden apartheid."[98] Though drawing attention to the persisting virulence of the problem, no viable solutions are thereby being proffered apart from addressing claims of victimhood and consequently calling for compensation. However, if more fundamental improvement is to be sought, rather than merely stigmatizing and transfixing caste as a racist institution, positive measures need to be taken to empower (politically, socially, and economically) the many disadvantaged groups so that the subcontinent's social, cultural, and ethnic diversity may finally shed the classifying trammels—in their Brahmanized and racist avatar—bequeathed by colonialism.

Notes

1. André Béteille, "Race and Caste," *The Hindu*, 10 March 2001.
2. United Nations, *Report of the World Conference against Racism, Racial Discrimination, Xenophobia and Related Intolerance*, Department of Public Information, News and Media Services Division (New York, 2002); Ambrose Pinto, "Caste Discrimination and UN," *Economic and Political Weekly* 37, no. 39 (2002): 3988–90.
3. A Marathi term meaning "broken" or "reduced to pieces," Molesworth's *Marathi–English Dictionary* (1975), cited in Eleanor Zelliot, "Dalit: New Cultural Context for an old Marathi Word," in *From Untouchable to Dalit* (Delhi, 2001), 267. The term came into general use through the literature of the *Dalit Panthers* in the early 1970s.
4. Soli J. Sorabjee, "The Official Position," *Seminar* 508 (December 2001): 14–16; M.N. Panini, "Caste, Race and Human Rights," *Economic and Political Weekly* 36, no. 35 (2001): 3344–46; P.N. Bhagwati, "The Caste and Race Debate," *PUCL Bulletin* 21, no. 7 (2001): 3–8.
5. D.L. Sheth, "Caste in the Mirror of Race," *Exclusion*, 50–55, citation on 55.
6. Sukhadeo Thorat and Umakant, eds., *Caste, Race and Discrimination: Discourses in International Context* (Jaipur, 2004); Ameena Hussein, ed., *Race, Identity, Caste & Conflict in the South Asian Context* (Colombo, 2004).
7. See the contributions in Crispin Bates, ed., *Beyond Representation: Colonial and Postcolonial Constructions of Indian Identity* (New Delhi, 2006), and Mohan Rao, "'Scientific' Skein," *Economic and Political Weekly* 38, no. 8 (2003): 697–700.
8. Crispin Bates, "Race, Caste and Tribe in Central India: The Early Origins of Indian Anthropometry," *Edinburgh Papers In South Asian Studies*, no. 3 (1995): 14; also Nicholas B. Dirks, *Castes of Mind: Colonialism and the Making of Modern India* (Princeton, 2001), 125–227.

9. Susan Bayly, *Caste, Society and Politics in India from the Eighteenth Century to the Modern Age* (Cambridge, 1999), 1.

10. Challenging this hegemonic interpretation, the sociologist Dipankar Gupta argues that any notion of a fixed hierarchy is arbitrary: Dipankar Gupta, *Interrogating Caste: Understanding Hierarchy & Difference in Indian Society* (New Delhi, 2000).

11. Louis Dumont, *Homo Hierarchicus: Essai sur le système des castes* (Paris, 1966).

12. Ronald Inden, *Imagining India* (Oxford, 1990), 57, 47–84.

13. Chris Smaje, *Natural Hierarchies: The Historical Sociology of Race and Caste* (Malden, 2002), 34. Smaje writes: "assumptions [made by orientalists] are systematically associated with European colonial domination in its attempt to characterise and control the non-European, by working the irreducibly manifold world of meanings, actions and intentions into a singularity which, through devices such as the concept of culture, constitutes the non-European as 'other.'"

14. The term "race" was apparently first used in the English language in 1508 in a poem by William Dunbar, but notably as a literary term denoting a class of persons or things. See Bill Ashcroft et al., *Key Concepts in Post-Colonial Studies* (London, 1998), 199. Etymologically derived from the Arabic *raz* (head, leader, or origin) and the Latin *radix* (root), it came to signify "race, breed, lineage," and was applied to designate a "people of common descent," or a "group of people with common occupation" and "generation" (c.1560). For details of the conceptual origin, see Christian Geulen, *Geschichte des Rassismus* (München, 2007), 14.

15. Henry Yule and A.C. Burnell, *Hobson-Jobson: A Glossary of Colloquial Anglo-Indian Words and Phrases, and of Kindred Terms, Etymological, Historical, Geographical and Discursive* (1886; reprint, Delhi, 1989), 170; for more details, cf. Gita Dharampal-Frick, *Indien im Spiegel deutscher Quellen der Frühen Neuzeit (1500–1750): Studien zu einer interkulturellen Konstellation* (Tübingen, 1994), 182.

16. Dharampal-Frick, *Indien im Spiegel*, 183. For a refutation of the interpretation of caste organization constituting "genetic segregation," see Morton Klass, *Caste: The Emergence of the South Asian Social System* (Philadelphia, 1980), 26.

17. The term race, moreover, in the sixteenth century did not yet designate a distinct category of human beings with physical characteristics transmitted by descent, and hence was without the later more pronounced "racist" implications.

18. Sanjay Subrahmanyam, *The Political Economy of Commerce: Southern India, 1500–1650* (Cambridge, 1990), 338. Subrahmanyam writes: "Indeed, early Portuguese uses of the term *casta* ... are notorious for being fluid as an organising rubric."

19. Yule and Burnell, *Hobson-Jobson*, 171. It is elaborated further here: "Barbosa ...[did not] apply the word *casta* to the divisions of Hindu society. He calls these divisions in Narsinga and Malabar so many *leis de gentios*, i.e., 'laws' of the heathen, in the sense of sectarian rules of life. But he uses the word *casta* in a less technical way, which shows how it should easily have passed into the technical sense."

20. This is quite an eye-opener for today's reader, too, bearing in mind the modern stereotypical notion of the sweeping profession in India being the preserve of low or out-caste untouchables.

21. Dumont, *Homo Hierarchicus*, 65, 78. Dumont writes: "L' ensemble est fondé sur la coexistence nécessaire et hiérarchisée des deux opposes: le pur et l'mpur." And continues later: "l'exécution des tâches impures par les uns est nécessaire au maintien de la pureté chez les autres."

22. Dharampal-Frick, *Indien im Spiegel*, 183. Reference to the reports of early modern travelers such as William Methwold, Antonio Schorer, and Pieter Gilliesz van Ravesteyn appear in W.H. Moreland, ed., *Relations of Golconda* (London, 1931).

23. For according to Montaigne, "Human eyes cannot perceive things but in the shape they know them by." Consequently, in the Indo-European interaction, the intellectual reservoir from which organizing principles have been drawn were, needless to say, Eurocentric. See his *Essais*, vol. 1 (Paris, 1962), 223.

24. Johannes Fabian, *Time and the Other: How Anthropology makes its Object* (New York, 1983), 31. Fabian argues that the "denial of coevalness" as a distancing device represents "a persistent and systematic tendency to place the referent(s) of anthropology in a time other than the present of the producer of anthropological discourse." In contrast to this later approach, though India in the early (pre-colonial) period was considered by European observers as existing on the same temporal level as pre-industrial Europe, the multi-dimensional nature of intercultural perception and its subsequent representation should not be underestimated; for explanatory details, with regard to the Spanish conquest of America, see Tzvetan Todorov, *La conquête de L' Amérique: la question de l'autre* (Paris, 1982), chap. 4.

25. Bartholomäus Ziegenbalg, *Malabarisches Heidenthum*, edited by W. Caland (1711; reprint of ms., Amsterdam, 1926), 195. For a detailed elucidation of Ziegenbalg's proto-ethnography of Tamil societal groupings, see Dharampal-Frick, *Indien im Spiegel*, 228–42.

26. Stanley J. Tambiah, "From Varna to Caste through Mixed Unions," in *Culture, Thought and Social Action. An Anthropological Perspective*, edited by Stanley J. Tambiah (Cambridge, MA, 1985), 212–51.

27. See Thomas R. Metcalf, *Ideologies of the Raj* (Cambridge, UK, 1998).

28. For empirical data on the first phase of British colonial conquest, see Ramsay Muir, *The Making of British India, 1756–1858: Described in a Series of Dispatches, Treaties, Statutes, and other Documents, selected and edited with Introduction and Notes* (Manchester, 1917).

29. For an analytical study of the modalities and repercussions of colonial rule, see Ranajit Guha, *Dominance without Hegemony: History and Power in Colonial India* (Cambridge, MA, 1997).

30. Brahma Nandal, *Famines in Colonial India* (New Delhi, 2007); Ranajit Guha, *Elementary Aspects of Peasant Insurgency in Colonial India* (New Delhi, 1983); Hamza Alavi, "Peasants and Revolution," in *Imperialism and Revolution in South Asia*, edited by Kathleen Gough (New York, 1973), 291–337.

31. Peter van der Veer, *Imperial Encounters: Religion and Modernity in India and Britain* (Princeton, 2001); Bernard Cohn, *Colonialism and its Forms of Knowledge* (Princeton, 1996).

32. Rosanne Rocher, "British Orientalism in the Eighteenth Century: The Dialectics of Knowledge and Government," in *Orientalism and the Postcolonial Predicament: Perspectives on South Asia*, edited by Carol A. Breckenridge (Philadelphia, 1994), 215–49.

33. Christopher A. Bayly, *Empire and Information: Intelligence Gathering and Social Communication in India, 1780–1870* (Cambridge, 1996), 56–97.

34. For a critical appraisal of colonial historiography with regard to the battle of Plassey, which marks a turning point in the colonial conquest of India, see Ram Gopal, *How the British Occupied Bengal: A Corrected Account of the 1756–1765 Events* (London, 1963); Biplab Dasgupta, "Palashi: The Inside Story of a Betrayal," in *The Making of History: Essays Presented to Irfan Habib*, edited by Kandiyur N. Panikkar (New Delhi, 2000), 202–36.

35. For details about the establishment of British rule in Bengal, see the study by Peter J. Marshall, *Bengal: The British Bridgehead. Eastern India, 1740–1828* (Cambridge, 1987).

36. Om P. Kejariwal, *The Asiatic Society of Bengal and the Discovery of India's Past, 1784–1838* (Delhi, 1988).

37. Henry Beveridge, ed., *Warren Hastings in Bengal* (Calcutta, 1978); for a recent critical examination of the ignominious actions of the first Governor-General, see Nicholas B. Dirks, *The Scandal of Empire. India and the Creation of Imperial Britain* (Cambridge, 2006), 87–131.

38. William Jones, Nathaniel Halhed, Henry Thomas Colebrooke, and Charles Wilkins were the first most prominent scholars; for an overview of British orientalism, see David Kopf, *British Orientalism and the Bengal Renaissance: The Dynamics of Indian Modernisation, 1773–1835* (Berkeley, 1969).

39. Ronald Inden, "Orientalist Constructions of India," *Modern Asian Studies* 20, no. 3 (1986): 401–46; Peter J. Marshall, *The British Discovery of Hinduism in the Eighteenth Century* (Cambridge, 1970); Sylvia Murr, "Les conditions d' emergence du discourse sur l' Inde au siècle des Lumières," *Collection Purusartha* VII (Paris, 1983), 233–84.

40. Patrick Olivelle, ed., *Manu: Manu's Code of Law: A Critical Edition and Translation of the Manava-Dharmasastra* (Oxford, 2005).

41. For a standard biography, see Garland H. Cannon, *The Life and Mind of Oriental Jones: Sir William Jones, the Father of Modern Linguistics* (Cambridge, 1990); for a critical contextualization of Jones's indological work, see S.N. Mukherjee, *Sir William Jones: A Study in Eighteenth Century British Attitudes to India* (Cambridge, 1968). See also, Sir William Jones, trans., *Institutes of Hindu Law: or, the ordinances of Menu, according to the gloss of Cullúca. Comprising the Indian system of duties, religious and civil* (Calcutta, 1794).

42. See the more recent critical edition, Wendy Doniger, trans., *The Laws of Manu, with an Introduction and Notes* (London, 1991).

43. Dirks, *Castes of Mind*, chap. 2.

44. Furthermore, in this connection, J. Duncan Derrett lists nearly fifty Sanskrit treatises of law known to have been produced for the British. See his "The British as patrons of the Sastra," in *Religion, Law and the State in India* (London, 1968), 225–69.

45. Thomas R. Trautmann, *Aryans and British India* (New Delhi, 1997), 58.

46. See Jones's third anniversary discourse delivered in 1786, cited in Trautmann, *Aryans and British India*, 38.

47. Trautmann, *Aryans and British India*, 42–61.

48. Maurice Olender, *The Languages of Paradise: Race, Religion and Philology in the Nineteenth Century* (Cambridge, 1992).

49. Gita Dharampal-Frick, "'India – what can it teach us?' – Neue Überlegungen zu einer alten Frage," *Saeculum* 57, no. 2 (2006): 255–68; Trautmann, *Aryans and British India*, 173–81.

50. This term refers to the theoretical concept of a fourfold division of society in varnas. A critique against the application of this concept to social reality can be found in Gerald D. Berreman, "The Brahmanical View of Caste," *Contributions to Indian Sociology* 5 (1971): 16–23.

51. It is doubtful whether prior to its canonization by British orientalists this myth had enjoyed pan-Indian validity. It was first published under British auspices as H.H. Wilson, trans., *Rig-veda-sanhita: A collection of ancient Hindu hymns of the Rig-Veda; the oldest authority on the religious and social institutions of the Hindus*, 4 vols. (London, 1854–57). This was later reedited by Friedrich Max Müller, ed., *Rig – Veda – Samhita. The sacred hymns of the Brahmans together with the commentary of Sayanakarya*, 4 vols. (London 1890–92).

52. A perception that was acerbated and intensified by the concomitant repercussions of economic exploitation and political subjugation as a result of colonial conquest.

53. William Ward, *A View of the History, Literature and Mythology of the Hindoos*, vol. 2 (London, 1822), 64–65.

54. See Sushil Chaudhury, *From Prosperity to Decline: Eighteenth Century Bengal* (Delhi, 1999).

55. William Carey (1761–1834), founder of the English Baptist Missionary Society in 1792; see Timothy George, *The Life and Mission of William Carey* (New Hope, 1998).

56. Cited by Duncan Forrester, *Caste and Christianity: Attitudes and Policy on Caste of Anglo-Saxon Protestant Missions in India* (London, 1980), 26; see also William Carey, *An Enquiry into the Obligations of Christians* (Leicester, 1792).

57. Cited by Dirks, *Castes of Mind*, 27.

58. Charles Grant, *Observations on the State of Society among the Asiatic Subjects of Great Britain Particularly in Respect of Morals and on the Means of Improving it* (London, 1793).

59. William Wilberforce (1759–1833), British politician and philanthropist who from 1787 was prominent in the campaign to abolish the slave trade and then slavery itself in British overseas possessions. Speaking in Parliament in favor of the Charter

Act 1813 and the concomitant Christianization of India, he condemned aspects of Hinduism including the caste system, infanticide, polygamy, and sati.

60. "On the Christianisation of India," (speech before the House of Commons, London), *Hansard* (London, 22 June 1813), cols. 831–72, quoted extracts, cols. 861, 71.

61. James Mill, *The History of India*, ed. H.H. Wilson, 6 vols., 5th ed. (1817; London, 1858); for a critical appraisal of utilitarian politics with regard to India, cf. Eric Stokes, *The English Utilitarians and India* (Oxford, 1959).

62. Mill, *The History of India*, vol. 1, 131.

63. Ibid., 128.

64. In colonial terminology this uprising is usually referred to as the Sepoy Mutiny, thereby denoting its illegitimacy and minimizing its extent, see George B. Malleson, ed., *History of the Indian Mutiny of 1857–58*, 6 vols. (London, 1897). Indian nationalists contest this view, in particular Vinayak D. Savarkar, *The Indian War of Independence 1857* (New Delhi, 1970); for a review of literature on the subject, see Biswamoy Pati, ed., *The 1857 Rebellion* (Delhi, 2007).

65. See the study by Thomas R. Metcalf, *Forging the Raj: Essays on British India in the Heyday of Empire* (Delhi, 2005).

66. See Trautmann, *Aryans and British India*, 209–11.

67. Cf. M. Monier-Williams, *English Sanskrit Dictionary* (New York, 1976), 652; Romila Thapar, "Durkheim and Weber on Theories of Society and Race Relating to Pre-Colonial India," in *Sociological Theories: Race and Colonialism* (Paris, 1980), 96.

68. For an in-depth discussion of the relationship between anthropology and imperialism, see Talal Asad, ed., *Anthropology and the Colonial Encounter* (London, 1973).

69. See Sanjay Nigam, "Disciplining and Policing the 'Criminals' by Birth," *Indian Economic and Social History Review* 27, no. 2–3 (1990): 131–65, 257–88. Moreover, Cesare Lobroso's theories "proving" criminality to be inherited found its codification in the Criminal Tribes Act of 1871 which, according to Bates "remained in force and was still being used actively in the Central Provinces and elsewhere in the late 1930s." See his "Race, Caste and Tribe in Central India," 25–26.

70. See *Ethnographic Survey of Castes and Tribes of India*, Census Department, 10/1901, Appendix, cited by Bates, "Race, Caste and Tribe in Central India," 35.

71. Bernard S. Cohn, "The Census, Social Structure and Objectification in South Asia," *An Anthropologist among the Historians and Other Essays* (Delhi, Oxford, New York, 1987), 224–54.

72. Bernard S. Cohn, "The Command of Language and the Language of Command," in *Subaltern Studies* 4, edited by Ranajit Guha (Oxford, 1985), 276–329.

73. Defined as the "measurement and estimation of physical data relating to people belonging to different races, castes and tribes", Dirks, *Castes of Mind*, 185. See Rashmi Pant, "The Cognitive Status of Caste in Colonial Ethnography," *Indian Economic and Social History Review* 24, no. 2 (1987): 145–62.

74. Paul Broca, professor of clinical surgery, who founded the Anthropological Society in Paris in 1859, was convinced that human races could be ranked on a linear

scale of mental capabilities; see Paul Broca, "Sur le volume et la forme du cerveau suivant les individus et suivant les races," *Bulletin de la Société d'Anthropologie de Paris* 2 (Paris, 1861).

75. Paul Topinard, student of Brocard, became one of the leading late-nineteenth-century anthropologists, see Paul Topinard, *Anthropology* (London, 1878).

76. Alphonse Bertillon (1853–1914), a French law enforcement officer, was the inventor of the first biometric method of identifying criminals.

77. Herbert H. Risley (1851–1911), census commissioner and superintendent of the Ethnographic Survey of Bengal.

78. Superintendent of the Madras museum from 1885, Thurston was subsequently in charge of ethnographical research for the Madras Presidency; see Edgar Thurston (assisted by K. Rangachari), *The Tribes and Castes of South India*, 7 vols. (Madras, 1909).

79. Christopher Pinney, "Colonial Anthropology in the 'Laboratory of Mankind,'" in *The Raj: India and the British, 1600–1947*, edited by C.A. Bayly (London, 1990), 252–63.

80. Herbert H. Risley, *The People of India*, 2nd ed. (London, 1915), 29.

81. Cited by Dirks, *Castes of Mind*, 185.

82. Ibid.

83. Herbert H. Risley, "The Study of Ethnology in India," *The Journal of the Royal Anthropological Institute of Great Britain and Ireland* 20 (1891): 259.

84. For a discussion of the influential racial and evolutionary theories of the age, see G.W. Stocking, *Victorian Anthropology* (London, 1987).

85. For a detailed discussion, see Trautmann, *Aryans and British India*.

86. Thapar, *Durkheim and Weber*, 96.

87. Ibid.; see also Léon Poliakov, *The Aryan Myth: A History of Racist and Nationalist Ideas in Europe* (London, 1975).

88. Trautmann, *Aryans and British India*, 12.

89. Archaeological and linguistic evidence for this has been seriously contested; see Colin Renfrew, *Archaeology and Language: The Puzzle of the Indo-European Origins* (London, 1987).

90. For a deconstruction of how Vedic texts were (mis)interpreted to construct the racist theory of Indian civilization, specifically a vehement contestation of the philological extrapolation of Dravidians as dark-skinned, flat-nosed savages, see Trautmann, *Aryans and British India*, chapter 7, 208.

91. Herbert H. Risley, *People of India*, 275.

92. Ibid. Contrary to this explanation, according to the popular emic view, *jatis* or subcastes are formed by the intermarriage of varnas, originating from the body of Purusha; hence all groups are considered as being of one "blood." See Arvind Sharma, *Hinduism and Human Rights: A Conceptual Approach* (Delhi, 2004), 179. To explain the origin of social groups other than those belonging to the four varnas, Risley is said to have coined the term *aprishya-shudra* (untouchable) which

appeared for the first time in print in 1902. Cf. Simon Charsley, "'Untouchable': What is in a Name," *Journal of the Royal Anthropological Institute* 2 (1996): 1–26.

93. Other ethnographic administrators such as J.C. Nesfield, D.C.J. Ibbetson and W. Crooke argued that caste, rather than being defined racially, was in fact the outcome of "a community of function and occupation." See Dirks, *Castes of Mind*, 79. Max Müller, who had initiated the language and race debate with regard to the Aryan origins of Indian civilization and Indo-European linguistic family, later warned against the dangers of mixing linguistics with anthropology. See Speech before the University of Stassbourg, 1872, cited in Nirad Chaudhuri, *Scholar Extraordinary: The Life of Professor the Rt. Hon. Friedrich Max Müller* (London, 1974), 313.

94. Risley, *People of India*, 272–73. See also Frederick G. Bailey, *Tribe, Caste, and Nation* (Manchester, 1971).

95. For instance, Jyotibai Phule in Maharashtra and E.V. Ramaswamy Naiker (alias Periyar) in the Tamil region laid claims to racial indigeneity or Dravidian origins through reassertion against Brahmanical or Aryan subjugation. See Dirks, *Castes of Mind*, chapters 7, 12.

96. Jürgen Stein, "Mahatma Gandhi's Evaluation of the Caste System as an Element of the National Independence Movement in India," *Journal of Religious Culture* 24 (1998): 1–7.

97. B.R. Ambedkar, *Who were the Shudras?* (1946; Bombay, 1970). In his meticulous exegesis of the Vedic scriptures, he convincingly shows that the implied hostility between different social groups was due to differing cultic practices and did not stem from racial animosity.

98. "Hidden Apartheid: Caste Discrimination against India's 'Untouchables,'" *Human Rights Watch* 19, no. 3 (New York, 2007), <http://www.hrw.org/reports/2007/india0207/>.

Chapter 10

The Making of a "Ruling Race": Defining and Defending Whiteness in Colonial India

Harald Fischer-Tiné

Introduction: Difficult Differences

It has become almost a cliché to claim that ideologies postulating an essential difference between rulers and ruled were the cornerstones of colonial regimes.[1] The picture becomes somewhat more complex, however, if one tries to discern exactly how this difference was constructed, or the extent to which upholding it was seen as indispensable—or even possible, for that matter. Taking the example of British India, the present chapter explores how the elusive quality of "whiteness" was defined and defended in a colonial setting. It first contextualizes this quality through a broad overview of the historical trajectory of ideologies used to account for racial divergence across British colonial possessions in South Asia. It demonstrates how the language of "scientific racism" gradually superseded environmentalist explanations of human diversity during the course of the nineteenth century. The second part presents a case study illustrating just how difficult it could be to uphold such racial ideologies given the existence of strict stratifications within India's "white" colonial society itself. Specifically, this section analyzes the mid-nineteenth-century controversy over how to deal with white criminals and convicts in a colonial setting. This debate—which eventually resulted in the construction of segregated European penitentiaries in the 1860s—points to the existence of conflicting hierarchies of race, class, and respectability that undermined British self-representations as a "ruling race" and rendered the defense of the image of a "white aristocracy" highly problematic.

Before these particular questions can be considered, however, it is important to understand the various ways in which Europeans justified their self-perceived exceptionalism. If we consider the entire period of British rule in India, it becomes clear that a single consistent ideology of racial difference did not exist. To the contrary, how the dissimilarity between Europeans and Indians was perceived and explained changed considerably over time. Broadly, however, we can distinguish two chief approaches to understanding the discrepancies between European and Indian bodies, mentalities, and social institutions.

Racial Differentiators and Colonial Realities

Differences of Degree? — Environmentalism and "Ethno-Climatology"

The pioneers of the East India Company (EIC) began experiencing India's topographical differences from Europe as early as the seventeenth century. Many travelers dreaded the climate in the maritime periphery of the subcontinent, where the EIC's initial settlements were located.[2] This association of India's climate with danger and personal peril was due largely to the prevalence of diseases that took a heavy toll on the Company's servants. The mortality rate was particularly high in the initial phase of the EIC's expansion,[3] although most Company employees certainly did not regard the country as uninhabitable.[4] Perceptions of climatic difference soon combined with contemporary medical theories, together triggering the belief that "human character and physical appearance was dependent upon the effects of heat and moisture."[5] In other words, the British came to believe Indians were different on the grounds of their constant exposure to a tropical climate.[6]

When it came to assessing this difference, opinions regarding its meaning and manifestation were far from unanimous. On the one hand, a number of powerful and persistent negative stereotypes developed, including the idea of the so-called "effeminate Bengali,"[7] who lacked manly qualities because he lived "in a constant vapour bath."[8] As Mrinalini Sinha and others have shown,[9] running tropes of this kind were crucial elements in emerging doctrines of the "white man's burden" that guided imperial trusteeship. As long as native elites could be presented as sensual, feckless and irrational, colonial rulers could sustain their own self-images as manly rulers and protectors of peoples wanting impartial and effective leadership. On the other hand, actual experiences on the ground soon led the British to revise their general assumptions regarding the Indian populace, resulting in a number of racial clichés about Indians that were not entirely negative. The efficiency and low mortality rates of Indian troops under British command,[10] for example, or the military skills of those communities who managed to resist British annexation produced positive images of resilient, warlike and manly "natives."[11]

Conversely, Europeans appeared physically weak and prone to disease because they were not sufficiently accustomed to the Indian environment. But as Mark Harrison has reminded us, the conviction that human bodies were malleable and that Europeans could therefore get acclimated to the new surroundings prevailed well into the nineteenth century. There were even proposals to "vaccinate" newly arrived Europeans by infusing a small quantity of "native" blood into their veins,[12] apparently an influence of the Hippocratic school of medicine. In short, differences between Europeans and Indians were not initially regarded as being fundamentally unbridgeable, and the boundaries between races were not conceptualized as being as rigid and impenetrable as they would later become in the "imperial heyday."[13]

The idea that both physical constitutions and characters were moulded by climate also had a profound effect on the politics of colonization. Throughout the late eighteenth and early nineteenth centuries, there was relative optimism regarding the capabilities for adaptation to the Indian environment, and accordingly, several detailed colonization schemes were developed. Europeans, it was believed, could live permanently in India as long as they adopted, to some extent, Indian diets and methods of bodily hygiene.[14] "Indianization" in homeopathic doses, as it were, thus promised to ensure European health and longevity in a hostile environment. Almost from the outset, however, this optimism went hand in hand with fears of being morally contaminated by Indian practices. The more intense the exposure to Indian life-worlds, the argument ran, the more dangerous this influence became for European bodies and minds. Poor whites compelled to live in Indian neighborhoods—mostly for economic reasons—and European orphans were particularly imperilled according to this line of reasoning.[15] Charitable institutions were established, in part, to keep these segments of the European colonial population away from the dangers of native influences. The Free School of Calcutta, for instance, was founded as early as the 1790s[16] with the avowed aim of protecting European and Eurasian children from these corrupting elements:

Here Christian children of whatever denomination among lower classes are exposed to difficulties and dangers, which could hardly occur in England[.] … Even under the most favourable circumstances, they are too much exposed to the contaminating vices of the natives with whom they are necessarily much associated, and are not seldom situated in places where instructian [sic] is not to be had. In all such cases it is not merely a question of instruction which is to be considered but of the preservation from Want, from Vice and … from the influence of superstition and idolatry.[17]

The emphasis placed on the "vices of the natives" points to another deep-seated anxiety that haunted colonial administrators: the spectre of miscegenation which, in turn, conjured anxieties of possible racial degeneration and the ensuing loss of the "imperial self." This suggests the second major differentiating ideology that became popular in Anglo-Indian circles in the last third of the nineteenth century: race. Especially influential was the school of so-called "scientific racism", which—in its more radical forms of expression—postulated a more or less permanent and unbridgeable biological difference between colonizers and colonized. It should be kept in mind, however, that racial ideologies did not completely supplant environmentalist theories.[18] Rather, the two discourses existed side by side and mutually influenced each other.

Differences of Kind? — Discourses of "Race" and British India

Recent scholarship has stressed the close entanglement between European expansion and the emergence of (pseudo-) scientific discourses concerned with "race" in Europe from the late eighteenth century onwards. The imperial penetration of the globe, of course, brought Europeans into contact with other ethnic groups and hence triggered the need to classify and categorize the varieties of the human species following the Enlightenment tradition.[19] Yet the state of affairs in British India demonstrates that racialism was not merely a corollary to colonialism. The imperial interchanges between colony and metropole can also be traced through the emergence of Western discourses on race. Almost from its inception, the colonial enterprise in the subcontinent existed in parallel with and was conditioned by myriad scholarly attempts in Britain and around Europe to come to terms with human diversity.

European racial thought had an early start in India. Interestingly enough, one of the most persistent and influential theories explaining the history of mankind and physical differences between various human groupings was first formulated in colonial Bengal. In the third of his annual "anniversary discourses," held before the "Asiatick Society of Bengal"[20] in 1786, William Jones—philologist and judge at the Supreme Court in Calcutta[21]—expounded a groundbreaking theory, claiming the existence of a set of closely related "Aryan" languages. From his discovery of striking linguistic similarities between Sanskrit, the language of the *Avesta*, Latin and Greek, he not only deduced the existence of an Indo-Aryan "language family," but also used it as a starting point for his well-received hypothesis locating humanity's common origin in Persia, from where it subsequently dispersed across the globe.[22] Jones's linguistic comparisons thus formed the nucleus of what later became known as the "Aryan race theory." Yet his speculation, deeply influenced by both Enlightenment universalism and Christian tradition, proved unsuitable for the legitimization of colonial rule, as the close relationship between Indians and Europeans the theory postulated made racially grounded distance between rulers and ruled difficult to justify.[23]

Like Jones, later champions of the Aryan myth were mostly philologists. The most prominent and sophisticated among them was the German Indologist Friedrich Max Müller, who elaborated and refined the theory of Indo-European kinship from the mid nineteenth century onwards.[24] Predictably enough, the emerging "Anglicized" Indian intelligentsia picked up his provocative statements claiming that the same blood ran through the veins of both the Indian "mutineers" of 1857 and the European soldiers who suppressed the rebellion.[25] However, they were not so well received in Britain[26] and even less so by the majority of European residents in British India.[27] Hence, the phrase "our Aryan brethren," by which Anglo-Indians occasionally referred to their "native" contemporaries, colleagues or competitors was almost exclusively used "with heavy irony."[28] In contrast, from the 1840s onwards, Anglo-Indians employed the term "nigger" frequently and apparently without even the slightest ironic overtones.[29]

The noticeable contradiction between the putative kinship of the British rulers with their (North-) Indian subjects on the one hand and the colonial establishment's need for clear markers of difference allowing for "imperial aloofness"[30] on the other posed a deeply unsettling ideological problem. Most frequently, British thinkers and administrators attempted to resolve this tension by focusing on the supposed "degeneration" of the Indian branch of the Aryan family, and posited two main explanations. One line of argument combined the Aryan race theory with the ethno-climatological discourse discussed above, ascribing the supposedly inferior physical development of the Indians to the long-term effect of "enervating" tropical climates.[31] The triumphant advance of evolutionism from the 1860s onwards further facilitated such exercises in squaring the Aryan circle by popularizing the concept of degeneration as the inevitable corollary of "progress."[32] Races and civilizations, even if they had been closely related originally, could now easily be ranked on different scales of the evolutionary ladder due to subsequent modifications or "mutations" caused by external influences.[33]

Yet the Aryan theory of race had come under attack even before the Darwinian revolution. By the mid nineteenth century, the nascent discipline of ethnology began contesting the monopoly of comparative philology on explaining the mystery of human diversity. Whereas early British ethnologists like James Cowles Prichard (1786–1848)[34] had consulted mostly philological and historical evidence to buttress their theories, a new current with the discipline tried to establish ethnology as a natural science, abandoning any kind of philological speculation based on linguistic affinities. Ethnology (or anthropology, as it came to be called) moved "from texts to bodies"[35] as the appropriate objects of scholarly interest. Again, from a very early point, data collected in India—the "great museum of races"[36]—proved crucial for the evolution of anthropology and closely-related disciplines.[37] Many of the leading early anthropologists were scholar-administrators, who had served in India and used the subcontinent as a laboratory for their ethnographical pursuits before establishing themselves in academia back home.[38]

It would be wrong to see later ethnology in colonial India as a monolithic project.[39] However, the fact that most of the empirical data collected in ethnographical surveys[40] and anthropological measurements[41] were easier to reconcile with the practical and ideological requirements of colonialism than the linguistic findings of the early Orientalists. Difference proved easier to define and defend on the basis of new craniological or anthropometrical data, which were combined with assessments of the intellectual and moral qualities of the "measured" population. In other words, the change of scientific paradigms substantially contributed to a general stiffening of racial attitudes.[42] John Crawfurd,[43] for instance, a leading anthropologist and one of the most outspoken critics of the linguistic approach to ethnic diversity, came to the following conclusion when comparing "European and Asiatic Races" in a paper read before the Ethnological Society of

London in 1866:

> Beauty and symmetry of a person would seem to decrease as we pro-
> ceed from West to East. The Persians are less handsome than the
> Georgians and Mingrelians, and the Hindus much inferior in this re-
> spect to the Persians. The Hindus, again, far surpass the Chinese, who,
> ill-favoured as they are, are exceeded by the Coreans ... . The differ-
> ences in the intellectual and moral qualities of the European and Asiatic
> races are of far more importance than those in their mere bodily struc-
> ture, and deserve to be considered in greater length. In understanding,
> in judgement, in taste, in invention, in reach of imagination, in enter-
> prise, in perseverance and in the moral sense, the European, placed
> under equal conditions, is greatly superior to the Asiatic.[44]

Anthropology and "race science" thus slowly replaced Oriental studies and comparative philology as the authoritative disciplines used to explain India and its people.

How was Anglo-Indian society affected by these ideological shifts? It comes as no surprise that the growing obsession with matters of race and the related sense of being "greatly superior" caused by the proliferation of racial discourses in the nineteenth century had a palpable effect on British India. They affected not only the everyday relationship between colonizers and colonized, but also imperial self-perceptions.[45] The drawing and polic-ing of racial boundaries—clearly demarcating the realm of the rulers from native life-worlds—was increasingly considered as vital to the success of the imperial enterprise. Before long, Europeans came to regard misce-genation as more dangerous to the colonizing "race" than even the most hostile tropical environments.[46] This "racial turn" in imperial self-definition can perhaps be most clearly discerned by looking at the changing percep-tion of people of mixed parentage: the so-called "Eurasians."[47]

Distrust of "East-Indians," also referred to as "Hindoo-Britons," was cer-tainly not an entirely new phenomenon by the late nineteenth century. Still, the late–Victorian scientific sanction of "racial purity" significantly rein-forced pre-existing fears of hybridity that had their origins in the initial period of colonial state formation in the late eighteenth century. Whereas the early East India Company had taken a relatively relaxed stance on con-cubinage and "cross-racial" sexual contact,[48] colonial officials gradually came to see "interracial" intercourse and the resulting offspring as prob-lematic by the beginning of the 1790s. Lord Governor-General Cornwallis (1786–1793, 1805) was the first to use the "heavy hand of repression"[49]

against Eurasians when he introduced a set of laws that significantly cur-
tailed the rights of the mixed descent population.[50] Consequently, the
Eurasian community, which had played a prominent role in the first phase
of empire building,[51] was gradually marginalized, both socially and economically, during the first half of the nineteenth century. Only the
mid-century introduction of the railway and telegraph services provided
many of its members with an economic niche that prevented their complete pauperization. Notwithstanding such new job opportunities and
various measures of "improvement," initiated either by the state or civil social agencies to keep Eurasians from becoming "social parasites,"[52]
ostracism continued to exclude the "racially mixed" population from the respectable "white society" until the end of the Raj.[53] The question to be
asked, then, is why the British in India had such trouble integrating their
Eurasian "cousins."[54]

To understand the marginalization of "Indo-Britons" in the late nineteenth century, it is important to note that late–Victorian "race
consciousness" dovetailed with pre-existing stereotypes, which painted the
mixed population as potentially dangerous, as they bore "the negative traits
of both races."[55] This trope subsequently influenced the cultural representation of the so-called "half-castes" in the metropolis.[56] In the colony, such
prejudices were underpinned by the results of pseudo-scientific surveys in-
quiring into the social and medical condition of these "inbetweens."[57] The
"Report of the Pauperism Committee" (1892) in Calcutta, for example, explained the exceptionally high unemployment rates among Eurasians by
pointing to the "defects of character" purportedly inherent in people of
mixed heritage.[58]

In summary, both differentiating ideologies employed by the colonizers
were extremely ambivalent and fragile. Environmentalist explanations of Indian difference raised the spectre of European "degeneration" in the hostile
environments, which ultimately meant that Europeans would become "na-
tivized" over time and therefore lose their imperial self-identity. Consequently,
keeping the "debilitating" influences at bay required strategies of isolation and
protection. In a similar vein, racial theories could be used not only for "oth-
ering" but also for "brothering." They certainly helped legitimate colonial
suppression and exploitation in the name of "benevolent despotism"—the
only form of rule deemed suitable for an inferior people. Yet concurrently, the
colonized population, to suit their own designs and ends, successfully appropriated at least some elements of the racial theories developed by the
colonizers; the Indian intelligentsia's use of the Aryan race theory provides a

case-in-point. But even the hardened "scientific racism" of the late Victorian era left some loopholes, if not always for counter-hegemonic appropriation,[59] at least for critiques exposing its internal contradictions.

The second half of this essay will consider these contradictions in much greater detail. For decades, critical race studies have pointed to the socially constructed character of racial categories and identities.[60] Admittedly then, simply calling attention to the socially constructed character of colonial whiteness would not be very original. The case of lower class and "disrespectable" Europeans in British India, nevertheless, offers a significant and striking example of the inner tensions of this racial category, demonstrating how it was continually modified and remolded in order to uphold the fiction of difference and guarantee the stability of colonial rule. The defense of the fragile "differentiators" that rendered the members of the "imperial race" superior, and underscored their responsibility to rule, ultimately remained an unfinished, and virtually unfinishable, project throughout the period of colonial rule in India. As the example of white convicts shows, ideologies proclaiming "white supremacy" came further under siege when other hierarchical taxonomies—in this case class and criminality—came into play. The remainder of this chapter briefly sketches out the colonial debate on a separate punishment regime for Europeans in India. It will become clear that both environmentalist arguments as well as the language of race were used to preserve some of the privileges associated with whiteness, even for those Europeans that were on the lowest rung of the social ladder.

Race and the "Just Measure of Pain"

Hierarchies of Punishment

Thomas Babington Macaulay, during his tenure as a member of Governor-General of India's Council in the 1830s, first addressed the delicate issue of how to punish Europeans appropriately in a colonial setting. As he shared the widespread view that "every Englishman participates in the power of the Government, though he holds no office,"[61] he advocated transporting Europeans who had committed felonies in India to Australia as a suitable means of punishment. Such a system would ensure that the crimes and vices of the felons did not "reflect disgrace on the Government."[62] For lesser crimes perpetrated by members of the "ruling race," his scheme suggested that in "one District Gaol, here and there, suitable accommodation should be provided … for one or two prisoners of European habits."[63]

The use of the term "European habits" is momentous, reflecting that even a Utilitarian thinker like Macaulay, who was generally inclined to believe in the universal character of the law, retained deep-seated presumptions regarding the essential cultural and physical differences between Western and Eastern "races." In addition to reflecting anxieties regarding the defense of racial prestige, Macaulay alludes to the second pervasive theme in the administrative discourse on "white" punishment in nineteenth-century India, namely if the same kind of punishment would result in the same effect on Indian prisoners in the colony as it presumably had on Englishmen in England. The statements of jail inspectors and magistrates that were attached to the 1838 *Report of the Committee on Prison-Discipline* expressed serious doubts on this matter.[64] Asked about the likelihood of character reformation by alterations to the penal system, Mr J. Dunbar, magistrate of Bhagaulpore, pointed to the unbridgeable difference between Englishmen and Indians in terms of their moral capabilities:

> Nine-tenths of those who fill our English Jails have at least had the seeds of virtue implanted in their breasts during childhood, and it is only through bad example or vicious habits that they have been seduced from the path of rectitude: the moral reformer therefore has something to work upon in an English Jail … [.] Widely different in every respect are the people with whom we have to deal in this country. The great mass of our prisoners are men advanced in life, their passions and their evil habits confirmed by time, and interwoven, as it were, to their very nature. To purge the bosoms of such men, destitute as they are, of every fine and manly feeling, of all the various motives of crime—to make them good and upright, and to endue them with a love of morality, would truly be an Augean task, more difficult of accomplishment, and certainly more worthy of commemoration, than that which Hercules performed of old.[65]

According to this logic, European convicts "natural" endowment with "fine and manly feelings" made them more worthy targets of rehabilitation than Indian criminals,[66] who, as a leading expert on colonial prison administration later put it, were sometimes "aboriginal savages, nearly as low in the scale of civilisation as any wild uncultivated people known to ethnologists."[67]

Their perceived moral superiority was not the only difference which qualified convicted European criminals for preferential treatment. In an era in which environmentalist theories exerted significant influence, many experts firmly believed in the fundamental physical disparities between the "imperial race" and the colonized population. Accordingly, in a minute written in 1844, Herbert Maddock, a member of the Governor-General's Council and one of the highest ranking officials in British India, declared it to be "absurd to sentence an Englishman and an Indian to the same term of confinement in Jail."[68] He regarded confinement in a crowded place as a minor evil for an Indian,[69] whereas a European inmate "deprived of exercise and exposed to all the heat of the climate within the walls of a jail" would suffer terribly.[70] In line with this logic, the Inspector-General of Prisons in Bengal argued in 1868 that the introduction of cellular jails would be much more efficient for Indian convicts than for Europeans because of the former's "cultural peculiarities." Complaining about the "demoralization" of male Indian prisoners and "abominations" in the native female wards he "cannot venture to avail," he explains: "The separation by night, which is the sole means of putting a stop to this immorality, would at once double the effect of every sentence. ... Natives of India are an eminently sociable people and any thing which interrupts their association, whether for good or evil, is regarded with dislike by them. This dislike would be intensified to a degree unintelligible to an [sic] European, if it were rigidly applied to the extinction of one of the vices which robs the prisons of many of their terrors."[71]

Reasoning along lines of crucial racial distinctiveness, which expressed itself not least in the allegedly unique Indian inclination towards the "unnatural vices" alluded to above, remained popular in British India throughout the nineteenth century and beyond.[72] From the mid-1880s onwards, the European and Anglo-Indian Defence Association, a body founded to fight for the interests of Europeans in British India, began to lobby for an extension of white privileges in jails.[73] Anxious about the health of white convicts, MP Samuel Smith asked the Secretary of State for India in the House of Commons in July 1899 if the British-Indian Government would "take into consideration the special hardships which long term European prisoners now suffer in India owing to their inability to bear the climatal [sic] effects under gaol conditions, as compared with the Native prisoners around them."[74] The Government of India reassured him that the "accommodation provided for European prisoners has been very favourably reported upon by expert authorities. It should also be remembered that the courts in sentencing Europeans, take into consideration the effects of climate, and that such prisoners, if their health requires it, can be transferred to the United Kingdom under an Act of 1884."[75]

A mixture of "racial prestige" and such "physical cum cultural differ-ence" arguments was brought forward in the controversy surrounding the use of flogging as a regular jail punishment for refractory European in-mates.[76] An anonymous European author writing under the pseudonym "The Reviewer" in the *Calcutta Review* criticized the practice as unwise, since it would diminish the authority of European convicts who often had the role of overseers, guarding Indian prisoners. Besides, he considered the whipping of Europeans as inadvisable for other reasons as well:

> The fact that British Sailors form a fair proportion of the pure-blooded Europeans imprisoned in India should give the subject a special claim for consideration ... [as] sailors are under very specially hard conditions in India and the manliness of their calling must ren-der prison a specially hard discipline for them, whilst their usual ignorance of the language renders them especially liable to suffer from the wily oriental. — Moreover, flogging is regarded by Jack as the last disgrace and it is notorious that in both Army and Navy flogging is the ruin of a man.[77]

The drastic inversion of roles and judgements stands out in this statement. European sailors were often a source of danger for the Indian population in seaport towns,[78] yet quite ironically, here the white seamen become vic-tims of the "wily Oriental." As if being compelled to live in India was punishment enough, the writer insinuates, they should not be treated too severely. At the same time the "manliness of their calling" entitles them to receive milder treatment. Such an argument does not come with regard for the "manly callings" of Indian inmates, nor does flogging seem to possess the same degrading character for natives.[79]

However, it must be stressed that this was a very contentious issue in terms of both official and public opinion. Indeed, this is a fine example of the fundamental "tensions of empire" European deviants could provoke. Not convinced by the arguments of "the Reviewer," another author writing in the same journal tries to remind his readers of the importance of taking the internal civilizing mission as seriously as possible. From his point of view, the moralizing impetus, based on class pretensions, outweighs the need to uphold the myth of an all-encompassing racial superiority:

> Criminals must to a large extent be treated as children; discipline to

be of any use must be firm[.] ... The maxim "spare the rod and spoil the child" still holds good and probably ever will. Corporal punishment is the only effectual treatment for crimes of violence, and crimes against the nature, not as a dignified indication of abstract virtue, but as most beneficial to society and the individual inasmuch as it is the only really deterrent punishment in the hands of those responsible for the good conduct and moral behaviour of our criminal classes either European or native.[80]

Crucially, the author admits the existence of "European criminal classes." This, of course, would not have been noteworthy in the metropolitan arena, where the colonial rhetoric of "criminal tribes" to denote the urban vagrant and/or criminal population had become deeply rooted by the middle of the nineteenth century.[81] Yet, it would have been quite unusual in a colonial setting, with the exception of the settler colony Australia.[82] Such striking contradictions remind us once more that colonialism did not speak with one voice. Quite the contrary: it was usually a rather polyphonic affair in which the transgressive acts of "white subalterns" frequently provoked the most dissonant utterances.

Imperial Imperatives and Moral Reservations: The Debate on "White Penitentiaries" in British India

The suggestion to erect a separate prison exclusively for European criminals was a logical outcome of and perfect solution to the conflicting interests of the colonial administration outlined above. A completely separate punishment for Europeans would allow for harsh handling of the "white criminal classes" while simultaneously removing them from the "native gaze" and maintaining "racial prestige." These advantages seemed all the more attractive against the backdrop of the demographic upheavals of the 1850s and 1860s, when the European civilian population in India swelled rapidly and reports on white crime regularly appeared in the English language newspapers. But these factors alone do not fully explain the sudden interest in the issue of "white punishment" in the mid nineteenth century. Several important developments in the wider imperial framework decisively influenced this debate.[83] For one, Britain largely terminated the transportation of convicts to Australia in 1853. This not only affected the penal system in the United Kingdom[84] but had strong repercussions in British India as well. For decades, convicts of "pure European extraction," who had been sentenced to transportation for terms exceeding seven years, had been sent from India to "the colonies."[85] Their first destination was New South Wales, then Van Diemen's Land (Tasmania) and later—and on a much smaller scale—Western Australia, where the last penal settlements closed in 1868.[86] Without this option, Act XXIV of 1855[87] replaced transportation to Australia (or Singapore) for punishment with penal servitude in Indian jails. Immediately, some of the existing Indian penitentiaries were selected as facilities suitable for the long-term confinement of Europeans.[88] It was at this moment that the idea of the "European penitentiary" appeared in the discussion.

The Government of Bengal first suggested opening such an institution: in 1854, it proposed constructing a jail for white convicts from the Bengal Presidency in Hazaribagh, but this was rejected "on sanitary grounds."[89] Until the 1850s, few Europeans and Americans had actually been sentenced to transportation abroad. Although the number of Europeans on the subcontinent rose constantly in those years, the Government of India nevertheless thought it sufficient "that if one jail were to be built for all India it should be capable of containing 100 convicts."[90] Governor-General Dalhousie wrote a letter to the Court of Directors announcing the plan to build "a general prison as in Scotland and England" for Europeans sentenced to penal servitude and reiterated the familiar environmentalist argument that the "jail should be erected at some hill stations and not in the plains of India seeing that the inmates will be Europeans and that the sentences for some of them will be for life or long terms of years."[91]

The EIC's Court of Directors eventually sanctioned the construction of a Central Penitentiary for Europeans in January 1857.[92] The question of exactly where to locate such an institution arose next. Dalhousie had originally recommended "a site on the Neilgherries which will be shortly reached by the Railways," but due to the outbreak of "Mutiny" later that year, the project was delayed for a while. It took until 1860 for the Madras Government to somewhat half-heartedly suggest a site for the proposed prison near the hill station of Ootacamund—situated seven thousand feet above sea level.[93] The reason for the provincial government's reluctance became clear in a letter written to the Government of India in September 1861, which raised serious objections to the Central European Penitentiary on numerous grounds, the first being that the cost for building the jail and maintaining the prisoners at a high altitude was "at least double that in the plains." The second argument is more interesting. The Government of Madras stated that the European community living in Ooty[94] felt a "great uneasiness … at the idea that a body of desperate European prisoners being placed among them."[95] The prevailing "uneasiness" was partly explained by

doubts surrounding whether it was really "necessary to make a point of selecting the very best climate in India"[96] for the "white criminal classes," and
partly by the absence of a European garrison in the station that could protect the local British community from their captive compatriots. A recent
violent mass breakout by European convicts confined in the Calcutta House
of Correction had not only demonstrated "the urgent necessity for the com-
pletion of the contemplated Jail for European Convicts," but had also shown
that European prisoners, some of them well-trained ex-soldiers, could become a source of danger for the colonial authorities.[97] The division between
the rulers and ruled was murky at best during this debate.

Since the Government of India did not react immediately, the administrators responsible in Madras sent another letter on 20 September 1861,
asking: "[W]hat is to become of the men when their sentences expire, or
they receive pardons? Are they to be turned loose upon the society in this
Presidency, or sent back to the Presidency whence they came? This is a serious question as respects Madras. Its own European criminal population
is small; but if that of the whole of India is to be poured into it, merely because it happens to have, in some localities, a good climate, the Madras
police system will be much enhanced."[98] Their resistance was only partly
successful: ultimately two European penitentiaries were built and opened
in the early 1860s. One opened in Ooty, accommodating prisoners from
the Bombay and Madras presidencies, and another in Hazaribagh, in the
Bengal Presidency, for those coming from the rest of British India.[99] The
colonial government's strong determination to realize its plans for segregated penal institutions for whites, which would allow for the thorough
re-education of European criminals securely hidden from the Indian gaze,
shows the sensitivity of the issue at stake: the need to defend the myth of
"white superiority." It is also clear that the debate surrounding hierarchies
of punishment put on full display the very contradictions within white society that made that myth so challenging to preserve.

Conclusion

This chapter has had a twofold aim. It first highlighted the ways in which
racial difference and particularly "whiteness" (often cast as "Europeanness")
were constructed in India, Britain's most important colony. We have seen
that there were two partly overlapping and partly contradictory ways of accounting for the differences between rulers and ruled. The language of
"scientific" racism that became dominant by the last third of the nineteenth

century was certainly more rigid and exclusionary than the environmentalist discourse that had been popular in the earlier phase, and hence better able to provide the ideological basis for a "rule of difference." However, the realities of colonialism, such as the existence of hybrid "Eurasian" communities and Indian resistance through the appropriation of elements of racial theories, constantly threatened this rule.

The analysis of the debate over how to punish European offenders living in the colony—the focus of the second part of this chapter—has shown that the clear-cut racial boundaries advocated by the champions of "race science" in British India were further threatened by the extreme stratification of the white colonial society along the axes of class and respectability. The decision to construct segregated penal institutions for European convicts can be interpreted as a frantic effort to defend those boundaries. However, this defensive strategy never fully succeeded, as criticism and dissenting voices even among the colonizers demonstrate. The debate over flogging and the trenchant refusal of the provincial Government in Madras to accommodate the "white trash" from other presidencies of British India powerfully illustrate the problems of coming to terms with the lower orders of their own community. The minuscule body of white criminals facing long-term penal servitude thus threw a spanner into the works of the British imperial machinery. On the one hand, prison sentences had to be dreadful deterrents; on the other, tribute had to be paid to the overarching ideology of European difference. The core of the colonial predicament caused by white criminals—and other disrespectable groups like European vagrants and prostitutes—lay in the fact that their mere existence undermined the simple equation of whiteness with "moral superiority." This complication of what it meant to be white in colonial India continually threatened to undermine the most salient ideological feature of colonial rule during the age of high imperialism: the belief in the existence of a monolithic and superior "ruling race."

Notes

1. This chapter draws to a large extent on various portions of my habilitation thesis "Low and Licentious Europeans: Race, Class, and White Subalternity in Colonial India," (New Delhi, 2009). Probably the most influential statement to that effect is the discussion of the "rule of difference" in Partha Chatterjee, *The Nation and its Fragments: Colonial and Postcolonial Histories* (Princeton, 1993), 16–34.
2. See the description of Indian port towns in William Milburn, *Oriental Commerce or the East India Trader's Complete Guide; containing A Geographical and Nautical*

Description of the Maritime Parts of India etc. (London, 1825).

3. Philip Mason, *The Men Who Ruled India*, repr. (Calcutta, 1992), 14. See also David Arnold, "Deathscapes: India in an Age of Romanticism and Empire, 1800–1856," *Nineteenth-Century Contexts* 26, no. 4 (2004): 340–43; Theo Wilkinson, *Two Monsoons: The Life and Death of Europeans in India*, 2nd ed. (London, 1987).

4. Mark Harrison, *Climates and Constitutions: Health, Race, Environment and British Imperialism in India 1600–1850* (New Delhi, 1999), 30.

5. Ibid., 56.

6. For a contemporary recapitulation and critique of this theory see James Hunt, "On Ethno-Climatology, or the Acclimatization of Man," *Transactions of the Ethnological Society of London* 2 (1863): 50–83.

7. See, for instance, Mrinalini Sinha, *Colonial Masculinity: The 'Manly Englishman' and the 'Effeminate Bengali' in the Late Nineteenth Century* (Manchester, 1995).

8. T.B. Macaulay quoted in Sudipta Sen, "Colonial Aversions and Domestic Desires: Blood, Race, Sex and the Decline of Intimacy in Early British India," *South Asia* 24 (2001): 25.

9. See for instance Indira Chowdhury, *The Frail Hero and Virile History: Gender and the Politics of Culture in Colonial Bengal* (Delhi, 1998), 120–49; John Rosselli, "The Self-image of Effeteness: Physical Education and Nationalism in 19th Century Bengal," *Past & Present* 86 (1980): 121–48.

10. Harrison, *Climates and Constitutions*, 114–23.

11. More recent studies on the constructions of these "martial races" include: Gavin Rand, "'Martial Races' and 'Imperial Subjects': Violence and Governance in Colonial India," *European Review of History* 13, no. 1 (2006): 1–20; Heather Streets, *Martial Races: The Military, Race and Masculinity in British Imperial Culture, 1857–1914* (Manchester, 2004); Pradeep Barua, "Inventing Race: The British and India's Martial Races," *Historian* 58, no. 1 (1995): 107–16.

12. Satoshi Mizutani, "The British in India and their Domiciled Brethren: Race and Class in the Colonial Context, 1858–1930" (Ph.D. diss., Oxford University, 2004), 60.

13. Harrison, *Climates and Constitutions*, 224.

14. E.M. Collingham, *Imperial Bodies: The Physical Experience of the Raj* (Cambridge, 2001), 33–34.

15. See also the insightful discussion in Teresa Hubel, "In Search of the British Indian in British India: White Orphans, Kipling's Kim and Class in Colonial India," *Modern Asian Studies* 38, no. 1 (2004): 227–51.

16. Anonymous, *Proposals for the Institution of a Free School Society in Bengal* (Calcutta, 1794).

17. Free School (Calcutta), *An Account of the Free School in Calcutta and of its Proceedings to Mid-summer, 1821* (Calcutta, 1821), 4–5.

18. See, for instance, Catherine Hall, "'From Greenland's Icy Mountains… to Africa's Golden Sand': Ethnicity, Race, and Nation in Mid-Nineteenth-Century England,"

Gender and History 5, no. 2 (1993): 221.

19. For such an approach see, for instance, George M. Frederickson, *Racism: A Short History* (Princeton, 2002), 57–63 and Immanuel Geiss, *Geschichte des Rassismus,* 2nd ed. (Frankfurt, 1989), 158–60.

20. See Thomas Trautmann, *Aryans and British India* (Berkeley, 1997), 37–41.

21. An excellent analysis of Jones's ambivalent role as colonial "scholar-administrator" can be found in Rosanne Rocher, "British Orientalism in the Eighteenth Century: The Dialectics of Knowledge and Government," in *Orientalism and the Postcolonial Predicament,* edited by Carol A. Breckenridge and Peter van der Veer (Philadelphia, 1993), 215–49.

22. William Jones, "On the Origin and Families of Nations," in *Race: The Origins of an Idea, 1760–1850,* edited by Hannah F. Augstein (Bristol, 1996), 40–50. This article is also based on a talk originally delivered in 1792 as an "anniversary discourse" before the Asiatick Society in Calcutta.

23. The literature on the Aryan Race theory and its implications for colonial India is vast. The more important titles include: Tony Ballantyne, *Orientalism and Race: Aryanism in the British Empire* (Basingstoke, 2002); Trautmann, *Aryans and British India*; Léon Poliakov, *Le Mythe Aryen: Essai sur les Sources du Racisme et des Nationalismes,* nouvelle éd. augmentée, (Bruxelles, 1987), 209–43; Joan Leopold, "The Aryan Theory of Race," *Indian Economic and Social History Review* 7, no. 2 (1970): 271–97; Joan Leopold, "British Applications of the Aryan Race Theory to India," *English Historical Review* 352 (1974): 578–603.

24. See Trautmann, *Aryans and British India,* 194–98; Dilip K. Chakrabarti, *Colonial Indology: Socio-politics of the Indian Past* (New Delhi, 1997), 80–81, 98–100.

25. Christophe Jaffrelot, "The Ideas of the Hindu Race in the Writings of Hindu Nationalist Ideologues in the 1920s and 1930s," in *The Concept of Race in South Asia,* edited by Peter Robb (Delhi, 1995), 330–32; Susan Bayly, "Race in Britain and India," in *Nation and Religion: Perspectives on Europe and Asia,* edited by Peter Van der Veer and Hartmut Lehmann (Princeton, 1999), 81–85, and Leopold, "The Aryan Theory of Race."

26. Thomas R. Trautmann, "Constructing the Racial Theory of Indian Civilization," in *The Aryan Debate,* edited by Thomas R. Trautmann (New Delhi, 2005), 99; Christine Bolt, *Victorian Attitudes towards Race* (London, 1971), 190.

27. Margaret MacMillan, "Anglo-Indians and the Civilizing Mission," in *Contributions to South Asian Studies,* edited by Gopal Krishna (Delhi, 1982), 86.

28. Ibid.

29. Francis G. Hutchins, *The Illusion of Permanence: British Imperialism in India* (Princeton, 1965).

30. Philipp Mason, *Prospero's Magic: Some Thoughts on Class and Race* (London, 1962), 1.

31. Thomas R. Metcalf, *Ideologies of the Raj* (Cambridge, 1995), 83–87; Susan Bayly, "Caste and Race in the Colonial Ethnography of India," in Robb, *The Concept of Race in South Asia,* 165–218.

32. Daniel Pick, *Faces of Degeneration: A European Disorder, ca. 1848–1918* (Cam-

bridge, 1989), 11–27. For an extensive treatment see also the articles in *Degeneration: The Dark Side of Progress,* ed. J.E. Chamberlin and S.G. Gilman (New York, 1985).

33. Crispin Bates, "Race, Caste and Tribe in Central India: The Early Origins of Indian Anthropometry," in Robb, *The Concept of Race in South Asia,* 226.

34. On Prichard, see George W. Stocking, *Victorian Anthropology* (New York, 1987), 48–53; and Nancy Stepan, *The Idea of Race in Science: Great Britain, 1800–1960,* repr. (Basingstoke, 1982), 31–40.

35. Peter Pels, "From Texts to Bodies: Brian Houghton Hodgson and the Emergence of Ethnology in India," in *Anthropology and Colonialism in Asia and Oceania,* edited by J.G. van Bremen and A. Shimizu (Richmond, 1998), 65–92.

36. John Marriott, *The Other Empire: Metropolis, India and Progress in the Colonial Imagination* (Manchester, 2003), 187. See also Bernard S. Cohn, "The Past in the Present: India as Museum of Mankind," *History and Anthropology* 11, no. 1 (1998): 29–35.

37. Jane Samson, *Race and Empire* (Harlow, 2005), 70.

38. See Mark Brown, "Ethnology and Colonial Administration in Nineteenth-Century British India: The Question of Native Crime and Criminality," *British Journal of the History of Science* 36, no. 2 (2003): 201–19.

39. Bayly, "Caste and Race in the Colonial Ethnography of India," 204–14.

40. See for example Herbert Hope Risley, *The People of India* (Calcutta, 1908).

41. A comparison based on measurements of European soldiers and Indians is undertaken by John Short, "Notes on Differences in Weight and Stature of Europeans and Some Natives of India," *Transactions of the Ethnological Society of London* 2 (1863): 213–16.

42. Ronald Hyam, *Britain's Imperial Century, 1815–1914: A Study of Empire and Expansion,* 3rd ed. (Houndmills, 2002), 155–64.

43. John Crawfurd (1783–1868) was the President of the Ethnological Society of London. Like many of his fellow ethnologists, he had an intimate knowledge of South Asia, since he had spent five years in northern India as a medical officer. See Trautmann, *Aryans and British India,* 178–81.

44. John Crawfurd, "On the Physical and Mental Characteristics of the European Asiatic Races of Man," *Transactions of the Ethnological Society of London* 5 (1867): 60.

45. See also the discussion in Benita Parry, *Delusions and Discoveries: India in the British Imagination, 1880–1930,* 2nd ed. (London, 1998), 39–41.

46. There was a long tradition of an "extinction discourse" in Europe, a strong undercurrent of which maintained not that the "inferior native" races would vanish in the course of protracted cultural contact with a "superior conquering" race, but vice versa. See Patrick Brantlinger, *Dark Vanishings: Discourse on the Extinction of Primitive Races, 1800–1930* (Ithaca-London, 2003), 191–93.

47. The community usually referred to as "Anglo-Indian" in twentieth-century parlance was known as "Eurasian" or by one of the other eighteenth- and

nineteenth-century epithets given above.

48. Percival Spear, *The Nabobs: A Study of the Social Life of the English in Eighteenth-Century India,* repr. (London-Dublin, 1980), 126–45; S.C. Ghosh, *The Social Condition of the British Community in Bengal, 1750–1800* (Leiden, 1970), 70–78.

49. Herbert A. Stark, *Hostages to India: The Life Story of the Anglo-Indian Race,* 2nd ed. (Calcutta, 1936), 50.

50. Sen, "Colonial Aversions and Domestic Desires"; Christopher Hawes, *Poor Relations: The Making of a Eurasian Community in British India* (Richmond, 1996), 57–59; Stark, *Hostages to India,* 50–67.

51. See also Peter Robb, "Children, Emotion, Identity and Empire: Views from the Blechyndens' Calcutta Diaries (1790–1822)," *Modern Asian Studies* 40, no. 1 (2006): 175–201.

52. John Macrae, "Social Conditions in Calcutta. I. The Problem for [*sic*] Charity among the Anglo-Indian Community," *The Calcutta Review* 271 (1913): 85.

53. For recent accounts of the fate of "Eurasians," see Alison Blunt, "Land of our Mothers: Home, Identity and Nationality for Anglo-Indians in British India," *History Workshop Journal* 54 (2002): 49–72; Laura Bear, "Public Genealogies: Documents, Bodies and Nations in Anglo-Indian Railway Family Histories," *Contributions to Indian Sociology* 35, no. 3 (2001): 355–58; Lionel Caplan, *Children of Colonialism: Anglo-Indians in a Postcolonial World* (Oxford, 2001).

54. Amicus [pseud.], "Our Cousins the Eurasians of India," *Calcutta Review* 121 (1905): 381–97.

55. Sudipta Sen, *Distant Sovereignty: National Imperialism and the Origins of British India* (New York, 2002), 141–43.

56. H.L. Malchow, "The Half-breed as Gothic Unnatural," in *The Victorians and Race,* edited by Shearer West (Aldershot, 1996), 101–11.

57. Waltraud Ernst, "Colonial Policies, Racial Politics and the Development of Psychiatric Institutions in Early Nineteenth-Century India," in *Race, Science and Medicine, 1700–1960,* edited by Waltraud Ernst and Bernard Harris (London, 1999), 92.

58. See Oriental and India Office Collection, India Office Records, British Library [hereafter cited as OIOC, IOR], P/4089GoBeng, General Dept. Progs.—Miscellaneous, 1892, no. 4C/1, September 1892, "Report of the Pauperism Committee," Calcutta, 1892; Macrae, "Social Conditions in Calcutta," I: 85–86.

59. On the appropriation of "scientific racism" by Indian elites for an affirmation of existing caste hierarchies, see also Sumit Guha, "Lower Strata, Older Races and Aboriginal People: Racial Anthropology and Mythical History Past and Present," *Journal of Asian Studies* 57, no. 2 (1998): 423–41.

60. See, for instance, Kenan Malik, *The Meaning of Race: Race, History and Culture in Western Society* (Basingstoke, 1996), 3–6. Specifically on the constructed character of "whiteness" in various contexts, see, for instance, W.P. Anderson, *The Cultivation of Whiteness: Science, Health and Racial Destiny in Australia* (Carlton, 2002);

Birgit B. Rasmussen, ed., *The Making and Unmaking of Whiteness* (Durham, NC, 2001); Matthew Frye Jacobson, *Whiteness of a Different Color: European Immigrants and the Alchemy of Race* (Cambridge, MA, 1998); Ruth Frankenberg, "Introduction: Local Whitenesses, Localizing Whiteness," in *Displacing Whiteness: Essays in Social and Cultural Criticism*, edited by Ruth Frankenberg (Durham, 1997), 1–33; Ann Laura Stoler, "Rethinking Colonial Categories: European Communities and the Boundaries of Rule," *Comparative Studies in Society and History* 31, no. 1 (1989): 134–61.

61. Macaulay, *Notes on the Indian Penal Code*, cited in Elizabeth Kolsky, "Codification and the Rule of Colonial Difference: Criminal Procedure in British India," *Law and History Review* 23, no. 3 (2005): 659.

62. Ibid.

63. *Report of the Committee on Prison-Discipline* (Calcutta, 1838), sec. 291.

64. *Report of the Committee on Prison-Discipline*, app. no. 4.

65. Ibid., app. no. 4, 124. Other administrators made many statements given to the same effect.

66. See Satadru Sen, *Colonial Childhoods: The Juvenile Periphery in British India, 1850–1945* (London, 2005), 85–87.

67. Frederic J.Mouat, "On Prison Discipline and Statistics in Lower Bengal," *Journal of the Statistical Society of London* 35, no. 1 (1872): 57.

68. Minute by H. Maddock, 4 September 1844, GoI, Legisl. Progs., Oct.–Dec. 1844, 12 October, no. 5, National Archives of India [hereafter cited as NAI]. I am grateful to Elizabeth Kolsky for informing me of this particular reference.

69. The prevalence of this view among British officials is shown in Mrinal Kumar Basu, "Food, Fatality and Deprivation in Bengal Prisons: A Study of the Santal Convicts," *Indian Historical Review* 32, no. 2 (2005): 122–41, see particularly 125–26.

70. Minute by H. Maddock, 4 September 1844, GoI, Legisl. Progs., Oct.–Dec. 1844, 12 October, no. 5, NAI.

71. F.J. Mouat, "Extract of the Report by F.J. Mouat," in A.P. Howell, *Note on Jails and Jail Discipline in India, 1867–68* (Calcutta, 1868), 156.

72. One witness gave evidence to the Jail Committee of 1919 that 80 percent of the inmates of a particular native jail were "either sodomites or catamites or both." *Report of the Indian Jails Committee, 1919–20* (London, 1921), 99–100.

73. "Communication to the Secretary to the European & Anglo-Indian Defence Organisation forwarding a copy of a Resolution on the differential treatment of prisoners," GoI, Home Dept. Progs., Publ., No. A-1-18, April 1893, NAI.

74. OIOC, IOR, L/PJ/6/516, GoI, Home Dept., Public & Judicial Progs., 1899, Question by Samuel Smith, MP, in the House of Commons, 31 July 1899.

75. Ibid., Reply of the Secretary of State for India. The Act referred to is the 'Colonial Prisoners Removal Act', 1884.

76. It is implicit in the discussion that the possession of tobacco and "crimes against nature" (i.e., homosexual activities) were the most frequent transgressions of jail rules

that resulted in flogging.

77. A Reviewer [pseud.], "Whipping as Jail Punishment. A rejoinder to J. M.," *The Calcutta Review* 117 (1903): 90.

78. For details on this point, see my essay "Flotsam and Jetsam of the Empire? European seamen and spaces of disease and disorder in mid-nineteenth century Calcutta" in *The Limits of British Control in South Asia: Spaces of Disorder in the Indian Ocean Region*, edited by Ashwini Tambe and Harald Fischer-Tiné (London, 2008).

79. On the debate over corporal punishment for Indians see also Satadru Sen's interesting discussion on flogging in reformatory schools. Sen, *Colonial Childhoods*, 103–13.

80. J. M. [pseud.], "Whipping as Jail Punishment," *The Calcutta Review* 116 (1903): 90. The same view had already become prominent decades earlier through the controversy over flogging as a punishment in the European regiments of the EIC's army. See Douglas Peers, "Sepoys, Soldiers and the Lash: Race, Caste and Army Discipline in India, 1820–50," *Journal of Imperial and Commonwealth History* 23, no. 2 (1995): 211–47, esp. 228–29.

81. See also Marriott, *The Other Empire*, 101–29, 160–86; Deborah E. Nord, "The Social Explorer as Anthropologist: Victorian Travellers Among the Urban Poor," in *Visions of the Modern City. Essays in History Art and Literature*, edited by William Sharpe and Leonard Wallock, repr. (Baltimore, 1987), 122–34; Seth Koven, *Slumming: Sexual and Social Politics in Victorian London* (Princeton, 2004).

82. See Ian Duffield and James Bradley, "Introduction: Representing Convicts," in idem, eds., *Representing Convicts: New Perspectives on Convict Forced Labour Migration* (London-Washington, 1997), 6–7.

83. If not indicated otherwise, the following is based on, "Closing of the European Jail at Hazareebagh," Letter No. 609 P, GoBeng to GoI, Home Dept., 26 May 1881, GoI, Home Dept. Progs., Judl., A-179–187, August 1881, NAI.

84. See McConville, "The Victorian Prison: England 1865–1965," in *The Oxford History of the Prison: The Practice of Punishment in Western Society,* edited by Norval Morris and David J. Rothman (New York, 1995), 135–36; Michael Ignatieff, *A Just Measure of Pain: The Penitentiary in the Industrial Revolution, 1750–1850* (London, 1978) 200–204.

85. Clare Anderson, *Legible Bodies: Race, Criminality and Colonialism in South Asia* (Oxford, 2004), 119–20. Anderson notes that only "European born British subjects" were sent to Australia, whereas Eurasians and "domiciled Europeans" (i.e., Europeans born in India) were invariably shipped to penal settlements in Mauritius and the Straits.

86. "Deportation of Military Convicts," Letter No. 1355, W. Grey, Secy. to GoI, to T. Pycroft, Chief Secy. to GoFort St. George, 9 July 1859, GoI, Home Dept. Progs., Judl., No. 5, 15 July 1859, NAI. For details on the penal regimes in the various Australian colonies, see Robert Hughes, *The Fatal Shore: A History of the Transportation of*

Convicts to Australia, 1787–1868, repr. (London, 2003).

87. OIOC, IOR, V8/35, "An Act to substitute penal servitude for the punishment of transportation in respect of European and American convicts, and to amend the law relating to the removal of such convicts," *India Acts 1854–57*.

88. See, for instance, OIOC, IOR, P/925 GoMad, Judicial Progs. 1876, Prog. No. 69, 11 August 1876, Govt. Order No. 1639, August 1876.

89. "Protest of Madras Government against having one Central Jail for all Europeans in India and the Decision of the Government of India to have one in each Presidency," Letter No. 1976, GoI, Judl. Dept. to E.H. Lushington, Secy. to GoBeng, 31 October 1861, GoI, Home Dept. Progs., Judl., No. A–30–35, 31 October 1861, NAI.

90. "Closing of the European Jail at Hazareebagh."

91. Ibid.

92. "Sanction to expenditure of Rs 30,000 for construction of a Jail at Ootacamund for Europeans under Penal servitude," GoI, Home Dept. Progs., Publ., No. A⊠10, 8 October 1858, NAI.

93. *The Imperial Gazetteer of India (new edition)* (Oxford, 1908), 12: 215.

94. For an interesting account of the small white community in Ooty and its internal stratifications, see Alexander Morrison, "'White Todas': The Politics of Race and Class Amongst European Settlers on the Nilgiri Hills, *c.*1860–1900," *Journal of Imperial and Commonwealth History* 32, no. 2 (2004): 54–85.

95. Letter No. 1106, J.D. Sims, Secy. to GoFort St. George, to GoI, 3 September 1861, Home Dept. Progs., Judl. Progs., No. A⊠30–35, 31 October 1861, NAI.

96. From 1870 onwards, Ootacamund served as the summer capital of the Madras Presidency and thus was the seat of government for five months a year.

97. See OIOC, IOR, P/206/64, GoI, Judl. Dept. Progs. 1861, Prog. No. 36, 16 April 1861, Letter No. 212, S. Wauchope, Commissioner of Police, Calcutta to the Secy. to the GoBeng, to W. Grey, Secy. to GoI, 13 March 1861.

98. "Closing of the European Jail at Hazareebagh." See also OIOC, IOR, P/206/64, GoI, Judl. Dept. Progs. 1861, Prog. No. 30, 3 September 1861, Letter No. 1106, J.D. Sim, Secy. to GoMad to W. Grey, Secy. to GoI, 3 September 1861.

99. Due to constraints of space it is impossible to elaborate further on the history of these institutions. The penal regime in European penitentiaries is analyzed in depth in my essay "Hierarchies of Crime and Punishment? European Convicts in Colonial India and the Racial Dividend," in *Empires and Boundaries: Rethinking Race, Class, and Gender in Colonial Settings*, edited by Harald Fischer-Tiné and Susanne Gehrmann (New York, forthcoming).

Chapter 11

Glocalizing "Race" in China: Concepts and Contingencies at the Turn of the Twentieth Century

Gotelind Müller

Introduction

This essay proposes to look at the process of introducing Western "scientific" concepts of "race" into China in terms of a negotiated process of "glocalization" (Robertson),[1] i.e., of being global and local *at the same time*. In comparison to other terms like indigenization, appropriation, adaptation etc., the advantage of the "glocalization" approach is to acknowledge the remaining link (and even at times contribution) to global discourse while at the same time focusing on a specific locality into which something is introduced and by which it is framed. This essay will demonstrate on the one hand in which ways linguistic, cultural and above all historical contingencies were of crucial importance in the process of glocalizing "race" in China; on the other it will show how the specific motivation of individual actors made for notable twists in this development. Thus, it will become evident that although the Western "race" concept was taken up by various Chinese, this should not just be interpreted as a passive submission to an "imposed hegemonic discourse" but rather as an active manipulation by different "glocalizers" with their own ends, at times consciously using the pseudo-scientificity of a global discourse to fight against local, i.e., inner-Chinese adversaries. For demonstrating the above, a close reading and a historical contextualization of texts and authors is proposed here, focusing on texts by Chinese intellectuals of the time.

China has often been cited as a case of "cultural ethnocentrism" (Sinocentrism) vs. "racial ethnocentrism." In fact, even though "racial" definitions of self are not totally absent in pre-modern China,[2] the historically dominant trend—in the sense of elite Confucian literati culture which produced the main sources that have been used up until today—was to define "Chineseness" in cultural terms. Basically, biological traits were not of primary concern.

The Western "scientific" theory of mankind being divided into "races," assigning the Chinese to the "mongoloid"/"yellow" race, was introduced in China in the late nineteenth century. The theory itself went back to Bernier, Buffon, Kant (the first to speak of a "yellow race," though not intending China) and Blumenbach, "father" of anthropology as a "scientific" discipline, who propagated the influential theory of mankind's division into five races, one of them being the "mongoloid"/"yellows" living in Asia. In the second half of the nineteenth century, Gobineau and Chamberlain popularized and systematically matched this concept with supposed mental and cultural characteristics to "demonstrate" the "inequality of races." Thus, at the time, more or less accepted "scientific knowledge" suggested the existence of differently colored "races" ranked in their "civilized" status and identified with certain parts of the world, with "whites" usually located in Europe, "yellows" in continental Asia, "blacks" in Africa, "reds" in America, and "browns" in maritime Asia, although a simpler threefold structure of the "whites," "yellows," and "blacks" was also current.

In the historical process of introducing Western "race" concepts to China, two kinds of influence played an important role: on the one hand, some Western missionary works started to make these ideas known via translations or summaries; on the other, and with much greater long-term effect, Japanese works and translations molded Chinese perceptions, so that the newly coined characters for "race" in China were almost exclusively graphical loans from Japanese. (This, of course, holds true for much of modern Chinese scientific vocabulary.) Terms used for "race" in China since the 1890s all transported specific shades of meaning via the characters chosen. *Renzhong* (man-kind) was the closest to a biological- anthropological interpretation. *Zhonglei* (kind-category) was a "neutral" categorization without specific reference to human beings. Both *zhongzu* (kind-lineage) and *minzu* (people-lineage, also used as a translation for "people" in the sense of *Volk* and "nation") included the lineage element. *Minzu* (adding the "people" character), however, provided the closest approximation to a purely social interpretation and sparked the most heated debates due to its ambiguous shifting between "race," "*Volk*," and "nation." This already hints at a certain malleability of the whole "race" concept in Chinese via "flexibility" in linguistic options.[3]

When linguistically introducing Western "race" concepts, just who was to be subsumed under these categories also became an issue—a question itself inconsistently answered in the West. Some authors, when speaking of "the yellows" or "mongoloids," generically intended "the Asians," while others excluded the Indians, and still others separated the Malays as a "race" in itself, etc. The Chinese in the late nineteenth century, in any case, found themselves grouped with (somewhat varying) others under the label of "yellow" or "mongoloid." How did they view and react to this? Two cases proved especially salient to the introduction of Western notions of "race." One was the grouping of the Han with the ruling Manchus and all (other) "minorities" in China. When anti-Manchu nationalism arose around 1900, Han nationalists began to see this as problematic since the question entailed the issue of domination, i.e., power relations. The other case was the grouping together of China and Japan—two countries whose relationship was undergoing a substantial shift at the time. This chapter focuses on the struggle with "glocalizing" the Western concept of "race" in China around the turn of the twentieth century, on the problems this generated, and the motives driving (or hampering) it.

Are We "Yellow"?

It came as quite a surprise when the Chinese found out in the late nineteenth century that the West defined them according to their supposedly "yellow" skin color. Skin color had not been an important issue, rather "fair" and "dark" complexion signified (as in early modern Europe) social distinction between the wealthy and the poor. If anything, the Chinese tended to see themselves as of "white complexion."[4] Apart from the fact that "yellow" has favorable symbolic connotations in Chinese traditional culture, being closely associated with the emperor, and from the possibility that Jesuit information about the symbolic value of "yellow" in China might have played a role in leading Westerners to finally opt for "yellow" as the supposed skin color of the Chinese,[5] this was clearly a heteronomous definition for the Chinese.[6] Consequently, Chinese reactions (amongst intellectuals) were divided: some pleaded for rejecting the label in favor of defining themselves as "white," others saw no problem in accepting a symbolically positive marker, though the realization of a hierarchy between the colors in this Western "race" concept (namely, since Gobineau's influential mid-nineteenth-century work on the "inequality of the races") complicated things. "Yellow" would be acceptable if it were not secondary to "white."

To cope with this situation, various strategies were available. One of them can be gleaned from an early reference to Western ideas on "race" in Chinese: the article "Ren fen wu lei shuo" (On the division of men into five categories/races) in the Western-directed, Chinese-language journal *Gezhi huibian* in 1892,[7] presented the Blumenbach classification (without mentioning the name) and started quite tellingly with the "Mongoloids"/"Yellows" before the "Caucasians"/"Whites," followed by the "Africans"/"Blacks," "Malayans"/"Browns," and finally the "Americans"/"Reds." (Blumenbach's original order had been: (1) Caucasians as the "primary" and "most beautiful," (2) Mongoloids, (3) Ethiopians, (4) Americans, (5) Malayans.) Thus, the article subtly changed the hierarchy implicit in numbering to suit Chinese readers (also upgrading the Asian Malayans vis-à-vis the far-away Native Americans). Both the fact that the "old" sequence of Americans-before-Malayans reappears in the text itself and the casual acknowledgement of less "favorable" Western schemes integrating the "Americans," "Malayans," and "Mongoloids" into one single "race" demonstrate that this hierarchical change was not accidental.[8] The drawing attached also presented the "Mongoloids"/"Yellows" in the "Chinese" fashion of the time (with the Manchurian queue obligatory for every male to wear under Qing rule), thus making the Manchu-Qing-dynasty subjects stand for "the Mongoloids." The article downplayed the negative physical or psychological features attributed to the "Mongoloids" in Blumenbach's (and his followers') scheme and presented an image of a race outstanding in wisdom and arts, though somewhat deficient in moral judgement and bound by conventions. Alongside the Chinese, it included Mongols as Manchus, Japanese as Koreans, and Tibetans as Vietnamese, who together made up this "most numerous race" on earth. The next group, the "Caucasians"/"Whites," were treated as especially skilled in material and practical matters, foreshadowing the later image of the "spiritual East vs. the material West," whereas the "Africans"/"Blacks" were invariably associated with slavery,[9] the "Malayans"/"Browns" deemed morally ignorant infants and the Native "Americans"/"Reds" considered hopelessly incapable of education. The main aim of the presentation, though, was to hammer home the transformative power of "today's civilization" as an implicit agenda to follow. Furthermore, the article is one of the rather rare instances where the term "Mongoloids" (in Chinese equalling "Mongol"/*menggu*) appears, a term increasingly superseded by "yellow race" (*huangzhong*) by the mid 1890s to resolve the "problematic" identification with a one-time enemy "invader" and current "minority."[10]

The argument for "reform," however, could also be made the other way round by using precisely the "secondary" status of "yellow" to "white" in this supposedly "scientific" and "universal" race concept. Calling for policies that would "whiten" China's future (and thus giving credit to the idea of an integral link between "race" and "survival" current with Gobineau and Social Darwinists), one could easily explain China's historically factual weakness by its "lack of whiteness." "Whitening" thus represented the only way to achieve an era of "equal strength of the whites and yellows,"[11] thereby safeguarding China's existence from the threat of "racial competition," which had already claimed several "victims" worldwide.[12] "Whitening" entailed efforts to copy Western institutions as well as more biological tactics, like intermarriage. (Not surprisingly, the latter tactic was highly controversial.) Reformer Yan Fu, for example, opted for this strategy in 1895 (after China's defeat in the war against Japan) when he urged educating the "yellow race" (obviously referring only to the Chinese) to prevent it from perishing.[13] Likewise, Kang Youwei rhetorically accepted the "priority" of "white" in his agenda, which culminated in his ill-fated 1898 reform endeavors. This later carried over to his work, *Datongshu* (Book of the Great Union), which advocated a program of racial amalgamation that would dissolve the "yellows" through intermarriage with the "whites" (again relegating the "hopeless" case to "inferior races," for example "the browns" and especially "the blacks," who would not be able to "whiten").[14] Apart from its final utopian rendering, Kang's argument was not intended to hail "whiteness" in a racial sense, but identified it, as did Yan Fu, with "civilization." (NB: He occasionally switched from "white"/"yellow" to "silver"/"gold," implying a reversed hierarchy of values.)[15] In this way, he always stayed true to his culturalist Confucian framework. Characterizing the "yellows" as equally spread over the globe as the "whites," and even superior to them in wisdom, amalgamating the two would not require bridging any major gaps. Kang supported his claims by citing Chinese living overseas who had adopted Western cultural habits without problems.

Another strategy for coping with imported race concepts was *accepting* "yellowness" and turning it into an asset. As revolutionary Liu Shipei stated: "In recent times … Chinese[16] are called the 'yellow race.' If we check with the Chinese ancient books, [we see] that among the five colours only yellow was adored … In old times, yellow was interpreted as the middle and harmonizing colour … It means also brightness and from this the meaning of 'China' is derived … The people on the yellow earth are the Han lineage people."[17] The focus in this process of "glocalizing" the foreign ascription was thus significantly shifted away from skin color—something the reformers cited above had already started to do—either towards a purely cultural definition of "yellowness" or a merger of "cultural" with "biological" descent. The latter was accomplished by tracing an elaborate lineage back to the "Yellow Emperor" (Huangdi), one of the mythical first rulers of China (NB: *di* in "Huangdi" originally meant "divine *ancestor*") in order to "reinvent" "Chineseness," which in turn could be used to identify the only "true Yellows," i.e., to separate the Han from non-Han.

Thus the figure of the Yellow Emperor turned into a symbol for political contestation among Chinese reformers, who had been the first to revive him in the 1890s, and among revolutionaries shortly thereafter. Hoping their ideas would help "preserve Chinese culture," the reformers stressed the cultural side, building up the Yellow Emperor as a symbol of pride for all people living in China as heirs to a "great civilization" set in motion by early cultural heroes like "Huangdi." The revolutionaries adopted this politically useful symbol but reinvented Huangdi as an "ancestor" exclusively of the Han, stripping him (also visually) of his emperorship and transforming him into a militaristic ancestor with the "conquering" abilities to take control of what was then "Chinese soil."[18] Thus, he was declared the founding father of the Chinese and their state, and the "first nationalist hero" (*minzuzhuyi daweiren*) on earth.[19] At times the revolutionaries also integrated another foreign theory into this vision, namely, that of the Han's "Western" origins and later migration to the East from Mesopotamia. This theory, proposed by the Frenchman Terrien de Lacouperie, implied that the Han had a common place of origin with the "Western whites" and—paralleling Aryan and Spanish conquests—the martial vigor of a moving conquering people who easily subdued the "natives" living in the territory making up modern "China."[20]

A further motivation for creating the "Yellow emperor myth" was the contemporaneous and parallel construction of "Japaneseness" through a supposed ancestor of the Japanese emperor: Jimmu. The Japanese even introduced a calendar that started with his "birth," which was then copied by the Chinese revolutionaries for Huangdi (though, as already mentioned, omitting the monarchical aspect).[21] Taking up the "challenge" of being defined as "yellow" led to conscious strategies for building up future nationalism around "yellowness" that took primarily either culturalist or racial approaches, the respective paths followed by the reformers and revolutionaries.

In one way or another, the blending of nationalism and "yellowness" was common to many reformers and revolutionaries around 1900. (It should be stressed, though, at the time "race" came to be used interchangeably with "nation" in the West as well,[22] thus undermining the categorical "unity" of a "white" or "Caucasian" "race"). Earlier reformers who followed Confucianism, like Kang Youwei, obviously viewed "race" in a larger, supranational context, even while China as a "cultural" category remained central to their political aims. But Liang Qichao, Kang's one-time disciple, modified this position after the turn of the century: he retained Kang's "larger" Confucian model but developed a more nationalistic interpretation. For example, he noted in 1903 that even though, in the West, Spaniards and Englishmen could not be physically differentiated at first glance as "whites" could from "blacks," they still constituted different "races" because "racial consciousness" was based on biological heredity *and* psychological features. Therefore the Spanish and English were different "races" due to the latter, separated by a psychological "heredity," which Liang explained manifested in cultural-moral traditions—a good example of the blending of "race" and "culture." Without this two-tiered "racial consciousness" no state could be set up.[23]

Significantly, Liang Qichao (basically a "reformer") and many revolutionaries who criticized reform were soon writing mainly in Japan and being influenced by Japanese publications and translations, though at times they used them in "creative" ways to meet their own respective agendas. Liang's approval of a piece by Japanese journalist Ishikawa Hanzan in 1900 provides a telling case in point. Ishikawa wrote about "the struggle in the racial world," arguing that although there were "three races" (white, yellow, and black), the "white race" actually should be subdivided into "red–white" (Westerners) and "yellow–white" (Chinese—named first in the Chinese version—Japanese, Koreans, Hungarians, and Turkish). Suprisingly, exactly who would remain to constitute the "yellow race" was not even discussed.[24] Here, again, we see an example of superficial acknowledgment of Western "scientific" theories and the changes made to them to meet particular agendas—a strategy already familiar to the Chinese and which made clear to Chinese readers that the Japanese had developed similarly flexible ways of glocalizing Western "race" concepts. Japan was obviously succeeding in her struggle for "racial survival" by "semi-whitening" *without* denying its "yellow" roots. China, Liang thought, needed to follow this example.

Who is "Us"?

The Sino-Japanese War of 1894–95 was linked to this whole scenario and provides important background to the sense of crisis shared by many Chinese intellectuals around the turn of the century. The war not only led to a perception of an urgent need for "reform" in China, but also gave the question of "race" a new turn: who should count as "our" race? Who would count among "the yellows"?

This problem functioned on two levels. One dealt with inclusion and exclusion *inside* China with regard to non-Han, particularly the ruling Manchus. The other considered the same issue *outside* China: who else would comprise "yellowness" or the "mongoloid" race (the latter term usually avoided in China, as already stated)? Asia or East Asia? More specifically, were the Chinese and Japanese members of one "race"?

With regard to the first level, in the early 1900s the debate focused on the "racial" relation between Manchu and Han, and sometimes extended to the Miao minority living in Southern China, depicted as the archetypical Chinese "barbarians" in need of being "civilized."[25] (Typically, this discussion was not politically "neutral" but rather intertwined "race" and "domination," including the problem of whether the Han themselves had been "imperialists" towards "their" minorities.) In a famous debate, Liang Qichao as spokesman of the reformers and proponents of a constitutional monarchy under the Manchus, argued for inclusion. On the other hand, anti-Manchu revolutionaries used precisely the "racial" difference theory to argue for toppling Manchu rule: the Manchus were a "racially retarded" or "lower level" ethnic minority who had unjustly usurped the Chinese throne. They claimed the "higher" Chinese "race" had lived through humiliation in the nineteenth century because the "barbarian" Manchus had obstructed "Chinese civilization." They were obstacles on the road to progress that had to be removed. In fact their incompetent rule was accused of putting the Chinese "race" in danger of extinction. Getting rid of them was thus necessary for "racial" survival in the Social Darwinist struggle setting of the time.[26]

The Kang/Liang camp, on the other hand, argued that there was no "racial" difference between the Manchus and the Han, since the Manchus lived out and practiced Chinese "cultural" norms. Their "sinicisation" guaranteed their "sameness"—here, the universalist Confucian background of the reformers became evident. In any case, one could argue that the Manchus had already been part of the Chinese empire before their conquest, which meant, in an interesting argumentative twist, that they need not to be considered "alien."[27] Since the current government included many Han, they had to be seen as "Chinese" for the same reason. On the other hand, the Miao were highly diverse,[28] thus not qualifying as a historical "parallel case." Therefore Liang suggested a "broad nationalism" (*da minzuzhuyi*) over a "narrow" Han-centered one in order to include all peoples living in China,[29] though in so doing he rejected the "race" argument altogether in favor of a common national interest in a multi-ethnic society. Obviously, then, when the revolutionaries started playing the "race" card to support their political ends, Liang retreated from the "race" concept, which had seemed useful to him insofar as it meant "the nation" in a political sense. The ambiguous term *minzu* (people-lineage, *Volk*, or nation) used by both sides, however, hid Liang's shift to a certain extent. But Liang had clearly distanced himself from a less ambiguous "race" definition connoted by the term *zhongzu* (kind-lineage) and attacked his opponents for the latter.

Liang alleged anti-Manchu "racism" in the revolutionaries' camp and implied it could be traced to envy and resentment. He focused these allegations mainly on Zhang Binglin, a fervent anti-Manchu intellectual who countered the Kang/Liang faction's "sinicization" thesis by pointing to the historical fact of Manchu rule and describing it as imperious (rather than the other way round)[30] and Zou Rong, who called for "killing the Manchus living in China."[31] In the face of Liang's criticisms, Liu Shipei tried to bolster the revolutionaries' position by integrating the whole question of minorities, mainly the Miao, into the debate.[32]

Since the Miao were not Han, Liu concluded that the Manchus were not either. But the Miao, who either migrated after Huangdi subdued them or assimilated into the Han, were less problematic. The Manchus, though, were a conquering people with a clear-cut identity and thus could not have assimilated into the Han at all. They, in fact, used the "white race" to help keep the "yellow race" down—thus excluding the Manchus from the "yellows" which in this formulation meant the Han.[33] The Han, then, were different in terms of geographic distribution, language, religion, and customs—the attributes necessary to constitute a distinct *minzu*—from the Mongols, Manchus, Hui, and Miao.[34] During the evolving debate with Liang Qichao, Zhang Binglin, in an interesting contradiction of his earlier hailing of both Lacouperie and Huangdi as a "conqueror," pointed out that even the argument for a parallel one-time Han "invasion" could not be proven. Therefore one could not—as the Liang camp had argued—say that the Han would have been "aggressors" as well.[35] In any case, even if the origin of all mankind were somewhere in the West, then the Miao as well were only immigrants.[36]

"Our race" thus became narrowly defined as "Han" and linked to an ancestry which Liu had already constructed via the "Yellow Emperor theory": the emperor, then, was only the progenitor of the Han, not of any of the minorities. According to Liu, who based his ideas on a Japanese source,[37] the subdivision of the "yellow race" into "Chinese" and "Siberians" identified the "Chinese" only as Han, Tibetans, and Indo-Chinese. The "Siberians" grouped together the Japanese,[38] Tungus (i.e., Manchus), Mongolian, and Turkish. Other revolutionaries, though, suggested a slightly different internal division in the larger "yellow race," further subdividing "Chinese" and "Siberians": according to Zou Rong's influential chart, the "Chinese race" included the Han and "others" (specified as Koreans, Burmese, Japanese, Tibetans, and "other East Asians"), and the "Siberian race" included the Mongols (including Mongols, Manchus, Siberians, and "other Asians") and the Turkish (including the Turkish, Hungarians, and "other European Yellows"). But Zou Rong himself gave a somewhat different categorization in the text preceding the chart, though he, like Liu, stressed Manchu exclusion from the "Chinese" category (though here keeping them in the "yellow" category, obviously due to a lack of alternatives). Still the contradictions revealed in the range of just two pages leaves a close reader of Zou Rong's inflammatory tract bewildered.[39] This, again, leads to the conclusion that this whole enterprise of glocalizing "scientific" "race" categories was highly malleable.[40]

Revolutionary par excellence, Sun Yatsen, and his followers provide additional telling examples of the "flexibility" of "racial" boundaries: first, when anti-Manchuism was on the main agenda, the principle of "nationalism" (*minzuzhuyi*) was clearly defined "racially" against inclusion of the Manchus. When the Manchu court abdicated and the Republic was established, the agenda shifted to arguments for the "inheritance" of all territory under the Manchu-Qing dynasty, including minority terrain. Then, the argument came to promote the "five races" of China (one of them the Manchus) as constituting the "nation." In other words, the "Han" were still seen as constituting a "race," but only as a part of the "Chinese" nation. Later, however, the trend changed to include minorities in a single "Chinese race" to bolster internal cohesion—ironically recalling reformer and one-time arch-rival Liang Qichao's call for a "broad" understanding of the race-nation.[41]

On the "outward" level, "racial" relations between China and Japan was a persistent issue. As long as Japan was in the position of a traditional "vassal" country, the question from the Chinese perspective was not pressing: the Japanese were usually called "dwarfs," which obviously had a "racist" implication.[42] But in terms of "culture," they were acceptable, since they had proven "receptive" to Chinese civilization. The First Sino-Japanese War turned China's relationship with Japan upside down. Significantly, only after the war, which was seen in the West as a war between the "yellows," did Japan replace China as a place-holder for the "the yellows" and the primary symbol of a "yellow peril" in Western minds,[43] a status in part attributable to Chinese emigration since the mid nineteenth century.[44] Around the time of the war, the term "yellow race" also became common in China.[45]

Those in China bent on reform argued that Japan provided the best model, precisely because it was culturally and "racially" "close": if the Japanese as "part of the yellow race" could "civilize" (i.e., Westernize), the Chinese could too. Thus Kang Youwei proposed the Japanese as an example in the 1890s. Similarly, Liang Qichao stated explicitly in 1896 that since the "whites" and "yellows" were close, whatever the "whites" could do, the "yellows" could as well, citing Japan as proof (without openly mentioning the recent Sino-Japanese War). He immediately went on to "conclude": "Since the Japanese race [*Riben zhi zhong*] originated in our country, it would be illogical to say that we cannot accomplish what they can!"[46] Thus he argued that China, like Japan, had the potential to rise in the future, if only that potential was developed properly. Soon large numbers of Chinese students would go to Japan to study, hoping their "Asian neighbor" would teach them a convenient "shortcut" to modernity.[47]

This wave of students, in turn, counterbalanced the "theoretical" model of Meiji Japan with personal experience. Like racial discriminatory language towards Japan common in China before the war ("apes," "dwarfs," etc.) and "racist" comments during the war (with the Japanese doing the same and both sides heavily influenced by Western stereotypes),[48] after the war the Japanese looked down on China and the Chinese students, for example calling them "chink" (*chanchan bôzu*).[49] The more intensive personal contact between the Chinese and Japanese after the war highlighted the problem of "sameness" or "difference," with daily life, to a certain degree, contrasting with "theoretical" discourse on "sameness" occasionally put forward by both sides, though with different motives. On the one hand, some Japanese argued for a "racial unity" between China and Japan paralleling a supposed "cultural–scriptural unity" (*dôbun dôshu*), whether it be an emotional attachment to Chinese traditional culture engendered by their own educational upbringing, a desire to further Japan's very rational interests on the continent, or a genuine belief in "(East) Asianness."[50] On the other hand, some Chinese argued for "sameness" with Japan in order to adopt reform methods that had obviously been successful, while others advocated it based on a genuine belief in Asianness. The latter, however, was much rarer in the Chinese case, as China had grudgingly emerged on the "receiving" end of their newly adjusted asymmetrical relationship.

This ambivalence of both countries vis-à-vis each other continued and was deeply influenced by the positions of the West: when the Boxers arose in China, the West, particularly the German Kaiser as spokesman for the "yellow peril" paradigm,[51] again associated China with the "yellow peril" at what was likely "the" historical moment the term gained real currency in Western politics. The Boxers, seen as a barbaric, oriental, and backward movement, threatened brute and blind force against the Allies as bearers of the torch of civilization. The Japanese in this case openly sided with the Allies, dispatched the biggest contingent of soldiers, and took pains to distinguish themselves from the Chinese. Still, Westerners hesitated to give the "yellow" Japanese full credit for their involvement in the Boxer War.[52]

When Japan won the Russo-Japanese War of 1904–5, Westerners again identified Japan as the "yellow peril"[53]—obviously since the Chinese threat had waned and Japan's adversary had been "Western." The Chinese widely applauded the Japanese victory, even though it had been achieved over Chinese soil (Manchuria), just as in the Sino-Japanese War ten years earlier. They self-servingly interpreted Japan's success as demonstrating the ability of "the yellows," which could again be used to argue for using the Japanese as a model to institute changes in China.[54] Japan, on the other hand, was not keen on "representing the yellows" with its victory, but chose to distance itself from the "weak" Chinese, who had played no role in the war apart from it being fought over Chinese territory.

The problem of "drawing the racial line" went on and, obviously, it shifted often due to historical power relations and the agenda of those who argued for or against including the other. When China could "use" Japan as a model or wanted to argue for its own potential, it included Japan. When China suffered under Japanese supremacy or aggression, "racial" difference was underlined. This became most evident during the course of the twentieth century. The Second Sino-Japanese War and Japanese war atrocities in China led to a strongly racialized view of the "Japs." The "cruelness" of Japanese character "by nature" has often been stressed in the commemoration of war atrocities, which has played a key role in the post-Mao era (since the 1980s) government's rhetoric legitimizing the People's Republic of China. They are not portrayed as individuals committing crimes, but rather as indiscriminate and unrestrained "devils," which contrasts with portrayals of the goodness of the "civilized," meek, and victimized Chinese.[55] The Chinese government promotes this basically "racist" view of the Japanese in textbooks, official television programs, and other media, and it is further sustained by popular nationalism, which often exceeds the level of anti-Japanese racism that the government can tolerate for diplomatic reasons[56]

Conclusion

From the above we may conclude that the Western concept of "race" introduced to China in the late nineteenth century confronted various problems that hampered and colored its glocalization. First of all, the term did not easily translate into Chinese characters, which always carried connotations that usually blended biology and culture into the Western term. Furthermore, due to contemporary translation practices, terms were mostly coined in Japanese before being transferred into Chinese, making race concepts doubly "alien" to China. For the term "race" itself, the question of Western racial taxonomies proved problematic, particularly with regard to the question of how to deal with the fact that "they" were calling "us" "yellow" in hierarchical assignment of "colors" with "white" at the top. As shown above, there were multiple ways of accepting, remolding, or rejecting this "color" definition as "yellow." All cases reinterpreted "yellow" as *not* (or not simply) connoting skin color, investing it with some kind of cultural or genealogical meaning, and generally avoiding the alternate term "mongoloid" for historical and cultural reasons. In the setting of the time, a purely "scientific" biological categorization was not primarily relevant and "science," in any case, was clearly not an "innocent" enterprise in the context of global imperialism. Thus, only the combination of "scientific" biology and Social Darwinism was received in China, a combination that raised the spectre of "races" in a mutual struggle for survival, thereby interlocking "race" with "cultural-civilizational abilities." It was therefore only logical that the categories of "race" and "nation" were soon conflated, as they were in the West around the turn of the twentieth century.

Furthermore, an uneasiness concerning the in- or out-group assigned by the West can be clearly detected in Chinese reactions to the "race" concept. If one accepted the "scientific" contention of mankind being divided into "races," it raised the question of who should count as "yellow." Within

China at the turn of the twentieth century, this problem revolved around two main issues: whether or not to include the Manchus (and other minorities) and whether or not to include the Japanese. Here, the central issue was locating a discursive line between "culture" and "race" with the ever-present issue of power relations involved. Thus, the Chinese, like the Japanese, struggled with an "unfavorable" foreign concept. But whereas Japan saw that concept endangering a rise in the international field already under way and thus largely avoided its use self-referentially,[57] the Chinese at times voluntarily embraced it, although twisting the concept according to their particular needs. The race concept could be used to explain *both* how the recent *past* had left them in a weak position and how either reform or revolution could allow them to design their own *future*. This discursive use of the "race" concept "from below" was addressed inward toward Chinese (if one includes the Manchus in this category) adversaries, *not* "outsiders." The "foreign concept" thus turned into a weapon primarily for political contests within China.

In any case, it is obvious that the question of where to draw the "racial" line was never definitively answered; various conclusions closely followed the agendas of the persons arguing. Chinese intellectuals—on whom the focus has been here—manipulated the "race concept" in various ways, often toying with its pseudo-scientific elements to win a game over opponents or at least to argue for one's own political aims. Thus, the "glocalizers" were active agents and not only "receiving ends" of a Western "hegemonic discourse" on "race." Consequently, the answer to the question of who was "yellow" or not, or who constituted "us," was constantly shifting, revealing the crucial importance of linguistic, cultural, and above all historical contingency to the specific motivation of individual actors in the "glocalizing" process.

Although more than a century has elapsed since the period focused upon here, the basic strategies of handling the "race" concept are still, or rather again, relevant. On the surface of today's discourse, however, the "outmoded" "race" paradigm has been superseded by the "culture" paradigm due to globally received concepts like Huntington's theses, which have to a certain extent substituted earlier "racial competition" with "civilizational clashes." Thus the modern Chinese "culture" paradigm is clearly different from the traditional Chinese Confucian one. After Mao and—*a fortiori*—after the Tiananmen massacre, "race" and "culture" have been consciously blended to bolster a newly defined "Chineseness" with integrative potential vis-à-vis Taiwan and all overseas Chinese in a hoped-for "rise of China" in the twenty-first century. Thus, China's current national-

ism presents itself under the label of "culture" but integrates racial elements,[58] and occasionally resurfaces as a latent confrontation with the
"racially-culturally" "different" West and the "similar" Japanese on the contemporary global scene.

Notes

This is an abridged version of my original paper "Are we Yellow? And Who is 'Us'?
China's Problems with Glocalizing the Concept of 'Race' (around 1900)" which appears
in full length in *Bochumer Jahrbuch zur Ostasienforschung*.

1. Roland Robertson, "Glokalisierung – Homogenität und Heterogenität in Raum
   und Zeit," in *Perspektiven der Weltgesellschaft*, edited by Ulrich Beck (Frankfurt,
   1998), 192–200.
2. See Frank Dikötter, *The Discourse of Race in Modern China* (London, 1992), chap.
   1. For more comments on the pre-modern situation, see the long version "Are we
   Yellow?" The term "racial" is understood here very broadly, in the sense of some
   perceived special biological traits common to groups of people.
3. For the different uses See also Kai-wing Chow, "Narrating Nation, Race, and National Culture: Imagining the Hanzu Identity in Modern China" in *Constructing
   Nationhood in Modern East Asia*, edited by Kai-wing Chow, Kevin M. Doak, and
   Poshek Fu (Ann Arbor, 2001), 47–83.
4. Dikötter, *The Discourse of Race*, 10.
5. As Walter Demel has demonstrated, it took some time to arrive at this. "Brown" etc.
   had been an option as well. See his "Wie die Chinesen gelb wurden," *Historische
   Zeitschrift* 255 (1992): 625–66.
6. Here I slightly disagree (see "Are we yellow?") with Frank Dikötter, "Racial Discourse in China: Continuities and Representations," in *The Construction of Racial
   Identities in China and Japan: Historical and Contemporary Perspectives*, edited by
   Frank Dikötter (London, 1997), 12–13.
7. *Gezhi huibian* [Chinese Scientific and Industrial Magazine] 7, no. 2: 227–30.
8. My reading of the article therefore differs from that of Yoshihiro Ishikawa, who sees
   it only as a faithful rendering of Blumenbach's outline but pays no attention to the
   subtle shifts in presentation. See his "Anti-Manchu Racism and the Rise of Anthropology in Early 20th Century China," *Sino-Japanese Studies* 15 (April 2003): 7–26.
9. The Western slave trade was well known in China (as was the earlier Arabian one),
   but the association of slavery and dark complexion incorporated some Chinese
   legacies as well. See Dikötter, *The Discourse of Race*, 14–17.
10. The term "mongoloid" (notably used by Blumenbach) necessarily evoked bad his-
    torical memories of Mongol domination (the first complete foreign domination of
    China, but different from the Manchus as the "second case" of complete domina-
    tion), degrading China to just a part of a world empire.

11. See, for example, the outline of the revolutionary 1904 treaties on "Chinese history" by Tao Chengzhang, *Tao Chengzhang ji* (Peking, 1986), 226.

12. The usual references were to the Indians, who lost their "nation to the British" in this competition, and the Native Americans, who were nearly extinguished as a "race." See, for example, "Yameilijia zhi xin induren [The New Indians of America]," *Xinmin congbao* 37, 5 September 1903, 71.

13. "Lun kai min zhi zhi [On educating the people]," *Shenbao*, 27 July 1895.

14. Kang Youwei, *Datongshu* (1935), part 4. For a translation, see Laurence G. Thompson, *Ta T'ung Shu: The One-World Philosophy of K'ang Yu-wei* (London, 1958), 140–48.

15. Strangely, existing scholarship seems to have overlooked this curious but telling switch, including the very recent discussion of Kang, even citing the passage, in Jing Tsu, *Failure, Nationalism, and Literature: The Making of Modern Chinese Identity, 1895–1937* (Stanford, 2005), 43–47.

16. Significantly, Liu here uses the Sanskrit rendering of "China" in Chinese translation (*zhendan*), implying an "outsider's view."

17. "Gudai yi huangse wei zhong [In old times only the colour yellow was revered]," *Guocui xuebao* [*Journal of National Essence*] 4 (1905): 499–500.

18. For the development of the image of the "Yellow Emperor" in this period see Sakamoto Hiroko, "Chûgoku minzokushugi no shinwa: shinkaron, jinshukan, hakurankai jiken [Myths of Chinese nationalism: evolution theory, racial views, and the exhibition incident]," *Shisô* [*Thought*] 849 (March 1995): 61–84; and especially the richly documented article by Shen Songjiao, "Wo yi wo xue jian Xuanyuan: Huangdi shenhua yu Wan-Qing de guozu jiangou [I offer myself and my blood to Xuanyuan: the myth of the Yellow Emperor and the construction of nationhood in the late Qing]," *Taiwan shehui yanjiu jikan* [Bulletin of Taiwan Social Studies] 28 (Dec. 1997): 1–77, plates on 23–24 and 39.

19. See a booklet assembling articles on Huangdi by the revolutionaries, *Huangdihun* [Soul of the Yellow Emperor] (1904; repr. Taipei, 1979).

20. See Shen, "Wo yi wo xue," 38, 40.

21. Liu Shipei, "Huangdi jinianshuo [On the calendar reckoning from Huangdi on]," in *Huangdihun*, 1–2. See also Martin Bernal, "Liu Shi-p'ei and National Essence," in *Limits of Change*, edited by Charlotte Furth (Cambridge, MA, 1976), 99. The reformers, instead, opted for a reckoning starting with Confucius.

22. See Werner Conze and Antje Sommer, "Rasse," *Geschichtliche Grundbegriffe*, vol. 5 (Stuttgart, 1984), 135–78, esp. 156 and 169.

23. "Guomin xinlixue yu jiaoyu zhi guanxi [Psychology of the national people and its relation to education]," *Xinmin congbao* 25, 2 Feb. 1903, 49–57, esp. 52–54.

24. "Lun zhongjie zhi jingzheng [On Competition in the Racial World]," *Qingyibao* [*The China discussion*] 48 (1900; reprint Taipei, 1967), 3097.

25. See Nora Diamond, "Defining the Miao: Ming, Qing, and Contemporary Views," in *Cultural Encounters China's Ethnic Frontiers*, edited by Steven Harrell (Seattle, 1995), 99–100.

26. See Mary B. Rankin, *Early Chinese Revolutionaries* (Cambridge, MA, 1971), 26–30.
27. See Liang Qichao, "Za da mou bao [Answers on various topics to a certain journal]," *Xinmin congbao* 84, 4 August 1906, 1–21. Liang aimed his attack at the *Minbao* whereas Wang Jingwei voiced the opposing view.
28. Liang, introduction to, and "S. C. Y.: Zhongguo yuanshi minzu zhi xianzhuang [The present situation of China's aborigines]," *Xinmin congbao* 60, 6 January 1905, 91–100.
29. See his "Zhengzhixue jia Bolunzhili zhi xueshuo [The theories of political scientist Bluntschli]," *Xinmin congbao* 38/39, 4 October 1903, 32, where he introduced these terms.
30. "Bo Kang Youwei shu [A refutation of Kang Youwei]" in *Wan-Qing geming wenxue* [Late–Qing revolutionary literature], edited by Zhang Yufa (1903; repr. Taipei 1981), 51–52.
31. See Zou Rong, *Gemingjun* [Revolutionary Army], in *Wan-Qing*, 125, 137.
32. See Liu's tract written in late 1903, *Zhongguo minzuzhi* [History of the Chinese nation-race], in *Liu Shipei quanji* [Collected Works of Liu Shipei], vol. 1 (Peking, 1997), 597–626, esp. chap. 2. The Mongols, another issue, but a historically more sensitive one, were occasionally integrated as well.
33. See ibid., 622.
34. See ibid., chap. 17.
35. This, in fact, had been promoted outright and in a positive sense by revolutionary Song Jiaoren in 1905. See Chow, "Narrating Nation," 62.
36. "Pai-Man pingyi [Balanced view on rejecting the Manchus]," *Minbao* 21 (June 1908), 2–3.
37. Liu only names "Kuwabara." His source was China historian Kuwabara Jitsuzô's (1870–1931) *Tôyô shiyô* [Historical outline of East Asia]. See Liu, *Zhongguo minzuzhi*, 599.
38. On the stakes for the Japanese in distancing themselves from the Chinese and the implications of devising schemes of differentiation in Asian populations, see Stefan Tanaka, *Japan's Orient: Rendering Pasts into History* (Berkeley, 1993); and Leo Ching, "Yellow Skin, White Masks: Race, Class, and Identification in Japanese Colonial Discourse," in *Trajectories: Inter-Asia Cultural Studies*, ed Kuan-Hsing Chen (London, 1998), 65–86.
39. See *Gemingjun*, in *Wan-Qing*, edited by Zhang Yufa, 129–30.
40. It should be noted that these utterances were made in polemical literature where logical consistency was not of primary concern, whereas the same authors often argued less "racially" in their other writings. The "intended audience" factor has often been disregarded hitherto in evaluating such "racist" comments.
41. See James Leibold, "Competing Narratives of Racial Unity in Republican China," *Modern China* 32, no. 2 (April 2006): 181–220.
42. The term has also been explained as a purely phonetic rendering for "Yamato" in the beginning, but clearly came to be understood as derogatory over time.

43. For the history of this term, see Heinz Gollwitzer, *Die Gelbe Gefahr: Geschichte eines Schlagworts* (Göttingen, 1962). For the shift toward Japan see Urs Matthias Zachmann, "China's Role in the Process of Japan's Cultural Self-Identification, 1895–1904" (Ph.D. diss., Heidelberg, 2007), 80–81, 108. Kaiser Wilhelm's Knack-fuss-painting of 1895 is well known enough. Significantly, Gobineau, writing in the mid 1850s, had not yet assigned the "yellow" category to the Japanese.

44. Due to Chinese emigration to the United States, anti-Chinese sentiment, notably man-ifesting in the Chinese Exclusion Act of 1882, gave rise to a series of fictional portrayals of the "yellow peril" (although not yet using that term). See William F. Wu, *The Yel-low Peril: Chinese Americans in American Fiction, 1850–1940* (Hamden, CT, 1982).

45. Earlier references are extremely scarce, but with the war the term *huangzhong* (yel-low race) gained currency in Chinese publications.

46. See Liang Qichao quanji, "Lun Zhongguo zhi jiang qiang" [On China Becoming Strong], in Liang Qichao quanji [Collected Works of Liang Qichao] vol. 1 (Beijing 1998), 99–101. Translated sentence from Tsu, *Failure*, 51.

47. See Paula Harrell, *Sowing the Seeds of Change: Chinese Students, Japanese Teachers, 1895–1905* (Stanford, 1992).

48. On the Western and Japanese perceptions of this war, see S.C.M. Paine, *The Sino-Japanese War of 1894–1895: Perceptions, Power, and Primacy* (Cambridge, 2003). For Chinese depictions of war scenes and comments in China, see, for example, the popular *Dianshizhai huabao* [Diahshizhai pictorial] of that period, using the derogatory terms *wo* (dwarfs) and *kou* (pirates) for the Japanese. Official docu-ments also used the term "dwarfs" and "head of dwarfs" for the Tennô and avoided the "normal" term "Japanese" (*Riben*). For a general overview, see Samuel C. Chu, "China's Attitudes toward Japan at the Time of the Sino-Japanese War," in *The Chi-nese and the Japanese: Essays in Political and Cultural Interaction,* edited by Akira Iriye (Princeton, NJ, 1980), 74–95.

49. See Donald Keene, "The Sino-Japanese War of 1894–95 and Its Cultural Effects in Japan," in *Tradition and Modernization in Japanese Culture,* edited by Donald Shiv-eley (Princeton, NJ, 1971), 121–75. Earlier images tended to be more positive.

50. See Kazuki Sato, "'Same Language, Same Race': The Dilemma of *Kanbun* in Mod-ern Japan," in *Construction of Racial Identities in China and Japan,* 118–35.

51. On the use of the "yellow peril" concept in Western politics, see Ute Mehnert, *Deutschland, Amerika und die "Gelbe Gefahr": Zur Karriere eines Schlagworts in der Großen Politik, 1905–1917* (Stuttgart, 1995).

52. See Zachmann, "China's Role," chap. 5.

53. For an illustration of this shift, see Sepp Linhart, *"Dainty Japanese" or Yellow Peril? Western War Postcards 1900–1945* (Vienna, 2005).

54. For Chinese reactions to the Russo-Japanese War, see my "Chinesische Perspek-tiven auf den Russisch-Japanischen Krieg," in *Der Russisch-Japanische Krieg 1904/05 – Anbruch einer neuen Zeit?,* edited by Maik Hendrik Sprotte, Wolfgang Seifert, and Heinz-Dietrich Löwe (Wiesbaden, 2007), 203–40.

55. See Peter Hays Gries, *China's New Nationalism: Pride, Politics, and Diplomacy* (Berkeley, 2004), 93.
56. Cases in point are anti-Japanese demonstrations, often connected to the Japanese invasion of China and the Nanjing Massacre of 1937, which tended to spin out of government control or were organized privately from the outset, and films like *Guizi laile* [The Devils have come] in the 1990s that were officially banished for being overly anti-Japanese.
57. See Zachmann's essay on the "race" concept as an "anathema" in this volume.
58. See Frank Dikötter, "Race in China," in *A Companion to Racial and Ethnic Studies*, edited by Theo Goldberg and John Solomos (Oxford, 2002), 495–510, esp. 507.

Chapter 12

Race without Supremacy: On Racism in the Political Discourse of Late Meiji Japan, 1890–1912

Urs Matthias Zachmann

Introduction

Although racism as an ideology is hard to define, most would agree that, at its core, racism—intentionally or not—includes some groups in the allocation of resources and services while excluding others, and does so by referring to a hierarchy defined by somatic differences.[1] Moreover, in the nineteenth century, this hierarchy was "scientifically" grounded on the concept of "races" as the immutable and inherent biological differences in mankind. Although the theory of evolution questioned the idea of fixed and immutable species in principle, Social Darwinism retained the idea of "race" by ranking it on an evolutionary scale.[2] "Racism" as a term was not used at the time,[3] the phenomenon hidden *avant la lettre* in the meaning of "race" itself. Moreover, in Germany at the turn of the nineteenth century, *Rassenphilosophie* was in vogue, and also known as such in Japan, albeit not accepted, as we shall see presently.

The discussion of racism in historical perspective often focuses on the European endeavor both to legitimate colonialism and to respond to their experiences with the populations they subjugated.[4] However, Japan constitutes a singularity in history in that it managed to establish "the only non-Western imperium in modern times"[5] during the late Meiji period (1868–1912). Much of this empire-building was done by emulating the Western powers, especially the leading power Britain. Thus, the assumption that Japan would not only emulate the outer vestiges but also the *spirit* of expansion, including racism, comes naturally and has been, in fact, quite dominant in the postwar historiography of Japan. Michael Weiner observed, for example: "Given the fact that Japan was consciously modeling its behaviour in other spheres of activity on its European and North American contemporaries, it is hardly surprising that Japanese 'racial' thought drew much of its inspiration from the most advanced Western nations and developed in response to it."[6] Consequently, Weiner sees the results of this response in an ideology:

> predicated on a conflict between the white and yellow 'races', while on the other it assumed distinct and immutable differences in intellectual and cultural capacities between the Yamato *minzoku* [race] and those of China and Korea. This allowed Japanese ideologues to conceive of the world's population as comprising three 'races', along the lines set out by Arthur de Gobineau and other European 'racial' theorists.[7]

The problem with this understanding lies in assuming too close and literal a translation of European racialist thought into the Japanese context and thus underestimating the different social, political, and economic environment into which this thought migrated. For one, it is difficult to say whether the official Japanese policy wanted to exclude Chinese and Koreans in the "homeland" and in the colonies, as racism does not legitimate all discriminatory practice, which makes the concept itself so hard to define.[8] Moreover, the Japanese themselves had to grapple with European racism that sought to exclude Japan from the concert of powers. Thus, the assumption that the Japanese accepted and internalized European racism without protest seems less intuitive.

Thus, after a short introductory section on the reception of "scientific" racism in Japan, this essay studies late–Meiji Japanese attitudes toward racism in three fields of publicly regulated human interaction where racialized views traditionally play a significant role: international relations, immigration policies, and colonial policies. Consequently, this chapter focuses on Japanese interactions with Europeans, Chinese, and Koreans, although a more complete discussion of attitudes toward racism would certainly include a section on the position of the Ainu in Japanese society.[9]

The Reception of "Scientific Racism" in Meiji Japan

The scientific notion of "race" entered Japan in the late 1870s through Darwin's theory of evolution. The American zoologist Edward Sylvester Morse (1838–1925), one of the many foreign employees in the service of the Japanese government at the time, first introduced the Japanese public to the rules of the "Preservation of Favoured Races in the Struggle for Life" (thus the alternative title of Darwin's *On the Origin of Species by Means of Natural Selection* 1859) in 1877.[10] Darwin's theories have since fascinated the Japanese intelligentsia considerably, and as Eikoh Shimao has observed, no "Western scientist's works have been translated into so many Japanese versions as Darwin's."[11] However, the attraction was less due to the "scientific" impact of evolutionism. Not until 1910, with the advent of Mendelism, did the biological sciences respond more positively to evolutionary theory,[12] although eugenics, as an offspring of evolutionary theory, for certain reasons later to be explained, did garner followers in academic circles even earlier.[13]

As in Europe and the United States, the Japanese general public was more interested in the "survival of the fittest" (Herbert Spencer) among mankind, i.e., with the social and political application of Darwin's theories, than "natural selection" in animal life. Thus, Spencer has been called "the most widely read and possibly the most influential Western social and political thinker in Japan during the 1880s."[14] During the struggle of oppositional groups against the oligarchic Japanese government for more political participation at the time, both sides invoked Spencer's ambiguous authority, either by stressing the individualistic, dynamic aspect of his theory and arguing for open political competition, or by stressing his organismic conception of society and thus legitimizing the status quo of social and political inequalities.[15] A similarly Janus-faced interpretation applied to international politics, as will be shown presently.

However, whereas European societies saw "survival of the fittest" in the framework of a racial hierarchy among the peoples of the earth, this view was not readily accepted in Japan, as evidenced by reactions to the thesis of Joseph Arthur Gobineau and his *Essai sur l'inégalité des races humaines* (1853–55). Gobineau was much less popular and introduced to Japan much later than Darwin and Spencer. His relative unpopularity may just mirror a similar situation in Europe,[16] or be the product of contingency. However, the fact that Gobineau so clearly stressed the superiority of the "Aryan" race in his *Essai*, placing the Japanese only as second-ranking, certainly did not endear him to the Japanese readership.

Thus, when the famous writer and Surgeon-General of the Japanese Imperial Army, Mori Ōgai (1862–1922), gave a lecture on Gobineau to an academic audience in June 1903, he supposed his listeners knew nothing about Gobineau and minutely described his life and arguments.[17] Only then did he add a brief comment of his own: Gobineau's theses were clearly self-serving, unfair, and prejudiced. If Gobineau had been of a different skin color, he would have argued differently. One should not give credence to such "âriocentrique" theories, nor to any other -centric thinking for that matter.[18] And although this kind of race philosophy seemed then in vogue in Germany, Mori Ōgai could not see any worth in it. Moreover, he interpreted this vogue as a sort of *Götterdämmerung* of European self-confidence. Thus, he concluded his lecture with the question: "When a race starts to be delighted in hearing that it is the only one with the power to civilize others, isn't that when it has already lost belief in its own uniqueness?"[19]

Racism in Japan's International Relations

Japan's international relations with the European powers for most of the latter half of the nineteenth century revolved around the renegotiation of its diplomatic and commercial treaties with the powers. These were concluded in the last years of the Tokugawa reign (a few of them in the Meiji era as well) and stipulated, among other things, consular jurisdiction for foreigners (i.e., the privilege of extraterritoriality), which was tallied, however, by a restriction of foreigners' residence and movement to Japan's treaty ports (the largest being Yokohama).[20] Commonly called the "unequal treaties" in Japan, it should be noted that Japan was certainly not the only non-European country to suffer under such agreements. When compared to the treaties with China, for example, which in effect granted free movement to foreigners, Japan received rather more favorable treatment by the European powers than other nations. Of course, in Japan's case, too, it is doubtful whether the rules confining foreigners to the ports were ever strictly enforced.[21] Thus, in the hot phase of treaty-related protests from 1889–1894, the protesters demanded strict observation of the rules to make the Europeans feel the actual inconvenience of the treaties and compel them to renegotiate. However, for a long time, the European powers remained adamant, and it took more than twenty years, starting in 1871, until the Japanese government finally concluded its first revised treaty with Britain in 1894.

Popular protest, of course, attributed the reluctance of the European powers to discrimination on the basis of race or religion (in fact, more the latter).[22] This may have well been a consideration on the part of the powers, although, on the surface, the negotiations always revolved around the question of whether or not Japan already met the "standard of civilization." As Eric Gong has demonstrated, this standard emerged in Europe (although of universal pretence) during the latter half of the nineteenth century—in fact, was made explicit largely due to the contact with Japan— and contained minimum requirements such as the effective protection of basic rights by the domestic legal system and adherence to international law (which, of course, was another European standard).[23]

Whatever one may think of the European powers' pretence to dictate standards, the Japanese government and, in fact, a majority of the Japanese people rapidly internalized this standard in its pursuit of equality with the powers, one of the primary goals of Meiji foreign policy. In 1894, Britain concluded a new treaty and thus issued, as one American observer put it, "a certificate of civilization" to the Japanese nation.[24] That same year, Japan also fought a spectacularly successful war against China to realize its second goal: to break the hegemony of China in East Asian waters and establish its own predominance.

Japan's success was against all foreign expectations, and although at first it may not have achieved its primary goal, it certainly led to a re-evaluation of its military capacity in the eyes of the Western powers.[25] However, the spectacular military success of a non–European nation also spread fear among some European observers, which in turn was soon noticed in Japan, as the following newspaper article shows, quoting the opinions of an unidentified Hungarian general:

The Rise of the Yellow Race really frightens a part of the people in Europe. General *Chuiiru* also observes: 'Japan in twenty-five years has made the same progress as other countries in centuries. If, on top of that, China too awakes from its slumber, then Europe certainly cannot sleep safely anymore. Do the European countries really have the time to sap each other's strength by internal fighting?'[26]

Graphically, the "yellow peril" found its most notorious expression in the so-called "Knackfuss painting," drawn by the academic painter Herman Knackfuß (1848–1915) after the design of Kaiser Wilhelm II sometime in the summer of 1895.[27] Under the heading "Ye nations of Europe, protect your most holy goods," the allegorical painting shows the European powers gather under the holy cross and the angelic leadership of Germany to fight against a golden Buddha riding a yellow dragon and leaving a trail of destruction. This painting, of which the German Kaiser distributed many copies to Western leaders, was also known in Japan from early on. Already in January 1903, a Japanese newspaper showed a redrawing of the painting with a short explanation of its meaning.[28]

Of course, the threat of Japan alone would not have caused such nightmares. Thus, the painting hints at a union between Japan and China. The combination of Chinese multitudes harnessed by Western military skill in Japanese hands constituted the ultimate embodiment of the "yellow peril." Other fictitious accounts played on this horror, such as the novel "The Yellow Danger" by pulp-fiction writer M.P. Shiel.[29] Shiel, who also wrote speeches for the British foreign minister and other influential politicians, using the a very realistic setting to develop the fantastical story of a Chinese-Japanese villain who, after uniting China and Japan under his leadership, almost succeeds in extirpating the "white race" before one young British hero turns the tables and brings the story to a happy ending. Of course, this fiction was supposed to be laughed at and about (which the *Times* in London did).[30] However, it can be imagined that Japanese observers were less enthusiastic about such fantasies.

As the diplomatic historian William Langer observed, "the cult of this [Gobineau's] extravagant racialism and nationalism came only in the last lustrum of the nineteenth century. In England as in Germany it was carried to absurd heights."[31] And for Japan, being one of the main targets of this racialism, this especially posed a problem. At the very moment that the Japanese government had finally succeeded in overcoming the barrier of "civilization" and reached the brink of being accepted into the concert of powers, new barriers arose and racism raised its head to drive Japan out again.[32] Although Japanese intellectuals considered these barriers "artificial," the problem was that they were, in fact, supposed to be "natural" and scientific, and therefore (the distant promises of eugenics aside) objective and insurmountable. As a reaction to these limitations, the Japanese public could only deny the validity of racism, insist on the universality of civilization with greater determination, and even denounce racism as the new "barbarism" of the self-styled civilized European countries.[33]

The Japanese government pursued the same course in its diplomacy, but in a less confrontational way. Thus, in order to facilitate Japan's acceptance into the concert of powers, it sought to dispel any fears that Japan would form an alliance with China against the West, and to broadcast the fact that it adhered steadfastly to the standard of civilization at every possible opportunity. Two conspicuous examples illustrate the former strategy. Firstly, when Germany occupied Qingdao (later turning it into a lease) in late 1897, the President of the Japanese House of Peers, Konoe Atsumaro (1863–1904) published an article calling for a "racial alliance" of the Asian nations against the West (with Japan and China at its core) in the popular magazine *Taiyō* in January 1898.[34] Based on the assumption of a "racial competition," Konoe predicted a "showdown" between the white and yellow races in which Japan would not stand aside. However, the article is less remarkable for its thesis than for the storm of protest that it elicited in Japan, and the suspicions and insinuations produced abroad.[35] Domestically, Konoe's proposal was seen as a "stupid idea" (*guron*): Why should a developed country like Japan ally itself with a country as backward as China, which would surely pull Japan back into a quagmire of stagnancy and corruption, and this simply for the sake of some romantic feelings of "same race, same culture" (*dōbun dōshu*)? The only criterion for alliance, his critics argued, was progress, which corresponded with the majority opinion that Britain was Japan's most desirable alliance partner, if anything at all. However, Konoe's article did more damage to Japan in Europe, where even local newspapers reported its contents.[36] The Japanese government eventually saw no other means to contain the damage than to have its minister to France issue a statement asserting that Konoe's opinions by no means represented the official position of Japan, but were rather the private opinion of a radical hothead who had only reached his government position of President of the House of Peers because of his high birth and family ties. Given the fact that the Japanese emperor intended Konoe to become prime minister in the future, this can only be seen as a desperate measure. However, Konoe soon recanted and subsequently became an ardent advocate of an alliance with Britain.[37]

Secondly, the further advance of the western powers into China following Germany's initiative led to a gradual rapprochement between Japan and China that eventually resulted in a flurry of cooperation on the semi-state and non-governmental level.[38] However, the Japanese government was intent on keeping these interactions informal and not rousing any suspicions among the Western powers of a formal alliance between China and Japan. Thus, when the leading statesman Yamagata Aritomo (1838–1922) heard in May 1899 of the imminent arrival of a special envoy from Beijing, he surmised that the Chinese government was going to ask Japan for its protection and an alliance against the encroachment of the powers.[39] He cautioned his colleagues that, in this case, the envoy should be turned away with the utmost politeness—so as not to hurt the Chinese government—but also with firmness for the following reasons:

> If our country and China were to enter a relationship which exceeded the degree of closeness and aroused the suspicion among the western powers of a Sino-Japanese alliance against Europe, this would not only eventually result in a battle of races [*jinshu no arasoi*], but it is difficult to tell if this would not also have consequences which would prove detrimental to our interests in the present Hague Peace Conference [1899]. Moreover, even if our financial, political, and military power were to allow it, I believe that to cooperate with China for the independence of East Asia is a poor strategy [*sessaku*]. China, as I have said before, like the Jewish race will continue as a race, but it will not long maintain its state as a whole. This is already the fixed opinion of the experts. Even if it can maintain it, it will not be able to maintain it with the present territory. It will save only a small fraction, and the rest will be divided among the powers. In East Asia, the only country which will be able to maintain its independence is only our empire.[40]

Yamagata's words reveal a certain ambiguity toward the concept of race when it came to nations considered inferior to Japan. This will be discussed in more detail presently. However, toward European countries, the Japanese government clearly tried to avoid any notion of racial antagonism and, in the following years, most notably during the Boxer expedition of 1900, tried to broadcast its firm allegiance to the European concert with mixed success.[41]

Western observers were, of course, conscious of this strategy and its aims. They fully understood that racism was limiting Japan's upward trajectory as an imperial power (this was racism's function in international politics in the first place). However, they also understood that Japan needed to overcome racial prejudice and earn the acceptance of the Western powers and its citizens if it wanted to expand. This applied to expansion by formal means (as the intervention of Russia, France, and Germany against Japanese expansion in China in 1895 had shown) as well as to "peaceful expansion," i.e., through emigration of Japanese laborers.[42] Thus, on the occasion of Japan's participation in the Boxer expedition, a British newspaper observed with considerable condescension:

> It may be said, indeed, without exaggeration, that on the conduct of her officers and men in the present war depends the whole future of Japan. If the British Tommy takes to the Japanese Tommy as he takes to the Ghurka, all will be well; but there is just the possibility that he may conceive as rooted a dislike for him as the white labourer in British Columbia and Seattle does for the Japanese coolie, who is, after all, about the same status as the Japanese soldier. In that case Japan's energies would be for ever circumscribed within her five hundred isles.[43]

Thus, in all cases in international affairs where Japan wanted to rise or expand and expected racially legitimated resistance by the Western powers, it sought to overcome this resistance by insisting on the prevalence of the standard of civilization.

Racism in Domestic Politics

Japan remained, in a sense, a "closed country" (*sakoku*) until 1899, when the revised treaties with Western powers finally came into effect and, in return for abolishing extraterritoriality, the restrictions were lifted on free movement and residence for foreigners in Japan. However, for the Chinese, significant restrictions remained in place, and the discussion of their status in contrast to Western and Korean foreigners in Japan sheds a revealing light on the basis for criteria the Japanese used to differentiate and deal with the Other inside their borders.

Considering that a statistically negligible number of foreigners resided among Japan's approximately forty million citizens (for example, in 1894, the Chinese as the largest foreign community numbered a little over five thousand),[44] the intensity of the debate on "mixed residence" (*naichi zakkyo*) in the 1880s and 1890s seems out of proportion and irrational. However, for most of the Japanese, mixed residence was a matter of principle, its introduction anticipated with many fears and hopes.

Mixed Residence with Western Foreigners

To begin with the discussion of "mixed residence" with Western foreigners: throughout the late 1880s and into the 1890s, a certain antipathy existed against the integration process, as it required large-scale legal reforms on the Japanese side, and the more nationalistically minded people saw it as undue interference with domestic politics by European powers.[45] Most controversial was the revision of the family law and the law of succession section in the Civil Code, so much so that conservative lawyers like Hozumi Yatsuka (1860–1912) exclaimed that "if the Civil Code comes through, loyalty and filial piety will perish."[46]

The very prospect of living next door to Western foreigners filled many observers with a sense of foreboding. A newspaper cartoon from 1877 illustrated their various fears, which depicted, under the title "When foreigners live among us,"[47] the evils of a poor country being held up on its long way to progress by rich Western foreigners buying up the land, exploiting Japanese workers, taking all their money, and luring women with riches, etc. Thus, the cartoon graphically played on the character *gai* (foreign) which as written could also be read as *dame* (no good).

Thus, there was a strong xenophobic current among the Japanese people against Western mixed residence that was, however, based on specific concerns about economic inequality rather than racial fears. This does not mean that such fears did not exist, rather that they were found more among the intellectual elite and in a minority of the population. Moreover, those who most prominently voiced racialized fears, such as the philosopher Inoue Tetsujirō (1855–1944) and the above-mentioned lawyer Hozumi Yatsuka, both pre-eminent in their respective academic fields, were conspicuously those with the most exposure to Europe through extended periods of study there. Thus, in their new environment, they seemed to have internalized the notion in their host country (mostly Germany) that their "race" was inferior to the Europeans, and they came to oppose mixed residence with Westerners in Japan. After all, this is what some foreign advisers did as well. None other than Herbert Spencer himself, who on several occasions advised the Japanese government on modernization and reform, wrote to the statesman Kaneko Kentarō (1853–1942) in 1892 that "the Japanese should, I think, be that of *keeping Americans and Europeans as much as possible at arm's length*. In presence of the more powerful races your position is one of chronic danger, and you should take every precaution to give as little foothold as possible to foreigners."[48]

Inoue Tetsujirō, for example, while still studying in Berlin in 1889, published a treatise "On Mixed Residence in the Interior" in which he made a similar argument. This treatise reacted to a previous essay written by the renowned liberal economic journalist Taguchi Ukichi (1855–1905), who argued in favor of "mixed residence," pointing out that Japan in former times, too, had profited from the importation of superior civilization from the Chinese and Koreans, who had since become fully assimilated.

Moreover he claimed that Japan would only benefit from the free inflow of foreign capital and workers. He denounced all limitations on free intercourse as neo-feudalistic. Thus, the argument between Taguchi and Inoue went back and forth, but the basic positions never wavered.[49] However, it should be noted that Taguchi rested his arguments on an assumption which he made much more explicit in later years and was hardly less racialized than Inoue's, namely that the Japanese race was not inferior to the Europeans because the Japanese, in fact, descended from the Aryan race. In this, Ukichi echoed the minority theory among Western scholars about the origins of the Japanese.[50] However, in Japan, Taguchi remained the theory's only prolific advocate. Mori Ōgai in the above lecture touched upon Taguchi's theory, but certainly did not commit himself to it.[51]

Another minority opinion embraced "mixed residence" with Westerners exactly because of the "racial gap," as it would give the Japanese a better opportunity to ameliorate their race through intermarriage. Such was the opinion of Takahashi Yoshio, who published a treatise entitled "On the Amelioration of the Japanese Race" in 1884.[52] This early example of eugenics in Japan, of course, attracted the harsh criticism of the above conservative thinkers such as Inoue Tetsujirō and Katō Hiroyuki (1836–1916), then the president of the Imperial University.

In the same vein as their arguments, Herbert Spencer, too, strictly opposed miscegenation: "Respecting the intermarriage of foreigners and Japanese … it should be strictly forbidden[.] … There is abundant proof, alike furnished by the intermarriages of human races and by the interbreeding, that when the varieties mingled diverge beyond a certain slight degree *the result is inevitably a bad one* in the long run."[53]

From Spencer's point of view, miscegenation was detrimental (to the "superior" race, that is) and thus to be opposed. From the Japanese point of view, however, embracing eugenics offered another strategy for the "underdog" to subvert strict biological determinism, which made it popular among some medical scholars in Japan.[54] One of the most prolific eugenicists, Ōsawa Gakutarō (1863–1920), also married a German while studying at the University of Freiburg, although one might hope that eugenic theory was not his primary motive.[55]

Eventually, the Japanese government heeded neither Spencer's advice nor that of mixed residence opponents in general, and succeeded in introducing "mixed residence" in 1899. In the meantime, Japan's success in the Sino-Japanese War (1894–95) seemed to have led to a new confidence among the Japanese.[56] The renowned journalist Tokutomi Sohō (1863–1957), for example, described the effects of the war as follows: "Before we did not know ourselves and the world did not yet know us. But now that we have tested our strength, we know ourselves and we are known by the world."[57] This newly gained confidence (whatever its claims of being justified) also eased the fear of contact with foreigners. Whereas the mood before the war had been rather against mixed residence, this changed and more favorable arguments were heard again. Moreover, especially in the period of postwar economic stagnation, the "introduction of foreign investment" (*gaishi yu'nyū*) became particularly attracted to the notoriously undercapitalized Japanese industry, which began to lobby heavily for the speedy introduction of mixed residence, helping to make it possible.[58] Thus, when mixed residence was finally introduced, it could be said that both pride and necessity had won over prejudice, and that race was hardly the issue.

Mixed Residence with Chinese

The Chinese, as previously mentioned, constituted the single largest group of foreigners in Japan, the majority of which resided in the two largest treaty ports, Yokohama and Kōbe.[59] Although their numbers were diminutive compared to the overall Japanese population, political relations with China and the image projected on the Chinese made the issue of mixed residence with Chinese the most controversial in the debate, which even continued after the settlement of all other mixed residence issues.

Japan had concluded the Treaty of Amity and Commerce with China in 1871, and it was in fact the first fully equal treaty with a foreign country, as it granted every privilege in reciprocity, notably the privilege of extraterritoriality. However, in the following decades, Japan actively challenged China's political position in East Asia, and this competition also further polarized the image of the Chinese in Japan. Thus, as early as the Tokugawa period, China constituted the essential Other upon which the Japanese projected the image of their own country, often by simple inversion.[60] This did not change in the Meiji Period, and as late as 1899, Tokutomi Sohō wrote: "I think that there are quite a lot of things which our Japanese people should learn from our neighbor's people. After all, what they lack, we have, and what we are weak in, is their strength. However, their points of strength are not just one or two."[61]

As to the ratio of what China lacked and Japan had (and vice versa), opinions of course differed. The picture of a weak and stagnant China, which had existed prior to the advent of the Western powers in East Asia, was reinforced by China's defeats at the hands of the British and French and by the "orientalized" picture of China in the West.[62] In daily practice, this image resulted in discrimination against Chinese people in Japan, especially for their "bad habits" which, of course, had all the characteristics universally attributed to socially discriminated groups (e.g., lack of hygiene, stinginess, lack of education and morals), but also some unique features such as addiction to opium and a total dedication to earning money, which suggested ruthless materialism.[63] The latter resulted, in part, from jealously of the many well-off Chinese merchants residing in Japan prior to the Sino-Japanese War who monopolized trade with China.[64]

However, the image of the Chinese also had a positive side, although the effect of this is open to debate as well, as it struck even more fear in the hearts of Japanese. Thus, Tokutomi Soho continued the above quote by enumerating the strengths of the Chinese people as follows: absolute reliability in commercial transactions, resilience and perseverance in the face of adverse circumstances and hostile environments, strong bonding power that allows them to draw on existing networks wherever they go, and finally the ability to make coolheaded and well-calculated decisions even in critical situations.[65]

This, of course, depicted the perfect merchant roving the globe. Combined with the negative side, it very much resembled the image of Jews in Europe, certainly a conscious rather than coincidental likening. Thus, in concluding a passage in a chapter on what the Japanese should learn from the Chinese, Tokutomi Soho made the following observation which, to a great degree, turned the positive aspects of this image of the Chinese into a threat:

> If China is being partitioned and will be effaced as the Chinese empire from the political map, the influence of the Chinese race in the world from that time on will increase even further. Once the Chinese, like the Jews, will have lost their state, there is absolutely no doubt that, like them, they will become parasites in every country of the world and will exercise their pressure and beneficence on the country where they temporarily reside in, at times as workers, at times as financiers, and at times as traders.
>
> In any case, numerically speaking, they are fifty times more than the Jews. How much more horrendous then must be their racial characteristics, which makes the world tremble?[66]

Thus, Japanese contemporaries not only made use of the "orientalized"

Western image of China, but also of European anti-Semitism to describe their tense relationship with the Chinese.[67] Since the Chinese (either through Christian missionaries or Japanese literature) knew this negative image of Jews well, the comparison must have been considerably galling.[68]

In his "Guide to the Implementation of the New Treaties" (1898/99), Hara Takashi observed that the population opposed Chinese mixed residence firstly because it feared that masses of Chinese laborers would flood the Japanese market and, being cheap, drive out the Japanese from their jobs.[69] Secondly, they feared that the Chinese, with their shrewd business sense, would eventually monopolize Japan's economy, and thirdly, that the bad customs and habits of the Chinese would debase Japanese society.[70] Thus, Hara observed that a majority still favored expelling the Chinese altogether rather than integrating them even with limitations (a view which Hara did not share).

Hara wrote at a time when the fate of the Chinese in Japan was still open to debate. Thus, whereas Japan concluded new treaties in 1894, the Sino-Japanese War in the same year voided the Sino-Japanese Treaty of Friendship and Commerce, and consequently extraterritoriality of the Chinese was rescinded, although limitations on residence and movement remained in place according to the new Japanese law.[71] As a result, the question of whether or not Japan should grant mixed residence to every nation but the Chinese remained in 1899. Hara argued for granting mixed residence to the Chinese as well, and significant within the context of Japan's immigration and colonial policies, the main thrust of his argument was based on "cultural assimilation". Thus he wrote:

> As a general rule in man's world, the minority does not take the majority for its enemy. ... Therefore, if—like in some places abroad or in our treaty ports—one segregates the Chinese completely from the citizens and keeps them locked in, that is exactly the reason why their customs and habits will be transmitted to their descendants as they are. However, if not, and they are granted free residence and made to live in the interior, then those Chinese will be influenced by our customs, but our people will not be influenced by theirs. Even if we look at the present state of Taiwan, although the Chinese clearly are in the majority, even now it is not hard to discern a tendency that they are gradually being influenced by our customs.[72]

Thus Hara argued for "assimilating" the Chinese and thereby elevating them to a higher level of civilization. The government, although apparently divided on the question (the Department of the Interior opposed, the Foreign Ministry favored Chinese mixed residence),[73] eventually leaned towards Hara's opinion and lifted the limitations on free movement and residence for Chinese, albeit with considerable exceptions for "foreign workers" (meaning Chinese), who had to get an official permit to stay and work in Japan's interior.

Mixed Residence with Koreans

The strict treatment and the rather negative image of the Chinese in Japan contrasts starkly with the case of the Koreans. In fact, since there existed no treaty that specifically regulated the presence of Koreans in the Japanese interior (the Kanghwa Treaty of 1876 only regulating the Japanese presence in Korea), Koreans could move freely in the country.[74] Hara in his "Guide" argued that the liberal treatment stemmed from Japan's wish to "support Korea" and lead it onto the path of civilization.[75] Moreover, one is struck by the extremely positive image which Hara reports that the Koreans have among the Japanese population:

> Fortunately, our people do not have such feelings against the Koreans as they have against the Chinese, and there has until now arisen no objection against them living among us. Although there are at present only a few of them here, if more Korean workers will be employed, there will be no need to change this situation even after the implementation of the New Treaties. Moreover, although I don't think that the Koreans are faultless in their nature, they don't have such bad habits as the Chinese do and also not such evil customs as other barbarian people. Especially if seen from the legal point of view, since they are second to none when it comes to obedience to the law, there is absolutely no objection to give them all the rights and privileges we have given other [Western] foreigners.[76]

One could argue that the liberal treatment and relatively positive image resulted from the fact that so few Koreans lived in Japan compared to Chinese. However, the situation did not change even after Korea had become a full-fledged colony of Japan in 1910. In fact, one can safely surmise that the positive image of Koreans in Japan related closely to Japan's policy toward Korea itself, as will be shown presently.

Racism in Japan's Colonial Policies

Japan's drive to territorial expansion in the nineteenth and early twentieth centuries is generally seen as motivated by two factors.[77] First, there was the overall concern for Japan's insular security. In the age of Social Darwinism, it was taken for granted that empires as much as individuals followed the principle of "the survival of the fittest"—which in Japanese was aptly rendered by the classical phrase "the flesh of the weak is meat for the strong" (*jakuniku kyōshoku*)—and would either expand like the European powers, or fall prey to territorial division by the other powers, potentially China. Whatever one might think of Japan's real endangerment in hindsight, military leaders such as Yamagata Aritomo soon developed the doctrine that Japan must establish a cordon of sovereignty around its borders. The annexation of Taiwan in 1895 hardly aligned with this argument, as it did not add much—apart from about 2.5 million new subjects—to Japan's security. However, since Taiwan was the bounty of the Sino-Japanese War, this decision resulted more from political expediency than strategic rationale.[78] Japan saw Korea under foreign influence, on the other hand, as a dagger pointed eternally at its throat. Thus, when Japan erected a protectorate over Korea in 1905 and annexed it formally in 1910, the acquisition of the new colony with about 30 million subjects marked a major step in Japan's security strategy, but, of course, also helped the country establish itself as a "respectable" colonial empire in the eyes of the European powers.[79]

The second factor that informed the thrust of Japan's territorial expansion was the presence of the European powers in East Asia and their opposition to Japan's policies. Apart from the fact that the European powers distrusted Japan's motives toward China, they were considerably invested in China themselves. Thus, the racialized opposition to a Sino-Japanese alliance also served as a convenient cloak to hide Europe's own interests in expansion. Consequently, Japanese scenarios of expansion always avoided the main body of China and either pointed northward to Korea and Manchuria (the "northern advance" favored by the army), or southward from Taiwan to Southern China and Southeast Asia (the "southern advance" favored by the navy).[80]

The above factors also shaped Japan's colonial policy with respect to the issue of racism. Firstly, since Japan hoped colonies would enhance its prestige in the eyes of the European powers, the colonial bureaucracy diligently studied the successful models of European colonial rule and applied their findings to Taiwan and Korea (in this respect, the formulation of colonial policy resembled that of the early Meiji reforms).[81] As Japan based this "scientific colonialism" on Western theories of colonialism which, despite a considerable latitude in content, were all predicated on "difference" reflecting the geographic diversity of homeland and colonies, it is no surprise that the Japanese colonial bureaucracy—although ruling geographically adjacent territories—usually assumed a similarly detached view of their subjects, often declaring them members of a wholly different (and inferior) race.[82] Thus colonial bureaucrats favored the gradualist approach, which envisioned the development of the colonies over many generations, but also tended to favor the status quo.

On the other hand, Japan's move into geographically contiguous regions also favored the early development of an expansionist ideology that stressed cultural and genetic affinities with colonized peoples.[83] Although theories of the mixed origins of the Japanese had existed prior to the Sino-Japanese War and even dominated academic circles, they gained wider currency in the public soon after the annexation of Taiwan and experienced a tremendous boost with the acquisition of Korea. These theories, although almost limitless in their variety and fantasy, consciously opposed an isolationist theory of the Japanese as a homogeneous, "pure blooded" nation and explained in "scientific" terms why the Japanese, as a hybrid nation, had a natural inclination to immerse themselves in their origins and were ideally fit to move beyond them.[84] Thus, almost all of these theories supposed that the Japanese nation was a composite of a northern and a southern element, the ratio of which was determined by the proponent's inclination to favor the "northern" or the "southern advance."[85] Conveniently, the most dominant theory saw Japan's origins as integrated in an empire that included South Korea and Southern China, and ruled by the ancestors of the Japanese emperor.[86] Not surprisingly, these theories elaborated more on Japan's affinities with the 30 million subjects in Korea than the 2.5 million Taiwanese. Consequently, it became generally accepted that Japanese and Koreans shared the same ancestors (*Nissen dōso ron*).[87] Only after Japan's occupation of Manchuria in 1931 and the beginning of the Sino-Japanese War in 1937 (also a propaganda war) did a concerted effort to win over the Chinese begin.[88] Thus, differing sympathies for the Chinese and the Koreans in domestic politics had their parallels in varying degrees of necessity to accommodate Chinese and Japanese in colonial policies.

As in its immigration policies, the Japanese government opted for assimilation (*dōka*) rather than segregation of its colonial subjects.[89] Consequently, the existing or alleged affinities between Japan and her colonial people, to quote Mark Peattie, "made possible the idea of a fusion of the two and suggested that ultimately Japanese colonial territories had no separate autonomous identities of their own, but only a destiny which was entirely Japan."[90] However, such an idea was not uncontroversial. Apart from introducing assimilation policies which concerned the outer vestiges of colonial life, such as on life style and language, colonial bureaucrats tended to oppose the idea on the principle of their gradualist beliefs, but even more so because they wanted to preserve the status quo and avoid granting privileges to the new citizens. Eugenicists in later stages of the Japanese empire opposed the promiscuous identity of a mixed nation in theory and of assimilation policies in practice, as they endangered the assumed "pure-bloodedness" of the Japanese nation.[91] By then, Japanese eugenicists had taken account of the ascent of the Japanese empire and assumed the superiority of the Japanese race, thereby taking the opposite stance of their predecessors in the mixed-nation debate. However, since insistence on homogeneity severely limited expansion prospects, it remained the stance of a minority.

Finally, although this section focused on racism in the "discourse" of policies, and not in actual colonial rule, it should be cautioned that, for all the ostentatious racial egalitarianism of Japan's colonial policies, colonial citizens did not enjoy the same rights and privilege as their homeland compatriots. As expected, lofty professions of affinity did not translate into full citizenship, and severe discrimination persisted on grounds that the colonial subjects were "not yet" ready for the full rights of a civilized citizen. Moreover, the number of intermarriages between Koreans and Japanese in Korea remained low for a long time and only rose significantly with official sponsorship of intermarriage after 1937.[92] This shows that despite the rhetoric of assimilation and racial equality, in practice social prejudice still imposed severe limitations. Thus, the colonial situation in many ways reflected the problem of foreigners at home, and vice versa.

Conclusion

Based on the above findings, the following conclusions can be drawn regarding Japanese attitudes toward racism in the late Meiji period. Although "race" as a scientific notion was known well enough in Japan and even accepted in some academic circles, by and large its implications for the political realm were rejected. Those who did accept the Western racial taxonomy belonged to a vociferous minority among Japan's intellectual elite (such as Katō Hiroyuki, Inoue Tetsujirō, or Hozumi Yatsuka) who had been exposed most and directly to European civilization. As a result, they showed strong symptoms of overcompensation or "over-assimilation" to the European standard. Only for them does the traditional view of a literal translation of European racism into the Japanese context hold true.[93]

The rejection of European racism was, of course, not a matter of beliefs and morals, but of political expediency. As a rule of thumb, whenever exclusion or inclusion by racialist designation threatened an important Japanese political agenda, racism was rejected. However, whenever inclusion or exclusion were indifferent or served a purpose, then discrimination entered political practice; in such cases drawing a line to racism, in fact, becomes a problem of definition.

Thus, Japan in its relations with the Western powers rejected racism, as it threatened Japan's rise to "great power" status and peaceful expansion through labor emigration. Instead, Japan insisted on the validity of the standard of civilization. By the same token, Japan lifted all restrictions on free movement and residence for citizens of European Treaty nations in 1899. All of this did not prevent the Western nations, of course, from continuing racist practices, or practices that "felt" racist to the Japanese public. The best-known instance of this was the rejection of Japan's motion for a so-called "racial equality clause" in the Covenant of the League of Nations in 1919.[94] However, U.S. immigration policies toward Japan arguably left the deepest imprint on Japanese public memory: traumatically for the Japanese, Congress passed a selective immigration bill in 1924 which effectively voided the Gentlemen's Agreement of 1907 and included the Japanese with other Asiatics as "undesirable aliens."[95]

Likewise, Japanese colonial policies toward Korea and Taiwan downplayed the exclusive aspect of racism and insisted on the enforced cultural assimilation of its subjects, although this did not go hand-in-hand with an enhancement of legal status. Again, colonial high bureaucrats steeped in the lore of Western colonial theory tended to insist on difference, which was also racially defined. However, it could be argued that the Japanese dogma of "common ancestors" with the Koreans, although not exclusive, was no less "racist" in the opposite direction. Typically, racism would result in the "exclusion" of a group, which at the same time would privilege another in the allocation of resources and services. However, the above dogma intended to "include" 30 million (unwilling) Koreans theoretically, if not actually, with the 40 million "motherland" Japanese in the Japanese nation, and did not concern itself with other groups. Thus, it is open to debate whether forceful "inclusion" of a group should fall under the definition of "racism" as well.

In contrast to Japanese attitudes toward Koreans, their attitudes toward the Chinese —evident in political indifference toward inclusion, accommodation in international politics, and resistance to domestic opposition groups through colonial policy—tipped the balance toward discriminatory immigration policies. However, it is difficult to decide whether this was also accompanied, if not driven, by "racialist" prejudice. The use of anti-Semitism branding the Chinese as "constitutive outsiders"[96] may point in this direction, although this alone does not reveal how far the analogy was intended to carry.

On the other hand, such statements as Hara Takashi's advocacy of "influencing" the Chinese and leading them toward civilization invoke the same assimilationist strategy pursued in colonial policies, i.e., enforced inclusion on the level of "civilization." Although some may want to belittle this as political "cant," which it might have been in many cases of practical application, it cannot be so facilely disowned on principle, for several reasons: firstly, for the fact that the Japanese leaders held onto assimilation as the official policy even against the vehement critique and resistance of the colonial bureaucracy and against Western precedent; secondly, the general tendency to reject the tenets of racism in political discourse in modern times; and finally (and probably most profoundly) the premodern interactions with China and Korea which, in the context of the Sino-centric international order, were ideologically predicated on civilization only.[97] Although path dependence itself is not a sufficient argument, combined with the other reasons, one is inclined to view Japanese attitudes in dealing with "other" people based on what must be termed "culturalism" rather than racism.[98]

Notes

1. Robert Miles, *Racism* (London, 1989), 3, 77–84; on the growth of the term, see 41–68. See also Pierre L. van den Berghe, *Race and Racism: A Comparative Perspective*, 2nd ed. (New York, 1978).
2. Miles, *Racism*, 31, 36.
3. Ibid., 42.
4. Ibid., 2, 25.
5. Mark Peattie, "The Japanese Colonial Empire, 1895–1945," in *The Cambridge History of Japan*, edited by Peter Duus (Cambridge, 1988), 6: 217.

6. Michael Weiner, "The Invention of Identity: Race and Nation in Pre-War Japan," in *The Construction of Racial Identities in China and Japan: Historical and Contemporary Perspectives*, edited by Frank Dikötter (London, 1997), 104.

7. Weiner, "Invention of Identity," 110; for an alternative view, see Kazuki Sato, "'Same Language, Same Race': The Dilemma of *Kanbun* in Modern Japan" in *Construction of Racial Identities*, 118–35, and Eiji Oguma, *A Genealogy of 'Japanese' Self-images*, trans. David Askew (Melbourne, 2002). Note that Japanese names in the main text and for citing authors of Japanese-language publications are given in the Japanese order, i.e., family name first. Japanese authors of English publications, however, are given in the order as their publishers chose to do so, i.e., family name last.

8. Miles, *Racism*, 3.

9. See, for example, Richard Siddle, "The Ainu and the Discourse of 'Race,'" in *Construction of Racial Identites*, 136–57.

10. Eikoh Shimao, "Darwinism in Japan, 1877–1927," *Annals of Science* 38, no. 1 (1981): 93; on the introduction of Darwinism to Japan, see also Hiroshi Unoura, "Samurai Darwinism: Hiroyuki Katō and the Reception of Darwin's Theory in Modern Japan from the 1880s to the 1900s," *History and Anthropology* 11, no. 2–3 (1999): 235–55; Watanabe Masao, *Dâwin to shinka-ron* (Darwin and evolutional theory) (Tokyo, 1984), 192–210.

11. Shimao, "Darwinism in Japan," 97; of the *Origins of Species* alone, Shimao counts eleven full translations to have appeared by 1963, see 98.

12. Unoura, "Samurai Darwinism," 239.

13. For the study of eugenics in Japan, see Sumiko Otsubo, "The Female Body and Eugenic Thought in Meiji Japan," in *Building a Modern Nation: Science, Technology, and Medicine in the Meiji Era and Beyond*, edited by Morris Lowe (New York, 2005), 61–81; Oguma, *Genealogy*, 203–36.

14. Michio Nagai, "Herbert Spencer in Early Meiji Japan," *The Far Eastern Quarterly* 14, no. 1 (1954): 55. Nagai counts at least thirty-two translations of Spencer's work between 1877 and 1900. See also Douglas Howland, "Society Reified: Herbert Spencer and Political Theory in Early Meiji Japan," *Comparative Studies in Society and History*, 42, no. 1 (2000): 67–86; Yamashita Jun'ichi, *Supensâ to Nihon kindai* (*Spencer and Japan's Modernity*) (Tokyo, 1983).

15. Nagai, "Herbert Spencer," 57.

16. John Bowle places the whole discussion of political thought in the latter half of the nineteenth century under the caption: "The political thought of the age of Darwin." On Spencer's eminent position, see his *Politics and Opinion in the Nineteenth Century* (London, 1954), 224–36.

17. The lecture was later published as *Jinshu tetsugaku kōgai* (An outline of racial philosophy) (Tokyo, 1903).

18. Ibid., 63–65.

19. Ibid., 67.

20. On these treaties, see Harald Kleinschmidt, *Das europäische Völkerrecht und die ungleichen Verträge um die Mitte des 19. Jahrhunderts* (Tokyo, 2007).

21. For a description of the extraterritoriality system in operation, see J.E. Hoare, *Japan's Treaty Ports and Foreign Settlements: The Uninvited Guests, 1858–1899* (Sandgate, UK, 1994), 66–105.

22. For Japanese intellectuals' reactions to the treaty revisions, see Kenneth B. Pyle, *The New Generation in Meiji Japan: Problems of Cultural Identity, 1885–1895* (Stanford, 1969), 99–117.

23. Gerrit W. Gong, *The Standard of 'Civilization' in International Society* (Oxford, 1984), 14–21, 25–35.

24. "The Japanese Treaties," *New York Times*, 12 June 1895. Of course, Britain's willingness to sign a new treaty was also an attempt to win Japan's favor as a counterweight to Russia in East Asia. This eventually resulted in the Anglo-Japanese Treaty of 1902.

25. For this, see S.M.C. Paine, *The Sino-Japanese War of 1894–1895: Perceptions, Power and Primacy* (Cambridge, 2003).

26. "Kōshoku jinshu no bokkō," *Kokumin shinbun*, 8 July 1895, 3.

27. Heinz Gollwitzer, *Die Gelbe Gefahr: Geschichte eines Schlagworts* (Göttingen, 1962), 206–8. On the history of the keyword, see also Ute Mehnert, *Deutschland, Amerika und die „Gelbe Gefahr“: Zur Karriere eines Schlagworts in der Großen Politik 1905–1917* (Stuttgart, 1995).

28. "Tōyō, Seiyō o osou no zu" ("A picture of the East attacking the West"), *Kokumin shinbun*, 8 January 1896, 3.

29. M.P. Shiel, *The Yellow Danger* (London, 1998). The novel was initially serialized under the title "The Empress of the Earth" (meaning Britain) in the all-fiction weekly *Short Stories* in 1898, and went into several reprints after.

30. See the review of Shiel's novel, "Recent Novels," *The Times*, 13 September 1898, 13.

31. William L. Langer, *The Diplomacy of Imperialism*, 2nd ed. (New York, 1965), 417.

32. On racism as a limitation to the historical "standard of civilization," see Gong, *Standard of 'Civilization'*, 48–50. On racism as a persistent factor in international politics, see R.J. Vincent, "Race in International Relations," *International Affairs (Royal Institute of International Affairs)* 58, no. 4 (1982): 658–670.

33. For such a reaction, see for example the journalist Kuga Katsunan's (1857–1907) commentary "Sekai bunmei no shogai" (Obstacles to universal civilization), *Nippon*, 11 February 1898. It should be noted that the particular "values" which constituted civilization were open to discussion; however, that such a standard existed and applied universally was not controversial in Japan.

34. Konoe Atsumaro, "Dō-jinshu dōmei, tsuketari Shina mondai kenkyū no hitsuyō" ("A racial alliance and the necessity of studying the Chinese Question"), reprinted in *Konoe Atsumaro nikki* (The diary of Konoe Atsumaro), edited by Konoe Atsumaro nikki kankō-kai (Tokyo, 1968–69), 5: 62–63.

35. For a detailed analysis of the reactions, domestic and international, see Urs Matthias Zachmann, *China's Role in the Process of Japan's Cultural Self-*

Identification, 1895–1904 (Ph.D. diss., University of Heidelberg, 2006), 141–49.

36. For an example, see the letter of Nakamura Shingo to Konoe in *Konoe Atsumaro nikki* 2: 47–52.

37. For a short portrait of Konoe's person and positions, see Marius B. Jansen, "Konoe Atsumaro," in *The Chinese and the Japanese: Essays in Political and Cultural Interaction*, edited by Akira Iriye (Princeton, 1980), 107–23.

38. On this, see Douglas R. Reynolds, *China, 1898–1912: The Xingzheng Revolution and China* (Cambridge, MA, 1993); Marius B. Jansen, *The Japanese and Sun Yat-sen* (Cambridge, MA, 1967).

39. Yamagata Aritomo, *Yamagata Aritomo ikensho* (The opinion papers of Yamagata Aritomo), edited by Ōyama Azusa (Tokyo, 1966), 251–53.

40. Ibid., 252–53.

41. See Robert B. Valliant, "The Selling of Japan: Japanese Manipulation of Western Opinion, 1900–1905," *Monumenta Nipponica* 29, no. 4 (1974): 415–38.

42. On the discourse on Japanese "peaceful expansion," see Akira Iriye, *Pacific Estrangement: Japanese and American Expansion, 1897–1911* (Cambridge, MA, 1972).

43. "Japan (From our Correspondent)," *The North-China Herald*, 25 July 1900, reprinted in *Gaikoku shinbun ni miru Nihon* (Japan as seen through foreign newspapers), edited by Kokusai nyūsu jiten shuppan iinkai (Tokyo, 1989–1993), 3: 243.

44. As of 1894, see Iwakabe Yoshimitsu, "Nisshin senji hōka no zainichi Chūgoku-jin mondai" (The legal problem of Chinese residing in Japan during the first Sino-Japanese War), in *Nisshin sensō to Higashi-Ajia sekai no hen'yō* (The first Sino-Japanese war and the transformation of East-Asia), edited by Higashi-Ajia kindai-shi gakkai (Tokyo, 1997), 2: 207.

45. See, for example, Kuga Katsunan, "Naichi kanshō-ron" (On intervention in domestic politics), *Nippon*, 22 August to 5 September 1889, reprinted in *Kuga Katsunan zenshū* (The Collected Works of Kuga Katsunan), edited by Nishida Taketoshi et al. (Tokyo, 1968–1985), 2: 197–221. It should be cautioned that the protest against intervention was often wielded as a weapon against the "oligarchic politicians" by playing the national card, and thus was motivated by purely political concerns. However, the case of Tane Tateki (Kanjō, 1837–1911), who left the cabinet in protest against its treaty policies, shows that there was also genuine concern (Kuga Katsunan, in consequence, became a supporter of Tani, and vice versa).

46. "Minpō idete chūkō horobu": this is the title of Hazumi's well-known diatribe against the French draft of the family and inheritance law section of the Code. See Oguma, *Genealogy*, 35.

47. "Gaijin zakkyo-chū," *Yubin hōchi shinbun*, 4 November 1877, reprinted in Maeda Ai and Shimizu Mikio, *Jiyū minken-ki no manga* (Tokyo, 1985), 14.

48. David Duncan, *Life and Letters of Herbert Spencer* (London, 1908), 321 (emphasis

in the original).

49. For the arguments on "mixed residence" between Inoue and Taguchi before the Sino-Japanese War, see Oguma, *Genealogy*, 16–30.

50. For this theory and Taguchi's advocacy, see Oguma, *Genealogy*, 143–55. For another specimen, see Morris Low, "The Japanese Nation and Evolution: W.E. Griffis, "Hybridity and the Whiteness of the Japanese Race," *History and Anthropology* 11, no. 2–3 (1999): 203–34.

51. Mori, *Jinshu tetsugaku*, 65.

52. "Nihon jinshu kairyō ron" (Tokyo, 1884). On Takahashi, see Otsubo, "The Female Body and Eugenic Thought," 63–64; Oguma, *Genealogy*, 143.

53. (Herbert Spencer quote): Letter to Kaneko Kentarō, August 1892, in Duncan, *Life and Letters*, 322.

54. For this argument, see Otsubo, "The Female Body and Eugenic Thought," 70.

55. Otsubo, "The Female Body and Eugenic Thought," 65.

56. See Donald Keene, "The Sino-Japanese War of 1894–95 and Its Cultural Effects in Japan," in *Tradition and Modernization in Japanese Culture*, edited by Donald Shively (Princeton, 1971), 121–75.

57. Tokutomi Sohō cited by James L. Huffman, *Creating a Public: People and Press in Meiji Japan* (Honolulu, 1997), 212.

58. Thus, Hara Takashi's guide to mixed residence for example, devoted only five chapters (15–19) to the question of foreign enterprises in Japan and the introduction of foreign investment. See his *Shin-jōyaku jisshi junbi* (Preparing for the implementation of the New Treaties), 2nd ed. (Osaka, 1899).

59. See Iwakabe Yoshimitsu, "Nisshin senji hōka," 207. For exact numbers, see Noriko Kamachi, "The Chinese in Meiji Japan: Their Interactions with the Japanese before the Sino-Japanese War," in *The Chinese and the Japanese*, 60–61.

60. See Harry D. Harootunian, "The Functions of China in Tokugawa Thought," in *The Chinese and the Japanese*, 9–36.

61. Tokutomi Sohō, *Shakai to jinbutsu* (Society and people) (Tokyo, 1899), 81.

62. See Bob Tadashi Wakabayashi, "Opium, Expulsion, Sovereignty. China's Lessons for Bakumatsu Japan," *Monumenta Nipponica* 47, no. 1 (1992): 1–25; on the impact of the Sino-French War 1884–85, see Sushila Narsimhan, *Japanese Perceptions of China in the Nineteenth Century: Influence of Fukuzawa Yukichi* (New Delhi, 1999), 106–16. On Japan's internalization of the Western China-image, see Zachmann, *China's Role*, 49–52.

63. On the discrimination of Chinese, see Kamachi, "The Chinese in Meiji Japan," 62–63, 66; Keene, "The Sino-Japanese War of 1894–95 and Its Cultural Effects in Japan," 138. For an example of denouncing the Chinese as opium smokers, see Hara, *Shin-jōyaku jisshi junbi*, 60.

64. See Kamachi, "The Chinese in Meiji Japan," 66.

65. Tokutomi, *Shakai to jinbutsu*, 81–84.

66. Tokutomi, *Shakai to jinbutsu*, 85. For other explicit comparisons of Chinese with Jews, see Yamagata Aritomo's opinion paper as quoted above or the chapter "Yūdaijin" (Jews) in the essay collection *Sanshi suimei* (The Glory of Nature), edited by Kuga Katsunan (Tokyo, 1897), 186–193, esp. 192. Judging by the style, this text was written by Miyake Setsurei (1860–1945).

67. For the role of anti-Semitism in Japan in general, see David G. Goodman, "Anti-Semitism in Japan: Its History and Current Implications," in *The Construction of Racial Identities*, 177–98.

68. See Zhou Xun, "Youtai: The Myth of the 'Jew' in Modern China," in *The Construction of Racial Identities*, 53–74. As Xun mentions, Liang Qichao, for example, lived for many years in Japan and was a major force in introducing Japanese knowledge to China.

69. Hara, *Shin-jōyaku jisshi junbi*, 57–58. See also Matsuoka Bunpei, "Reimei-ki rōdō kumiai undō no tokushitsu: 'Rōdō sekai' to Chūgoku zakkyo mondai" ("The characteristics of the early labor movement: the magazine 'Rōdō sekai' [The working world] and the Chinese mixed residence problem"), *Shisen* 48 (1974): 15–32.

70. Hara, *Shin-jōyaku jisshi junbi*, 59–61. See also "Shinajin no naichi zakkyo" (Mixed residence of Chinese), *Jiji shinpō*, 27 February 1894, 2.

71. For details, see Matsuoka, "Reimei-ki rōdō kumiai," 18; Hara, *Shin-jōyaku jisshi junbi*, 52–55.

72. Hara, *Shin-jōyaku jisshi junbi*, 60–61.

73. Matsuoka, "Reimei-ki rōdō kumiai," 22.

74. Hara, *Shin-jōyaku jisshi junbi*, 62.

75. Ibid., 63.

76. Ibid., 63.

77. Peattie, "The Japanese Colonial Empire," 218–23.

78. Edward I-te Chen, "Japan's Decision to Annex Taiwan: A Study of Mutō-Itō Diplomacy," *Journal of Asian Studies* 37, no. 1 (1977): 62.

79. On this process, see Peter Duus, *The Abacus and the Sword: The Japanese Penetration of Korea, 1895–1910* (Berkeley, 1995), 201–41.

80. On the debate between *hokushin* and *nanshin* advocates, see Hata Ikuhiko, "Continental Expansion, 1905–1941," in *Cambridge History of Japan*, 6: 271–76.

81. For the "European impress," see Mark Peattie, "Japanese Attitudes Toward Colonialism, 1895–1945," in *The Japanese Colonial Empire, 1895–1945*, edited by Ramon H. Myers and Mark R. Peattie (Princeton, 1984), 82–96.

82. Peattie, "Japanese Attitudes Toward Colonialism, 1895–1945," 95–96.

83. This is the central argument of Oguma, *Genealogy*, 321.

84. For a detailed description of the theories in the Meiji period, see Oguma, *Genealogy*, 3–92.

85. However, in times when the "northern advance" was the politically predominant opinion, favoring the "southern" theory could also mean taking a proto-pacifistic,

isolationist stance, as in the case of the famous ethnographer Yanagita Kunio (1875–1962), see Oguma, *Genealogy*, 175–202.

86. Ibid., 73–75.
87. Ibid., 64–80.
88. See Akira Iriye, *China and Japan in the Global Setting* (Cambridge, MA, 1992), 74–88.
89. For a discussion of assimilation policies, see Peattie, "Japanese Attitudes Toward Colonialism, 1895–1945," 96–103.
90. Ibid., 96.
91. On the position of eugenicists toward colonial policies, see Oguma, *Genealogy*, 203–36.
92. According to Oguma, as late as 1925 the annual rate of marriages was only 404; by 1937, the number had risen to above 1,200 couples. See his *Genealogy*, 206.
93. See Weiner, "Invention of Identity," 102.
94. See Ōnuma Yasuaki, "Haruka naru jinshu byōdō no risō: Kokusai renmeikiyaku e no jinshu byōdō jōki teian ti Nihon no kokusaihō-kan" (The remote ideal of racial equality: the proposition of a racial equality clause to the Covenant of the League of Nations and Japan's view on international law), in *Kokusaihō, Kokusai Rengō to Nihon* (International Law, the League of Nations, and Japan), edited by Ōnuma Yasuaki (Tokyo, 1987), 427–80; Naoko Shimazu, *Japan, Race and Equality: The Race Equality Proposal of 1919* (London, 1998).
95. Ian Nish, *Japanese Foreign Policy: Kasumigaseki to Miyakezaka* (London, 1977), 144; on the San Francisco School debate of 1906, which eventually led to the Second Gentlemen's Agreement of 1907, see Mehnert, *Deutschland, Amerika und die "Gelbe Gefahr,"* 82–87. See also Roger Daniels, *The Politics of Prejudice: The Anti-Japanese Movement in California and the Struggle for Japanese Exclusion* (Berkeley, 1962).
96. See Xun, "Youtai," 54.
97. On culture as the ideological foundation of relations in the Sino-centric world order, see John K. Fairbank and S.Y. Teng, "On the Ch'ing Tributary System," *Harvard Journal of Asiatic Studies* 6, no. 2 (1941): 137–39. Japan may have excluded itself from the political order, but certainly not from its cultural foundations, see Marius B. Jansen, *China in the Tokugawa World* (Cambridge, Mass., 1992) and Ronald P. Toby, *State and Diplomacy in Early Modern Japan: Asia in the Development of the Tokugawa Bakufu* (Stanford, 1984).
98. For a similar assessment of Japanese attitudes, see Sato Kazuki, "'Same Language, Same Race': The Dilemma of Kanbun in Modern Japan," in *Construction of Racial Identities in China and Japan*, 135.

Chapter 13

Hendrik Verwoerd's Long March to Apartheid: Nationalism and Racism in South Africa

Christoph Marx

Before 1948 South Africa was not noticed as a special case internationally. In fact its policy of segregation fell more or less in line with that of other set- tler colonies in Africa—like Rhodesia (Zimbabwe), South West Africa (Namibia), Kenya, and Algeria—where minority settler populations had exclusive access to government.[1] Even in the United States, where people of African origin were a minority and carried the historical stigma of slavery, the politics of segregation introduced after the Civil War shared a number of similarities with South Africa. Segregation measures concerning public amenities and signs drawing attention to separate facilities closely resem- bled those in South Africa. George Fredrickson, however, drew attention to the main difference between the forms of racism in the Deep South and South Africa: in South Africa segregation could draw on cultural differ- ences and therefore pretend its main object was the conservation of organically grown cultures, whereas in the United States blacks were largely acculturated to white ways of living, religion, and language. As a result, seg- regation in the United States was "a much more nakedly and overtly racial form of domination."[2]

From the 1930s onward, these differences became visible: in South Africa, Afrikaner intellectuals developed a form of nationalism that emerged as the vanguard in promoting racist policies that drew on cultural differences for political legitimacy, whereas in the United States notions of biological inferiority were much more prevalent.[3] Within Afrikaner na- tionalist circles, organized through the secret society of the Afrikaner Broederbond, these intellectuals devised a new policy called apartheid. At first, apartheid was more of a claim than a concept, since the term was sim- ply an Afrikaans translation of "segregation" adapted to signal a new political movement. Nevertheless, until 1950, the contours of this policy remained remarkably blurred, except for public claims that Afrikaner nationalism would replace the present patchwork of individual measures with a policy devoted to general principles.

In 1948, the National Party won the elections as the main political representative of Afrikaner nationalism, largely because the majority of the population was disfranchised. The incompetence of the former United Party government under the internationally acclaimed General Smuts, economic problems after World War II, increasing urbanization of blacks during the war, and the failures by the government to re-integrate white war veterans all probably had a greater impact on the vote than the National Party's apartheid slogans. Immediately after assuming power the new government began to implement a policy intended to go far beyond radicalizing segregation. But the aging Prime Minister Daniel Malan was apparently more interested in achieving and maintaining the unity of his "volk" than giving shape to the new policy of apartheid. He gave the portfolio of Native Affairs to the rather conservative political stalwart Ernest Jansen, who had previously run the department. Jansen's political course, therefore, differed very little from the old policy of segregation. This caused a group of radical politicians to urge Malan to promote Jansen to the post of Governor-General and to give a cabinet seat to Hendrik Verwoerd, who had a reputation as an uncompromising nationalist. As Minister of Native Affairs from 1950 to 1958, Verwoerd fulfilled the expectations of his colleagues by simultaneously implementing apartheid policy in different fields, including education, housing, labor relations, church matters, and African political structures. He proved himself a politician with extraordinary political acumen, shrewdness, and an unbending will. After he joined the cabinet, it quickly became clear that the new policy differed considerably from all recent forms of racial segregation. Verwoerd gave apartheid a much more radical impulse by providing it with a comprehensive and systematic approach. Driven by both personal ambition and a sense of executing a historical mission, he helped apartheid develop into nothing less than an attempt to rebuild a postcolonial state on racism and to refashion a complex multiethnic society according to racist assumptions.

As Minister of Native Affairs, Verwoerd transformed a department hitherto regarded as second rank into a key institution. The department increasingly adopted the character of a state within the state, because it developed univeral competences for the administration of the African population. Native Affairs usurped the responsibility for African education from other departments and began to resemble a government for the African majority, without being beholden to this majority. Verwoerd was mainly responsible for initiating and implementing these changes, which increasingly demoted other departments to auxiliary functions. Of even greater impact beyond these questions of departmental responsibilities was the all-encompassing character of the administrative transformation of South African society. Verwoerd's main impact on the policy of apartheid was on its remarkably ruthless implementation, which contrasted with the accompanying propaganda praising the often brutal interventions into the daily affairs of many people as benevolent and well meaning. His forcefulness and inflexibility earned him the nickname "man of granite." When Prime Minister Hans Strijdom suddenly died in 1958, Verwoerd joined the small circle of promising candidates for the nation's most influential political post. The National Party caucus elected him in a second round of voting as the new party leader, which meant he would automatically succeed Strijdom. However, his inability to win decisively and the presence of a substantial minority opposing him within the National Party weakened his position somewhat.

As Prime Minister (1958–1966), he still paid attention to various aspects of apartheid, but the creation of a white nation-state remained his main goal. The transformation of the Union of South Africa into an independent republic in 1961 marked a major step in this direction. Verwoerd shrewdly planned South Africa's exit from the Commonwealth during the same year,[4] although the official version of history presented it as a move forced upon him by the other Commonwealth members. In order to strengthen his position within his own party, he brought in a number of right-wing people, like John Vorster and Nicholas Diederichs, who had been marginalized after World War II for their anti-parliamentary and anti-party stance. Verwoerd also started expanding his cabinet by creating junior minister posts, which extended his patronage. The growth of parastatal enterprises also opened opportunities for him to provide followers with well-paid jobs. After the first assassination attempt in 1960 his position within the party became undisputed and his survival of the two close-range shots fired into his head hardened his conviction to fulfill his mission. At the apex of his power and influence, however, an allegedly insane messenger murdered him on 6 September 1966 in parliament. Neither assassin was ever brought to trial, as both were declared insane and locked away in a prison psychiatric department. Consequently, nothing substantial is known about their motivations besides rumors about the involvement of Verwoerd's political opponents.

Verwoerd's years in journalism from 1937–48 and his following career in government have already been researched fairly extensively.[5] Scholars know much less about his earlier career; his time at university and his academic career, in particular, have for the most part received scant attention. Nevertheless, time and again there has been speculation about the influence of National Socialism on the apartheid policies introduced in 1948. To date there are only three biographies of Verwoerd in existence,[6] all of which, strangely, in large part omit treatment of Verwoerd's life before the start of his journalistic career. Two other authors, however, offer completely different interpretations of this period.

In his pioneering 1975 history of the nationalist ideology of the Afrikaners, the sociologist Dunbar Moodie ascribed Verwoerd to the "neo-Fichteans," a group of young intellectuals who had studied in Germany in the 1920s and 1930s, supposedly bringing back a radicalized nationalism to South Africa.[7] Unfortunately, apart from its plausibility, Moodie produced no proof, which nonetheless did not deter several authors from treating his claim as an established fact.[8] While it is true that many Afrikaans-speaking intellectuals studied at German universities with academics from very different political camps, they all obtained their degrees in the 1920s, not during the Third Reich.

Similarly wanting is the evidence produced by the American social scientist Roberta Balstad Miller in a 1993 essay in which, contrary to Moodie, she claims that Verwoerd was neither a racist nor a nationalist at the start of his active political career in 1937. She maintains that his move toward nationalism and advocacy of apartheid resulted from opportunism more than anything else.[9] Although Miller claims to have drawn on rich source material, an attentive reading of her essay and the alleged sources reveals that her reading was very superficial. Moreover, her selective approach ignored known sources contradicting her thesis. Miller's claim that Verwoerd suddenly underwent a conversion to racism and nationalism in 1937 contradicts all the biographical research on the powerful influence of his adolescent years.

In this chapter I develop my own interpretation of Verwoerd's long march to apartheid, between the two unfounded and extreme views of Moodie and Miller. No evidence suggests a substantial German influence on Verwoerd's ideological stance. In my view, the history of Afrikaner nationalism already contained seeds of radicalization during the 1930s.[10] For this reason, outside influences are of subordinate importance to this analysis of Afrikaner nationalism and its apartheid ideology. The case of

Verwoerd substantiates my claim, since Verwoerd was fairly consistent in his nationalist views from his early youth onwards. This makes examining his early career especially worthwhile. I will therefore concentrate on Verwoerd's time as a student and university lecturer, with particular attention to the basic structure of views. His work on behalf of the "poor whites" is central to understanding his thinking, as it explains his shift toward the politics of racial segregation.

Verwoerd the Psychologist (1919–1932)

Verwoerd studied applied psychology at Stellenbosch from 1919–24, completing his studies with a dissertation entitled "Die Afstomping van die gemoedsaandoeninge" (The Blunting of the Emotions).[11] Extensive notes and records exist for the lectures he gave from 1925 onward. They demonstrate that Verwoerd found no particular grounds for a definitively racist approach in psychology. In 1925 Stellenbosch University granted him a research scholarship that enabled him to travel to Germany, where he attended the leading institutes of psychological research. He spent a semester at the universities of Leipzig, Berlin, and Hamburg, respectively, each of which took very different approaches to psychology. Apart from his registration, Verwoerd left no trace in the archives of these universities, so that the influence of his stay can only be intimated from the surviving notes and lecture manuscripts from the period before his journey and after his return.

All three institutions were interested in applied psychology, a discipline referred to as "psychotechnik" by one of its pioneers, Hugo Münsterberg, who taught at Harvard. Münsterberg understood this as a technical science that could contribute to work place efficiency in the field of business management.[12] Psychotechnik was in fact very similar to Taylorism in the United States and found support in Germany in entrepreneurial circles, where its advocates hoped it would help reduce class polarization and social conflict, or at least cushion them.[13] At the time of Verwoerd's stay in Germany, confidence in laboratory experiments was still completely unscathed,[14] although the three German psychological institutes differed in their theoretical underpinning. Pinpointing a clear trend is most difficult in the case of the Hamburg Institute, since the head of department, William Stern, was involved in many fields of psychological research, as well as one of the first court psychologists. Stern's "differential psychology" opened the path to the further development of psychotechnik.[15] In later years two different approaches developed, the so-called subject and object oriented psychotechniks. The former aimed to manipulate human beings into adapting to the conditions of the workplace, while the latter tried to modify the workplace and conditions according to workers' needs.[16] Verwoerd clearly belonged to the latter school. As an academic and later as a politician he always strove to change the social environment in order to further the well-being of the people concerned. This outlook also indicates why he was uninterested in eugenics.

The Berlin Institute represented the forward-looking direction of gestalt psychology headed by Wolfgang Köhler starting in 1922.[17] The Berlin psychologists developed gestalt psychology because they did not believe Wilhelm Wundt's explanation was sufficient. Wundt, one of the founding fathers of academic psychology, had taught that psychic elements—the smallest units conceivable, which could be compared to atoms—constituted the human psyche. This resulted in an inductive method centered on collecting as much data and statistically valuable material as possible, then using it to draw conclusions. Repudiating this explanation, the gestalt psychologists claimed that sensual perceptions were always structured. To them the human being as an *individuum*—in the literal sense of the word—remained the object of their study and research. They wanted to analyze the human psyche scientifically by taking these structures as their point of departure.[18]

Gestalt psychology had developed in a move away from Wundt's inductive method and his adoption of psychological atom-like elements.[19] Wundt's disciple Felix Krüger, who succeeded him in his chair in Leipzig, vehemently rejected his mentor's approach. He went beyond gestalt psychology, developing a holistic psychology that extended beyond the individual psyche to encompass the community.[20] Whereas William Stern as well as the Berlin gestalt psychologists were politically rooted in a moderate liberalism, the Leipzig psychologists stood much closer to the political right. Felix Krueger was a conservative German nationalist whose influence on Verwoerd is as difficult to trace as that of his younger colleagues, some of them being far more radical than Krueger himself.

In his notes, Verwoerd repeatedly referred to Adolf Ehrhardt, who taught at the Leipzig Institute and had worked on typologies and, in this context, racial stereotyping. Although Erhardt did not hold a professorial chair at the Psychological Institute in Leipzig, he was certainly representative of the holistic psychology that it fostered. When he applied character types to collectivities, he generalized them in a way that was typical of the Leipzig Institute, which charged them with an ethnic and racial outlook.[21]

Verwoerd took an interest in Erhardt's character types but not in their racist consequences. Racial stereotyping apparently did not interest him that much, for he was still speaking out against biological-determinist assumptions in his sociology lectures in the early 1930s. He even emphasized "that there are no biological differences between the great races which could be one of the causes for the development of a higher social civilisation of the caucasian race as has been alleged."[22] At the same time, he concerned himself with research into character types, following the trend in international psychology from psychotechnik to characterology.[23] In this context he adapted the study of types and temperaments developed by the German psychiatrist Ernst Kretschmer. He assiduously referred to Kretschmer's textbook *Physique and Character (Körperbau und Charakter)*, which, incidentally, continued to be reprinted after World War II.[24] Kretschmer referred back to the ancient teachings of the four temperaments, further differentiating them and trying to link them to particular physical features. He combined elements of heredity, psychology and physiognomy into a theory that claimed to be able to gauge basic character traits from the human physique.

Nevertheless, Kretschmer rejected conclusions that he regarded as too one-dimensional. He instead applied inductive methods: "The types … are no 'ideal types' having been constructed through the application of certain leading ideas or values. They have been developed in the following way: Whenever a number of morphological similarities can be seen at a larger number of individuals, we take this as a starting point to establish the scaling. As soon as we calculate the average values, all the common features come to the fore, whereas the differences of individual cases become blurred." This is why "in each concrete case study we find the typical usually masked and even blurred by heterogeneous, 'individual' features."[25] Notwithstanding this cautious methodological reasoning, Kretschmer illustrated his book with photographs of individuals representing the typical.

Kretschmer's temperament and type theories were very susceptible to racist thinking because they believed people to be dominated by a basic character trait, permitting classification on the basis of alleged characteristic behavior. Verwoerd himself was convinced that it was possible to develop an objective method for identifying character traits.[26] Notwithstanding this line of reasoning, he proved more keenly interested in the stereotyping itself than in its possible biological and racial implications, since he was working in the field of the psychology of advertising in the late 1920s.[27] He concerned himself with tests of job suitability, a classical application of psychotechnik, trying to refine the methods for measuring. He aimed to find the right persons for certain occupations.[28] This interest already foreshadows his transfer to sociology and practical social work a few years later. It is therefore not really surprising that his nationalistically motivated involvement in what contemporaries referred to as the "poor white problem" would lead him into politics.

Verwoerd the Sociologist (1932–1937)

In 1932, Verwoerd took over a newly created chair for applied sociology and social work at Stellenbosch University, the first of its kind in South Africa. For the most part Verwoerd embraced the ideas of American sociologists dealing with the same topic that had occupied him for a long time: white poverty.

The Afrikaners' idea of themselves as an egalitarian frontier society long concealed the appearance of white poverty in South Africa as early as the late nineteenth century. The number of whites without their own land had increased in several phases, particularly after the South African War (1899–1902) and as a result of the Great Depression, until a considerable number of white families were eking out livings through casual work in a semi-nomadic existence. A five-volume investigation, entitled the *Carnegie Report* (after its sponsor), caused quite a stir when it appeared in 1932. The researchers who carried out the investigation were mainly from Stellenbosch University, and the author of the psychological report, R.W. Wilcocks, had supervised Verwoerd's Ph.D. thesis.

As a student, Verwoerd discovered white poverty, the lode star of his future academic and political career. He was inspired in this by Afrikaner nationalism, which up until the 1940s was mainly directed against the British Empire. According to statements by a former schoolmate, Verwoerd had followed the rise of the National Party with enthusiasm and a sympathetic eye as early as the age of sixteen.[29] His first publication, which the 19-year-old published in a student newsletter of his alma mater, dealt with white poverty. Shortly before, Verwoerd had visited the poor white suburbs of Woodstock and Salt River in Cape Town for the first time, and the distress he felt clearly had an impact on his report. He began with an ironic, though seriously meant, appeal to the patriotism of his readers: "Day after day, even hour after hour we hear people talking about patriotism, nationalism etc., but we really start to have doubts if these people have an idea about what love for the fatherland in the true sense of the word means."[30] He criticized white South Africans who did not care about the fate of the "poor whites" and he identified white poverty as the major problem of South African society and particularly of the Afrikaner "volk."

On taking up the chair of sociology approximately ten years later, Verwoerd returned to his old theme. Most of his lectures dealt directly with the "poor white problem" or closely related topics, such as juvenile delinquency.[31] This commitment to the cause reveals both Verwoerd's academic conception of himself as well as his racism.

In his sociology and social work lectures Verwoerd kept a conspicuous distance from eugenic theories and racist social technologies, emphasising environmental influences rather than hereditary abilities. In fact, the large number of poor whites offered little cause to make a Social Darwinistic argument.[32] As about a quarter of Afrikaners lived below the poverty line and theories linking impoverishment and anthropological degeneration were very popular in South Africa, the nationalist Verwoerd emphasized the dangers associated with this view, pointing out that environmental influences played a much greater role than heredity. The cause of white destitution lay in environmental factors and could be eradicated. He stressed that there was no significant connection between poverty and mental retrogression. Thus he also rejected the genetic theses that drew on Lamarck, according to whom acquired traits were passed on, as, in this case, was so-called "degeneration": "The question of possible transmittance of acquired psychic traces is still undecided. Therefore we have to draw the conclusion that the role of racial or ethnic traits which were once so much emphasised are physically and psychically unproven."[33] By contrast, Verwoerd argued that it was no coincidence that many underachievers and people with below average intelligence could be found among the poor whites, as they were the ones most likely to get caught up in the spiral of destitution. Low intelligence, in his view, helped cause poverty rather than resulted from it. He therefore aimed to transform the social environment of poor whites in a sustainable manner, in order to ensure that they would never sink into impoverishment again.

This was why he rejected charity as inadequate, criticizing the politicians' view that white poverty was solely a problem of unemployment and therefore a short-term consequence of the Depression. Rather, at issue was a highly complex set of conditions that thrust people into their wretched situation and kept them there. This is where the psychologist who had dealt with the blunting of emotions in his dissertation could come to the aid of the sociologist. Verwoerd stressed that miserable living conditions caused people to become emotionally blunted and physically lethargic. Furthermore, he claimed to be able to detect a typical sign of impoverishment in racial mixing, when whites lived cheek by jowl with the native African population in the poorer quarters of the cities. Here he thought mainly of Cape Town, which he knew particularly well. The hallmark of poverty was a loss of self-respect, which he diagnosed when whites and blacks transgressed the racial boundaries in their sexual behavior.[34]

Here only a comprehensive approach could bring a remedy, namely one that assessed the precise combination of factors in each individual situation that kept a family in poverty, in order to demonstrate a way out. And because he expressed his dissatisfaction with single and uncoordinated measures, striving instead for more fundamental changes, Verwoerd had to rely on help from the state. His strategy aimed at building up an educational system that could ensure once and for all that the children of poor whites would never fall into poverty again. To improve their chances, however, competition with low-paid and badly educated blacks in the job market had to be eliminated by privileging whites. This would become Verwoerd's main task as a nationalist politician in his later years.

A big conference on the problem of white poverty was held in Kimberley in 1934. Verwoerd, who was one of the principal organizers,[35] held the keynote address,[36] which introduced him to a broader public for the first time and attracted the attention of politicians. His speech contains several signs of his later politics, primarily his faith in a powerful state and the belief in planning and plannability, and demonstrates a thoroughly technocratic approach to social problems.

In the early 1930s the South African press lauded the Stellenbosch professor as one of the few who had developed a comprehensive, well-thought-out approach to solving the white poverty problems.[37] In the years that followed he was active as an assiduous lobbyist who urged the Minister of Labour to set up a separate Department of Social Welfare.[38] The sociologist Verwoerd did not wait for the opinions of politicians but became active himself. He led a follow-up committee to the Kimberley Conference, laying the cornerstone for its extension to an Institute for Social Welfare. This soon fell under the control of the Afrikaner nationalists and the secret organization of the Afrikaner Broederbond.[39] He was also active in other related organizations like "The Citizens Housing League Utility Company" of Cape Town and the Cape Town Charity Commission.[40] His rise to prominence and the involvement of intellectuals in relief work for poor whites "drew psychologists into the cause of Afrikaner nationalism and assisted in shaping racist ideology."[41] Even in the late 1940s just before he became a cabinet minister Verwoerd was still very much involved in social work, although then as a political lobbyist in parliament.[42]

Verwoerd's Racism

Verwoerd's rejection of "miscegenation" can be traced to his cultural racism. For him, biology—evident in skin color—determined cultural belonging. Consequently, "coloreds" as a "mixed race" population were seen as a special problem. Racist ideologues like Geoffrey Cronjé,[43] a professor of sociology at the University of Pretoria and an extreme right-wing political activist, alleged that "coloreds" showed a special disposition for alcoholism and psychological instability.[44] Verwoerd on the other hand never stated anything in this vein; for him the mixture of cultures was socially destabilizing.

Racial mixing was not the cause of social instability but its result. Based on his findings about poor whites, Verwoerd wrote in a National Party election pamphlet on race mixing: "Such marriages are mainly contracted by aliens who know no colour bar, by people who are sexually abnormal or mentally deficient or by degenerates who have long lived in close contact with non-Europeans."[45] Just as the white state, in its capacity as a trustee, had to protect Africans from themselves, so it had to protect the white race from its deficient members and racial mixing. Remarkably, for Verwoerd degeneration was not inherited but acquired during the lifetime of individuals.

When people of different races came together in their daily lives, conflict inevitably resulted: "The fundamental principles on which the policy of the Government is built is that nowhere in history or in present Africa has multi-racialism in any form or degree proved a success."[46] Verwoerd repeated his conviction again and again in his speeches as if it was a proven fact. Apartheid only made sense if the different cultures in South Africa were seen as fundamentally different and irreconcilable. He wrote to one of his critics that their government was convinced

that its policy is the only one which can ensure the preservation of Christianity in South Africa since it seeks to develop a situation in which both Bantu and White can be contented and prosperous and without the danger of one being absorbed by the other. It is their firm conviction that this was the divine purpose in bringing the White man to South Africa, namely to civilize and Christianise the black man and then to preserve this by ensuring the continued co-existence of both. The necessary steps to achieve this can be understood wrongly through lack of full knowledge of the facts as is clear in your case.[47]

This explains his later policy of "influx control," which aimed to keep the black population out of urban centers through use of the pass laws.[48] The towns and cities were meant for whites; Africans were supposed to develop their own urban structures out of their own cultural heritage in the homelands. In Verwoerd's eyes, the destabilization of family life, alcoholism, and criminality as well as the consequences of migrant labor and exploitation were the result of a cultural clash and unassimilability. To Verwoerd, urban racial segregation was only part of the solution and he ultimately aimed to return a large part of the black population to the rural regions. The rest, he argued, should lose their nationality when they became citizens of the homelands. Afterwards urban segregation could be legitimized as separate settlement of "foreigners." He directed specific enmity against the African-educated elite, because in his eyes these people were merely uprooted, looking for a place in society which was not theirs. In apartheid plans they were singled out as people who should be resettled into the homelands because they were not needed in the "white" cities. When they lived Western lifestyles and propagated African nationalism instead of an ethnic "Bantu" identity, they were nothing but "traitors to their own people," according to Verwoerd.[49] This shows clearly that to him cultural and ethnic communities were the fundamental social units. He never problematized them as a sociologist, but rather took them as given. In other countries even racial theoreticians could not avoid the conclusion that no pure nations existed. For this reason, they viewed race as an abstract construct that they used in order to identify empirically racial contributions and proportions within single peoples.[50] In contrast, Verwoerd always deferred to the nation as the main unit, with racial segregation deemed a means to an end: the conservation of Afrikaner nationhood. One of his political opponents called it a "kind of racial and superiority nationalism."[51]

Verwoerd's ideas clearly went beyond the welfare state since he foresaw the need for intensive intervention in the private sphere of the poor whites to help them out of poverty. His interest in a powerful state can also be found in his research into juvenile crime, whose traces can be found in a series of authoritarian re-education measures that he later planned as Minister.[52] This exposes a further essential feature of Verwoerdian politics, namely its totalitarian scope. In terms of Verwoerd's integral nationalism, the individual was only a part of a greater whole, someone who should fit into and be of service to the community.[53] This justified authoritarian control through state officials. The paternalism that caringly turned its attention to the poor whites was essentially no different from the cold bureaucratic control of the pass laws that restricted the freedom of movement of Africans.

It is striking that Verwoerd's interest in the literature of biological determinism and racial theory was rather peripheral, playing an insignificant role in his sociological argumentation. Nonetheless, Verwoerd's lectures and writings at this stage already revealed his racism, though he argued culturally and ethnically rather than according to biological determinism.

In his sociology lectures Verwoerd presented an evolutionist approach in the form of a cultural-historical theory of phases. Accordingly, this theory not only inexorably trapped the so-called primitives in religious-magical thinking but also afforded them only a rudimentary division of labor.[54] Alongside this, especially after he started in earnest with his "homeland" policy in 1959, he also subscribed to a cultural-relativistic model in which the black population did not constitute a lower stage in the progression of civilization. Instead, black South Africans were part of a completely different civilization, one largely incompatible with the West. Very often, though, both models were used at the same time, without Verwoerd or other proponents being aware of their inherent contradictions.

Verwoerd adopted the findings of contemporary ethnology transmitted to him by Werner Eiselen, his colleague at Stellenbosch University and later his Secretary of Native Affairs. For Verwoerd the idea of hermetically sealed cultures would always be linked to race. In his extensive correspondence, he repeatedly doubted that Africans would ever be in a position "to develop along their own lines." Officially he proclaimed his policy of "separate development" as offering a fair chance to everybody:

> The policy of South Africa is not one of suppression but of separating people who are so very different as the Whites and the Blacks. Besides colour, the mental differences, traditions and culture are so different that there is far more justification for separate States to be created here than between the English and the Dutch and the Germans or the French and the Swiss and the Belgiums [sic], or the various nations of Slovakian [sic] origins in Europe. This is all that 'Apartheid' or separate development means, namely the gradual development of separate nations on their own and in their own areas.[55]

In order to understand Verwoerd's position, it is necessary to describe the notion of racism more precisely. A minimal definition of racism could describe it as the causal linkage of biology and culture. In this context racial theorists more involved with the population to which they themselves belong reveal a tendency to emphasize the biological side. This is why they advocate eugenic means to curb what they perceive as decadence and degeneration within their own nation. On the other hand, theorists tracing the identity of their own population through difference and alterity by drawing boundaries against other population groups place culture in the foreground. This second explanation, with its emphasis on population groups as cultural units that can also be biologically distinguished from other groups, usually through skin color, appears mainly in the colonial context. In its practical application it aims at racial segregation to conserve one's own population group as a cultural entity. Nevertheless, even when the argument is mainly cultural, biology remains decisive, because both are causally linked. The fact that Verwoerd saw whites and blacks as belonging to different cultures was not in itself racist, but his perception of each as captive to these cultures was.

Verwoerd belonged to the second group, since he wanted to conserve his own Afrikaner culture through segregation.[56] The national socialists in Germany on the other hand were part of the first group, because they aimed at the inner purity of the Germanic race. They wanted to achieve this by racial hygienic and eugenic measures against so-called intruders and "parasites." Even today, many Germans still conceive of Jewish Germans in ethnic rather than religious terms, seeing them as a different people. Verwoerd's anti-Semitism, which he revealed most clearly in his first article in the daily newspaper *Die Transvaler*, a paper he edited from 1937–48, indicates that he did not always fit squarely into the culturalist group.[57] Yet in the context of his later apartheid policy cultural racism proved decisive.

The composition of the South African population kept Verwoerd away from eugenics. The fact that the whites constituted a minority encouraged him to favor a social-technocratic solution rather than a biological-technocratic one. It also kept him from biological determinism in his justifications and it explains why his statements on apartheid from 1948 onwards contained virtually no direct references to race or racial theories. Since he wanted to conceal the social-technocratic nature of his measures, he had to find another explanation. Therefore he used an essentialist cultural relativism that saw people's social practices and behavior as rooted in their culture. Accordingly, Verwoerd the sociologist only went half way, because he dropped the sociological argument when he made assumptions about the irreconcilable cultural differences between white and black. He came to believe that whites would be driven towards destitution due to competition from cheap black labor, a point he analyzed sociologically only in part, attributing it to essential cultural differences. Verwoerd instrumentalized ethnology where others used biological determinism. This was why his solution was not eugenics but racial discrimination, not sterilization and breeding but a technocratic transformation of South African society according to ethnic principles.

Science and Politics

Verwoerd's understanding of social science can also explain his cultural racism and simultaneous distance to genetic theories. Social Darwinism had given a teleological twist to Darwin's theory of the mechanisms of selection and adaptation through its discussion of degeneration or enhancement through breeding.[58] By starting from unproven basic assumptions, proponents of the various forms of Social Darwinism always argued deductively. The more self-critical amongst them perceived the lack of an empirical basis as a desideratum, but certainly not as a deficit. In fact, eugenicists, like protagonists of other racial theories, remained captive to circular arguments when they constructed a causal linkage of social observations to biological assumptions.

Verwoerd, on the other hand, remained true to an inductive, positivist way of thinking. Miller alleges that Verwoerd's methodology improved remarkably after his stays in Germany and the United Sates. The evidence does not support this, because to him introspection remained the most important method. Although it was regarded as outdated in European psychology, Verwoerd clung to and even propagated it in some of his publications. For him, introspection was a method for collecting data during serial tests that could be treated as objective facts.[59] In its practical implementation positivism has always proved conservative and committed to the existing order. Verwoerd combined his marked hostility towards theory with the idea that the right explanation for reality would emerge as soon as enough data had been collected. Thus he favored disseminating statistical material in his lectures, announcing to his students that in a three-year BA course in industrial sociology two and a half years would be devoted to the techniques of data-gathering and only half a year to the theories underpinning it.[60]

Right up until his years as prime minister, Verwoerd derided theories in various contexts, and especially people whom he considered mere theoreticians. Among the latter were clearly those who supported the rights of the black majority. Thus it was to his advantage that the "theoretical human being" had already been categorized in his 1925 lectures as its own character type, therefore making it thoroughly predictable. Likewise, he rejected well-meaning critics of his policies in much-repeated catchphrases, maintaining that they could only have arrived at their opinions because they did not have the necessary facts.

Conversely, whoever had the necessary facts would automatically come to the same conclusion as himself, Hendrik Verwoerd, for in his research he always assumed the existence of an objective truth only kept concealed by unknown facts: "I only wish to point out that where criticism in the newspapers often leads people to accept a certain view-point, this cannot often be retained when the full facts become known to them."[61] Hendrik Verwoerd, a workaholic and maniac for facts was firmly convinced that he possessed this knowledge. He would rail against those who criticized certain aspects of his policies in schoolmasterly fashion, regularly pointing out that they did not know the "true facts." So he lectured the Fédération Internationale des Droits de l'Homme, who had dared to criticize his authoritarian politics, that his government "is best able to judge ... because it has all the facts at its disposal, which is not the case with organisations who have been incited by interested parties to take part in an agitation against the Government's carefully considered decision."[62] He insinuated that there was an objective truth, which those who stuck to the true facts would be able to recognize without difficulty. Whoever still refused to share his opinion could only be ideologically blinded, or plain pigheaded—making further dialogue unnecessary. Verwoerd believed in this form of politics, free from opinions and oriented to the truth, and from it he drew his distinctive missionary zeal. This inspired him to push through his policies against all odds. It also allowed him to be totally unflinching in his choice of means.

Verwoerd began as a psycho-technician and developed into a technocratic politician. A continuous line leads from his attempts to create and measure emotions in the laboratory via the assignment of people to certain character types to the politics of apartheid.[63] On the basis of his ethnological presumptions and sociological research he assumed the necessity of fundamentally restructuring society in order to preserve the identity of the white race on the southern tip of Africa. As a result of his unwavering belief in an objective truth, the product of his positivism, Verwoerd developed a type of substitute theory in which the real secret of his political success presumably lay, namely his logic. One of his political opponents, Japie Basson, wrote in his memoirs that it was impossible to prove Verwoerd wrong on account of his clear logic. To achieve this, one would have had to examine the premises of his thinking much more meticulously.[64] For a positivist like Verwoerd, dialectic thinking was as accessible as the far side of the moon. He was and remained an advocate of formal logic. In his dissertation he had already shown a conspicuous eagerness to arrive at non-contradictory statements and conceptualizations. The conviction that the world was logically ordered and without contradictions fuelled his search for pure and clear concepts. The only problem lay in recognizing this order. Thus, when contradictions arose, they could not have been from the real situation but rather must have resulted from terminology unable to adequately depict the truth. In his dissertation, as in one of his few published essays,[65] he invested a great deal of energy in the development of precise terminology. These endeavors are all the more striking, since it never occurred to Verwoerd that the human psyche in its complexity could contain contradictions. His obsession with dividing the world into concepts, people into types, and the psyche into clearly distinguishable areas reveals an affinity for essentialist ideas of ethnicity. Strikingly, he never, not even partially, questioned the concept of organic communities. Verwoerd presumed he was depicting the true picture of the world by developing his watertight categories and following his belief that the absence of contradictions constituted the logical order of the inner world of the human psyche just as it shaped the outer world of human society. As a result he was predestined to legitimize the politics of apartheid as a justifiable and natural necessity. The purity of principles as an essential feature of his thinking could be easily extended to the purity of races and the nation. Thus, contrary to Miller's thesis that Verwoerd changed political direction out of opportunism, and to Moodie's contention that he had a Damascus experience in Germany, one can recognize a basic continuity in Verwoerd's thinking. The orientation to the state, the striving towards totalitarian measures—which did not stop at the private sphere—the faith in planning, and the resultant technocratic access to politics, as well as the reduction of reality to social categories and the belief in objective truth, characterized Verwoerd both as an academic and a politician.

This indeed allows for a comparison of Verwoerd with ideologues of all sorts, and permits one to identify him as a representative of the "age of extremes," as Eric Hobsbawm named the twentieth century. The belief in historical laws, objective truths, and the conviction that it was possible to plan and implement completely new social orders marked this era.[66] Verwoerd did not want to create a new human being with the help of eugenics but to establish a new society whose essential feature was ethnic-racial segregation through political-technocratic action. This substantiates once again that national socialist racial ideologies did not influence apartheid to a noteworthy extent. Verwoerd was a "white revolutionary" in both senses of the word: of the revolution in the original meaning of "turning back," understood as the reestablishment of a golden age, of an imaginary world of clear ethnic categories, of an unspoilt world of separate nations which included that of the black ethnos. At the same time this way of thinking and acting was modern, apartheid was an authoritarian modernization of state and society. Thus he was convinced that he was acting rightly, establishing a just order for all through his politics.

Notes

1. Christoph Marx, "Siedlerkolonien in Afrika - Versuch einer Typologie," in *Rassenmischehen – Mischlinge – Rassentrennung: Zur Politik der Rasse im deutschen Kolonialreich*, edited by Frank Becker (Stuttgart, 2004), 82–96.
2. George M. Fredrickson, *White Supremacy: A Comparative Study in American and South African History* (New York, 1981), 250.
3. Jürgen Heideking, *Geschichte der USA* (Tübingen, 1996), 214.
4. Japie Basson, *Politieke kaarte op die tafel: Parlementêre en ander herinneringe* (Cape Town, 2006), 113.
5. Dioné Prinsloo, *Die Johannesburg-periode in Dr H.F. Verwoerd se loopbaan* (Ph.D. diss., Rand Afrikaans University, Johannesburg 1979 and Prinsloo 1981).
6. Alexander Hepple, *Verwoerd* (Harmondsworth, 1967); Gert Daniel Scholtz, *Dr Hendrik Frensch Verwoerd, 1901–1966*, 2 vols. (Johannesburg, 1974); Henry Kenney, *Architect of Apartheid - H.F. Verwoerd: An Appraisal* (Johannesburg, 1980).
7. T. Dunbar Moodie, *The Rise of Afrikanerdom: Power, Apartheid and the Afrikaner Civil Religion* (Berkeley, 1975), 154.
8. Patrick Furlong, *Between Crown and Swastika: The Impact of the Radical Right on the Afrikaner Nationalist Movement in the Fascist Era* (Johannesburg, 1991), 80.
9. Roberta B. Miller, "Science and Society in the Early Career of H.F. Verwoerd," *Journal of Southern African Studies* 19, no. 4 (1993): 660.
10. Christoph Marx, *Im Zeichen des Ochsenwagens: Der radikale Afrikaaner-Nationalismus in Südafrika und die Geschichte der Ossewabrandwag* (Münster, 1998), 202.
11. Hendrik Verwoerd, *Die afstomping van die gemoedsaandoeninge* (Ph.D. diss., Stellenbosch University, 1924). See also Hendrik Verwoerd, "A Method for the

Experimental Production of Emotions," *The American Journal of Psychology* 37 (1926): 357–371.

12. Hugo Münsterberg, *Psychologie und Wirtschaftsleben* (1912; repr., Weinheim, 1997), 21.

13. Peter Hinrichs, *Um die Seele des Arbeiters: Arbeitspsychologie, Industrie- und Betriebssoziologie in Deutschland* (Köln, 1981), 125.

14. Monika Schubeius, *Und das psychologische Laboratorium muss der Ausgangspunkt pädagogischer Arbeiten werden! Zur Institutionalisierungsgeschichte der Psychologie von 1890–1933* (Frankfurt, 1990); Friedrich Dorsch, *Geschichte und Probleme der angewandten Psychologie* (Bern, 1963), 88.

15. Gerald Bühring, *William Stern oder Streben nach Einheit* (Frankfurt, 1996); Norbert Kleinefeld, *Wiederentdeckung der Ganzheit: Zur Bedeutung idealistischer Ganzheitsansätze im Deutschen Reich am Ende des 19. Jahrhunderts und zum Begriff der Ganzheit bei William Stern* (Oldenburg, 1997); Helmut Moser, "Zur Entwicklung der akademischen Psychologie in Hamburg bis 1945: Eine Kontrast-Skizze als Würdigung des vergessenen Erbes von William Stern," in *Hochschulalltag im "Dritten Reich": Die Hamburger Universität 1933–1945. Teil II: Philosophische Fakultät, Rechts- und Staatswissenschaftliche Fakultät*, edited by Eckart Krause, Ludwig Huber, and Holger Fischer (Berlin, 1991), 487–92.

16. Ulfried Geuter, *Die Professionalisierung der deutschen Psychologie im Nationalsozialismus* (Frankfurt, 1988), 148.

17. Siegfried Jäger, "Wolfgang Köhler in Berlin," in *Zur Geschichte der Psychologie in Berlin*, edited by Lothar Sprung and Wolfgang Schönpflug (Frankfurt, 1992); Siegfried Jäger, "Wolfgang Köhler," in *Illustrierte Geschichte der Psychologie*, edited by Helmut E. Lück and Rudolf Miller (Weinheim, 2005).

18. Lothar Sprung and Helga Sprung, "Die Berliner Schule der Gestaltpsychologie," in *Illustrierte Geschichte der Psychologie*; Martin Leichtman, "Gestalt Theory and the Revolt against Positivism," in *Psychology in Social Context*, edited by Allan R. Buss (New York, 1979), 59, 67; Edwin G. Boring, *A History of Experimental Psychology* (Englewood Cliffs, NJ, 1950), 587.

19. Dorsch, *Geschichte und Probleme der angewandten Psychologie*, 70.

20. This becomes evident in an article by Hans Volkelt, one of Krüger's collaborators and certainly the one who was ideologically closest to the extreme right wing. He explicitly draws the connection between the holistic approach of the Leipzig psychologists and the idea of "Volksgemeinschaft." See Volkelt, *Über die Forschungsrichtung des Psychologischen Instituts, Literarische Berichte a.d. Gebiet der Philosophie* 6 (1925): 14, Philosophische Fakultät, No. B1/14:37, vol. 1, Psychologisches Institut, 1911, 1925, 1931–41, Leipzig University Archive; Albert Wellek, *Die Wiederherstellung der Seelenwissenschaft im Lebenswerk Felix Krügers* (Hamburg, 1950), 20; Steffi Hammer, "Felix Krueger," in *Illustrierte Geschichte der Psychologie*.

21. Adolf Ehrhardt, "Typus," in *Wege zur Ganzheitspsychologie*, ed. Otto Klemm, 2nd rev. ed. (München, 1954).

22. Hendrik Verwoerd, "Eerste jaar Sociologie: Algemene kursus" (Lecture notes, Stellenbosch University), 22, PV 231/2/1/2, Verwoerd Collection, Archive for Contemporary Affairs, University of the Free State, Bloemfontein, South Africa (hereafter cited as Verwoerd Collection).
23. Peter Hinrichs, *Um die Seele des Arbeiters*, 208.
24. See Verwoerd's notes on lectures and books (1932), PV 93/1/33/3, Verwoerd Collection.
25. Ernst Kretschmer, *Körperbau und Charakter: Untersuchungen zum Konstitutionsproblem und zur Lehre von den Temperamenten*, 3rd ed. (Berlin, 1922), 14.
26. Hendrik Verwoerd, "Oor die opstel van objektiewe persoonlikheidsbepalingskemas," *South African Journal of Science* 27 (1930): 583.
27. Hendrik Verwoerd, "'n Bydrae tot die metodiek en probleemstellings vir die psigologiese ondersoek van koerante-advertensies," *South African Journal of Science* 25 (1928): 469–80.
28. Hendrik Verwoerd, "The Distribution of 'Attention' and its Testing," *The Journal of Applied Psychology* 12, no. 5 (1928): 495–510; Hendrik Verwoerd, "Effects of Fatigue on the Distribution of Attention," *The Journal of Applied Psychology* 12, no. 6 (1928); Saul Dubow, *Scientific racism in modern South Africa* (Cambridge, 1995), 230.
29. J.F.J. van Rensburg to Hendrik Verwoerd, September 1958 PV 93/1/11/5, Verwoerd Collection. In this letter congratulating Verwoerd for becoming Prime Minister, van Rensburg identified himself as a classmate from Brandfort and reminded Verwoerd: "Hoe intens was ons jong penkoppe se belangstelling in die tussenverkiesing van 1917 te Calvinia waar Dr Malan teen Sen. Conroy gestaan het en met 80 stemme verslaan is" (How intensely we were interested as youngsters in the by-election of 1917 in Calvinia, when Dr Malan stood against Sen. Conroy and lost with 80 votes).
30. Hendrik Verwoerd, "Die veragterdes in ons midde," *Stellenbosch University Magazine* 21, no. 4 (1920): 123.
31. O. Wagner, "Prof. Dr. H.F. Verwoerd," *Die Stellenbossche Oudstudent* 7, no. 1 (1937): 10. See Verwoerd's lecture notes, and "Armoede en sy bestriding" and "Sociopsigologie van misdaad" (Lecture manuscripts, Stellenbosch University), PV 231/2/4/1 and PV 231/2/3, Verwoerd Collection. Verwoerd applied for funding for a research project on "Crime and Punishment in South Africa." See his proposal in PV 93/1/33/1, Verwoerd Collection. The Research Grants Board refused the application in 1929. See Saul Dubow, *A Commonwealth of Knowledge: Science, Sensibility, and White South Africa, 1820–2000* (Oxford, 2006), 232.
32. See Johann Louw, "Social Context and Psychological Testing in South Africa, 1918–1939," *Theory & Psychology* 7, no 2. (1997): 251.
33. Verwoerd, "Eerste jaar Sociologie: Algemene kursus," 26.
34. Verwoerd, "Die veragterdes in ons midde," 124.
35. Correspondence, notes, and memoranda on the Congress and the follow-up committee, PV 93/1/67, Verwoerd Collection.

36. Hendrik Verwoerd, "Die bestryding van armoede en die herorganisasie van wel-vaartswerk," in *Verslag van die volkskongres oor die Armblanke-vragstuk gehou te Kimberley 2 tot 5 Okt. 1934*, edited by P. Du Toit (Cape Town, 1934), 30–40.

37. Collection of newspaper clippings, mostly undated (1932–35), PV 93/1/29/3, Ver-woerd Collection.

38. Correspondence with the Department of Labour and Memoranda on the poor white problem (1932–35), PV 93/1/29/2, Verwoerd Collection. See Erika Theron and A.A. Stulting, *Maatskaplike dienste in Suid-Afrika* (Stellenbosch, 1961), 25f.

39. Meeting of a group of delegates of the follow-up committee with the Minister of Labour on 26 February 1935, notes, PV 93/1/67/6, doc. 36, Verwoerd Collection. Verwoerd was the main speaker of the delegation.

40. Kaapstadt se Liefdadigheidskommissie (January 1933), 53–55, PV 93/1/19/1, Ver-woerd Collection; Behuisingsbond (1936), PV 93/1/5/1, doc. 39, Verwoerd Collection; Behuisingskonferensie (1934–1937), PV 93/1/6/1, Verwoerd Collec-tion. The latter comprise various papers related to a conference on slums.

41. Don Foster, "Race and Racism in South African Psychology," *South African Jour-nal of Psychology* 21 (1991): 205.

42. Armesorgraad (1948–50), PV 93/1/4, Verwoerd Collection. On Verwoerd's in-volvement in charity organisations and social work cf. Erika Theron, *H.F. Verwoerd as welsynbeplanner 1932–1936* (Stellenbosch, 1970).

43. Dirk van Zyl Smit, "Adopting and adapting criminological ideas. Criminology and Afrikaner nationalism in South Africa," *Contemporary Crises* 13 (1989): 229.

44. John M. Coetzee, "Apartheid thinking," *Giving Offense. Essays on Censorship* (Chicago, 1996): 171.

45. Hendrik Verwoerd, *Look at the Facts about mixed marriages* [1947] (National Party, [1947]).

46. Hendrik Verwoerd to D. Green, 18 September 1963, Aug–Sept. 1963, PV 93/1/30/1/22, Verwoerd Collection.

47. Hendrik Verword to Miss Olive Warner, 26 June 1959, April–June 1959, PV 93/3/1/23, doc. 178, Verwoerd Collection.

48. Deborah Posel, *The Making of Apartheid, 1948–1961: Conflict and Compromise* (Oxford: 1997).

49. A.N. Pelzer, ed. *Verwoerd aan die woord. Toesprake 1948–1962* (Johannesburg, 1963), 12.

50. Stefan Kühl, *Die Internationale der Rassisten: Aufstieg und Niedergang der interna-tionalen Bewegung für Eugenik und Rassenhygiene im 20. Jahrhundert* (Frankfurt, 1997), 70.

51. Basson, *Politieke kaarte op die tafel*, 102.

52. He planned to establish work camps for *tsotsis*, young black criminals, see PV 276/I/17/1, Verwoerd Collection.

53. Marx, *Im Zeichen des Ochsenwagens*, 194.

54. Verwoerd, "Eerste jaar Sociologie: Algemene kursus," 10. He refers to the German psychologist Hellpach and his theories about geographical and climatic influences on cultural development. See ibid., 19.

55. Hendrik Verwoerd to John McKenzie, 10 November 1964, 1964–65, PV 93/1/30/1/29, doc. 5, Verwoerd Collection.

56. Although some South African psychologists did research on differences in abilities between blacks and whites, especially in the field of intelligence testing, Verwoerd never displayed any marked interest. The ethnologist Werner Eiselen, who became his Secretary of Native Affairs in later years, even doubted the results. See his preface to M. Laurence Fick, *The Educability of the South African Native* (Pretoria, 1939). Verwoerd himself was skeptical of the results of intelligence testing because it neglected a number of variables. See Verwoerd, "Eerste jaar Sociologie: Algemene kursus," 25.

57. "Die Joodse Vraagstuk," *Die Transvaler,* 1 October 1937. See also Milton Shain, *The Roots of Antisemitism in South Africa* (Johannesburg, 1994), 146.

58. Peter Weingart, Jürgen Kroll, and Kurt Bayertz, *Rasse, Blut und Gene: Geschichte der Eugenik und Rassenhygiene in Deutschland* (Frankfurt, 1992), 76.

59. Verwoerd, "The Distribution of 'Attention' and its testing"; Verwoerd, "'n Bydrae tot die metodiek en probleemstellings vir die psigologiese ondersoek van koerante-advertensies"; Verwoerd, *Die afstomping van die gemoedsaandoeninge.* See Hendrik Verwoerd, "Metodes van sociologiese navorsing" (Lecture manuscript, Stellenbosch University), PV 231/2/2, Verwoerd Collection.

60. Hendrik Verwoerd, "Inleiding tot die Sociologie," (Lecture manuscript, Stellenbosch University), 3, PV 231/2/1/1, Verwoerd Collection.

61. Hendrik Verwoerd to Mrs R.A. Budd, 13 March 1962, PV 93/3/1/5, Verwoerd Collection.

62. Hendrik Verwoerd to Fédération Internationale des Droits de l'Homme, 7 November 1959, PV 93/3/1/25, Verwoerd Collection.

63. Verwoerd, "A Method for the Experimental Producation of Emotions."

64. Japie Basson, *Raam en rigting in die politiek: En die storie van Apartheid* (Cape Town, 2004), 146.

65. Hendrik Verwoerd, "Oor die persoonlikheid van die mens en die beskrywing daarvan," *South African Journal of Science* 27 (1930): 577–80.

66. James C. Scott, *Seeing Like a Stat:. How Certain Schemes to Improve the Human Condition Have Failed* (New Haven, 1998).

Chapter 14

The "Right Kind of White People": Reproducing Whiteness in the United States and Australia, 1780s–1930s

Gregory D. Smithers

Writing in the annual report of the Department of Indian Affairs for 1900, Joseph Hall, the principal of the Coqualeetza Industrial Institute in British Columbia, praised the educational progress of indigenous children under his charge.[1] Like so many of his contemporaries in the British Empire and the United States, Hall devoted himself to the task of transforming the world's purportedly "doomed" Aboriginal children into civilized adults.[2] The key to "civilizing" Aboriginal children, Hall instructed, was to have indigenous and white children interact from a young age. In Hall's words, "the more our [Indian] children are brought into contact with the right kind of white people, the better it is for them, and the more sympathy is felt for them, and for the work which we are striving to do."[3]

Hall's emphasis on "the right kind of white people" reveals as much about the late nineteenth- and early twentieth-century racialization of "Indian" reform efforts as it does about the construction of whiteness and the extension of settler colonial civilization. In settler colonies such as Canada, British East Africa, South Africa, the United States, and Australia, whiteness was imagined as both a powerful and fragile human category. This dual and contradictory construction of whiteness reflected how white settler colonial identities became entwined in the same transnational racial discourses that defined and redefined "blackness," "redness," and myriad other racial designations after the eighteenth-century Enlightenment.[4] At stake in the transnational debates that missionaries, scholars, and political leaders conducted was the viability of Western civilization in far-flung and expanding settler colonies. Of great importance to the participants in these debates was the reproduction of "the right kind of white people." After surveying the scholarship on "whiteness," this chapter focuses on the racial construction of white identity in the United States and Australia between the 1780s and 1930s. A chronological and geographical analysis of this nature provides a glimpse into how different English-speaking settler colonies shared, and ultimately applied, racial ideologies in different ways to define "the right kind of people."

The Historiography of Whiteness

The historical study of whiteness in colonies of settlement has focused on white identity as a "signifier of power."[5] Scholars of the United States and Australia, such as David Roediger, Matthew Frye Jacobson, Ian F. Haney-Lopez, and Warwick Anderson, have demonstrated the importance of labor relations, immigration patterns, legal definitions, and advances in tropical medicine to definitions of whiteness. The majority of these scholars observe that over the course of the eighteenth, nineteenth, and twentieth centuries, European immigrants—or "white ethnics"—improved their socio-economic standing in settler societies by coalescing around a white identity. This identity represented an oppositional marker to the "dark smudge" of enslaved blacks, Chinese and Indian coolies, Polynesian plantation laborers, and purportedly transient indigenous tribes.[6] Whiteness therefore constituted an identity that was defined in relation to the socio-economic mobility, political power, and disease environments which European immigrants and settlers colonized.[7]

Settler colonies like the United States and Australia have never been racially and ethnically homogenous spaces. The imperial drive to acquire land rich in mineral resources, establish plantation agriculture, and for European settlers, aspire to a life of social and economic independence, resulted in whiteness being invested with different degrees of social, economic, and political power.[8] At the same time, the kaleidoscope of racial and ethnic groups that settler colonial expansion brought together prompted political leaders to draw from different racial ideologies to structure political and geographical space, thereby differentiating the powerful from the powerless. In the American South, for instance, political participation involved the creation of a space reserved for a select few educated and financially independent white men—"the right kind of white people"—at the expense of poor whites and Southern blacks.[9]

Defining whiteness according to political participation and economic independence did not always provide a clear map of who was and was not entitled to the socio-economic and political privileges associated with whiteness. The ordering of geographical space during the nineteenth century was designed to provide a clearer racial mapping of whiteness and white privilege. From Montgomery, Alabama, to Sydney, Australia, the architects of settler colonialism ordered space along racial lines.[10] Closely related to the ordering of physical space was the concern of settler colonial officials, community leaders, and family patriarchs for the reproductive health of white women. Of particular concern to white patriarchs was the perceived threat posed to white women from the "black male rapist."[11] By the early twentieth century, white men in the United States and Australia had anointed themselves the protectors of white "purity" and the chivalrous guardians of domestic spheres in which white women would reproduce and nurture future generations of the white race.[12]

The anxiety that European settlers expressed as they attempted to establish and reproduce settler colonial societies across the continents of North America and Australia has provided cultural analysts and historians with ample scope to emphasize the cultural significance of whiteness as a "signifier of power." Rebecca Aanerud, Ruth Frankenburg, and Richard Dyer, for example, have argued that the power of whiteness is reflected in the way that it evades racial definition. Accordingly, whiteness is "empty or absent," lacks "content," is "unmarked" and, as Jennifer Morgan has argued of the English Caribbean in the seventeenth century, was stabilized by images of black women as either lascivious or grotesque.[13] Such analysis reinforces the findings of scholars of labor, immigration, and law, and historians of science through its characterization of whiteness as an oppositional category. In other words, whiteness exists only where a racialized "other" is present to enslave, to caricature, to perform medical and anthropological experiments on, and, as Patrick Wolfe has argued, to "eliminate" from land coveted by European settlers.[14] This vast literature has provided some original and thoughtful insights into white identity in British and formerly British settler colonies. Still, the questions of just who "the right kind of white people" were, and how such white people were reproduced culturally and biologically requires further historical investigation. In the final analysis, the architects of settler colonies tended to believe that the societies they were helping to create would not endure without the reproduction of a population that had a clear set of shared racial and cultural ideals.

Cultivating Whiteness in the American Republic

The 1780s witnessed the birth of the republic of the United States and the founding of a British colony on the southeastern coast of Australia. These two events were not unrelated, as British defeat in the American Revolutionary War prompted an urgent search for a new imperial frontier where convicts could safely be deposited and confined to an open-air prison far from the British metropole.[15] Both the United States and Australia therefore sprang from the Revolutionary convulsions in the Atlantic World during the 1770s and 1780s. The United States and Australia were also the products of British cultural, social, and economic roots, and had the "Anglo-Saxon" re-writing of history at the core of a white racial identity. Historians typically date the Anglo-Saxon re-writing of political history to the first half of the nineteenth century.[16] However, as early as 1771 political philosophers, such as William Smith, linked Anglo-Saxon government with whiteness and justice. Smith claimed that in Saxon England "there is mention of the *whites,* or *wise men,* ... [who were] judges, or men learned in the law."[17] By the 1830s and 1840s, the conviction that the "glorious institutions of our Anglo-Saxon ancestors" gave law and order to the United States and Australia became central to white racial and sexual identity.[18] Whiteness, though, was far from a rigid, unchanging, and monolithic racial identity with roots in the mist of "Anglo-Saxon" ancestry.[19]

British Americans forged an independent republic in the 1780s on the back of military success over the British. In spite of a new constitution and a beloved president, George Washington, the leaders of the American Revolution and early republic worried about the type of society that they now had sole political responsibility for. This anxiety, the historian Gordon Wood has written, led to a call for virtue, honor, and public displays of morality, qualities that would define republican citizenship in the United States.[20] The political leaders of the early republic turned to John Locke, one of England's greatest political and social theorists, to craft the ideological parameters of a virtuous citizenry and give meaning to Anglo-Saxon whiteness in the early American republic.

Locke's *Some Thoughts Concerning Education* (1693) proved to be a highly influential guide to the United States' literate elite as it provided lessons on how the masses might cultivate the qualities of virtue and personal morality. Locke referred to virtue and morality as character traits belonging to gentlemen of "good breeding," defined as not merely the outer appearance of virtue, but the cultivation of inner moral character. To cultivate the inner qualities of good breeding, he instructed that young children be taught to discipline their passions. As children grew into young adulthood and attained mastery over their violent and carnal impulses, careful observation of the social customs and etiquette of society should be encouraged. Locke believed that travel abroad offered the best opportunity for young gentlemen to hone those inner qualities of moral self-restraint and usefulness to society.[21]

Thomas Jefferson, the third president of the United States, epitomized the American elites' commitment to the Lockean principles of good breeding.[22] To ensure that white citizens became useful members of the republic, Jefferson proposed a three-tiered system of education. At the elementary level, he suggested three years of free education in which students learned the rudiments of reading, writing, and arithmetic. The second level involved a grammar school curriculum. Here students honed language skills, expanded their geographical knowledge of the world, and mastered mathematics. The final level of education involved a combination of college instruction, where scientific skills deemed useful to society were learned, and the future leaders of the United States traveled abroad and cultivated an ease of manner that would make conversation with foreign dignitaries pleasurable.[23]

Jefferson did not design his educational system to ensure socio-economic equality between all white Americans. Instead, he envisioned American whiteness being divided into gradations, each man performing those tasks best fitted to his educational level and deemed useful to society as a whole. In addition, Jefferson counseled that each man in American society must select his marriage partner wisely, thereby preserving the stability of the social order and ensuring the happiness of future generations of white citizens. In an October 1813 letter to John Adams, Jefferson instructed that "the organs and desires of coition have not been given by God to man for the sake of pleasure, but for the procreation of the race."[24] Jefferson thus believed that the peopling of the American republic with "the right kind of white people" involved a combination of education, sexual reproduction within marriage, and a strict adherence to the boundaries of class.[25]

However, reproducing the different classes of "the right kind of white people" in the United States was complicated by the expansive geographical nature of republican settler colonialism. Like other global sites of settler expansion, the nineteenth-century United States bore witness to rapid, and often aggressive, territorial expansion. Such expansion involved scientific expeditions; missionary efforts to convert the "native" to Christianity and bourgeois standards of morality and virtue; the "elimination" of Aboriginal peoples so that Europeans could survey, squat on, fence in, and settle "unoc-cupied" lands; and the extension of coerced forms of labor, including racial slavery.[26] What Thomas Jefferson, like so many of the architects of global set-tler colonialism understood, was that the relative strength or weakness of settler colonial cultures, political systems, and economic structures relied as much on the reproduction of a virtuous white body politic, comprising use-ful classes of citizens, as it did on the containment and exploitation of wilderness spaces and destruction of indigenous cultures and peoples.[27]

Settler colonialism in the United States created and reproduced, as much as it destroyed, new cultures and peoples. Just as racialist and exploitative motives helped to rationalize the removal of Aboriginal peoples from their ancestral lands and justify the coerced labor of African, Asian, and Poly-nesian peoples, so did the creation and reproduction of new cultures and "the right kind of white people" prove equally portentous to non-European races. In the early republic, the federal government adopted a policy of "ex-pansion with honor" towards Native Americans. For men like Jefferson, "expansion with honor" involved the extension of a uniquely virtuous American culture and social structure in which moral European and in-digenous peoples intermixed to create a harmonious republic that extended from the Atlantic to the Pacific. Jefferson thus speculated that American settlers and Native Americans should "harmonize as much as possible in matters which they must necessarily transact together."[28]

Jefferson's speculations on the mixing of European settlers and Native Americans rested on the assumption that the most virtuous individuals from each race amalgamated cultures and reproduced new generations of Americans within marriage. Early nineteenth-century missionaries worked hard to make such speculation a reality, encouraging indigenous Ameri-cans, particularly "half-breeds," to adopt Christianity, and bequeath a Western cultural, economic, and political way of life to future generations of progressively lighter-skinned Native Americans. The monogenesis and evolutionary ethnological theories of James Cowles Pritchard, a dedicated English abolitionist and advocate of indigenous rights, helped to shape mis-sionary work. Pritchard's encyclopedic ethnological writings were inspired by the reformist zeal of trans-Atlantic abolitionism, the Aboriginal Protec-tion Society, and the Ethnological Society of London.[29] However, like Jefferson, a belief in the cultural and biological efficacy of reproducing whiteness shaped Pritchard's racial reformism. Pritchard argued that "all races and varieties are equally capable of propagating their offspring by in-termarriage."[30] The hope that cultural and sexual intermixture would produce a progressive homogenization in society reinforced his commitment to the idea that culture and biology could be harnessed to reproduce human populations united by social ideals and racial descent.[31]

At the Brainerd Mission in Tennessee, devout members of the American Board of Commissioners for Foreign Missions in the South, attempted to apply Pritchardian evolution. American Board missionaries were "the right kind of white people," their Christian piety, virtue, morality, and commitment to agricultural and economic development making them models of "good breeding." Of particular interest to missionaries at Brainerd were mixed-race children, particularly "half-breed" Cherokee children. Missionaries claimed that mixed-race children exhibited an aptitude for learning and a phenotypic make-up that would "make them useful citizens and pious Christians" in the American republic.[32] Hyperbolic reports of missionary success in "harmonizing" mixed-race Cherokee children with the expanding white republic were common. For example, missionaries described John Ridge, a Cherokee "half-breed" and political leader, as "a young man of good talents, good information, good manners, and honorable standing among his own people." In echoes of Pritchardian evolutionary language, missionary reports unflinchingly celebrated the power of whiteness to redefine Native American cultures and reconstitute human biology. John Ridge thus symbolized and embodied a gentleman "worthy of respect in any community."[33]

Applying evolutionary principles to the republic's African-American population proved an entirely different matter. In 1815, Thomas Jefferson suggested to Frances Gray that he had faith in the robust and transformative powers of whiteness. Jefferson argued that if "equally cultivated [with white society] for a few generations," African-Americans could be made to harmonize with the white republic. According to Jefferson's mathematics, "a third cross clears the [black] blood."[34] Pritchard shared Jefferson's perspective on the transformative powers of whiteness. According to Pritchard, "Instances are not infrequently observed in different countries in which Negroes gradually lose their black colour, and become white as Europeans."[35]

As tensions between Northern and Southern states increased over slavery during the early nineteenth century, Jefferson's speculations, and Pritchard's evolutionary theories, became untenable in American political and social life. According to the proslavery defenders of Southern slavery, whiteness, and by extension the American republic, depended on the cultural and biological segregation of blacks from whites. The American School of Ethnology, led by the likes of Josiah Nott and George Gliddon, popularized the "scientific" work of phrenologists such as Samuel George Morton, emphasizing the cultural and biological frailty of American whiteness. The members of the American School of Ethnology, determined to counter abolitionist attacks on the western expansion of the Southern slave system, insisted that the "white [man] alone possesses the intellectual and moral energy which creates that development of free government, industry, science, literature, and the arts, which we all call civilization."[36] Without the reproduction of culturally and biologically "pure" white people, the virtue and morality—indeed, the "good breeding"—of the republic's white body politic would be inexorably compromised. A central component of upward socio-economic mobility in the wake of the Jacksonian era and the expansion of the franchise to poorer white men was the belief that all white American men could aspire to economic independence and the status of a well-bred gentleman.[37] To abolish slavery, the ideologues of the American School of Ethnology argued, was to unstitch the cultural fabric of white society, the basis for political and economic mobility, and to invite the reputedly unnatural mixing of black and white Americans. As Jeff Forret has argued, "Whiteness conferred upon even poor whites certain social privileges, including the expectation of respect and deference from slaves."[38]

The American Civil War and the bloody period of Reconstruction that followed in the late 1860s and 1870s, led to an unstable transition period in American race relations.[39] Despite these decades bearing witness to the diminishing racial power of whiteness, American whiteness emerged in the late 1870s and 1880s as an even more important racial identity than it had been during the antebellum era. Writing at the height of the Civil War, the proslavery propagandist John Van Evrie captured the importance of whiteness in the United States when he claimed that the "presence of the negro was and always must be a test that shows the insignificance and indeed nothingness of those artificial distinctions which elsewhere govern the world, and constitute the basis of the political as well as social order." In the United States, race defined one's "breeding," one's cultural acceptance as an "American," and prescribed one's ability to acquire economic independence and a shared interest in the American political system. Thus, while immigrants from Ireland before the Civil War, and from southern and eastern Europe after the war, endured episodes of violence and persecution, they, their children, and their grandchildren did not so much "become white" as become able to tap into the political, social, and cultural advantages of "already being white." The assimilation of European immigrants reproduced a racial dynamic that prized whiteness above all other racial categories and continued to marginalize African-Americans.[40] As the black travel writer Juanita Harrison understood, class, politics, and gender may stratify "white" communities, but at the end of the day an "acquaintance-ship with the right kind of white people ... [produces] a mutual community of interest."[41]

As the nineteenth century entered its final two decades, white Americans, both native-born and immigrant, expressed growing pessimism about the possibility of reproducing a republican culture within a population that included mixed-race Native Americans, and blacks of all "mixtures." At the heart of this pessimism was the way in which many Americans incorporated Charles Darwin's theory of evolution into American culture. In *The Origin of Species* (1859), Darwin referred to his theory of evolution as "natural selection." Darwin's "natural selection" embodied the patriarchal tradition of nineteenth-century biology, as it involved the male of a species selecting a female sexual partner for the purpose of reproducing offspring best suited to a given environment. The most vigorous males, Darwin argued, take "possession of the females" and reproduce the species.[42] Turning in a later work to human reproduction, Darwin argued that to succeed in the "general struggle of life, ... men must use their higher powers of imagination and reason" to select, marry, and reproduce with women who added to the happiness of the family, community, and society at large. Darwin's cousin, Frances Galton, added that it was essential for "eminent kinsfolk"— what we might call the "right kind of white people"— to reproduce children within Christian marriages. Galton christened such marriages as *eugenic*, arguing that the children of "eminent kinsfolk" would inherit the necessary "endowment" of "character, disposition, energy, intellect or physical power" to ensure "the cultivation of the [white] race."[43]

In the United States, Darwinian evolution was interpreted through the lens of another Englishman, Herbert Spencer. Spencer's phrase, "survival of the fittest," proved particularly attractive to white Americans who had grown tired of the "infernal negro problem" by the final two decades of the nineteenth century.[44] Accompanying Spencer's infamous phrase was the Englishman's argument that "humanity must in the end become completely adapted to its conditions," which, in the hard-bitten era of Gilded Age economics, was often interpreted as excluding the "doomed" race of Native Americans and marginalizing the formerly enslaved African-American population.[45] Whereas immigrants from southern and eastern Europe acquired the privileges of whiteness by accessing industrial jobs, acquiring educations that emphasized "Americanization," and participating in trade unions and political parties, Native Americans were confined to mission schools and reservations, or dispersed on individual allotments, and black Americans of all hues and levels of cultural sophistication were marginalized through Jim Crow laws in the South and West as "the wrong type of people."[46] Thus, fears for the posterity of the American republic that emerged after the arrival of southern and eastern European immigrants paled in comparison to the over-arching fear of "Africanization." As John Yule of Placer County, California, crudely stated in 1862: "It is 'nigger' in the Hall of Congress, 'nigger' in the camps of our armies, 'nigger' in the legislature of California, 'nigger' everywhere. The everlasting nigger permeates the whole atmosphere of the entire country."[47]

By the 1890s, American eugenicists, social commentators, and lawmakers highlighted the influence of Spencer's "survival of the fittest" rhetoric on white racial identity. "The white people of America," one writer warned, "are dying for want of fresh blood."[48] Such statements were far removed from Thomas Jefferson's speculation on the power of whiteness to blanch the color out of Native Americans and blacks. Indeed, the popular and widely read eugenic writer, Lothrop Stoddard, captured the fear that the "right kind of white people" were not doing their racial duty to reproduce the white race. The "New woman's" alleged obsession with unbridled consumerism and leisure, combined with declining marriage rates, and the general neglect of Anglo-Saxon white Americans to reproduce their number, Stoddard argued, resulted in "Racial impoverishment ... with its twin symptoms of extirpation of superior strains and the multiplication of inferiors."[49]

Thus, by the late nineteenth and early twentieth centuries, an era that Rayford Logan has referred to as "the nadir" of race relations in the United States, many segments of American society saw whiteness as a fragile racial category.[50] The cultural and sexual mixing of white and non-white races, eugenicists told Americans with increasing regularity, had transformed the "spotless race" of white Americans and plunged whiteness into the "hopeless depths of hybridization."[51] While historians have correctly observed that American eugenicists expressed concern over the impact that immigrants from southern and eastern Europe would have on American whiteness, early twentieth-century eugenicists insisted that the most dire consequences for white identity came from people of "color."[52] For example, Stoddard warned that "crosses between White and Negro are biologically undesirable, ... produce highly disruptive effects ... and threatens our social order."[53] In Spencerian language, another eugenicist argued, "due to many centuries of natural selection, the races of men have not now equal capacity to adapt themselves to the same environmental conditions nor to attain the same accomplishments."[54]

By the 1930s, with Jim Crow segregation legally entrenched in southern, and many western, states, Native Americans confined to reservations or dispersed on individual allotments, and Japanese and Chinese immigration restricted (as well as the placement of quotas on migrants from southern and eastern Europe), the vocal protestations of American eugenicists discomfited any thought of reproducing a white race that incorporated "Indian" or "African" blood. Whiteness was too fragile and the risks to American civilization too great for Jeffersonian ideas about biological assimilation and reproduction to be even idly considered by the early twentieth century. American whiteness may have been robust enough to assimilate southern and eastern European immigrants, but the alleged "thriftlessness," "criminality," and "immorality" of "half-breeds," "mulattoes," and mixed-blood Chinese, was too potent a threat to American civilization and the fragile whiteness of the United States.[55]

Cultivating Whiteness in Australia

Unlike their American cousins, a number of early-twentieth-century Australian authorities adopted a very different approach to whiteness. Australia was founded in the wake of the American Revolutionary War. In January 1788, some fifteen hundred convicts and crew under the command of Captain Arthur Phillip disembarked at Sydney Cove and established a tottering convict colony. Racked by hunger, disease, and ill-discipline, the colony of New South Wales, located on the southeastern coast of Australia, was far removed from the virtuous society imagined by the founding fathers of the United States; it was even further from the model of good breeding outlined by John Locke. Nonetheless, Australia's founders brought Lockean, and later Jeremy Bentham's, ideas about social and penal reform to the southwest Pacific. What the British called "Australia" after 1829, could not, as critics of the convict colony often warned, remain "buryed [*sic*] in ignorance and hardened in sin."[56]

The racially idealized whiteness that emerged in the American republic was shaped as much by the United States' colonial past as it was by the vicissitudes of the Revolutionary War. The founders of British Australia, in contrast, confronted neither the instability of war nor the political and social traditions that American colonists had developed for over a century. Australia, in British eyes, was a blank colonial slate. Therefore, in an age of reform and abolitionism in Britain, Australia's founders believed that they had a unique opportunity to draw from their experiences in North America, the Caribbean, southern Africa, and India, and apply their Enlightenment knowledge to carve out of the Australian "bush" a uniquely moral, well-ordered society of "ranks and orders."[57] Making the ideal of a well-ordered antipodean settler society a reality, Australia's colonial founders strove to implement a program of town planning, education, and moral improvement.

British officials saw town planning as a means of disciplining the natural environment and a population comprised overwhelmingly of criminals. For example, land was set aside for agricultural purposes, and the growing of crops such as Indian corn was encouraged. Similarly, to combat drunkenness and address reported cases of sexual immorality, town planners set about systematizing the layout of streets, dividing towns according to their intended use, and numbering homes and other structures.[58] Drawing inspiration from the writings of Locke, Bentham, and myriad other reform theorists in Britain, Australia's colonial leaders hoped to provide the foundations for a moral society where each individual worked to ensure the common good.[59] The first emancipated convict, John Irving, embodied the type of well-bred individual that the British hoped to reproduce in Australia. According to Governor Phillip, Irving had "been bred to surgery, and merited from his exemplary conduct what has been done for him."[60]

Educating men in useful trades and professions represented one important means of reforming convicts and bringing order to British colonial Australia. A related approach involved British officials using offers of land to encourage well-bred British immigrants to make the long journey to Australia, and to reward good conduct among convicts. For example, officials in New South Wales offered emancipated convicts thirty acres of land. To encourage marriage and reproduction, an additional ten acres was offered for each additional child in a household. Thus, from the earliest days of settlement, British officials in colonial Australia tied settler expansion, agricultural development, and the dispossession of the Australian Aborigines to patriarchal ideals about marriage and the reproduction of the settler population.[61]

In articulating these measures, colonial officials made it clear that "the right kind of white people" to help British settler civilization expand beyond the then Australian frontier region must receive an education that gave them the knowledge to practice a "useful" trade or profession, be self-restrained and Christian in their conduct, and ideally, be married. The reality was far different. As in other settler societies, the Australian frontier was largely a white man's domain. On occasion, officials celebrated the virtue of Australian "squatters," contrasting the Australian frontiersman with their allegedly immoral cousins in the United States.[62] Such boosterism, however, was belied by missionary and Aboriginal complaints that white frontiersmen were excessively violent, ill-bred, and sexually exploitative of Aboriginal women. In 1844 the settler Edward Mayne testified that white men "kept a number of Gins [Aboriginal women] away from their Blackmen and tribe, and was the cause of considerable disturbance amongst them."[63] Acts of this nature flew in the face of Colonial Office instructions for the settlement of Australia. Governor Phillip, for example, received instructions that colonists and convicts must live in "amity and kindness" with the Australian Aborigines. Similarly, Governor Lachlan Macquarie wrote in 1812 that the Australian Aborigines must "be treated in every respect as Europeans."[64] With these egalitarian sentiments guiding colonial policymaking, reports of racial violence and sexual immorality undermined efforts to create an ordered society comprised of "the right kind of white people." Missionaries therefore stepped onto the Australian colonial stage and urged British colonists to live up to their own ideals. Missionaries also maintained that the Australian Aboriginal people must be encouraged to evolve toward white standards of settler colonial civilization.

Using the language of Pritchardian evolution, missionaries approached the education of Aboriginal people with evangelical zeal. Many missionaries contended that Aboriginal people had the capacity to rise to the level of the white proletarian classes. Echoing the Pritchardian conviction that the human brain in all races possesses malleable qualities, colonial reformers claimed that Australian Aborigines had the brain capacity "of an untutored child."[65] William Broughton, the Archdeacon of Sydney, informed the 1836 Select Committee on Aborigines that indigenous children, like their white counterparts, needed the missionary to "restrain and redirect certain tendencies," thereby helping indigenous children to grow to adulthood and become useful members of settler society.[66] Lancelot Threlkeld hoped to implement such ideals. Threlkeld, a former actor, established a mission to the Awabakal Aborigines at Lake Macquarie in New South Wales. His work attracted visits from ethnologists from around the world, the most famous being the American Horatio Hale.[67] Like so many other colonial missionaries, Threlkeld failed to convince Aboriginal parents to part with their children—particularly mixed race, or "half-caste," children—so that they could receive a Western education, and become devout Christians, practitioners of monogamous marriage, and useful proletarian workers.

Undeterred by the failures of the early nineteenth century, the reformist imagination of Colonial Office officials, missionaries, and a number of colonial liberals, continued to press for the acculturation, and increasingly in the second half of the nineteenth century, biological assimilation of indigenous children with whites. Reformers argued that Aboriginal children, particularly "half-caste" children, should receive the necessary training that would enable them to become the kind of people who could set a moral and virtuous example for other indigenous Australians to emulate. Unlike the United States, which experienced the upheaval of a Civil War and a tumultuous period of Reconstruction, Australian reformers did not have to alter their goals dramatically for Aboriginal children because there were no such wartime disruptions. Instead, the Australian colonies experienced a short burst of immigration from North America and Europe following the discovery of gold in the late 1850s. The sudden increase in European immigration altered, albeit temporarily, the overwhelmingly Anglo-Celtic nature of Australian whiteness.[68] Similarly, individual conflicts between gold miners and colonial authorities over issues such as taxation, or divisions between labor and capital interests, constituted episodic fissures in white racial solidarity. However, in Australia, more so than the United States, whiteness remained a solidly homogenous cultural and biological category through the gold rush era and beyond.

The cultural and biological homogeneity of Australian whiteness constituted one of the cornerstones of the emerging "white Australia ideal" during the latter half of the nineteenth century. As the colonies acquired self-government after the 1850s, a nascent Australian nationalism emerged that emphasized the racial solidarity of the Australian colonists. Looking back over the development of the "white Australia ideal," the historian A. Wyatt Tilby wrote in 1912 that the "White Australia ideal [was] at once democratic and exclusive, postulating a white Australian nation as an aristocracy of humanity, untouched or uncontaminated by the admixture of its blood with any inferior breed from without, yet a nation organised on democratic lines from within."[69] But to maintain a society structured around democratic ideals "from within," white Australians had to reproduce in greater numbers. Just as fears of race suicide gripped the United States and spawned dire eugenic warnings of "race suicide" during the late nineteenth and early twentieth centuries, so did Australian policymakers worry about the declining birthrate among white people. Octavius Charles Beale, whose work proved influential among both Australians and Americans like Theodore Roosevelt, warned that "Self-induced abortion, or abortion produced by fashionable or fad doctors, is, as we know, a fruitful cause of horrible pus cases in which we are now and then called to operate." Abortion, Beale added, compromised the reproduction of a "white Australia," something that could only be remedied by the immigration of the right kind of white people, or as Beale put it, the penetration of *"new blood into the country by immigration."*[70]

The "white Australia ideal" had two significant racial consequences for people of "color" and what we might call "the wrong type of white people" (such as Jewish and "swarthy" Italian immigrants). Firstly, restrictive immigration laws were passed in an effort to preserve the imagined purity of white Australia and emphasize the benefits of Anglo-Celtic immigration to the reproduction of a "white Australia." Secondly, a number of Aboriginal Protectors, missionaries, and scholars believed that white "blood" was so powerful and transformative that a program of education and the careful management of marriages, or "breeding out the colour," would eventually result in "half-caste" Aborigines being bred white.[71]

The idea of "breeding out the colour" can be traced to seventeenth century English thought, if not earlier.[72] In late-nineteenth-century Australia, however, the scientific confidence to "breed" mixed-race people with whites came from Darwin's theory of evolution, the assumption that the white race in Australia was uniquely unified and possessed of transformative cultural and biological powers, and the belief that the Australian Aborigines descended from an Indo-Aryan race. The idea that Australian Aborigines possessed "Aryan," or white, blood, galvanized reformers in support of proposals to apply "natural selection" to all races of humankind. For example, John Mathew, a staunch supporter of Aboriginal rights, insisted that Australian Aborigines descended from the Dravidian peoples of India, a degraded branch of the Indo-Aryan race. Writing in 1889, Mathew summarized two decades of Orientalist speculation on the Indo-Aryan ancestry of the Australian Aborigines, claiming that "a true relationship subsists between the Australians and the Dravidians of India." The Australian Aborigines therefore had "Aryan" blood flowing through their veins, making the careful management of interracial marriages a positive evolutionary practice for "white Australia." The only problem, Mathew noted, was the Northern Territory, in Australia's tropical north, where "Dravidian and Malay blood" had mixed, producing a "composite" race.[73] For the "White Australia ideal" to become a reality in all corners of the continent, an infusion of white "blood" was needed in the Australian tropics.

Before officials in the Northern Territory had an opportunity to test the ideas associated with "natural selection," the transformative cultural and biological powers of whiteness, and the Indo-Aryan migration theory, the colonial government of Victoria, in southeastern Australia, took tentative steps toward applying these ideas to mixed-race Aboriginal people. The historian Katherine Ellinghaus has outlined in lucid detail the changes in Aboriginal legislation during the late nineteenth century.[74] The Victorian government's main objective in reforming Aboriginal legislation was to reduce expenditure on Aboriginal affairs. A related goal involved drawing on evolutionary and Dravidian migration theories to engineer a homogenous colonial society. The 1869 Act for the Protection and Management of Aboriginal Natives of Victoria (and amendments to the act in 1871, 1886, and 1890), was designed to facilitate the evolution of the half-caste Aborigine to white settler society, and at the same time provide the "doomed" race of "full-blood" Aborigines humane conditions in which to spend their last days.[75] Aboriginal children, particularly half-caste children, were the main targets of the Victorian Board's approach to Aboriginal evolution to white cultural standards and phenotype. The Board thus gained the power to take "any Aboriginal child neglected by its parents, or left unprotected, to any of the residences specified ..., or to an industrial or reformatory school."[76] The emphasis here was on cultivating in Aboriginal children those skills that would make them reliable proletarian workers. On the reproduction of the right kind of proletarian workers, the Board's members exhibited a willingness to incorporate Dravidian migration theory and Darwinian evolution. In 1888, for example, the Board insisted that the "marrying of half-caste girls to pure blacks ... should be discouraged as much as possible." Such statements reflected the Board's belief that white men must be the active sexual agents, and half-caste women the receptacles, of future generations of white proletarians.[77]

In the tropical north, the British settled the Northern Territory in 1869. From the earliest years of settlement, administrators expressed concern about the reproduction of the white population because of reports about the prevalence of mixed Aboriginal-Malay communities. To the founders of British settler society in the tropics, the "white Australia ideal" hung in the balance. Thus, proposals for monitoring, in addition to educating and whitening, people of Aboriginal descent were made in the late nineteenth and early twentieth centuries. For example, in 1911, Herbert Basedow, the Northern Territory Protector of Aborigines, recommended that a "slight lesion in the superficial skin" of the Aborigine be made for monitoring purposes. Basedow added, "This can be done in an absolutely painless way and without disfigurement. The space occupied by the mark need not exceed one or two square inches and would be chosen in quite an inconspicuous position."[78]

One of Basedow's most prominent successors to the position of Aboriginal Protector was Cecil Cook. Cook shared Basedow's concern about monitoring Aboriginal people, and he concurred with popular sentiment that restrictive immigration laws—the so-called "white Australia policy"—was "good for the world, good for the empire, and good for ourselves."[79] However, Cook also offered his full-throated support for schemes to "breed out the colour" among "half-caste" Aborigines. Cook and his Western Australian counterpart, A.O. Neville, became the most prominent public servants to advocate "breeding out the colour." Both Cook and Neville worried that interracial sex, decoupled from the didactic restraints of marriage, had produced "kombo-ism" (sex between white men and Aboriginal women) in the Northern Territory and Western Australia. Critics claimed that "Kombo-ism" had produced an unwieldy mixture of races and an ungovernable "hybrid colored population of low order."[80] Despite reports of this nature, white Australians remained divided about the efficacy of "breeding out the colour." Some eugenicists, for example, warned that interracial marriage produced "dysgenic" offspring. Other scholars, such as Dr. Cyril Bryan, believed that a managed program of interracial marriage would have a positive impact on Australia and was welcomed by half-caste Aborigines because they wanted to "lose their 'dash of colour.'"[81]

Cook took a pragmatic approach to the "science" of "breeding out the colour." He argued that "unless the matter of his [the half-caste's] propagation be dealt with immediately, Northern Australia will be faced in the course of a few decades with an insuperable problem necessitating the admission of a preponderating number of frankly coloured citizens to full social and economic equality."[82] Cook warned that an unmanaged population of mixed-race people would strain government finances, and "is likely to be attended by very grave consequences to Australia as a nation."[83] Cook therefore favored a program in which Aboriginal Protectors had the authority to determine who an Aboriginal "half-caste" could and could not marry. A "half-caste" girl, for example, should ideally marry a "half-caste" or white man. She should also receive an education that would mold her into a good and faithful worker "so that there may be no question of her impairing the social or economic status of her [white] husband."[84]

Missionary groups applauded Cook for what they saw as his foresight and progressivism. For instance, the Aborignes' Friends' Association (AFA) declared approvingly in 1934:

319

The authorities intend to try to inter-marry these half-castes, and to marry the surplus to white men, for whom, in the outback areas, they make very competent wives. This is a far-sighted policy. It looks toward breeding the Aborigine white, instead of letting the half-castes become black. Blood tests appear to show that the Aborigine is akin to the white man. There are no records of throwbacks. The black strain breeds out relatively quickly, and the slight evidence available indicates that the octoroon is of good type. One feels that Australia should support the Federal authorities in their policy, which is in accordance with racial tendencies; for if a country contains a large majority of one colour and a small minority of another the majority will always tend to breed the minority out.[85]

Just as popular opinion viewed restrictive immigration laws as a progressive policy, so too did reform groups and Aboriginal welfare organizations insist that modern "science" held the key to eliminating racial tension and forging a white nation that was ordered by gender roles, education, and work. After 1901, with the creation of an Australian Commonwealth, the federal government expressed its support for such reformism. While never officially embarking on a policy to "breed out the colour," a 1933 memorandum makes the federal government's position clear. The memorandum reads: "The policy of the [Commonwealth] Government is to encourage the marriage of half-castes with whites or half-castes, the object being to 'breed out' the colour as far as possible."[86]

Conclusion

Why did a number of important Australian government officials embrace "breeding out the colour" as a means of reproducing their version of the "right kind of white people?" Several factors account for this approach. Among the most important were an overwhelmingly homogenous white settler population; government officials with experience in, and connections to, other parts of the British Empire; and a colonial history of reform that included a willingness to experiment with the newest theories in racial "science." By the 1930s, the Australian population had 86.3 percent who were native-born, 99.1 percent who were subjects of the British Empire, and, according to the 1933 census takers, most Australians were "fundamentally British in race and nationality."[87] Demographic solidarity on this scale provided the racial foundation for government officials like Cook to champion a program of managed education and intermarriage that harnessed, in their minds, the best cultural and biological qualities of the white race. By nurturing future generations of Australians so that they conformed to the "white Australia ideal," those Australians who shared Cook's racial convictions worked to help create an island of whiteness in the South Pacific.

By the early twentieth century, the United States' population was much larger, and more diverse, than Australia's settler colonial population. The United States comprised people of British, German, Scandinavian, and French ethnicity, and struggled during the late nineteenth and early twentieth centuries to assimilate a perceived influx of Mediterranean, Slavic, and Jewish immigrants. The perception of large migrations of people from non-traditional (i.e., non-West European) ethnic backgrounds placed pressure on what had become a fragile American whiteness struggling to inoculate itself against the threats posed by Asian immigration and Mexican Americans in the West, and the "Negro problem" in the South.[88] By the early twentieth century, the rhetoric of the "survival of the fittest" and eugenics helped to open the boundaries of whiteness to the children of southern and eastern European immigrants, but at the same time erected a racial wall around whiteness that prevented Native Americans, Asian Americans, Mexican Americans, and especially African Americans, from aspiring to the status of "the right kind of white people."

American and Australian constructions of whiteness reflected, as Hsu-Ming Teo has argued in a different context, white racial identity as "an unstable fantasy existing along a spectrum."[89] However, the "fantasy" of whiteness had very real implications, as it prescribed social and economic mobility, and gave people a collective investment in American and Australian territorial expansion (and the political structures that oversaw expansion). To achieve all of this, settlers needed to reproduce their own kind, or at least an idealized vision of the "right kind of white people." While the architects of settler colonialism in the United States and Australia shared many of the same international ideas about race, sexuality, and human reproduction, only in Australia did a select few and important officials attempt to reproduce "the right kind of white people" by mixing white men with mixed-race women. Thus, like all racial categories, whiteness was a malleable ideal, a "fantasy," and a social construct; but in colonies of settlement like the United States and Australia, racial constructs had very real implications, inspiring "scientific" experimentation in the hope of engineering an ideal white settler population, and having an enduring legacy on those individuals who today are categorized as "black," "brown," "mixed-race," and "white."

Notes

1. Dominion of Canada, *Annual Report of the Department of Indian Affairs for the Year Ending 1900* (Ottawa, 1901), 428–29.
2. See for example Russell McGregor, *Imagined Destinies: Aboriginal Australians and the Doomed Race Theory, 1880–1939* (Carlton South, VIC, 1998); Louise Michele Newman, *White Women's Rights: The Racial Origins of Feminism in the United States* (New York, 1999); Myra Rutherdale, *Women and the White Man's God: Gender and Race in the Canadian Mission Field* (Vancouver, 2002); Norman Etherington, ed., *Missions and Empire: Oxford History of the British Empire* (New York, 2005); Gregory D. Smithers, *Science, Sexuality, and Race in the United States and Australia, 1780s–1890s* (New York, London, 2008), 146–47.
3. Dominion of Canada, *Annual Report*, 429.
4. For further analysis of this point see John Gascoigne, *The Enlightenment and the Origins of European Australia* (Cambridge, 2002); Nancy Shoemaker, *A Strange Likeness: Becoming Red and White in Eighteenth-Century North America* (New York, 2004); Tony Ballantyne, *Orientalism and Race: Aryanism in the British Empire* (New York, 2002); Allison Games, *The Web of Empire: English Cosmopolitans in an Age of Expansion, 1560–1660* (New York, 2008); Smithers, *Science, Sexuality, and Race*.
5. For the "signifier of power" see Catherine Hall, "Of Gender and Empire: Reflections on the Ninteteenth Century" in *Gender and Empire: The Oxford History of the British Empire*, ed. Philippa Levine (Oxford, 2004), 49. See also Caroline Knowles, *Race and Social Analysis* (Thousand Oaks, CA, 2003), 16, 199; Marilyn Lake and Henry Reynolds, *Drawing the Global Colour Line: White Men's Countries and the International Challenge of Racial Equality* (Cambridge, 2008), Part 3; Melissa Steyn, "Whiteness in the Rainbow: Experiencing the Loss of Privilege in the New South Africa" in *Beyond Racism: Race and Inequality in Brazil, South Africa, and the United States*, edited by Charles V. Hamilton, Lynn Huntley, Wilmot James (Boulder, CO, 2001), 86–87.
6. For the "dark smudge" see Kendall Johnson, *Henry James and the Visual* (Cambridge, 2007), 4. See also David R. Roediger, *The Wages of Whiteness: Race and the Making of the American Working Class*, rev. ed. (London, 2003), 13; David R. Roediger, *Working Toward Whiteness: How America's Immigrants Became White: The Strange Journey from Ellis Island to the Suburbs* (New York, 2005), 45; Noel Ignatiev, *How the Irish Became White* (New York & London, 1995); Jack Metzger, "Politics and the American Class Vernacular" in *New Working-Class Studies*, edited by John Russo & Sherry Lee Linkon (Ithaca, NY, 2005), 189–208.
7. Roediger, *Working Toward Whiteness*, 95; Jacobson, *Whiteness of a Different Color*, 22–24; Knowles, *Race and Social Analysis*, 180; Peck, *Reinventing Free Labor*, 168; Warwick Anderson, *The Cultivation of Whiteness: Science, Health, and Racial Destiny in Australia* (Carlton, VIC, 2005), 257; Susanne Schech and Jane Haggis,

"Migrancy, Whiteness and the Settler Self in Contemporary Australia" in *Race, Colour and Identity in Australia and New Zealand,* edited by John Docker, Gerhard Fischer (Sydney, 2000), 231–39.

8. Reginald Horsman, *Race and Manifest Destiny: The Origins of American Racial Anglo-Saxonism* (Cambridge, MA, 1981), 3–6; Amy S. Greenberg, *Manifest Manhood and the Antebellum American Empire* (New York, 2005), 18, 280–82; Carolyn Sorisio, *Fleshing Out America: Race, Gender, and the Politics of the Body in American Literature, 1833–1879* (Athens, GA, 2002), 74, 95, 142.

9. H. Bailey Thomson, for instance, observes that in the American South during the Jim Crow era of the late nineteenth and early twentieth centuries, both African-Americans and poor whites were restricted from political participation. As Bailey argues, the framers of Jim Crow laws and constitutions established "rule not just for whites but for only the right kind of white people." H. Bailey Thomson, "Constitutional Reform in Alabama: Long Time Coming" in *State Constitutions for the Twenty-First Century: The Politics of State Constitutional Reform*, eds. G. Alan Tarr, Robert F. Williams (Albany, 2006), 116.

10. David Theo Goldberg, *The Racial State* (Malden, MA, 2002), 171; See also Knowles, *Race and Social Analysis*, 100–101; Wendy Leo Moore, *Reproducing Racism: White Space, Elite Law Schools, and Racial Inequality* (Lanham, MD, 2007), 24–32.

11. Nancy MacLean, *Behind the Mask of Chivalry: The Making of the Second Ku Klux Klan* (New York, 1994); Jan Jindy Pettman, "Race, Ethnicity and Gender in Australia" in *Unsettling Settler Societies: Articulations of Gender, Race, Ethnicity and Class*, eds. Daiva Stasiulis, Nira Yuvul-Davis (Thousand Oaks, CA, 1995), 72; Jock McCulloch, *Black Peril, White Virtue: Sexual Crime in Southern Rhodesia, 1902–1935* (Bloomington, IN, 2000); Diane Miller Sommerville, *Rape and Race in the Nineteenth-Century South* (Chapel Hill, 2004).

12. Newman, *White Women's Rights*, 156; Nathan Stormer, *Articulating Life's Memory*, 86; Natalia Molina, *Fit to be Citizens? Public Health and Race in Los Angeles* (Berkeley, 2006), 110–11; Allison Berg, *Mothering the Race: Women's Narratives of Reproduction, 1890–1930* (Urbana, IL, 2002), 4–6; Angela Woollacott, *To Try Her Fortune in London: Australian Women, Colonialism, & Modernity* (Oxford, 2001), 34; Kay Schaffer, "Handkerchief Diplomacy: E.J. Eyre and Sexual Politics on the South Australian Frontier" in *Colonial Frontiers: Indigenous-European Encounters in Settler Societies*, ed. Lynette Russell (Manchester, 2001), 134–35.

13. Ruth Frankenberg, *White Women, Race Matters: The Social Construction of Whiteness* (Minneapolis, 1993), 1, 49, 115; Rebecca Aanerud, "Fictions of Whiteness: Speaking the Names of Whiteness in U. S. Literature," in *Displacing Whiteness: Essays in Social and Cultural Criticism*, ed. Ruth Frankenberg (Durham, NC, 1997), 47; Richard Dyer, *White* (New York & London, 1997), 11–12, 30; Steyn, "Whiteness in the Rainbow," 88; Jennifer L. Morgan, *Laboring Women: Reproduction in New World Slavery* (Philadelphia, 2004), 15.

14. Patrick Wolfe, *Settler Colonialism and the Transformation of Anthropology: The Politics and Poetics of an Ethnographic Event* (New York, 1999), 2, 27–30; Patrick Wolfe, "Land, Labor, and Difference: Elementary Structures of Race," *American Historical Review* 106, no. 3 (June 2001): 866–905.

15. Stephen Nicholas, *Convict Workers: Reinterpreting Australia's Past* (Cambridge, 2007), 17–18.

16. Horsman, *Race and Manifest Destiny*, chap. 1; Mark M. Carroll, *Homesteads Ungovernable: Families, Sex, Race, and the Law in Frontier Texas, 1823–1860* (Austin, TX, 2001), 33, 64–65.

17. William Smith, *The Nature and Institution of Government; Containing an Account of the Feudal and English Policy*, vol. II (London, 1771), 35–36. See also Robert Beatson, *A Political Index to the Histories of Great Britain and Ireland; Or a Complete Register of the Hereditary Honours, Public Offices, and Persons in Office, From the Earliest Periods to the Present Time*, vol. II (London, 1788), 329.

18. *Register of Debates in Congress, Comprising the Leading Debates of the First Session of the Twenty-Fourth Congress*, vol. XII (Washington, 1836), 1000; Martha Hodes, "The Mercurial Nature and Abiding Power of Race: A Transnational Family," *American Historical Review* 108, no. 1 (February 2003): 107.

19. Horsman, *Race and Manifest Destiny*, 3, 9–11, 93; Jacobson, *Whiteness of a Different Color*, chap. 1; Andrew Hassam, *Through Australian Eyes: Colonial Perceptions of Imperial Britain* (Brighten, 2000), 16.

20. Gordon Wood, *The Creation of the American Republic, 1776–1787* (Chapel Hill, 1969), 34, 65, 92.

21. John Locke, *Some Thoughts Concerning Education* (London, 1693), 157.

22. Peter Novak, *That Noble Dream*, 82–83.

23. Thomas Jefferson, *Notes on the States of Virginia*, ed. William Peden (1787; Chapel Hill, 1982), 146–47; Smithers, *Science, Sexuality, and Race*, 21–22.

24. Merril D. Peterson, ed., *The Portable Thomas Jefferson* (New York, 1988), 533.

25. These issues are explored in greater detail in Smithers, *Science, Sexuality, and Race*, chap. 1.

26. Bernard W. Sheehan, *Seeds of Extinction: Jeffersonian Philanthropy and the American Indian* (New York, 1974), 140; John and Jean Comaroff, *Of Revelation and Revolution: Christianity, Colonialism, and Consciousness in South Africa*, vol. I (Chicago, 1991), 62–65; Ann Laura Stoler and Frederick Cooper, "Between Metropole and Colony: Rethinking a Research Agenda" in *Tensions of Empire: Colonial Cultures in a Bourgeois World*, eds. Ann Laura Stoler and Frederick Cooper (Berkeley, 1997), 1–5; Wolfe, *Settler Colonialism*, 2–3; Norman Etherington, "Introduction," in *Missions and Empire*, 6–7; Norbert Finzsch, "'The Aborigines … Were never Annihilated, and Still they are Becoming Extinct': Settler Imperialism and Genocide in Nineteenth-Century America and Australia," in *Empire, Colony, Genocide: Conquest, Occupation, and Subaltern Resistance in World History*, ed. A. Dirk Moses (New York, 2008), 254.

27. John Wood Sweet, *Bodies Politic: Negotiating Race in North America, 1730–1830* (Baltimore, 2003), 308.

28. Jefferson, *Notes*, 84.

29. Gregory Smithers, "'Black Gentleman as Good as White': A Comparative Analysis of African American and Australian Aboriginal Political Protest, 1830–1865," *Journal of African American History* 93, no. 3 (Summer 2008), 316.

30. Smithers, *Science, Sexuality, and Race*, 50.

31. Ibid., 51.

32. Ibid., 101.

33. Ibid., 102.

34. Ibid., 30.

35. Smithers, "Black Gentleman," 318; Smithers, *Science, Sexuality, and Race*, 51.

36. *The Laws of Race as Connected With Slavery* (Philadelphia, 1860), 9–10.

37. Joseph L. Blau, ed., *Social Theories of Jacksonian Democracy: Representative Writings of the Period, 1825–1850* (Indianapolis, IN, 2003), 22, 85; Lee Benson, *The Concept of Jacksonian Democracy: New York as a Test Case* (Princeton, NJ, 1961); Charles Sellers, *The Market Revolution: Jacksonian America, 1815–1846* (New York, 1991).

38. Jeff Forret, *Race Relations at the Margins: Slaves and Poor Whites in the Antebellum Southern Countryside* (Baton Rouge, 2006), 166. See also David T. Gleeson, *The Irish in the South, 1815–1877* (Chapel Hill, 2001), 120–122.

39. James Wilfred Vander Zanden, *Race Relations in Transition: The Segregation Crisis in the South* (New York, 1965); Joel Williamson, *The Crucible of Race: Black-White Relations in the American South Since Emancipation* (New York, 1984), 50–52.

40. Gleeson, *The Irish in the South*, 121.

41. Juanita Harrison, *My Great, Wide, Beautiful World* (New York, 1936), 120.

42. Charles Darwin, *The Origin of the Species: By Means of Natural Selection*, ed. J.W. Burrow (1859; London, 1985), 135–36, 148–49; Charles Darwin, *The Descent of Man* (1874; Amherst, NY, 1998), 585; Smithers, *Science, Sexuality, and Race*, 72–75.

43. Smithers, *Science, Sexuality, and Race*, 76.

44. Norah Davis, *The Northerner* (New York, 1905), 194.

45. S. Elizabeth Bird, *Dressing in Feathers: The Construction of the Indian in American Popular Culture* (Boulder, CO, 1996), 8–9, 82, 249; Smithers, *Science, Sexuality, and Race*, 78.

46. See Franz Boas in Julia E. Johnson, ed., *Selected Articles on the Negro Problem* (New York, 1921), 116–17; Alford A. Young, *The Minds of Marginalized Black Men: Making Sense of Mobility, Opportunity, and Future Life Chances* (Princeton, 2003), 60.

47. San Francisco *Bulletin*, (2 March 1862), 3, in San Francisco Negro Historical and Cultural Society, Monograph 3, no. 2 (July 1968), 11.

48. Frederick L. Hoffman, *Race Traits and Tendencies of the American Negro* (New York, 1896), 191.

49. Lothrop Stoddard, *The Revolt Against Civilization: The Menace of the Under Man* (New York, 1924), 88. See similarly J.M. Stone, "Lessened Fertility of Women, Especially American Women," *American Journal of Obstetrics*, lxxiv (1916): 454–58.

50. Rayford W. Logan, *The Negro in American Life and Thought: The Nadir, 1877–1901,*

51. William Montgomery Brown, *The Crucial Race Question: Where and How Shall the Color Line be Drawn* (Little Rock, 1907), 105–7.

52. John Higham, *Strangers in the Land: Patterns of American Nativism, 1860–1925* (New York, 1963), 150–53; David Harry Bennett, *The Party of Fear: From Nativist Movements to the New Right in American History* (Chapel Hill, 1988), 283.

53. Lothrop Stoddard, "The Impasse at the Color-Line," *Forum*, LXXVIII, no. 4 (October 1927), 511, 513.

54. W.A. Dixon, "The Morbid Proclivities and Retrogressive Tendencies in the Offspring of Mulattoes," *Medical News*, 13 August 1892, 1–2, in Series I, A: 1225, "Mulattoes," Ms. Coll. 77, Eugenics Record Office, American Philosophical Society.

55. See for example, Charles Davenport to Ales Hrdlicka, 5 May 1915, Charles Benedict Davenport Papers, 1874–1944, B D27, Series I, American Philosophical Society; Earl F. Zinn, *History, Purpose, and Policy of the National Research Council's Committee for Research on Sex Problems* (New York, 1924), 6.

56. Rev. William Henry to the London Missionary Society, 29 August 1799, in F.M. Bladen, ed., *Historical Records of New South Wales*, vol. III (Sydney, 1892), 715. [Hereafter cited as *HRNSW*]. See also Gascoigne, *The Enlightenment and the Origins of European Australia*, 1–3; Smithers, *Science, Sexuality, and Race*, 32–33.

57. Smithers, *Science, Sexuality, and Race*, 31–33.

58. Government and General Order, 9 November 1796, *HRNSW*, III, 165.

59. Rowan Strong, *Anglicanism and the British Empire, c.1700–1850* (Oxford, 2007), 234–35.

60. Gov. Phillip to Lord Sydney, 16 May 1788, *HRNSW*, I, Part 2, 139; Smithers, *Science, Sexuality, and Race*, 33–34.

61. Phillip's Instructions, 25 April 1787, *HRNSW*, I, Part 2, 90; Jan Kocumbas, *The Oxford History of Australia: Possessions, 1770–1860* (Melbourne, 1992), 16–17; Rob Linn, *Battling the Land: 200 Years of Rural Australia* (Crows Nest, NSW, 1999), 7–8.

62. Smithers, *Science, Sexuality, and Race*, 60–61.

63. Edward Mayne to the Commissioner of Crown Lands, Gipps Despatches, Vol. 46, September–December 1844, ML, a1235, 189. See also Anna Haebich, *Broken Circles: Fragmenting Indigenous Families, 1800–2000* (Fremantle, 2000), 80.

64. Instructions Given to Governor Phillip, 23 April 1787, *HRNSW*, I, 485; Governor Macquarie to the Earl of Liverpool, 17 November 1812, *Historical Records of Australia: Governors Despatches to and from England*, ser. 1, vol. VII (Canberra, 1916), 661.

65. Smithers, *Science, Sexuality, and Race*, 64.

66. British Parliamentary Papers, *Report from the Select Committee on Aborigines (British Settlements); Together with Minutes of Evidence, Appendix and Index, 1836,* vol. I (Shannon, 1968), 13–14, 16–17, 487–88.

67. Smithers, *Science, Sexuality, and Race*, 126.

68. James Jupp, *From White Australia to Woomera: The Story of Australian Immigration* (Cambridge, 2007), 10.

69. A. Wyatt Tilby, *The English People Overseas, Volume V: Australasia, 1688–1911* (Boston, 1912), 311–12.

70. Octavius Charles Beale, *Racial Decay: A Compilation of Evidence from World Sources* (London and Sydney, 1911), 89–90, 236, 243–44. See also Theodore Roosevelt, *An Autobiography* (New York, 1913), 598; Elting E. Morrison, ed., *The Letters of Theodore Roosevelt* (Cambridge, 1954), 1356; David Walker, *Anxious Nation: Australia and the Rise of Asia, 1850–1939* (St. Lucia, QLD, 1999), 114.

71. Marilyn Lake, "The White Man Under Siege: New Histories of Race in the Nineteenth Century and the Advent of White Australia," *History Workshop Journal* 58 (2004): 56; Alison Bashford, "World Population and Australian Land: Demography and Sovereignty in the Twentieth Century," *Australian Historical Review* 38, no. 130 (October 2007): 211–26.

72. Late-nineteenth- and early-twentieth-century exponents of "breeding out the colour" can be viewed as the intellectual descendents of seventeenth-century thinkers who hypothesized that it was possible to take children and "breed them up to Learning," something that, if the Lord of tenanted families allowed, would put the children at "Liberty." The blanching of color from the skins of black people over the course of two or three generations was also seen as a progressive development. Edward Phillips, *The New World of Words: Or, Universal English Dictionary* (London, 1720), LI; Peter Heylen, *Cosmographe in Foure Books Contayning the Chorographie & Historie of the Whole World, & All the Principall Kingdomes, Provinces, Seas, & Isles, Thereof* (London, 1666), 966, 1004.

73. John Mathew, "The Australian Aborigines," *Journal and the Proceedings of the Royal Society of New South Wales* XVI (1882): 193–233. Russell McGregor dates the Indo-Aryan – Australian Aboriginal link to the early twentieth century. See his "An Aboriginal Caucasian: Some Uses for Racial Kinship in Early Twentieth-Century Australia," *Australian Aboriginal Studies* 1 (1996): 11–20.

74. Katherine Ellinghaus, *Taking Assimilation to Heart: Marriages of White Women & Indigenous Men in the United States & Australia, 1887–1937* (Lincoln, 2006), chap. 9.

75. Smithers, *Science, Sexuality, and Race*, 173.

76. *An Act for the Protection and Management of the Aboriginal Natives of Victoria* (16 December 1886); Smithers, *Science, Sexuality, and Race*, 173.

77. *Twenty-Fourth Report of the Central Board Appointed to Watch Over the Interests of the Aborigines in the Colony of Victoria* (Melbourne, 1888), 3; Smithers, *Science, Sexuality, and Race*, 174–75.

78. In making this recommendation, Basedow rejected other schemes, such as the injection of paraffin wax beneath the skin. See Herbert Basedow to the Acting Minister of External Affairs, 6 May 1911, A1, 1911/8705, Australian Archives (AA), Canberra.

79. *Argus*, 9 May 1901, in F.K. Crowley, ed., *Modern Australia in Documents: Volume 1, 1901–1939* (Melbourne, 1973), 6.

80. For "Kombo-ism" see *The West Australian*, 30 January 1905, in ACC 5086, Item 1, Western Australian State Archives; Commonwealth Bureau of Census and Statistics, *Official Year Book of the Commonwealth of Australia, 1901–1912*, vol. 6 (1913), 109.

81. For eugenic opposition to "breeding out the colour" see Alan Carroll, "The Australian Blacks, As Known to Science," *Sydney Quarterly Magazine* IX, no. 4 (December 1892): 289; Charles Davenport, "Notes on Physical Anthropology of Australian Aborigines and Black-White Hybrids," *American Journal of Physical Anthropology* VIII, no. 1 (January–March 1925): 79–80, 83, 87–88; Basil Matthews, *The Clash of Colour: A Study in the Problem of Race* (London and Edinburgh, 1925), 49–50. For Bryan's remarks see *Sydney Morning Herald*, 23 March 1934, 12.

82. AA, CRS A659 (A659/1) 1940/1/408.

83. Ibid.

84. C.E. Cook to the Administrator of the Northern Territory, 27 June 1933, AA, CRS A659 (A659/1) 1940/1/408; *Sydney Sun*, 2 April 1933, in Rowena MacDonald, ed., *Between Two Worlds: The Commonwealth Government and the Removal of Aboriginal Children of Part Descent in the Northern Territory* (Alice Springs, NT, 1995), 25; Anna Haebich, *Broken Circles*, 131, 156–61, 401–2. "Full-blood" men had no sexual role to play in the "breeding out of colour." In fact, both "half-caste" and "full-blood" boys were encouraged to live away from "half-caste" and white girls, and instructed to be stockmen or gain menial employment. See Smithers, *Science, Sexuality, and Race*, 185–86.

85. Aborigines' Friends' Association, *The Aborigines: A Commonwealth Problem and Responsibility* (1934), 6, indented quote on 15.

86. Department of the Interior, Memorandum – "Intermarriage of Coloured and Foreign Races with Aborigines," 25 May 1933, AA CRS A659 (A659/1), 1940/1/408.

87. Commonwealth Bureau of Census and Statistics, *Official Year Book of the Commonwealth of Australia* (Canberra, 1939), 381, 383, 384.

88. Higham, *Strangers in the Land*, 88, 168.

89. Hsu-Ming Teo, "The Romance of White Nations: Imperialism, Popular Culture, and National Histories" in *After the Imperial Turn: Thinking with and through the Nation*, edited by Antoinette M. Burton (Durham, NC, 2003), 281.

Chapter 15

Race and Indigeneity in Contemporary Australia

A. Dirk Moses

Race and Ethnicity in Australia

Race remains a term of public discourse in twenty-first-century Australia long after natural science and anthropology abandoned their belief in the existence of biologically distinct human species. Ideals of "whiteness," culminating in the "White Australia Policy" between 1901 and the early 1970s, were designed to keep out non-whites, especially Asians, and keep down Indigenous blacks who, it was hoped, would ultimately be "absorbed" or assimilated into the broader population.[1] But whiteness has been difficult to maintain in a globalizing world. As a classical country of immigration, Australia's population of some 21 million now comprises people from around the world. For decades, about 22 percent of its population has been born overseas, increasingly in non-European countries. Whereas British and Irish migrants constituted 58 percent and 22 percent respectively of all overseas-born Australians in 1901, those figures had declined to 27 percent and 1 percent by 1996. After a postwar immigration surge from Britain and non-British Europe, it has been migration from Asian countries that has increased considerably since the 1980s.

These changes are often understood in racial terms. Asian-Australians, who now comprise about 8.5 percent of the population, were sometimes feared to be "taking over."[2] The violent attack on Australians of so-called "middle-eastern appearance" by hundreds of Anglo-Australians on a Sydney beach in December 2005 was immediately dubbed a "race riot," as are the occasional clashes between Indigenous and Anglo-Australians in rural towns and inner-city Sydney.[3] Race remains a marker of difference for a public that regards "people," "ethnicity," and "race," and sometimes even "nation," as rough synonyms.

Even during the years of the "White Australia Policy," the population was never exclusively British and Celtic. Indigenous people(s), who have lived on the continent for tens of thousands of years, grew in number after their catastrophic decline during the nineteenth century.[4] Their enduring presence has been a feature of the Australian racial imagination, which fantasized the total disappearance of Aborigines until the 1940s, if not longer. They now constitute 2.5 percent of the population.[5] The colored and colorful language of racial distinction remains common, especially in rural areas. "Blackfellas" live alongside "whitefellas," referring to one another with these group designates, while other terms are loaded with disdain, and often used, though not in "polite society." They are widely regarded as "racist."[6]

Some language is deemed racist by Australian law. The relevant government agency, the Human Rights and Equal Opportunity Commission, describes the law thus: "The *Racial Discrimination Act 1975* protects individuals across Australia from discrimination on the grounds of race, colour, descent, or national or ethnic origin." In 1995, the national parliament passed the *Racial Hatred Act*, which covers "racially offensive or abusive behaviour" that is "done, in whole or in part, because of the race, colour, or national or ethnic origin of a person or group": it must also be "reasonably likely in all the circumstances to offend, insult, humiliate or intimidate that person or group."[7]

Arab and Muslim Australians felt offended, insulted, humiliated, and intimidated when they became the objects of intense media scrutiny as potential security threats after the terrorist attacks in the United States on 11 September 2001 and in Bali a year later.[8] The public spotlight was already on Muslim Arabs after the gang rape of Anglo-Australian women by Lebanese-Australian youths in Sydney in 2000. The rapists highlighted their Lebanese identity during the crime, leading to media observation that the rapes were "racist."[9]

Ubiquitous as racialized language is in popular and legal discourses in Australia, many historians would deny that race is actually at stake in these controversies. Racism implies biological distinction and domination. As George Fredrickson defines it, "[r]acism exists when one ethnic group or historical collectivity dominates, excludes, or seeks to eliminate another on the basis of differences that it believes are hereditary and unalterable."[10] Since almost no one any longer believes in unalterable, hereditary traits, we are usually confronted with xenophobia, they say, an unremarkable form of prejudice that characterizes virtually every society.[11] Alternatively, some commentators have preferred to regard these kinds of discrimination as manifestations of a "new racism," which marks difference by culture rather than genetic inheritance. Cultural incompatibility, not biological contamination, is the perceived social threat according to this constructivist methodology.[12]

Whether the old and new racisms can be distinguished so neatly has been questioned by British sociologists who point out that difference continues to be indicated by skin color: groups still possess a "racialized ethnicity" even though very few believe in inheritable and unalterable traits of character or culture.[13] For instance, a Jew or Muslim is racialized to the extent that his/her culture is marked by physical appearance. On these terms, to refer to people as of "middle-eastern appearance" (which excludes Jews in Australia) is to racialize them. But that would depend, Kwame Anthony Appiah might contend, on whether inferiority is ascribed to signs of physical difference; otherwise we are dealing with "racialism"—a mode of categorization that links culture to bodily inscription of individual and group otherness—rather than racism, which is necessarily discriminatory.[14]

The evidence is that many Australians think in racialist terms, and often in racist ones.[15] But if race is a social rather than biological fact, why the persistence of this category of difference at all? A global perspective is necessary to answer this question according to Immanuel Wallerstein, because the rapidly expanding and integrating world capitalist system has so undermined the ability of nation-states to deliver their promise of economic security that citizens resort to compensatory racial modes of identification. Identity politics and multiculturalism are the consequence of this transition.[16]

For critical race theorists, even liberal multiculturalism is suspect, because it suits the transcultural composition of the new global managerial class that insists on cosmopolitanism and interesting ethnic restaurants in their habitats while ignoring, or even contributing to, the international, racialized division of labor.[17] This reading of the relationship between globalization and racism is consistent with the neo-liberal opposition to the "old racism," because high levels of skilled, often non-white immigration are needed for economic growth. Thus *The Australian* newspaper's editors declined to follow the controversial argument of the Sydney-based legal academic, Andrew Fraser, who complained that "white Australians now face a life-or-death struggle to preserve their homeland" against "the Third World colonisation of Australia."[18] Hardcore racists such as Fraser are easy pickings for practitioners of "white studies," but few escape unscathed in this discipline which defines even multicultural liberals as purveyors of "benign whiteness."[19] Whites are invited by those in the know to become "race traitors" or "new Abolitionists" so they can relinquish their colonialist selves. Or they are condemned to be forever white, despite their anti-racist commitment, at best self-conscious of their inherited privilege.[20]

Indigenous Crisis?

These debates may appear like intellectual parlor games in light of the intensifying public discussion about the state and future of remote Indigenous communities.[21] Sharing headlines with stories about local Muslim "terror" suspects in the lead-up to the 2007 federal election, the reported problems in these communities—sexual violence against children, substance abuse, mismanagement, and economic stagnation—were highlighted by both Indigenous and non-Indigenous leaders and intellectuals. As usual, polarized positions characterized the field. Was the dire situation the consequence of colonialism's genocidal trauma or the Indigenous failure to fully embrace modernity? Had governments since the 1970s rashly encouraged the attempt of Aborigines to live apart from settler Australians while accelerating the erosion of essential social mores by providing excessive welfare benefits? Or were these remote communities in fact the victims of government neglect, a chronic underfunding of health and education services ascribable to a racist undervaluing of these particular citizens?

Most commentators, including a few progressive white and Indigenous leaders, supported the conservative federal government's military and bureaucratic "intervention" into the communities of the North Territory, which was announced in June 2007. As might be expected, most Indigenous leaders and others on the left opposed it, raising the spectre of neo-assimilation, neo-paternalism, and even genocide. They pointed out that the media's obsessive focus on "Aboriginal dysfunction" obscures white Australia's own identity anxieties, its hegemonic project of domination, and its denial of unrelinquished Indigenous sovereignty.[22]

And yet, the dysfunction is real, insist the minority of Indigenous leaders. To reject paternalist government measures, even if they are politically opportunistic, will affect Indigenous survival in parts of the country.[23] Inverting the usual compatibility between Indigenous and leftist political fronts, these intellectuals and leaders have accused white progressives of infantalizing Indigenous people by casting them as agentless victims of colonialism and rendering them dependent on welfare and white liberal beneficence, much to the delight of conservatives who claim that their positions have been vindicated.[24] These new fronts signal a major shift in the terms of debate about "the Indigenous question" in Australia. If the old progressive and Indigenous hope posited land rights, self-determination (or self-management), and civic equality as the high road to Aboriginal modernity, its apparent failure has not yet given birth to a new answer. In this chapter, we will see that the question of racial identity—framed in terms of "indigeneity"—is a central trope through which this crisis is framed by Aboriginal intellectuals. The survival of racial identity against the governmentality of the Australian state that seeks to aid Indigenous people can trump the imperative for "bare life"—but not for all Indigenous intellectuals.

The Question of Indigeneity

The settler colonial structure of Australian society results in an intense attachment to Indigeneity and the historical perspective that underwrites it, because this colonial modality seeks to replace them with a settler presence rather than exploit their labor, as in other colonial forms.[25] In such circumstances, one of the few strategies available to Aboriginal intellectuals is making moral claims to survival and, perhaps, some autonomy. The degree to which notions of Indigeneity persist as a discourse of self-identification mirrors the extent to which the labor of self-creation and self-preservation is necessary for a tiny population in the face of a white settler colony determined to assimilate the "native" other. Cultural survival is, then, a pressing issue for Indigenous leaders and intellectuals.[26] "Aboriginal culture and identity continue to be under increasing pressure," observed Indigenous academic Eleanor Bourke.[27]

It is not surprising that a large section of the Indigenous intelligentsia is preoccupied with articulating an emphatic sense of Indigeneity, particularly in the university environment where Aboriginal or Indigenous studies centers have been established only since the 1980s. Indeed, the Indigenous intelligentsia, comprising an impressive number of women,[28] is overwhelmingly situated in the academy, a social location that has led to reflection on Indigenous standpoints in relation to western knowledge. This novel situation is not always easy to negotiate. Confronted with often overtly racist white students, having to meet the expectations of the others who desire "postmodern primitivity where an *educated black* speaks 'their' English," and needing to rely on western scholarship to teach their subject while balancing the competing imperatives of objectivity and an Indigenous standpoint, Aboriginal academics have reported teaching and research to be a "sometimes traumatic experience" that can entail "outrage, pain, anger, humiliation, guilt, anxiety and depression."[29]

What is more, the academy's norms and imperatives function to accelerate assimilation and can thereby be a technique of "internal colonialism."[30] The challenge has been expressed by Bourke in the following terms:

> Appropriate education is critical in the survival of Aboriginal Australia but only if it is in harmony with Aboriginal aspirations and cultural contexts. The alternative is to lose Aboriginal values and lifestyles and to become Europeanised. Aboriginal people have to find the balance between gaining the necessary degree of expertise from western education and the enhancement of Aboriginality at the same time.[31]

Defining this balance has been anything but straightforward. This section identifies a number of answers to the question of Indigenous knowledge and identity, ranging from assertive challenges to "white" epistemology and calls for resistance in the name of unyielded sovereignty, to equally assertive questionings of stark polarities in the name of non-sovereign "peoplehood." As might be expected, both approaches differ markedly in their assessment of the federal government "intervention" into remote Indigenous communities, and in their comportment to history.

Indigeneity as Resistance to Colonial "Whiteness"

A defiant gesture of resilience is the emotional entailment of the project to invest Aboriginal difference with ontological status. Anita Heiss's poem, "We Have Survived," captures the sensibility in stark yet elegant terms.

> You may have tried to
> eliminate us
> assimilate us
> reconciliate us
> But you only managed to alienate us.
> And as Indigenous peoples united
> You will never totally
> eradicate us
> For our spirit has survived
> And we will remain, now and forever.[32]

Ensuring this survival is the task at hand rather than building a non-racial polity. The legal scholar Irene Watson speaks for many when she asks: "How do we, the minority, ensure Aboriginality? If we are cannibalised and utilised to Aboriginalise the majority, how do we as individuals and communities sustain our own vulnerable Aboriginality?"[33] A common strategy is to insist that the sovereignty of the Australian continent remains Aboriginal, and that Aborigines have not been defeated. It links Aboriginality to the international Indigenous movement that has emerged since the 1960s. Characterized by a shared sense of victimization by settlers, such movements now engage in "resistance to the hegemony of nations-states," unlike, say, the African postcolonies, which *are* nation-states.[34] This movement supplies a vocabulary and method for asserting Aboriginality as indigeneity, as evidenced in the many citations of Native American, Canadian First Nation, African-American, and Maori writers. Prominent among them is the Maori academic, Linda Tuhiwai Smith, whose book *Decolonizing Methodologies: Research and Indigenous Peoples* (1999) has been hugely influential in Australia and North America.[35] Its purpose has been to provide the intellectual tools to challenge the normative status of western knowledge so as to overcome the "fragmentation" of Indigenous culture: "the greater project is about recentering Indigenous identities on a larger scale" after the dislocation wrought by colonialism.[36]

We are witnessing not merely a defense or rescue of extant Indigenous culture, then. This is a project of regeneration, revitalization, and rehabilitation. "For us," writes the Torres Strait Islander academic Martin Nakata, "the field of Indigenous Studies is part of a broader landscape that includes not just Indigenous Studies, but ... the rebuilding of Indigenous communities and future."[37] These are common sentiments in Indigenous circles. "Indigenist research is research which gives voice to Indigenous people," writes Lester-Irabinna Rigney.[38] For Native American scholars Taiaiake Alfred and Jeff Corntassel even their own identity is a process of self-creation: "*being Indigenous* means thinking, speaking and acting with the conscious intent of regenerating one's indigeneity."[39]

Indigenous scholarship is therefore necessarily activist, and as such runs into western academic protocols of objectivity or neutrality. But that is not all. Western scholarship is experienced as a tool of colonial domination. The scholarly depiction of Aborigines over the centuries has been not only degrading in its arrogant assumption of white superiority; it defines Aboriginality as the negation of whiteness and colonizes knowledge about Aborigines, constraining the imaginaries of Aborigines themselves. The

Aborigine has to understand him/herself with the language of the colonizer in the manner of Du Bois's "double consciousness" and Frantz Fanon's *Black Skin, White Masks*.[40] This consciousness is a burden that non-Indigenous and non-black people can barely appreciate. Reading about "hybrid" Aborigines as bereft of history and as belonging to neither race, a teenage Ian Anderson experienced "something like grieving; but a grieving over a tremendous loss which is in itself then denied as being yours."[41] As might be expected, these Indigenous academics are suspicious of an institutional and cultural formation—the academy and modern science—that has been so complicit in the subjugation of their people.

Such suspicion extends to white academics who all too often have taken it upon themselves to "speak for" Aborigines, thereby compromising Indigenous agency while soothing their consciences. The struggle to claim a voice has extended to feminist circles, where Indigenous women have set clear boundaries about the priorities of race and gender.[42] Above all, white academics, however well-intentioned, could never relate the lived experience of Indigenous people, and this distance told in their historical reconstructions. Wendy Brady echoed a common complaint when she said that she was "tired of reading about us by people who are concerned about creating a new picture of Australia's past, yet are unable to make the connection with those of us who have experienced it."[45] Jackie Huggins was making the same point when she wrote that "Whites must not ignore this [distance between black and white positions] by taking advantage of their privileged speaking positions to construct an external version of 'us' which may pass for our 'reality'. There must be limits to the ways our worlds are re-written or placed in conceptual frameworks which are not our own."[44] Such "imposed labels and structures," writes Michael Dodson, have "[n]early suffocated" Indigenous people.[45] Not for nothing does Linda Tuhiwai Smith begin her book by noting that "'[r]esearch' is probably one of the dirtiest words in the Indigenous world's vocabulary."[46]

If these Indigenous scholars sometimes differ in the extent of their hostility to Western science, they do agree that they should no longer interpolate them as hybrid subjects, part Aboriginal, part non-Aboriginal—but not as emphatically *Indigenous*. It is not surprising, then, that they are hostile to the postcolonial and postmodern trend in the humanities, with its simultaneous celebration of cultural difference—which lends itself all too well to an immigrant settler society—and rejection of essentialisms of any kind, including, by implication, Indigeneity.[47] They want to control knowledge production about Aborigines so that Indigeneity can be (re)constructed. As Dodson puts it, "Self-representations of Aboriginality are always also acts of freedom."[48]

One strategy of Indigenous intellectuals has been to place intellectual authority in the hands of particular Aboriginal peoples in the interests of authentic and responsible cultural transmission and survival. Karen L. Martin–Booran Mirraboopa, for example, advocates an Indigenist research program that reflects a distinct Aboriginal ontology of natural and human parity and connectedness. A full-blown re-enchantment of the world, this program is designed for "protection and preservation of our country and its Entities and the protection and preservation of our Ways of Knowing, Ways of Being and Ways of Doing." Research requires a listening countenance towards organic totalities rather than their forensic dissection. Messages "may occur as dreams" or in the quotidian warp and woof of everyday life. Research "has less to do with capturing 'truth' or drawing general conclusions, than the reconnecting of self, family, community and Entities that can be claimed and celebrated."[49]

To decolonize higher education means that Aborigines become the authors rather than the object of research. The academy becomes a vehicle for Indigenous recovery. Lester-Irabinna Rigney uses the term "intellectual sovereignty," while Victor Hart refers to "knowledge governance" and "Indigenous standpoint pedagogy."[50] An explicitly philosophical defense of this position has been mounted by Aileen Moreton-Robinson. Against the utopian fantasies of Australian multiculturalism, she claims that Aborigines possess "ontological belonging," a prior rootedness to the land that subsequent migrant-settlers cannot cancel. She rejects the postcolonial literature that, as she accurately observes, focuses on countries like India and Algeria that have cast out the settler and become sovereign. Aborigines are still asserting their sovereignty against the settler, after all, and they remain Indigenous despite any seeming hybridity and loss of tradition. "Indigenous people may have been incorporated in and seduced by the cultural forms of the colonizer but this has not diminished the ontological relationship to land. Rather, it has produced a doubleness whereby Indigenous subjects can 'perform' whiteness while being Indigenous."[51]

This ontologically distinct Indigenousness consists in "relationship to country, derived from the Dreaming," the "original form of social living created by ancestral beings." Like Martin–Booran Mirraboopa, Moreton-Robinson emphasizes the unity of creation, and asserts that Aborigines today believe that they reincarnate "these ancestral beings," via which they "derive their sense of belonging to country through and from them."

She dismisses the critique of essentialism by positing the radical incommensurability of the Indigenous self, which, as part of creation, is immune to charges of essentialism. Western knowledge cannot comprehend it and should not try. "Questioning the integrity and legitimacy of Indigenous ways of knowing and being has more to do with who has the power to be knower and whether their knowledge is commensurate with the West's 'rational' belief system." How seriously she takes this argument about the non-translatability of Indigenous knowledge and culture-boundedness of Western rationality is unclear when she cites Western thinkers and qualifies her statements about the Dreaming by writing that "it is believed to have occurred."[52] Such tensions are inherent in any attempt to rationally base a claim of "strategic essentialism" on ontologically grounded indigeneity.[53]

Given the difficulty of defining Indigeneity in the international literature, some scholars have tried to distinguish it from the aspiration of peoples for autonomy and self-determination, goals that do not need to be grounded in Indigeneity per se.[54] Other researchers committed to an Indigenous research methodology implicitly accept this distinction by making less ambitious epistemological claims. Martin Nakata, for instance, sees an Indigenous standpoint not in privileged access to esoteric knowledge—as Martin and Moreton-Robinson aver—but in a "distinct form of analysis" that must be "rational and reasoned" and not "beyond the scrutiny of others." Such an analysis entails reflection on experience. The special Indigenous experience means that the Indigenous perspective lays bare that which is ignored by the powerful. In keeping with other Indigenous scholars, he prescribes lived experience as the starting point for investigation rather than abstract concepts and categories, although in his hands experience is a conduit for insight rather than an end in itself.[55]

He is not alone. Lester-Irabinna Rigney agrees that Indigenism "cannot afford hegemonic and simplistic generalisations and conclusions." Indigenous intellectual sovereignty selectively adapts Western critical theory's rejection of positivism by embedding it in, recovering, and honoring Indigenous experience. "The struggle for Indigenous intellectual sovereignty is to move our humanness, our scholarship, our identities and our knowledge systems from invisible to visible."[56]

As might be expected, scholars from this tradition tend to deplore the federal government's intervention into the remote communities of the Northern Territory. Like many anti-racist whites, they mock the proposition that these communities should join the "real economy" as a tawdry consolation for unjust dispossession. Land rights, the symbol of sovereignty and Indigeneity, cannot be relinquished or compromised for the sake of social order. The construction of these communities' problems as a national emergency or crisis displaces the deeper problem of illegitimate British conquest.[57] If intra-Aboriginal violence is regrettable, they continue, it is ultimately the fault of the colonialists who undermined traditional law. Aboriginal culture is not pathological and should not be blamed. "Our living Aboriginal being is alive and awake causing a disruption to the colonial project," announced Irene Watson defiantly when confronted with depictions of communal disintegration. Such depictions are mischievous, these thinkers retort, because they merely confirm the worst racist stereotypes of whites and serve to distract attention away from government underfunding of Indigenous services. The government's rhetoric of Aboriginal "responsibility" neglects the root causes of Indigenous disadvantage—colonial dispossession and trauma—and plays into the hands of racists who resent government assistance to remote communities. The intervention is above all an exercise in neocolonialism and neo-assimilation.[58]

This defensive perspective is indentured to a particular relationship to time. The traumatic past is the traumatic present. The colonialism that began in 1788 persists today. Indigenous people were victims then and they are now. Victor Hart's rejection of postcolonial studies is paradigmatic. The postcolonial gaze, he thinks, "implies history no longer has an effect on the present and that history is only relevant for *understanding* the present, rather than in transforming it."[59] The trauma was eloquently articulated by Kevin Gilbert in 1990:

> In attempting to present the evidence we are furiously attacked by white Australians and white converts, whatever their colour, as "Going back two hundred years … the past is finished …!" Yet, cut off a man's leg, kill his mother, rape his land, psychologically attack him and keep him in a powerless position each day—does it not live on in the mind of the victim? Does it not continue to scar and affect his thinking? Deny it, but it still exists.[60]

The persistence of this traumatic consciousness is a function, at least in part, of the denial of original Indigenous sovereignty and the genocidal effects of British settlement.[61] But if Hart's contention that the past affects the present is undeniable, one could ask whether freedom is thereby compromised. Does not Gilbert's self-reflexive consciousness demonstrate the capacity not to be determined by this past? By recognizing the temporal space between past and present—identifying the trauma as trauma means one has begun to overcome its spell—different questions can be asked of Aborigine-settler encounters. They would include the question, popular among historians, about "accommodation" between Aborigines and settlers, but also questions of the kind posed regarding the participation of some Aborigines in the extermination of others (like the Mounted Native Police in Queensland), and the origins of intra-black violence and exploitation.[62] Answering such questions would interrupt the heteronymous flow of historical relations, question the status of victimhood, enable a different comportment to historical responsibility, and open up space for a different language of identity. These, at least, seem to be the hopes of a small number of Indigenous intellectuals, to whom I now turn.

Peoplehood and Responsibility

We have seen why the transcendence of Aboriginal liberation narratives is difficult in Australia: holding fast to Indigeneity is the inevitable response of a tiny minority in the face of a settler majority intent on integrating Aborigines on its own terms. As Indigenous historian John Maynard, observes, "Historically, the Aboriginal political voice was silenced and in the contemporary setting it continues to be."[63] And yet, the much-discussed crisis of remote communities has led some Indigenous leaders to abandon the liberation narrative and to question the terms of conventional Aboriginal politics. They are, in the words of the African philosopher Achilles Mbembe, "revisiting this archive of abjection, no longer in the context of the call to murder the settler, but at a time when brother and enemy have become one, and in an age in which the sovereign right to ill is exercised against one's own people first—the violence of brother towards brother."[64]

Perhaps the most publicly prominent figure is Noel Pearson, an Indigenous leader who, as a lawyer in the 1980s and 1990s, was at the forefront of the land rights debate, and has since led the Cape York Institute in far-north Queensland to advance the welfare of his people.[65] Equally significant is Marcia Langton, a pioneer of the university-based Aboriginal intelligentsia who has written extensively about Indigenous ontology, sovereignty, and treaties, as well as about representations of Aborigines and the limits of the white academy.[66] Both of them, in addition to political leaders like Warren Mundine, national president of the Australian Labor Party, are trying to reshape the Indigenous political imaginary, and to that end have been given considerable space in Australia's public affairs journals and newspapers.

They support the intervention despite its origins with the conservative coalition government of John Howard. In fact, their targets are its white— liberals and "the old left"—and black opponents and the ideology of victimhood, entitlements, and rights that unite them. These targets are, in the first place, white "romantic defenders of Aboriginal self-determination" who "need perpetual victims for [their] analysis to work."[67] Although he acknowledges the support of white liberals for Indigenous rights over the decades, Pearson goes so far as to suggest that they present a greater threat to Aborigines than racist conservatives. The construction of Aborigines as perpetual victims of colonialism robs them of agency and renders them dependent on white liberal beneficence, resulting in a destructive co-dependency in which the white conscience is soothed[68] Consequently, the biggest danger for Indigenous people now, Langton thinks, "is that the old-left thinking will again prevail."[69]

Fellow Aborigines are not spared either. Langton is scathing about "the 'big men' in Aboriginal communities who harvest votes for their Labor mates," but also about women who oppose the intervention, because "they undermine attempts to prevent rape of Aboriginal children and other crimes against our most vulnerable citizens."[70] Both Pearson and Langton reject the argument that colonialism can be blamed entirely for the Indigenous predicament:

> Many of the strongest critics of the intervention have a sense of identity and dignity based on being in an oppressed 'racial' collective. As Aboriginal people, they feel they share the suffering of other Aboriginal people. I cannot quibble with this basic ontological characteristic of being a member of an oppressed group. The problem arises when there is a presumption of shared experience and willingness to overlook the moral, ethical or even rational view of particular behaviours. Solidarity for its own sake takes pre-eminence, and does not permit a clear-cut rejection of wrong doing.[71]

For the same reason, Pearson rejects the argument that structural disadvantages can account for Indigenous behavior in these communities. The "symptom theory" of destructive behavior, which refers, say, to alcoholism or sexual abuse to historical trauma or structural disadvantage disempowers Aborigines by suggesting that they cannot take responsibility for their actions and therefore that nothing can be done. These problems, he argues, are the poisoned fruit of Indigenous traditions distorted by substance abuse, which is also perpetuated in the name of those traditions, such as reciprocity among kin-members.[72]

Aboriginal freedom to forge an autonomous destiny is his goal. Their history cannot ultimately condemn his people to perpetual victim status:

> The disorder in our community is the symptom in the sense that it is a product of our history and marginalisation. It is a different question to what extent our history *maintains* the social chaos ... Inherited trauma is an issue, as we have seen in the Jewish experience. But the same experience shows us that trauma is not in itself enough to debilitate a people.[73]

The regeneration of his people requires the ascription of personal responsibility. These remote communities (or postcolonies), he has pointed out on many occasions, have become anarchic "outback hellholes" and cannot be spaces of regeneration until passive welfare is ended and social order is re-established.[74] Challenging the "whiteness studies" paradigm, he is dismayed that so many Aborigines decry the virtues of thrift and education as "white," implying that dissolute behavior and dropping out of school are characteristically black. Himself an accomplished university student and then lawyer, he does not share the suspicion of the academy: "Indigenous children will be able to choose their own life path only after they have received the best education and have been protected from ill health and neglect."[75] To that end, he also urges that remote communities integrate into the "real economy" by developing partnerships with the private sector, a position directly at odds with the oppositional posture that regards such collaboration as craven capitulation to white-settler colonialism, neo-liberalism, and globalization.[76]

Langton, too, rejects the avoidance of Indigenous responsibility that ascribes contemporary intra-Aboriginal violence to colonialism. "One of the sustained fantasies about traditional Aboriginal society," she notes, "is that, until colonisation, life for Aboriginal people was peaceful and idyllic."[77] She and Pearson extend the auto-critique of Kevin Gilbert who in 1978 punctured the Aboriginal myths about Indigeneity and communal and kinship solidarity by writing that "you only have to go to any Aboriginal mission or reserve to see the truth: the lack of community spirit, the neglect and abuse of tiny children, and all the rest of it."[78] This self-critical posture has led Pearson to question the metaphysics of Indigeneity proposed by Moreton-Robinson and others. Literate in the North American debates on race consciousness, he proposes "peoplehood" as an alternative to "nationhood" or, by implication, Indigeneity for Aboriginal peoples in Australia. Nationhood implies state sovereignty, which is not an option for Aborigines in Australia, but peoplehood underlines the pan-Aboriginal sense of common identity and history. At the same time, it is sufficiently open a concept to admit of layered identities for Aborigines, an approach inspired by the philosopher Amartya Sen. Rather than the stark and rigid opposition of black and white and its "illusion of singular identity," Pearson urges a complex amalgam of layers based on cultural and linguistic groups, religion, place of birth, residence, professional group, and so forth. "A pluralist and united world is one which has strong bonding identities between those who know each other, and bridging identities with strangers."[79] Such a view would accord with Duncan Ivison's argument about the consistency of Aboriginal group rights and individual freedom.[80]

Independent of this program, Yin Paradies, a Melbourne-based research scientist who identifies himself as "Aboriginal-Anglo-Asian Australian," has also mounted a trenchant critique of the Indigenity case. Exploding "fantasies of indigeneity," he points out that he himself is "[d]escended from both Indigenous and Euro-Australian ancestors," and is therefore "both colonizer and colonized, both Black and consummately White." The discourse of Indigeneity results in constructed boundaries of inclusion and exclusion, policed by whites and blacks alike, one demanding performances of race, the other questioning whether one is sufficiently black.[81] Such fantasies of alterity, in Paradies's view, ignore the fact that most Aborigines do not speak an Indigenous language, live on ancestral lands, or identify with them. Neither can they underwrite an illegitimate assumption of Indigenous superiority and access to truth that he perceives in claims by some Aboriginal intellectuals. Like Appiah, Paradies thinks such protocols of belonging, though understandably fashioned to ensure cultural survival, "end up replacing 'one form of tyranny with another.'" They have become maladaptive and outdated.[82] And like Pearson, he wants to reconcile the persistence of Aboriginal peoplehood with a diversity of identities, and thereby relinquish romantic notions of singular Indigenous selfhood. Hybridity, defined in this way rather than as a synonym for deracination as Ian Anderson experienced as a teenager, ought to be permitted to describe Aborigines as well.[83]

Conclusion

In many ways, these revisionist intellectuals are seeking to replace the language of authenticity with practices of sincerity that the African-American anthropologist John L. Jackson has theorized in his book *Real Black: Adventures of Black Sincerity*.[84] An opponent of strategic essentialism as well as anti-essentialist constructivism, he proposes a critical ontology of racial being in which performances of blackness negotiate, though never harmonize, the tension between black particularity and universal human subjectivity. The freedom of sincerity inheres in cracking open closed racial objectifications, in replacing the language of unchanging racial substance with that of becoming, and in rejecting the racially limited space of human meaningfulness prescribed by inherited regimes of power.

Converging arguments are being made in other disciplines. The African-American political scientist Tommie Shelby, inspired by Appiah, distinguishes between black solidarity and black identity—existence and essence, if you like—by arguing that struggles for justice against racism need not entail an emphatic sense of racial being. If African-Americans are disadvantaged because they are racialized as black, they can develop a "pragmatic nationalist conception of political solidarity," in other words, a political rather than racial identity committed "to eliminating unjust racial inequality." Like Pearson and Jackson, then, he is not a radical constructivist: he wants *black* political mobilization and he defends black group differentiation. But such mobilization and differentiation is hard to base philosophically on racial—rather than political—difference. Shelby's vision of black self-realization is "forthrightly anti-essentialist," then, because it "subordinate[s] questions of who blacks are as a people to questions about the ways in which they have been and continue to be unfairly treated."[85]

An Australian rendition might separate Aboriginal solidarity and political mobilization from pseudo-philosophical claims to Indigenous ontological difference. Pearson and Langton seem to imply that reclaiming freedom is only possible by challenging heteronymous formations. In this case, reflexivity about one's agency requires a new approach to both the self and to group membership. Moving beyond a view of the self based on "victimhood and mutilation" is as important, in the words of Mbembe, as "a revisiting of our own fables and the various grammars that, under the pretext of authenticity or radicalism, prosaically turn Africa into yet another deadly fiction."[86] This critical task in Australia is being undertaken principally by a small number of insider intellectuals, as it is in other national historiographies, such as Saul Friedländer's dismay at the lack of Jewish solidarity during the Holocaust, and Edward Said's call for a critical historical consciousness among Arabs "and Palestinians in particular," who "must also begin to explore our own histories, myths, and patriarchal ideas of the nation … [a task that]… cannot either be left unanswered or postponed indefinitely under the guise of national defense and national unity."[87] As the Jewish and Palestinian cases show, such a self-critical comportment is particularly challenging when the group itself feels beleaguered and stigmatized.

Notes

My thanks are extended to Gillian Cowlishaw, Ned Curthoys, Duncan Ivison, Olaf Kleist, Shino Konishi, Emma Esther Kowal, Neil Levi, Saadi Nikro, Paul Patton, Tim Rowse, Anja Schwarz, Lorenzo Veracini, and Natasha Wheatley for candid critique and valuable suggestions. Needless to say, they are not responsible for the views expressed here, with which they do not necessarily concur.

1. For background, see Raymond Evans, "'Pigmentia': Racial Fears and White Australia," in *Genocide and Settler Society: Frontier Violence and Stolen Indigenous Children in Australian History*, edited by A. Dirk Moses (New York, 2004), 103–124.
2. Two-thirds of this population lives in Sydney and Melbourne: Australian Bureau of Statistics, 2006 Census Data. "20680–Ancestry (Region) by Country of Birth of Parents–Australia," <http://www.censusdata.abs.gov.au>, viewed 9 February 2008; Department of Immigration and Multicultural Affairs, *Immigration: Federation to Century's End, 1901–2001* (Canberra, October 2001): <http://www.immi.gov.au/media/publications/statistics/federation/federation.pdf>, viewed 6 February 2008. An example of anxiety about Asian immigration is Geoffrey Blainey, *All for Australia* (Sydney, 1984).
3. For analyses of the Cronulla beach riot, see Gregory Noble, ed., *Lines in the Sand: The Cronulla Riots and the Limits of Australian Multiculturalism* (Sydney, 2009), and Scott Poynting, "What Caused the Cronulla Riot?," *Race & Class* 48, no. 1 (2006): 85–92. On Indigenous people and racial rhetoric, Joanna Atherfold, "Redfern: the 'Riot' and the Reporting," *Australian Studies in Journalism* 17 (2006): 41–53.
4. They declined in number from perhaps 750,000 to around 90,000 in the century after the British arrival/invasion in 1788. The complexity of defining, categorizing, and counting the Indigenous population is carefully set out in Tim Rowse, "Notes on the History of the Aboriginal Population of Australia," in Moses, *Genocide and Settler Society*, 312–325. Figures from this period need to be treated as rough estimates.
5. They are not evenly distributed throughout the country. For instance, 31.6 percent of Northern Territorians are Indigenous, while only 0.6 percent of Victorians. In-

digenous Australians numbered 517,200 in the 2006 census: Australian Bureau of Statistics, *Population Distribution, Aboriginal and Torres Straight Islander Australians*, Document 4705.0 (Canberra, 15 August 2007), <http://www.ausstats.abs.gov.au>, viewed 9 January 2008.

6. Gillian K. Cowlishaw, "Censoring Race in 'Post-Colonial' Anthropology," *Critique of Anthropology* 20 (2000): 101–23; Faye V. Harrison, "The Persistent Power of 'Race' in the Cultural and Political Economy of Racism," *Annual Review of Anthropology* 24 (1995): 47–74.

7. <http://www.humanrights.gov.au/racial_discrimination/about_race.html>, viewed 8 February 2008.

8. Andrew Jakubowicz, "Political Islam and the Future of Australian Multiculturalism," *National Identities* 9, no. 3 (2007): 265–80.

9. Miranda Devine, "Racist Rapes: Finally the Truth Comes Out," *Sydney Morning Herald*, 14 July 2002; Sarah Crichton and Andrew Stevenson, "When Race and Rape Collide," *The Age*, 17 September 2002.

10. George M. Fredrickson, *Racism: A Short History* (Princeton, 2002), 170. Still other historians concede that race/ism is a "moving and fuzzy target," and so take a broad definition for research purposes: Colin Kidd, *The Forging of Races: Race and Scripture in the Protestant Atlantic World, 1600–2000* (Cambridge, UK, 2006), 2.

11. This is the position of the conservative Australian broadsheet, *The Australian*. See its editorial, "Racism not Endemic," 14 December 2005.

12. Michael Humphrey, "Culturalising the Abject: Islam, Law and Moral Panic in the West," *Australian Journal of Social Issues* 42, no. 1 (2007): 9–25. The founding text of this distinction is Martin Barker, *The New Racism* (London, 1981); Barker, "Biology and the New Racism," in *Anatomy of Racism*, edited by David Theo Goldberg (Minneapolis, 1990), 18–37.

13. Tariq Modood, Richard Berthoud, and James Nazroo, "'Race', Racism and Ethnicity: A Response to Ken Smith," *Sociology* 36, no. 2 (2002): 419–27.

14. Kwame Anthony Appiah, "Racisms," in Goldberg, *Anatomy of Racism*, 3–18.

15. James Forrest and Kevin Dunn, "Racism and Intolerance in Eastern Australia: a Geographic Perspective," *Australian Geographer* 37, no. 2 (2006): 167–86.

16. Immanuel Wallerstein, "Comment" on Eric J. Wolfe, "Perilous Ideas: Race, Culture, People," *Current Anthropology* 35, no. 1 (1994): 9–10.

17. Ghassan Hage, *Against Paranoid Nationalism: Searching for a Home in a Shrinking Society* (Sydney, 2002).

18. Editorial, "The Racism Furphy," *The Australian*, 22 December 2005; Andrew Fraser, "Rethinking the White Australia Policy," *The Australian*, 21 September 2005. In the interests of "open debate," however, the newspaper was happy to publish Fraser's racist hysteria. Fraser was subject to disciplinary action from his employer, Macquarie University in Sydney, for suggesting that African immigrants were racially inclined to criminality.

19. The North American field is examined in Peter Kolchin, "Whiteness Studies: The New History of Race in America," *The Journal of American History* 89, no. 1 (2002): 154–73. On Australia, see Suvendrini Perera, "Race Terror, Sydney, December 2005," *borderlands e-journal* 5, no. 1 (2006); Rachel Standfield, "'A Remarkably Tolerant Nation'?: Constructions of Benign Whiteness in Australian Political Discourse," *borderlands e-journal* 3, no. 2 (2004). For high-level theorization of multiculturalism in Australia, see Geoffrey Brahm Levey, ed., *Political Theory and Australian Multiculturalism* (New York, 2008).

20. Jane Haggis, "Beyond Race and Whiteness? Reflections on the New Abolitionists and an Australian Critical Whiteness Studies," *borderlands e-journal* 3, no. 2 (2004). See the excellent discussion in Emma Esther Kowal, "The Proximate Advocate: Improving Indigenous Health on the Postcolonial Frontier" (Ph.D. diss., University of Melbourne, 2006), 42–44.

21. E.g., Richard Trugden, *When Warriors Lie Down and Die: Towards an Understanding of Why the Aboriginal People of Arnhem Land Face the Greatest Crisis in Health and Education Since European Contact* (Darwin, NT, 2001); Rosemary Neill, *White Out: How Politics Is Killing Black Australia* (Sydney, 2002); Michael Gordon, "Sweeter Dreaming," *The Age*, 19 July 2003.

22. E.g., Jon C. Altman, "The Howard Government's Northern Territory Intervention: Are Neo-Paternalism and Indigenous Development Compatible?" Centre for Aboriginal Economic Policy Research, Topical Issue No. 16/2007: <http://www.anu.edu.au/caepr/>. Former Indigenous member of parliament in the Northern Territory, John Ah Kit, linked the federal intervention to genocide: see "Indigenous Intervention 'Genocide,'" *The Daily Telegraph*, 7 August 2007.

23. Noel Pearson, "Passive Welfare and the Destruction of Indigenous Society in Australia," in *Reforming the Australian Welfare State*, edited by Peter Saunders (Melbourne, 2000), 136–55: Pearson, "Vale Hope in Outback Hellhole," *The Australian*, 17 February 2007; Marcia Langton, "Stop the Abuse of Children," *The Australian*, 12 December 2007; Langton, "Real Change for Real People," *The Australian*, 26 January 2008.

24. The former prime minister John Howard's praise of Noel Pearson is typical of this phenomenon, as is the decision of the conservative newspaper, *The Australian*, to devote much column space for Pearson and Marcia Langton.

25. Patrick Wolfe, "Structure and Event: Settler Colonialism, Time, and the Question of Genocide," in *Empire, Colony, Genocide: Conquest, Occupation, and Subaltern Resistance in World History*, edited by A. Dirk Moses (New York and Oxford, 2008), 102–32.

26. For a brilliant discussion of how international organizations participate in the construction and persistence of Indigeneity, see Tim Rowse, "Indigenous Culture: The Politics of Vulnerability and Survival," in *The Sage Handbook of Cultural Analysis*, edited by Tony Bennett and John Frow (Los Angeles, 2008), 406–26.

27. Eleanor Bourke, "The First Australians: Kinship, Family and Identity," *Family Matters*, no. 25 (1993): 6.

28. Mary Ann Bin-Salik, ed., *Aboriginal Women by Degrees: Their Stories of the Journey Towards Academic Achievement* (Brisbane, 2000).

29. Victor Hart, "Teaching Black and Teaching Back," *Social Alternatives* 22, no. 3 (2003): 13; Martin Nakata, "Anthropological Texts and Indigenous Standpoints," *Australian Aboriginal Studies* 3, no. 1 (1998): 4.

30. Tracey Imtoual Bunda, "Why Indigenous Programs Cannot Succeed Without a Critically Reflective Teaching Practice," *Professional Voice* (Institute of Koorie Education, Deakin University), 4, no. 3 (2007): 19–22.

31. Eleanor Bourke, "Aboriginal Australia," *Kaurna Higher Education Journal*, no. 2 (1992): 17. For similar fears about primary schools, see Lester-Irabinna Rigney, "Indigenous Education and Treaty: Building Indigenous Management Capacity," *Balayi: Culture, Law and Colonialism* 4 (2002): 73–82.

32. Antia Heiss, *Token Koori* (Sydney, 1998), 13.

33. Irene Watson, "Legitimising White Supremacy," *Online Opinion*, 28 August 2007, viewed on 13 April 2008, <www.onlineopinion.com.au/view.asp?article=6277>.

34. Ronald Niezen, *The Origins of Indigenism* (Berkeley, 2003), 207.

35. E.g., S. Masturah Ismail and Courtney B. Cazden, "Struggles for Indigenous Education and Self-Determination: Culture, Context, and Collaboration," *Anthropology and Education Quarterly* 36, no.1 (2005): 88–92.

36. Linda Tuhiwai Smith, *Decolonizing Methodologies: Research and Indigenous Peoples* (London, 1999), 97–98.

37. Martin Nakata cited in Jean Phillips, Sue Whatman, Victor Hart, and Greg Winslett, "Decolonising University Curricula – Reforming the Colonised Spaces Within Which We Operate," in *Proceedings The Indigenous Knowledges Conference – Reconciling Academic Priorities with Indigenous Realities*, Victoria University, Wellington, 2005; Aileen Moreton-Robinson, "Introduction: Resistance, Recovery, and Revitalisation," in *Blacklines: Contemporary Critical Writing by Indigenous Australians*, edited by Michelle Grossman (Melbourne, 2003), 127–31.

38. Lester-Irabinna Rigney, "Internationalisation of an Indigenous Anti-Colonial Cultural Critique of Research Methodologies: A Guide to Indigenist Research Methodology and its Principles," *The Journal for Native American Studies* 14, no. 2 (1997): 109–21.

39. Taiaiake Alfred and Jeff Corntassel, "Being Indigenous: Resurgence Against Contemporary Colonialism," *Government and Opposition* 40, no. 4 (September 2005): 614. Emphasis in original.

40. Aileen Moreton-Robinson, "Whiteness, Epistemology, and Indigenous Representation," in *Whitening Race: Essay in Social and Cultural Criticism*, edited by Aileen Moreton-Robinson (Canberra, 2004), 75–88; Martin Nakata, "Commonsense, Colonialism and Government," in *Woven Histories, Dancing Lives: Torres Strait Islander Identity, Culture and History*, edited by Richard Davis (Canberra, 2004), 154–73; Michael Dodson refers to such images as "the enemy within": "The End in the Beginning: Re(de)finding Aboriginality" in Grossman, *Blacklines*, 33, 38; W.E.B.

Du Bois, *The Souls of Black Folk* (1903; New York, 1996), 3. Frantz Fanon, *Black Skin, White Masks*, trans. Charles M. Larkmann (New York, 1967).

41. Ian Anderson, "Black Bit, White Bit," in Grossman, *Blacklines*, 46–47.

42. Jackie Huggins, "Black Women and Women's Liberation," *Hecate* 13, no. 1 (1987): 77; Aileen Moreton-Robinson, *Talkin' Up to the White Woman: Aboriginal Women and Feminism* (Brisbane, 2000).

43. Wendy Brady, "Indigenous Insurgency Against the Speaking for Others," *UTS Review* 7, no. 1 (2001): 28.

44. Jackie Huggins, Rita Huggins, and Jane M. Jacobs, "Kooramindanjie: Place and the Postcolonial," *History Workshop Journal*, no. 39 (1995): 167.

45. Dodson, "The End in the Beginning," 28.

46. Smith, *Decolonizing Methodologies*, 1.

47. Hart, "Teaching Black and Teaching Back," 14; Ian Anderson, "Re-Claiming TRU-GER-NAN-NER: Decolonising the Symbol," in *Speaking Positions. Aboriginality, Gender and Ethnicity in Australian Cultural Studies*, edited by Penny van Toorn and David English (Melbourne, 1995), 38.

48. Dodson, "The End in the Beginning," 39.

49. Karen L. Martin–Booran Mirraboopa, "Ways of Knowing, Ways of Being and Ways of Doing: A Theoretical Framework and Methods for Indigenous Research and Indigenist Research," *Journal of Australian Studies* 76 (2003): 203–14. For reflections on the distinction between time and place in Indigenous philosophy, see Stephen Muecke: *Ancient & Modern: Time, Culture, and Indigenous Philosophy* (Sydney, 2004).

50. Lester-Irabinna Rigney, "A First Perspective of Indigenous Australian Participation in Science: Framing Indigenous Research Towards Indigenous Australian Intellectual Sovereignty," *Kaurna Higher Education Journal*, no. 7 (2001): 1–13. He borrows the term from Osage First Nations scholar Robert Warrior. Victor Hart, "Mapping Aboriginality," in *Investigating Queensland's Cultural Landscapes. Report 1: Setting the Theoretical Scene*, edited by Helen Armstrong (Brisbane, 2001), 49–50.

51. Ailene Moreton-Robinson, "'I Still Call Australia Home': Indigenous Belonging and Place in a White Postcolonizing Society," in *Uprootings/Regroundings: Questions of Home and Migration*, edited by Sara Ahmed, Claudia Cantaneda, Anne-Marie Fortier, and Mimi Sheller (Oxford and New York, 2003), 31; Irene Watson, "Aboriginal Law and the Sovereignty of *Terra Nullius*," *borderlands e-journal* 1, no. 2 (2002); Ian Anderson, "I, the 'Hybrid' Aborigine: Film and Representation," *Australian Aboriginal Studies* 1 (1997): 4–14.

52. Moreton-Robinson, "'I Still Call Australia Home," 31–32; Moreton-Robinson, "Towards a New Research Agenda? Foucault, Whiteness and Indigenous Sovereignty," *Journal of Sociology* 42, no. 4 (2006): 383–95. Somewhat inconsistently, she also rejects what she calls the "racialized binary" of the white female researcher and Indigenous women: Aileen Moreton-Robinson, "Tiddas Talkin' Up to the White Woman: When Huggins et al. Took on Bell," in Grossman, *Blacklines*, 76. Michael

Dodson shares her belief about the untranslatability of Indigenous knowledge and consciousness. See his "The End in the Beginning," 39.

53. One might raise the issue of performative contradiction that cannot be wished away by claims that advancing and defending arguments is merely "performing whiteness." See Martin Jay, "The Debate Over The Performative Contradiction: Habermas Versus the Poststructuralists," in *Philosophical Interventions in the Unfinished Project of Enlightenment*, edited by Axel Honneth, Thomas McCarthy, Claus Offe, and Albrecht Wellmer (Cambridge, MA, 1992), 261–79.

54. John Bowen, "Should We Have a Universal Concept of 'Indigenous Peoples' Rights? Ethnicity and Essentialism in the Twenty-First Century," *Anthropology Today* 16, no. 4 (2000): 12–16; Ian McIntosh, "Defining Oneself, and Being Defined as, Indigenous: A Comment," *Anthropology Today* 18, no. 3 (2002): 23–24.

55. Martin Nakata, *Disciplining Savages–Savaging the Disciplines* (Canberra, 2004), 214. He has always rejected "intellectual separatism": Nakata, "Anthropological Texts and Indigenous Standpoints."

56. Rigney, "A First Perspective of Indigenous Australian Participation in Science," 1–13.

57. Aileen Moreton-Robinson and Fiona Nicoll, "We Shall Fight Them on the Beaches: Protesting Cultures of White Possession," *Journal of Australian Studies* 89 (2006): 160. Tracey Bunda rebuked Noel Pearson at the Adelaide Festival of Ideas on 8 July 2007 for counter-posing land rights and social order in certain circumstances. Aileen Moreton-Robinson, "The House that Jack Built: Britishness and White Possession," *Australian Critical Race and Whiteness Studies Association Journal* 1 (2005): 21–29.

58. Irene Watson, "Response to Peter Sutton," *Macquarie Law Journal* 6 (2006): 184; Larissa Behrendt and Nicole Watson, "Good Intentions Are Not Good Enough," 2 May 2007, Australians for Native Title <www.antar.org.au/content/view/382/127/>, viewed 13 April 2008; Larissa Behrendt, Address to the Indigenous Labor Network, 13 July 2005, <www.jumbunna.uts.edu.au/research/alpiln_13_07_05.pdf>, viewed 18 April 2008. Rebecca Stringer, "A Nightmare of the Neocolonial Kind: Politics of Suffering in Howard's Northern Territory Intervention," *borderlands e-journal* 6, no. 2 (2007). See also <www.womenforwik.org>.

59. Hart, "Teaching Black and Teaching Back," 14–15: "Postcolonial studies are becoming a celebratory cover-up of a dangerous period in Aboriginal peoples' lives and especially a cover-up on the 'hows' and 'whys' relating to the genocide of Aboriginal people past and present."

60. Kevin Gilbert quoted in Philip Morrissey, "Dancing with Shadows: Erasing Aboriginal Self and Sovereignty," in *Sovereign Subjects: Indigenous Sovereignty Matters*, edited by Aileen Moreton-Robinson (Sydney, 2007), 73.

61. On genocide in Australia, see A. Dirk Moses, "Moving the Genocide Debate Beyond the History Wars," *Australian Journal of Politics and History* 54, no. 2 (2008): 248–70.

62. Jonathan Richards, *The Secret War: A True History of Queensland's Native Police* (Brisbane, 2008); Margaret Fels, *Good Men and True: The Aboriginal Police of the Port Phillip District, 1837–1853* (Melbourne, 1988).

63. John Maynard, "Australian History: Lifting Haze or Descending Fog?" *Aboriginal History* 27 (2003): 139.

64. Achille Mbembe, "*On the Postcolony*: A Brief Response to Critics," *African Identities* 4, no. 2 (2006): 153. The quotation would need to be amended from killing one's brother to sexually exploiting one's sister.

65. Cape York Institute for Policy and Leadership: <www.cyi.org.au>. Pearson's commitment to the rights agenda and frustration with conservative government ministers led him once to call them "racist scum."

66. Marcia Langton, "An Aboriginal Ontology of Being and Place: The Performance of Aboriginal Property Relations in the Princess Charlotte Bay Area of Eastern Cape York Peninsula, Australia" (Ph.D. diss., Macquarie University, 2005); Langton, "Dominion and Dishonour: A Treaty Between our Nations?" *Postcolonial Studies* 4, no. 1 (2001): 13–26.

67. Marcia Langton, "Real Change for Real People," *The Australian*, 26 January 2008. Mundine likewise opposes "this romantic bullshit about Aboriginal culture," quoted in Stuart Rintoul, "Chance to Cut PC Rubbish: Mundine," *The Australian*, 4 February 2008.

68. Noel Pearson, "White Guilt, Victimhood, and the Quest for the Radical Centre," *Griffith Review*, no. 16 (2007).

69. Marcia Langton, "Trapped in the Aboriginal Reality Show," *Griffith Review*, no. 19 (2008): 8.

70. Ibid., 4, 8.

71. Ibid., 10.

72. Noel Pearson, "Light on the Hill," Ben Chifley Memorial Lecture, 2000, <www.capeyorkpartnerships.com/team/noelpearson/lightonhill-12-8-00.htm>, viewed 8 April 2008; Pearson, "Land Rights and Progressive Wrongs," *Griffith Review* 2 (2003), available at <www.capeyorkpartnerships.com/team/noelpearson/pdf/NPlandRIGHTSandProgWrongs2003.pdf>, viewed 8 April 2008; Pearson, "Reciprocity Resurrected," *The Australian*, 12 May 2007.

73. Noel Pearson, "Underlying Principles of a New People for the Restoration of Indigenous Social Order," 23 July 2003, <www.capeyorkpartnerships.com/team/noelpearson/pdf/np-restore-social-order-23-7-03.pdf>, viewed 8 April 2008.

74. Noel Pearson, *Our Right to Take Responsibility* (Cape York, 2000); Pearson, "Vale Hope in Outback Hellhole."

75. Noel Pearson, "Choice is Not Enough," *The Australian*, 28 April 2007.

76. Noel Pearson, "Peace and Prosperity for Indigenous Australians," *Online Opinion*, 28 October 2005.

77. Langton, "Trapped in the Aboriginal Reality Show," 9.

78. Kevin Gilbert, *Living Black: Blacks Talk to Kevin Gilbert* (London and Melbourne, 1978), 1.
79. Pearson, "White Guilt, Victimhood, and the Quest for the Radical Centre," 22–23. In this discussion, I do not treat Pearson's dismissal of social democratic philosophies of redistributive and historical justice, which he effectively equates—in terms of danger and damage to Aborigines—with conservative, often racist philosophies. In fact, at times he suggests that social democrats are *greater* threats to Aborigines because they pose as friends. Such arguments, which do not adequately understand the social democratic engagement in these areas, are doubtless driven by the desperate situation of the communities he is trying to rescue.
80. Duncan Ivison, "The Logic of Aboriginal Rights," *Ethnicities* 3, no. 3 (2003): 321–44.
81. Yin Paradies, "Beyond Black and White: Essentialism, Hybridity and Indigeneity," *Journal of Sociology* 42, no. 4 (2006): 357. This point is also made by Terry Moore, "Problematising Identity: Governance, Politics and the 'Making of the Aborigines,'" *Journal of Australian Studies* 80 (2005): 177–88.
82. Paradies, "Beyond Black and White," 361. He quotes Kwame Anthony Appiah, "Identity, Authenticity, Survival: Multicultural Societies and Social Reproduction," in *Multiculturalism: Examining the Politics of Recognition*, edited by Amy Gutmann (Princeton, NJ, 1994), 163.
83. On this point, see also Arlif Dirlik, "Rethinking Colonialism: Globalization, Postcolonialism, and the Nation," *Interventions* 4, no. 3 (2002): 428–48.
84. John L. Jackson, *Real Black: Adventures of Black Sincerity* (Chicago, 2005).
85. Tommie Shelby, *We Who Are Dark: The Philosophical Foundations of Black Solidarity* (Cambridge, MA, 2005), 3–4. Thanks to Duncan Ivison for drawing Shelby's work to my attention. Space limitations prevent me from elaborating his argument here.
86. Mbembe, "*On the Postcolony:* A Brief Response to Critics," 181–82.
87. Saul Friedländer, *Nazi Germany and the Jews: The Years of Extermination, 1939–1945* (New York, 2007); Edward Said, "New History, Old Ideas," *Al-Ahram Weekly On-line*, 21–27 May 1998: <http://weekly.ahram.org.eg/1998/378/pal2.htm>, accessed 8 February 2005.

Notes on Contributors

Boris Barth is a Professor of History at the Jacobs University of Bremen. His research focuses on the history of genocide and genocide theories as well as German history of the nineteenth and twentieth centuries. His most recent book is *Genozid: Völkermord im 20. Jahrhundert. Geschichte, Theorien, Kontroversen* (Munich, 2006).

Manfred Berg is Curt Engelhorn Professor of American History at the University of Heidelberg. Before he came to Heidelberg, he taught at the Free University of Berlin. From 1992 to 1997, he was a research fellow at the German Historical Institute in Washington, DC. From 2003 to 2005, he served as the executive director of the Center for USA Studies at the Leucorea in Wittenberg. Berg is a specialist in the history of the African–American civil rights movement and race relations. He has published numerous books and articles on American and international history.

Benjamin Braude is Professor of History at Boston College. He researches and teaches the history of the Middle East as well as the history of European–Middle Eastern relations. He has written numerous articles, among them "The Sons of Noah and the Construction of Ethnic and Geographical Identities in the Medieval and Early Modern Periods," *William and Mary Quarterly* 54 (January 1997): 103–42.

Claudia Bruns is Professor at the Humboldt University of Berlin, where she teaches gender studies and the history of knowledge. Her research focuses on European cultural history with a particular focus on gender. Her current research focuses on transatlantic history of racism and anti-Semitism. Her most recent book publication is *Politik des Eros: Der Männerbund in Wissenschaft, Politik und Jugendkultur, 1880–1934* (Köln, 2008).

Harald Fischer-Tiné is Professor of the History of the Modern World at the Swiss Federal Institute of Technology Zurich, in Switzerland. His research concentrates on modern South Asian history. He is the co-editor of *Empires and Boundaries. Rethinking Race, Class and Gender in Colonial Settings* (New

York, 2008) and the author of *Low and Licentious Europeans: Race, Class and White Subalternity in Colonial India* (New Delhi, 2009).

Gita Dharampal-Frick studied literature, philosophy (Manchester and Leipzig), social anthropology (Cambridge) and Indian cultural history (SOAS London, and Paris Sorbonne, Ph.D.), and completed her Habilitation in early modern history (Freiburg). Her published research on pre- and early-colonial European documentation of India underscores the continuities and discontinuities between early proto-ethnography and later scientific Indology. As a Heisenberg Fellow, she examined modernizing processes and resistance movements in post-independence India. Her current interests, as Head of the History Department, South Asian Institute, Heidelberg University, include Indian Ocean cultural history, medical history, ritual transformations (1500–2000) and the socio-cultural and political history of the colonial period in general, with a special focus on Gandhi.

Frank Dikötter is Chair Professor of Humanities at the University of Hong Kong. He has pioneered the use of archival sources and published nine books that have changed the way historians view modern China, from the classic *The Discourse of Race in Modern China* (1992) to *China before Mao: The Age of Openness* (2007). His last book, entitled *Mao's Great Famine*, was published with Bloomsbury.

Christian Geulen is Professor of Modern History at the University of Koblenz. His research focuses on the history of German nationalism and racism. He is the author of *Wahlverwandte: Rassendiskurs und Nationalismus im späten 19. Jahrhundert* (Hamburg, 2004) and *Geschichte des Rassismus* (Munich, 2007).

Katja Götzen is a graduate student in the South Asian Institute of the University of Heidelberg.

Paul A. Kramer is Professor of History at Vanderbilt University. His primary research interests are in modern U.S. history, with a special emphasis on transnational, imperial and global histories as well as the politics of race and gender. His first book, *The Blood of Government: Race, Empire, the United States and the Philippines* (Chapel Hill, 2006), was awarded the Organization of American Historians' James A. Rawley Prize and the Society for Historians of American Foreign Relations' Stuart L. Bernath Book Prize.

Christoph Marx is Professor of History at the University of Duisburg-Essen. He studied History and Musicology at the University of Freiburg and at Rhodes University in Grahamstown, South Africa. His research interests focus on Southern African history, especially the history of apartheid, comparative approaches to frontier history and the history of diasporas. He is the editor of the Journal *Periplus: Jahrbuch für außereuropäische Geschichte*. Among his most recent publications are *Oxwagon Sentinel: Radical Afrikaner Nationalism and the History of the Ossewabrandwag* (Münster, 2008) and *Pelze, Gold und Weihwasser: Handel und Mission in Afrika und Amerika* (Darmstadt, 2008).

A. Dirk Moses is Professor of History at the European University Institute in Florence, Italy. He is the author of *German Intellectuals and the Nazi Past* (2007). The current research interests of Moses are in world history, genocide, the United Nations, colonialism/imperialism and terror, about which he has published a number of anthologies, including *Genocide and Settler Society: Frontier Violence and Stolen Indigenous Children in Australian History* (2004), *Empire, Colony, Genocide: Conquest, Occupation and Subaltern Resistance in World History* (2008), and *The Oxford Handbook of Genocide Studies* (co-edited with Donald Bloxham, 2010).

Gotelind Müller is Professor of Chinese Studies at the University of Heidelberg. Her main research interests are modern Chinese history, the history of ideas, and Sino-Japanese cultural exchange. She has authored several books, including her published Ph.D. thesis on Buddhism and Modernity in early-twentieth-century China (in German) and her published Habilitation monograph on China, Kropotkin and Anarchism (in German). Her most recent monograph is *Representing History in Chinese Media: The TV Drama "Zou Xiang Gonghe" (Towards the Republic)* (Berlin, 2007).

John David Smith is Charles H. Stone Distinguished Professor of American history at North Carolina State University-Charlotte. His research interests are the Civil War and Reconstruction, slavery and emancipation, and the history of racism. John David Smith is currently working on a history of the slave reparations movement and an intellectual biography of the Austrian anthropologist Felix von Luschan (1854–1924). He is the author or editor of numerous books, among them *Black Judas: William Hannibal Thomas and The American Negro* (Athens, 2000), *The Negro in the American Rebellion* (Athens, 2003), *Black Soldiers in Blue: African American*

Troops in the Civil War Era (Chapel Hill, 2002), and *History Teaches Us to Hope: Reflections on the Civil War and Southern History* (Lexington, 2007).

Gregory D. Smithers is Lecturer of American History at the University of Aberdeen in Scotland. He is the author of *Science, Sexuality, & Race in the United States & Australia, 1780s–1890s* (New York, 2009), and co-author (with Clarence E. Walker) of *The Preacher & the Politician: Jeremiah Wright, Barack Obama, and Race in America* (Charlottesville, VA, 2009).

Simon Wendt is Professor of American Studies at the University of Frankfurt. His research interests are African-American history, gender and memory, nationalism, and the history of heroism and hero-worship. Simon Wendt is the author of *The Spirit and the Shotgun: Armed Resistance and the Struggle for Civil Rights* (Gainesville, 2007). He is currently working on a history of the Daughters of the American Revolution.

Urs Matthias Zachmann is Professor of Japanese History at the University of Munich. His research focuses on the intellectual and political history of modern Japan as well as the history of Japan's foreign relations. He is the author of *China and Japan in the Late Meiji Period: China Policy and the Japanese Discourse on National Identity, 1895–1904* (London, 2009).

Michael Zeuske is Professor of Latin American History at the University of Cologne. His research interests focus on the history of slavery as well as the history of Cuba, Venezuela, and the Caribbean. Among his numerous publications are *Sklaven und Sklaverei in den Welten des Atlantiks, 1400–1940* (Münster, 2007), *Von Bolívar zu Chávez: Die Geschichte Venezuelas* (Zuerich, 2008), and *Schwarze Karibik: Sklaven, Sklavenkultur und Emanzipation* (Zurich 2004).

Select Bibliography

Adams, Mark B., ed. *The Wellborn Science: Eugenics in Germany, France, Brazil, and Russia*. New York, 1990.

Adas, Michael. *Machines as Measures of Men: Science, Technology, and Ideologies of Western Dominance*. Ithaca, 1990.

Anderson, Clare. *Legible Bodies: Race, Criminality and Colonialism in South Asia*. Oxford, 2004.

Anderson, Warwick. *Colonial Pathologies: American Tropical Medicine, Race, and Hygiene in the Philippines*. Durham, NC, 2006.

———. *The Cultivation of Whiteness: Science, Health and Racial Destiny in Australia*. Carlton, 2002.

Ashcroft, Bill, et al. *Key Concepts in Post-Colonial Studies*. London, 1998.

Augstein, Hannah F., ed. *Race: The Origins of an Idea, 1760–1850*. Bristol, 1996.

Bailey, Frederick G. *Tribe, Caste, and Nation*. Manchester, 1971.

Balibar, Etienne, and Immanuel Wallerstein. *Rasse, Klasse, Nation: Ambivalente Identitäten*. Hamburg, 1990.

Ballantyne, Tony. *Orientalism and Race: Aryanism in the British Empire*. New York, 2002.

Banton, Michael. *Racial theories*. 2nd ed. Cambridge, UK, 1998.

Barkan, Elazar. *The Retreat of Scientific Racism: Changing Concepts of Race in Britain and the United States between the World Wars*. Cambridge, UK, 1992.

Barker, Martin. *The New Racism*. London, 1981.

Barth, Boris. *Genozid: Völkermord im 20. Jahrhundert, Geschichte, Theorien, Kontroversen*. München, 2006.

———. and Jürgen Osterhammel, eds. *Zivilisierungsmissionen: Imperiale Weltverbesserung seit dem 18. Jahrhundert*. Konstanz, 2005.

Bartlett, Robert. *The Making of Europe: Conquest, Colonization, and Cultural Change, 950–1350*. Princeton, 1993.

Bates, Crispin, ed. *Beyond Representation: Colonial and Postcolonial Constructions of Indian Identity*. New Delhi, 2006.

Bayly, Susan. *Caste, Society and Politics in India from the Eighteenth Century to the Modern Age*. Cambridge, UK, 1999.

Becker, Frank, ed. *Rassenmischehen–Mischlinge–Rassentrennung: Zur Politik der Rasse im deutschen Kolonialreich*. Stuttgart, 2004.

Bederman, Gail. *Manliness & Civilization: A Cultural History of Gender and Race in the United States, 1880–1917*. Chicago, 1995.

Bell-Fialkoff, Andrew. *Ethnic Cleansing*. Basingstoke, 1996.

Bennett, David Harry. *The Party of Fear: From Nativist Movements to the New Right in American History*. Chapel Hill, 1988.

Berg, Allison. *Mothering the Race: Women's Narratives of Reproduction, 1890–1930*. Urbana, 2002.

Bergmann, Werner. *Geschichte des Antisemitismus*, 3rd ed. München, 2006.

Berlin, Ira. *Many Thousands Gone: The First Two Centuries of Slavery in North America*. Cambridge, MA, 1998.

Bird, Elizabeth S. *Dressing in Feathers: The Construction of the Indian in American Popular Culture*. Boulder, CO, 1996.

Blee, Kathleen M. *Inside Organized Racism: Women in the Hate Movement*. Berkeley, 2003.

———. *Women of the Klan: Racism and Gender in the 1920s*. Berkeley, 1991.

Bloxham, David. *The Great Game of Genocide: Imperialism, nationalism and the destruction of the Ottoman Armenians*. Oxford, 2005.

Böhlke-Itzen, Janntje. *Kolonialschuld und Entschädigung: Der deutsche Völkermord an den Hereros, 1904–1907*. Frankfurt, 2004.

Bolt, Christine. *Victorian Attitudes towards Race*. London, 1971.

Brantlinger, Patrick. *Dark Vanishings: Discourse on the Extinction of Primitive Races, 1800–1930*. Ithaca, 2003.

Briggs, Laura. *Reproducing Empire: Race, Sex, Science, and US Imperialism in Puerto Rico*. Berkeley, 2002.

Broberg, Gunnar, and Nils Roll-Hansen, eds. *Eugenics and the Welfare State: Sterilization Policy in Denmark, Sweden, Norway, and Finland*. East Lansing, MI, 1996.

Brown, William Montgomery. *The Crucial Race Question: Where and How Shall the Color Line be Drawn*. Little Rock, 1907.

Browning, Christopher. *The Path to Genocide: Essays on Launching the Final Solution*. Cambridge, UK, 1992.

Budde, Gunilla-Friederike, Sebastian Conrad, and Oliver Janz, eds. *Transnationale Geschichte: Themen, Tendenzen und Theorien*. Göttingen, 2006.

Burleigh, Michael, and Wolfgang Wippermann. *The Racial State: Germany 1933–1945*. Cambridge, UK, 1991.

Cell, John W. *The Highest Stage of White Supremacy: The Origins of Segregation in South Africa and the American South*. Cambridge, UK, 1982.

Chakrabarty, Dipesh. *Provincializing Europe: Postcolonial Thought and Historical Difference*. Princeton, 2000.

Chatterjee, Partha. *The Nation and its Fragments: Colonial and Postcolonial Histories*. Princeton, 1993.

Cohen, Deborah, and Maura O'Connor, eds. *Comparison and History: Europe in Cross-National Perspective*. New York, 2003.

Conrad, Sebastian. *Deutsche Kolonialgeschichte*. München, 2008.

———. Andreas Eckert, and Ulrike Freitag, eds. *Globalgeschichte: Theorien, Ansätze, Themen*. Frankfurt, 2007.

————. and Jürgen Osterhammel. *Das Kaiserreich transnational: Deutschland in der Welt 1871–1914*. Göttingen, 2004.

————. and Shalini Randeria, eds. *Jenseits des Eurozentrismus: Postkoloniale Perspektiven in den Geschichts- und Kulturwissenschaften*. Frankfurt, 2002.

Daniels, Roger. *The Politics of Prejudice: The Anti-Japanese Movement in California and the Struggle for Japanese Exclusion*. Berkeley, 1962.

De la Fuente, Alejandro. *"A Nation for All": Race, Inequality, and Politics in Twentieth-Century Cuba*. Chapel Hill, 2001.

Delgado, Richard, and Jean Stefancic. *Critical White Studies: Looking Behind the Mirror*. Philadelphia, 1997.

Des Forges, Alison. *Kein Zeuge darf überleben: Der Genozid in Ruanda*. Hamburg, 2002.

Dietrich, Anette. *Weiße Weiblichkeiten: Konstruktion von "Rasse" und Geschlecht im deutschen Kolonialismus*. Bielefeld, 2007.

Dikötter, Frank. *Imperfect Conceptions: Medical Knowledge, Birth Defects, and Eugenics in China*. New York, 1998.

————. ed. *The Construction of Racial Identities in China and Japan: Historical and Contemporary Perspectives*. London, 1997.

————. *The Discourse of Race in Modern China*. London, 1992.

Diner, Dan. ed. *Ist der Nationalsozialismus Geschichte? Zu Historisierung und Historikerstreit*. Franfurt, 1987.

Dirks, Nicholas B. *The Scandal of Empire: India and the Creation of Imperial Britain*. Cambridge, MA, 2006.

————. *Castes of Mind: Colonialism and the Making of Modern India*. Princeton, 2001.

Dower, John W. *War Without Mercy: Race and Power in the Pacific War*. New York, 1987.

Dubow, Saul. *A Commonwealth of Knowledge: Science, Sensibility, and White South Africa, 1820–2000*. Oxford, 2006.

————. *Scientific Racism in Modern South Africa*. Cambridge, UK, 1995.

Duus, Peter. *The Abacus and the Sword: The Japanese Penetration of Korea, 1895–1910*. Berkeley, 1995.

Efron, John M. *Defenders of the Race: Jewish Doctors and Race Science in fin-de-siecle Europe*. New Haven, 1994.

Ellinghaus, Katherine. *Taking Assimilation to Heart: Marriages of White Women & Indigenous Men in the United States & Australia, 1887–1937*. Lincoln, 2006.

El-Tayeb, Fatima. *Schwarze Deutsche: Der Diskurs um "Rasse" und nationale Identität, 1890–1933*. Frankfurt, 2001.

Fanon, Frantz. *Black Skin, White Masks*. trans. Charles. M. Larkmann. New York, 1967.

Fellman, Michael. *Inside War: The Guerrilla Conflict in Missouri during the American Civil War*. New York, 1990.

Fels, Margaret. *Good Men and True: The Aboriginal Police of the Port Phillip District, 1837–1853*. Melbourne, 1988.

Ferber, Abby L., ed. *Home-Grown Hate: Gender and Organized Racism*. New York, 2004.

Ferrer, Ada. *Insurgent Cuba: Race, Nation, and Revolution, 1868–1898*. Chapel Hill, 1999.

Finley, Moses I. *Ancient Slavery and Modern Ideology*. Expanded ed. Princeton, 1998.

Finzsch, Norbert, and Dietmar Schirmer, eds. *Identity and Intolerance: Nationalism, Racism, and Xenophobia in Germany and the United States*. New York, 1998.

Forrester, Duncan. *Caste and Christianity: Attitudes and Policy on Caste of Anglo-Saxon Protestant Missions in India*. London, 1980.

Forret, Jeff. *Race Relations at the Margins: Slaves and Poor Whites in the Antebellum Southern Countryside*. Baton Rouge, 2006.

Frankenberg, Ruth. *White Women, Race Matters: The Social Construction of Whiteness*. Minneapolis, 1993.

Frederickson, George M. *Diverse Nations: Explorations in the History of Racial and Ethnic Pluralism*. Boulder, 2008.

———. *Racism: A Short History*. Princeton, 2002.

———. *The Comparative Imagination: On the History of Racism, Nationalism, and Social Movements*. Berkeley, 1997.

———. *White Supremacy: A Comparative Study in American and South African History*. Oxford, 1981.

———. *The Black Image in the White Mind: The Debate on Afro-American Character and Destiny, 1817–1914*. New York, 1971.

Friedländer, Saul. *Das Dritte Reich und die Juden: Verfolgung und Vernichtung 1933–1945*. München, 2007.

———. *Nazi Germany and the Jews: The Years of Extermination, 1939–1945*. New York, 2007.

Friedrichsmayer, Sara, et al., eds. *Imperialist Imagination: German Colonialism and its Legacy*. Ann Arbor, 1998.

Furlong, Patrick. *Between Crown and Swastika: The Impact of the Radical Right on the Afrikaner Nationalist Movement in the Fascist Era*. Johannesburg, 1991.

Garner, Steve. *Whiteness: An Introduction*. New York, 2007.

Gascoigne, John. *The Enlightenment and the Origins of European Australia*. Cambridge, UK, 2002.

Gates, Henry L. Jr., and Dominik LaCapra, eds. *The Bounds of Race*. Ithaca, 1991.

Geiss, Immanuel. *Geschichte des Rassismus*. Frankfurt, 1988.

Gerlach, Christian. *Kalkulierte Morde: Die deutsche Wirtschafts- und Vernichtungspolitik in Weißrußland, 1941 bis 1944*. Hamburg, 1999.

———. *Krieg, Ernährung, Völkermord: Forschungen zur deutschen Vernichtungspolitik im Zweiten Weltkrieg*. Hamburg, 1998.

Geulen, Christian. *Geschichte des Rassismus*. München, 2007.

Gilman, Sander. *Freud, Race, and Gender*. Princeton, 1993.

———. *Difference and Pathology: Stereotypes of Sexuality, Race, and Madness*. Ithaca, 1985.

Gilmore, Glenda Elizabeth. *Gender and Jim Crow: Women and the Politics of White Supremacy in North Carolina, 1896–1920*. Chapel Hill, 1996.

Gilroy, Paul. *The Black Atlantic: Modernity and Double Consciousness*. London, 1996.

Goldberg, David Theo. *The Racial State*. Malden, 2002.

Gollwitzer, Heinz. *Die Gelbe Gefahr: Geschichte eines Schlagworts. Studien zum imperialistischen Denken.* Göttingen, 1962.

Gossett, Thomas F. *Race: The History of an Idea in America.* New York, 1963.

Grant, Madison. *The Passing of the Great Race.* New York, 1916.

Greenberg, Amy S. *Manifest Manhood and the Antebellum American Empire.* New York, 2005.

Griffin, Roger, and Matthew Feldman, eds. *Fascism: Critical Concepts in Political Science.* 5 vols. London, 2004.

Grosse, Pascal. *Kolonialismus, Eugenik und bürgerliche Gesellschaft in Deutschland, 1850–1918.* Frankfurt, 2000.

Guglielmo, Thomas A. *White on Arrival: Italians, Race, Color, and Power in Chicago, 1890–1945.* New York, 2003.

Guha, Ranajit. *Dominance without Hegemony: History and Power in Colonial India.* Cambridge, MA, 1997.

Gupta, Dipankar. *Interrogating Caste: Understanding Hierarchy and Difference in Indian Society.* New Delhi, 2000.

Harrison, Mark. *Climates and Constitutions: Health, Race, Environment and British Imperialism in India, 1600–1850.* New Delhi, 1999.

Hassam, Andrew. *Through Australian Eyes: Colonial Perceptions of Imperial Britain.* Brighton, 2000.

Haupt, Heinz-Gerhard, and Jürgen Kocka, eds. *Geschichte und Vergleich: Ansätze und Ergebnisse international vergleichender Geschichtsschreibung.* Frankfurt, 1996.

Heideking, Jürgen. *Geschichte der USA.* Tübingen, 1996.

Hein, Annette. *"Es ist viel 'Hitler' in Wagner": Rassismus und antisemitische Deutschtumsideologie in den Bayreuther Blättern, 1878–1938.* Tübingen, 1996.

Hentges, Gudrun. *Die Schattenseiten der Aufklärung: Die Darstellung von Juden und "Wilden" in den philosophischen Schriften des 18. und 19. Jahrhunderts.* Schwalbach/Ts., 1999.

Hering Torres, Max S. *Rassismus in der Vormoderne: Die 'Reinheit des Blutes' im Spanien der Frühen Neuzeit.* Frankfurt, 2006.

Herrnstein, Richard J., and Charles Murray. *The Bell Curve: Intelligence and Class Structure in American Life.* New York, 1994.

Higham, John. *Strangers in the Land: Patterns of American Nativism, 1860–1925.* New York, 1963.

Hoffman, Frederick L. *Race Traits and Tendencies of the American Negro.* New York, 1896.

Hoganson, Kristin. *Fighting for American Manhood: How Gender Politics Provoked the Spanish-American and Philippine-American Wars.* New Haven, 1998.

Horsman, Reginald. *Race and Manifest Destiny: The Origins of American Racial Anglo-Saxonism.* Cambridge, MA, 1981.

Hosfeld, Rolf. *Operation Nemesis: Die Türkei, Deutschland und der Völkermord an den Armeniern.* Köln, 2005.

Hundt, Wulf D. *Rassismus.* Bielefeld, 2007.

Huntington, Samuel. *The Clash of Civilization and the Remaking of World Order*. New York, 1996.

Hussein, Ameena, ed. *Race, Identity, Caste and Conflict in the South Asian Context*. Colombo, 2004.

Huttenback, Robert A. *Racism and Empire: White Settlers and Colored Immigrants in the British Self-Governing Colonies, 1830–1910*. Ithaca, 1976.

Hutton, Christopher M. *Race and the Third Reich: Linguistics, Racial Anthropology and Genetics in the Dialectic of Volk*. Cambridge, UK, 2005.

Ignatiev, Noel. *How the Irish Became White*. New York, 1995.

Isaac, Benjamin. *The Invention of Racism in Classical Antiquity*. Princeton, 2004.

Jacobson, Matthew Frye. *Barbarian Virtues: The United States Encounters Foreign Peoples at Home and Abroad, 1876–1917*. New York, 2000.

———. *Whiteness of a Different Color: European Immigrants and the Alchemy of Race*. Cambridge, MA, 1998.

Jacoby, Russel, and Naomi Glauberman, eds. *The Bell Curve Debate: History, Documents, Opinions*. New York, 1995.

Jones, Cecily. *Engendering Whiteness: White Women and Colonialism in Barbados and North Carolina, 1627–1865*. Manchester, 2007.

Jordan, Winthrop D. *White over Black: American Attitudes toward the Negro, 1550–1812*. Chapel Hill, 1968.

Judson, Pieter M. *Guardians of the Nation: Activists on the Language Frontiers of Imperial Austria*. Cambridge, MA, 2007.

Jupp, James. *From White Australia to Woomera: The Story of Australian Immigration*. Cambridge, UK, 2007.

Kaelble, Hartmut, and Jürgen Schriewer, eds. *Vergleich und Transfer: Komparatistik in den Geschichts-, Sozial- und Kulturwissenschaften*. Frankfurt, 2003.

Kenney, Henry. *Architect of Apartheid - H.F. Verwoerd: An Appraisal*. Johannesburg, 1980.

Kidd, Colin. *The Forging of Races: Race and Scripture in the Protestant Atlantic World, 1600–2000*. Cambridge, UK, 2006.

Klass, Morton. *Caste: The Emergence of the South Asian Social System*. Philadelphia, 1980.

Klee, Ernst. *Euthanasie im NS-Staat: Die "Vernichtung lebensunwerten Lebens."* Frankfurt, 1985.

Knowles, Caroline. *Race and Social Analysis*. Thousand Oaks, 2003.

Kohn, Marek. *The Race Gallery: The Return of Racial Science*. London, 1996.

Kramer, Paul. *Blood of Government: Race, Empire, the United States, and the Philippines*. Chapel Hill, 2006.

Kretschmer, Ernst. *Körperbau und Charakter: Untersuchungen zum Konstitutionsproblem und zur Lehre von den Temperamenten*. 3rd ed. Berlin, 1922.

Krüger, Gesine. *Kriegsbewältigung und Geschichtsbewusstsein: Realität, Deutung und Verarbeitung des deutschen Kolonialkrieges in Namibia, 1904–1907*. Göttingen, 1999.

Kühl, Stefan. *Die Internationale der Rassisten: Aufstieg und Niedergang der internationalen Bewegung für Eugenik und Rassenhygiene im 20. Jahrhundert*. Frankfurt, 1997.

———. *The Nazi Connection: Eugenics, American Racism, and German National Socialism*. New York, 1994.

Kundrus, Birthe, ed. *Phantasiereiche: Zur Kulturgeschichte des deutschen Kolonialismus*. Frankfurt, 2003.

Lake, Marilyn, and Henry Reynolds. *Drawing the Global Colour Line: White Men's Countries and the International Challenge of Racial Equality*. Cambridge, UK, 2008.

Larson, Edward J. *Sex, Race, and Science: Eugenics in the Deep South*. Baltimore, 1996.

LeBlanc, Lawrence. *The United States and the Genocide Convention*. Durham, 1991.

Levey, Geoffrey Brahm, ed. *Political Theory and Australian Multiculturalism*. New York, 2008.

Lewis, Bernard. *Race and Slavery in the Middle East: An Historical Inquiry*. New York, 1990.

Lilienthal, Georg. *Der Lebensborn e.V.: Ein Instrument nationalsozialistischer Rassenpolitik*. Stuttgart, 1985.

Linhart, Sepp. *"Dainty Japanese" or Yellow Peril? Western War Postcards, 1900–1945*. Vienna, 2005.

Litwack, Leon F. *Trouble in Mind: Black Southerners in the Age of Jim Crow*. New York, 1998.

Logan, Rayford W. *The Negro in American Life and Thought: The Nadir, 1877–1901*. New York, 1965.

Love, Eric T.L. *Race Over Empire: Racism & U.S. Imperialism, 1865–1900*. Chapel Hill, 2004.

MacDonald, Rowena, ed. *Between Two Worlds: The Commonwealth Government and the Removal of Aboriginal Children of Part Descent in the Northern Territory*. Alice Springs, NT, 1995.

MacLean, Nancy. *Behind the Mask of Chivalry: The Making of the Second Ku Klux Klan*. New York, 1994.

MacMaster, Neil. *Racism in Europe, 1870–2000*. Houndmills, 2001.

Mann, Michael. *The Dark Side of Democracy: Explaining Ethnic Cleansing*. Cambridge, UK, 2005.

Marriott, John. *The Other Empire: Metropolis, India and Progress in the Colonial Imagination*. Manchester, 2003.

Martin, Peter. *Schwarze Teufel, edle Mohren: Afrikaner in Geschichte und Bewusstsein der Deutschen*. Hamburg, 2001.

Marx, Anthony W. *Making Race and Nation: A Comparison of South Africa, the United States, and Brazil*. New York, 1997.

Marx, Christoph. *Im Zeichen des Ochsenwagens: Der radikale Afrikaaner-Nationalismus in Südafrika und die Geschichte der Ossewabrandwag*. Münster, 1998.

Mason, Philipp. *Prospero's Magic: Some Thoughts on Class and Race*, London, 1962.

Maß, Sandra. *Weiße Helden, schwarze Krieger: Zur Geschichte kolonialer Männlichkeit in Deutschland 1918–1964*. Köln, 2006.

Matthews, Basil. *The Clash of Colour: A Study in the Problem of Race*. London, 1925.

May, Glenn Anthony. *Social Engineering in the Philippines: The Aims, Execution, and Impact of American Colonial Policy, 1900–1913*. Westport, CT, 1980.

Mazlish, Bruce. *The New Global History*. New York, 2006.

———. and Akira Iriye, eds. *The Global History Reader*. New York, 2005.

McCulloch, Jock. *Black Peril, White Virtue: Sexual Crime in Southern Rhodesia, 1902–1935*. Bloomington, 2000.

McGregor, Russell. *Imagined Destinies: Aboriginal Australians and the Doomed Race Theory, 1880–1939*. Carlton South, 1998.

Mehnert, Ute. *Deutschland, Amerika und die "Gelbe Gefahr": Zur Karriere eines Schlagworts in der Großen Politik, 1905–1917*. Stuttgart, 1995.

Melamed, Abraham. *The Image of the Black in Jewish Culture: A History of the Other*. London, 2002.

Memmi, Albert. *Rassismus*. Frankfurt, 1987.

Metcalf, Thomas R. *Forging the Raj: Essays on British India in the Heyday of Empire*. Delhi, 2005.

Michaels, Walter B. *Our America: Nativism, Modernism, and Pluralism*. Durham, 1995.

Miller, Stuart Creighton. *"Benevolent Assimilation": The American Conquest of the Philippines, 1899–1903*. New Haven, 1982.

Moodie, T. Dunbar. *The Rise of Afrikanerdom: Power, Apartheid, and the Afrikaner Civil Religion*. Berkeley, 1975.

Moore, Wendy Leo. *Reproducing Racism: White Space, Elite Law Schools, and Racial Inequality*. Lanham, MD, 2007.

Moreton-Robinson, Aileen. *Talkin' Up to the White Woman: Aboriginal Women and Feminism*. Brisbane, 2000.

Morgan, Jennifer L. *Laboring Women: Reproduction in New World Slavery*. Philadelphia, 2004.

Morrison, Elting E., ed. *The Letters of Theodore Roosevelt*. Cambridge, MA, 1954.

Moses, A. Dirk, ed. *Empire, Colony, Genocide: Conquest, Occupation, and Subaltern Resistance in World History*. New York, 2008.

———. ed., *Genocide and Settler Society: Frontier Violence and Stolen Indigenous Children in Australian History*. New York, 2004.

Mosse, George L. *Die Geschichte des Rassismus in Europa*. Frankfurt, 1990.

———. *Toward the Final Solution: A History of European Racism*. London, 1978.

Naimark, Norman. *Fires of Hatred: Ethnic Cleansing in Twentieth-Century Europe*. Cambridge, MA, 2001.

Nakayama, Thomas K., and Judith N. Martin. *Whiteness: The Communication of Social Identity*. Thousand Oaks, 1999.

Narsimhan, Sushila. *Japanese Perceptions of China in the Nineteenth Century: Influence of Fukuzawa Yukichi*. New Delhi, 1999.

Naudh, H[einrich]. *Die Juden und der Deutsche Staat*, 3rd rev. ed. Berlin, 1861.

Neill, Rosemary. *White Out: How Politics Is Killing Black Australia*. Sydney, 2002.

Newby, Idus A. *Jim Crow's Defense: Anti-Negro Thought in America, 1900–1930*. Baton Rouge, 1965.

Newman, Louis Michelle. *White Women's Rights: The Racial Origins of Feminism in the United States*. New York, 1999.

Ngai, Mae. *Impossible Subjects: Illegal Aliens and the Making of Modern America.* Princeton, 2004.

Nicholas, Stephen. *Convict Workers: Reinterpreting Australia's Past.* Cambridge, UK, 2007.

Niezen, Ronald. *The Origins of Indigenism.* Berkeley, 2003.

Noble, Gregory, ed. *Lines in the Sand: The Cronulla Riots and the Limits of Australian Multiculturalism.* Sydney, 2008.

Oguma, Eiji. *A Genealogy of 'Japanese' Self-images.* trans. David Askew. Melbourne, 2002.

Olender, Maurice. *The Languages of Paradise: Race, Religion, and Philology in the Nineteenth Century.* Cambridge, MA, 1992.

Omi, Michael, and Howard Winant. *Racial Formation in the United States: From the 1960s to the 1980s.* New York, 1986.

Osterhammel, Jürgen. *Geschichtswissenschaft jenseits des Nationalstaats: Studien zu Beziehungsgeschichte und Zivilisationsvergleich.* Göttingen, 2001.

Paquette, Robert L. *Sugar Is Made With Blood: The Conspiracy of La Escalera and the Conflict between Empires over Slavery in Cuba.* Middletown, 1988.

Paredes, Ruby, ed. *Philippine Colonial Democracy.* Quezon City, Philippines, 1989.

Parry, Benita. *Delusions and Discoveries: India in the British Imagination, 1880–1930.* 2nd ed. London, 1998.

Patel, Kiran Klaus. *Nach der Nationalfixiertheit: Perspektiven einer transnationalen Geschichte.* Berlin, 2004.

Paul, Heike. *Kulturkontakt und Racial Presences: Afro-Amerikaner und die deutsche Amerika-Literatur, 1815–1914.* Heidelberg, 2005.

Pick, Daniel. *Faces of Degeneration: A European Disorder, ca. 1848–1918.* Cambridge, UK, 1989.

Plummer, Brenda Gayle. *Rising Wind: Black Americans and U.S. Foreign Affairs, 1935–1960.* Chapel Hill, 1996.

Poliakov, Léon. *The Aryan Myth: A History of Racist and Nationalist Ideas in Europe.* London, 1975.

Popovic, Alexandre, *The Revolt of African Slaves in Iraq in the 3rd/9th Century.* trans. Léon King. Princeton, 1999.

Posel, Deborah. *The Making of Apartheid, 1948–1961: Conflict and Compromise.* Oxford, 1997.

Pulzer, Peter G.J. *Die Entstehung des politischen Antisemitismus in Deutschland und Österreich, 1867–1914.* Göttingen, 2004.

Pyle, Kenneth B. *The New Generation in Meiji Japan: Problems of Cultural Identity, 1885–1895.* Stanford, 1969.

Rafael, Vicente L. *The Promise of the Foreign: Nationalism and the Techniques of Translation in the Spanish Philippines.* Durham, 2005.

Rasmussen, Birgit B., ed. *The Making and Unmaking of Whiteness.* Durham, 2001.

Renda, Mary A. *Taking Haiti: Military Occupation and The Culture of US Imperialism, 1915–1940.* Chapel Hill, 2001.

Renfrew, Colin. *Archaeology and Language: The Puzzle of the Indo-European Origins.* London, 1987.

Richards, Jonathan. *The Secret War: A True History of Queensland's Native Police.* Brisbane, 2008.

Roediger, David R. *Working Toward Whiteness: How America's Immigrants Became White: The Strange Journey from Ellis Island to the Suburbs.* New York, 2005.

———. *Colored White: Transcending the Racial Past.* Berkeley, 2002.

———. *The Wages of Whiteness: Race and the Making of the American Working Class.* Rev. ed. New York, 1999.

Roosevelt, Theodore. *An Autobiography.* New York, 1913.

Rose, Paul Lawrence. *Revolutionary Antisemitism in Germany from Kant to Wagner.* Princeton, 1990.

Rubinstein, William D. *Genocide: A History.* Harlow, 2004.

Rummel, Rudolph J. *Lethal Politics: Soviet Genocide and Mass Murder since 1917.* New Brunswick, 1996.

Rutherdale, Myra. *Women and the White Man's God: Gender and Race in the Canadian Mission Field.* Vancouver, 2002.

Saffar, Muhammad. *Disorienting Encounters: Travels of a Moroccan Scholar in France in 1845–1846: The Voyage of Muhammad as-Saffar.* trans. Susan Gilson Miller. Berkeley, 1992.

Salman, Michael. *The Embarrassment of Slavery: Controversies over Bondage and Nationalism in the American Colonial Philippines.* Berkeley, 2001.

Samson, Jane. *Race and Empire.* Harlow, 2005.

Sanders, Ronald. *Lost Tribes and Promised Lands: The Origins of American Racism.* 1978, repr. New York, 1992.

Saniel, Josefa M., ed. *The Filipino Exclusion Movement, 1927–1935.* Quezon City, Philippines, 1967.

Savarkar, Vinayak D. *The Indian War of Independence, 1857.* New Delhi, 1970.

Schabas, William A. *Genocide in International Law: The Crime of Crimes.* Cambridge, UK, 2000.

Scherer, Christian P. *Ethnisierung und Völkermord in Zentralafrika: Genozid in Rwanda, Bürgerkrieg in Burundi und die Rolle der Weltgemeinschaft.* Frankfurt, 1997.

Schivelbusch, Wolfgang. *Three New Deals: Reflections on Roosevelt's America, Mussolini's Italy, and Hitler's Germany.* New York, 2006.

Schumacher, John N. *The Propaganda Movement, 1880–1895: The Creation of a Filipino Consciousness, the Makers of Revolution.* Manila, 1973.

Scott, James C. *Seeing like a State: How Certain Schemes to Improve the Human Condition Have Failed.* New Haven, 1998.

Sen, Saradru. *Colonial Childhoods: The Juvenile Periphery in British India, 1850–1945.* London, 2005.

Sen, Sudipta. *Distant Sovereignty: National Imperialism and the Origins of British India.* New York, 2002.

Shain, Milton. *The Roots of Antisemitism in South Africa*. Johannesburg, 1994.

Sharma, Arvind. *Hinduism and Human Rights: A Conceptual Approach*. New Delhi, 2004.

Sheehan, Bernard W. *Seeds of Extinction: Jeffersonian Philanthropy and the American Indian*. New York, 1974.

Shelby, Tommie. *We Who Are Dark: The Philosophical Foundations of Black Solidarity*. Cambridge, MA, 2005.

Shiel, Matthew P. *The Yellow Danger*. London, 1998.

Shimazu, Naoko. *Japan, Race and Equality: The Race Equality Proposal of 1919*. London, 1998.

Shoemaker, Nancy. *A Strange Likeness: Becoming Red and White in Eighteenth-Century North America*. New York, 2004.

Sinha, Mrinalini. *Colonial Masculinity: The 'Manly Englishman' and the 'Effeminate Bengali' in the Late Nineteenth Century*. Manchester, 1995.

Smaje, Chris. *Natural Hierarchies: The Historical Sociology of Race and Caste*. Malden, 2002.

Smedley, Audrey. *Race in North America: Origin and Evolution of a Worldview*. 3rd ed. Boulder, 2007.

Smith, Linda Tuhiwai. *Decolonizing Methodologies: Research and Indigenous Peoples*. London, 1999.

Smithers, Gregory D. *Science, Sexuality, and Race in the United States and Australia, 1780s–1890s*. New York, 2009.

Snowden, Frank M. Jr. *Before Color Prejudice: The Ancient View of Blacks*. Cambridge, MA, 1983.

Sobich, Frank Oliver. *"Schwarze Bestien, rote Gefahr": Rassismus und Antisozialismus im deutschen Kaiserreich*. Frankfurt, 2006.

Solomos, John. *Race and Racism in Britain*. 3rd ed. New York, 2003.

———. *Race and Racism in Contemporary Britain*. London, 1989.

———. and Les Beck. *Racism and Society*. London, 1996.

Sommerville, Diane Miller. *Rape and Race in the Nineteenth-Century South*. Chapel Hill, 2004.

Sorisio, Carolyn. *Fleshing Out America: Race, Gender, and the Politics of the Body in American Literature, 1833–1879*. Athens, 2002.

Southern, David W. *The Progressive Era and Race: Reaction and Reform, 1900–1917*. Wheeling, 2005.

Stannard, David E. *American Holocaust: The Conquest of the New World*. New York, 1992.

Stepan, Nancy Leys. *"The Hour of Eugenics": Race, Gender, and Nation in Latin America*. Ithaca, 1991.

Stern, Alexandra Minna. *Eugenic Nation: Faults and Frontiers of Better Breeding in Modern America*. Berkeley, 2005.

Stoddard, Lothrop. *Clashing Tides of Color*. New York, 1935.

———. *The Revolt against Civilization: The Menace of the Under Man*. New York, 1922.

———. *The Rising Tide of Color against White Supremacy*. New York, 1920.

Stokes, Eric. *The English Utilitarians and India.* Oxford, 1959.

Stoler, Ann Laura. *Carnal Knowledge and Imperial Power: Race and the Intimate in Colonial Rule.* Berkeley, 2002.

Streets, Heather. *Martial Races: The Military, Race and Masculinity in British Imperial Culture, 1857–1914.* Manchester, 2004.

Sudipta, Sen. *Distant Sovereignty: National Imperialism and the Origins of British India.* New York, 2002.

Sweet, John Wood. *Bodies Politic: Negotiating Race in North America, 1730–1830.* Baltimore, 2003.

Taguieff, Pierre-André. *The Force of Prejudice: On Racism and Its Doubles.* Minneapolis, 2001.

Tanaka, Stefan. *Japan's Orient: Rendering Pasts into History.* Berkeley, 1993.

Tatz, Colin. *With Intent to Destroy: Reflecting on Genocide.* London, 2003.

Terkessidis, Mark. *Kulturkampf: Volk, Nation, der Westen und die Neue Rechte.* Köln, 1996.

Theodore, Allen. *The Invention of the White Race.* New York, 1994.

Thomas, Nicholas. *Colonialism's Culture: Anthropology, Travel and Government.* Princeton, 1994.

Thorat, Sukhadeo, and Umakant, eds. *Caste, Race and Discrimination: Discourses in International Context.* Jaipur, 2004.

Toby, Ronald P. *State and Diplomacy in Early Modern Japan: Asia in the Development of the Tokugawa Bakufu.* Stanford, 1984.

Todorov, Tzvetan. *La conquête de L' Amérique: la question de l'autre.* Paris, 1982.

———. *The Conquest of America: The Question of the Other.* Norman, 1999.

Tomich, Dale W. *Through the Prism of Slavery: Labor, Capital and the World Economy.* Boulder, 2004.

Totten, Samuel, William S. Parsons, and Israel W. Charney, eds. *Genocide in the Twentieth Century: Critical Essays and Eyewitness Accounts.* New York, 1995.

Trachtenberg, Joshua. *The Devil and the Jews: The Medieval Conception of the Jew and its Relation to Modern Antisemitism.* 2nd paperback ed. Philadelphia, 1983.

Trautmann, Thomas R. *Aryans and British India.* New Delhi, 1997.

Trugden, Richard. *When Warriors Lie Down and Die: Towards an Understanding of Why the Aboriginal People of Arnhem Land Face the Greatest Crisis in Health and Education Since European Contact.* Darwin, 2001.

Tsu, Jing. *Failure, Nationalism, and Literature: The Making of Modern Chinese Identity, 1895–1937.* Stanford, 2005.

Tucker, William H. *The Science and Politics of Racial Research.* Urbana, 1994.

Tyrrell, Ian. *Transnational Nation: United States History in Global Perspective since 1789.* Basingstoke, 2007.

Valentino, Benjamin A. *Final Solutions: Mass Killing and Genocide in the Twentieth Century.* Ithaca, 2004.

Valls, Andrew. *Race and Racism in Modern Philosophy.* Ithaca, 2005.

Van den Berghe, Pierre L. *Race and Racism: A Comparative Perspective.* 2nd ed. New York, 1978.

Van der Veer, Peter. *Imperial Encounters: Religion and Modernity in India and Britain.* Princeton, 2001.

Vander Zanden, James Wilfrid. *Race Relations in Transition: The Segregation Crisis in the South.* New York, 1965.

Vaughan, Alden T. *Roots of American Racism: Essays on the Colonial Experience.* New York, 1995.

Voegelin, Eric. *Rasse und Staat.* Tübingen, 1933.

Wade, Peter. *Race and Ethnicity in Latin America.* London, 1997.

Walgenbach, Katharina. *"Die Weiße Frau als Trägerin deutscher Kultur": Koloniale Diskurse über Geschlecht, "Rasse" und Klasse im Kaiserreich.* Frankfurt, 2005.

Walkenhorst, Peter. *Nation - Volk – Rasse: Radikaler Nationalismus im Deutschen Kaiserreich 1890–1914.* Göttingen, 2007.

Walker, David. *Anxious Nation: Australia and the Rise of Asia, 1850–1939.* St. Lucia, 1999.

Ward, William. *A View of the History, Literature and Mythology of the Hindoos.* Vol. 2. London, 1822.

Weber, Eugen. *Peasants into Frenchmen: The Modernization of Rural France, 1870–1914.* Stanford, 1976.

Weikart, Richard. *From Darwin to Hitler: Evolutionary Ethics, Eugenics, and Racism in Germany.* New York, 2004.

Weingart, Peter, Jürgen Kroll, and Kurt Bayertz. *Rasse, Blut und Gene: Geschichte der Eugenik und Rassenhygiene in Deutschland.* Frankfurt, 1992.

Weitz, Eric D. *A Century of Genocide: Utopias of Race and Nation.* Princeton, 2003.

Wellek, Albert. *Die Wiederherstellung der Seelenwissenschaft im Lebenswerk Felix Krügers.* Hamburg, 1950.

Wexler, Laura. *Tender Violence: Domestic Visions in an Age of US Imperialism.* Chapel Hill, 2000.

Wickberg, Edgar. *The Chinese in Philippine Life, 1850–1898.* New Haven, 1965.

Wildenthal, Lora. *German Women for Empire, 1884–1945.* Durham, 2001.

Wildt, Michael. *Volksgemeinschaft als Selbstermächtigung: Gewalt gegen Juden in der deutschen Provinz, 1919–1939.* Hamburg, 2007.

Wilkinson, Theo. *Two Monsoons: The Life and Death of Europeans in India.* 2nd ed. London, 1987.

Williamson, Joel. *The Crucible of Race: Black–White Relations in the American South since Emancipation.* New York, 1984.

Wolfe, Patrick. *Settler Colonialism and the Transformation of Anthropology: The Politics and Poetics of an Ethnographic Event.* New York, 1999.

Wood, Gordon. *The Creation of the American Republic, 1776–1787.* Chapel Hill, 1969.

Woollacott, Angela. *To Try Her Fortune in London: Australian Women, Colonialism, & Modernity.* Oxford, 2001.

Wu, William F. *The Yellow Peril: Chinese Americans in American Fiction, 1850–1940.* Hamden, CT, 1982.

Young, Alford A. *The Minds of Marginalized Black Men: Making Sense of Mobility, Opportunity, and Future Life Chances.* Princeton, 2003.

Young, Robert J.C. *Colonial Desire: Hybridity in Theory, Culture and Race.* London, 1995.

Zantop, Susanne. *Kolonialphantasien im vorkolonialen Deutschland (1770–1870).* Berlin, 1999.

Zimmerman, Andrew. *Anthropology and Antihumanism in Imperial Germany.* Chicago, 2001.

Zimmermann, Moshe. *Wilhelm Marr: The Patriarch of Anti-Semitism.* New York, 1986.

Index

www.ingramcontent.com/pod-product-compliance
Lightning Source LLC
Chambersburg PA
CBHW060022030426
42334CB00019B/2134